# Perspectives and Strategies for Promoting Safe Transportation among Older Adults

# Perspectives and Strategies for Promoting Safe Transportation among Older Adults

*David W. Eby*
Research Professor, UMTRI and Director, ATLAS Center

*Lisa J. Molnar*
Associate Research Scientist, UMTRI and Associate Director, ATLAS Center

*Renée M. St. Louis*
Research Area Specialist, UMTRI and Education Coordinator, ATLAS Center

ELSEVIER

Elsevier
Radarweg 29, PO Box 211, 1000 AE Amsterdam, Netherlands
The Boulevard, Langford Lane, Kidlington, Oxford OX5 1GB, United Kingdom
50 Hampshire Street, 5th Floor, Cambridge, MA 02139, United States



**British Library Cataloguing-in-Publication Data**
A catalogue record for this book is available from the British Library

**Library of Congress Cataloging-in-Publication Data**
A catalog record for this book is available from the Library of Congress

ISBN: 978-0-12-812153-5



*Publisher:* Jonathan Simpson
*Acquisition Editor:* Brian Romer
*Editorial Project Manager:* Charlotte Rowley
*Production Project Manager:* Surya Narayanan Jayachandran
*Cover Designer:* Greg Harris and Lidia P. Kostyniuk

Typeset by MPS Limited, Chennai, India

# Contents

# About the authors

**David W. Eby, PhD**, is a Research Professor, Head of the Behavioral Sciences Group at the University of Michigan Transportation Research Institute (UMTRI), and an Adjunct Research Professor of Psychology at the University of Michigan. Dr. Eby earned a doctorate degree in experimental psychology from the University of California, Santa Barbara and held a postdoctoral fellowship in the Department of Cognitive Sciences at the University of California, Irvine. From 2005 to 2015, Dr. Eby served as an associate editor of the journal *Accident Analysis & Prevention*. He is a former convener of the Transportation and Aging Interest Group of the Gerontological Society of America (GSA) and was awarded a fellow of the GSA in 2008. Dr. Eby was the founding director of the University Transportation Center (UTC) called the Michigan Center for Advancing Safe Transportation throughout the Lifespan (M-CASTL) which was sponsored by the US Department of Transportation from 2007 to 2012. Dr. Eby is currently the director of another UTC called the Center for Advancing Transportation Leadership and Safety (ATLAS Center), a collaboration between UMTRI and the Texas A&M Transportation Institute (TTI). The primary focus of his research is to enhance the safe mobility of people by conducting and reporting behavioral studies. Dr. Eby's work at UMTRI has encompassed a number of topics in traffic safety and mobility, including occupant protection, impaired driving, distraction, young driver issues, risky driving, and the use of technology to enhance safety and comfort. A strong focus of Dr. Eby's work in the past 20 years has been in aging and mobility where he has conducted projects in medical conditions and driving, aging and safe mobility, older driver self-screening, older driver use of technologies, rural transportation, driving self-regulation, and older adult travel training. His older driver work has been sponsored by the AAA Foundation for Traffic Safety, AARP, Alzheimer's Association, Federal Highway Administration, National Science Foundation, the US Department of Transportation, Centers for Disease Control and Prevention; Toyota Collaborative Safety Research Center, Toyota Research Institute, General Motors Corporation, Michigan Department of Transportation, and the Transportation Research Board. Dr. Eby has managed more than 65 projects as a principal investigator, and he has authored more than 300 scholarly publications.

**Lisa J. Molnar, PhD**, is an Associate Director of UMTRI and an Associate Research Scientist in the Behavioral Sciences Group of UMTRI. Dr. Molnar is also an Adjunct Associate Research Scientist of Psychology at the University of Michigan. She is the Associate Director of the Center for Advancing Transportation Leadership and Safety and served as an Associate Director of the former Michigan Center for Advancing Safe Transportation throughout the Lifespan. Dr. Molnar holds a doctorate degree from Monash University in Australia with a concentration in road safety. She also holds a Masters in Health Services Administration from the University of Michigan School of Public Health and a BA in Sociology from Michigan State University. Her primary research interests are driver behavior and traffic safety. She has led or been involved in a variety of research projects focusing on older driver safety and mobility, development and evaluation of traffic safety programs and policies, social and behavioral factors associated with advanced vehicle technologies and vehicle automation, pedestrian and bicycle safety, primary prevention of alcohol-impaired driving, occupant protection, and adolescent/young adult driving behavior. Her work on aging and mobility has included survey research, naturalistic driving, and simulation studies to better understand older adult behaviors and perceptions as well as to assess health and functioning. Dr. Molnar is the Secretary of the Transportation Research Board's Committee on Safe Mobility of Older Persons (TRB ANB60) and the Chair of the TRB Joint Subcommittee on Senior Mobility Options. She is also a fellow of the Gerontological Society of America (GSA) and a past convener of GSA's Transportation and Aging Interest Group. Dr. Molnar has authored more than 200 scientific articles, technical reports, and book chapters.

**Renée M. St. Louis, MPH**, is a Research Area Specialist in the Behavioral Sciences Group at the University of Michigan Transportation Research Institute where she has worked since 2004. She is also the Education Coordinator for the Center for Advancing Transportation Leadership and Safety. Ms. St. Louis holds a BA in Psychology and a Masters of Public Health in Health Behavior and Health Education from the University of Michigan. She is also currently working on a PhD at the Monash University Accident Research Centre. While at UMTRI, Ms. St. Louis has managed numerous projects focused on older adult safety and mobility and has also participated in a variety of projects to evaluate the effectiveness of statewide policies and community-based programs aimed at changing traffic safety–related behaviors such as the use of seat belts and child safety seats, aggressive driving and impaired driving. Ms. St. Louis also has extensive experience coordinating and implementing research with a variety of stakeholders including law enforcement officials, legal representatives, health-care providers, community members, and government officials throughout the United States. Ms. St. Louis' research interests include program and policy evaluation, driver and passenger safety and mobility throughout the lifespan, psychosocial factors that influence driving behavior, and occupant protection issues.

# Preface

*Two wrongs don't make a right, but three lefts do.*

*Jason Love*

This book is about the safe transportation of older adults, a wide-ranging societal issue that has its roots in history. Prior to the 1900s, roadway transportation for most everyone, including older adults, generally involved equine- and human-powered modes (e.g., horses, walking, or bicycling). These transportation modes were relatively safe and affordable, but also limited. This all changed when the first automobiles were developed in the late 19th century, and particularly so since the introduction of mass-produced automobiles in the early 20th century. Since that time, society has been grappling with the mobility and safety implications of this unprecedented transformation in how people and goods are transported.

The ability to meet transportation needs through the personal automobile produced dramatic societal changes for all ages (Foner & Garraty, 1991). The value of the personal automobile was recognized early on, and as automobiles that were affordable to the middle-class started to be produced, they turned from being a novelty for the wealthy to a necessity for all of society. The automobile industry stimulated global economies and created new industries, such as motor hotels (motels), auto repair, gas stations, roadway construction, and drive-in restaurants (Melosi, 2010; UShistory.org, 2015).

The automobile revolution exposed people to new products and ideas and also changed people's thinking about where and how they would live their lives (Solsson, 2012). Prior to the 1920s, the average person lived their lives relatively near their home. The personal automobile expanded this living space, giving people the opportunity to live outside of cities and towns and to regularly interact with a greater variety of people—teenagers no longer had to date others in their own town and older adults had greater control in meeting their needs. The delivery of goods and services also improved. For example, with farmers able to get their goods to farther away markets the distribution for perishable produce expanded and with automobiles physicians could more rapidly reach patients to provide emergency care.

Along with the benefits of access to personal automobiles came the now modern problems of congestion, pollution, and crash-related deaths and injuries. Indeed, as early as 1905, reports of the "appalling" causalities of automobile crashes in the United States were published (Anonymous, 1905). According to that author's opinion, the main cause of these crashes was "high-speed automobiling." During the first few decades of the 1900s, the antecedents of some of the critical issues associated with safe driving among older adults were discussed, including reports of the relationship between poor vision and traffic crashes (e.g., Anonymous, 1907a; Bonner, 1923; Clements, 1906), physician reporting of unfit drivers (Anonymous, 1907b), and setting functional standards for a driver license (Kessler, 1924).

Within 30 years of the automobile first being generally available to large portions of society, the "older driver" was identified as being at higher risk of crashing (DeSilva, 1938, 1939; DeSilva & Forbes, 1937; Forbes, 1938). In the DeSilva (1939) study, 56 drivers who had been in multiple crashes (repeaters) based on Department of Motor Vehicle records were compared to 199 volunteer drivers (whose crash records were not reported, but presumably had no crashes) on a number of functional tests and a set of demographics variables. Comparisons were made between both groups, and the results showed that the repeaters exhibited poorer performance on several functional tests including vision, hearing, and reaction time. Both groups were also analyzed by age group and the study found that functional deficits (called efficiency in the paper) declined with increasing age for both groups, but there was a much steeper decline for the repeaters. The author concluded the following:

> *This indicates that the decrease in ability of the older driver is a factor related to accident history to some degree. It should be pointed out, however, that our experience elsewhere has shown that if this decreased efficiency is recognized, a large proportion of the drivers are able to compensate for it and to drive safely thereafter. (DeSilva, 1939, p. 341).*

These conclusions are remarkable not only for the insights that they reveal but also for being made more than 75 years ago. Current thinking about older drivers also concludes that it is not age per se that causes driving difficulties, but rather medical conditions and medication use that occur more frequently as one ages that leads to declines in functional abilities needed for safe driving (e.g., Dickerson et al., 2007; Eby, Molnar, & Kartje, 2009). It is also known today, as it was suggested in 1939, that some older drivers have awareness of functional declines and will attempt to compensate by driving less or trying to avoid driving in circumstances that are challenging for them given their functional declines—a behavior now known as self-regulation (Gwyther & Holland, 2012; Molnar et al., 2015; Wong, Smith, & Sullivan, 2012). As discussed in this book, there is still much to learn about the extent and efficacy of self-regulation for improving transportation safety.

The overarching objective of this book is to provide a concise, comprehensive, and up-to-date resource on aging and transportation. Specifically, this book has the following goals:

- Enable readers to understand the issues that are important to preserving safe mobility for older adults;
- Educate readers about a comprehensive framework for maintaining safe mobility into older adulthood;
- Enable readers to understand the perspectives of the critical groups of people involved in keeping older people safely mobile;
- Explore existing strategies by which an aging individual can maintain safe mobility;

- Provide information to help older adults transition out of driving to using non-driving means to satisfy mobility needs.

To this end, we divide the book into four broad sections. The first is the *Background*. This section has three chapters that provide the groundwork for understanding the many issues that relate to safe transportation for older adults, including population trends, crash data, common declines in driving abilities, consequences of driving cessation, licensing and driving trends, self-regulation, and detailed information about older adults' use of non-driving transportation options. The background section also has a chapter that describes a comprehensive framework for promoting safe older adult transportation. The next section is titled *Perspectives*. This section is based on the knowledge that solving the problems of older adult transportation require multidisciplinary research and a wide variety of perspectives (see, e.g., Classen, Eby, Molnar, Dobbs, & Winter, 2011; Dickerson et al., 2007). Seven chapters describe what is known about the older adult transportation issues facing: older adults themselves, family members and friends, health-care professionals, licensing agencies, law enforcement, transportation services providers, and governments. The third section, *Strategies*, addresses the various countermeasures and programs that show promise for achieving one or more of the following goals for promoting safe transportation among older adults (Eby et al., 2009; Molnar & Eby, 2008; Molnar, Eby, & Dobbs, 2005): keeping older adults driving for as long as they can safely drive; helping older drivers transition to non-driving as they become increasingly unsafe drivers; and providing/facilitating safe transportation options for those who no longer drive. This section is divided into three chapters that address strategies that are focused on automotive technologies, roadways and infrastructure, and age-friendly communities. The final section asks the question: *Where do we go from here?* This section is a single chapter that brings together the other three sections of the book and draws conclusions that address the question. While the field of transportation safety has continued to evolve since the introduction of the automobile, the societal need for safe mobility has persisted and will continue to be a critical issue for older adults.

**David W. Eby, Lisa J. Molnar, and Renée M. St. Louis**
*University of Michigan Transportation Research Institute, Ann Arbor, MI, United States*

# References

Anonymous. (1905). Auto casualties. *Journal of the American Medical Association, 44*(20), 1620–1621.

Anonymous. (1907a). Visual errors and automobile accidents. *Journal of the American Medical Association, 48*(4), 332.

Anonymous. (1907b). Another medicolegal point settled. *Journal of the American Medical Association, 48*(7), 616.

Bonner, W. F. (1923). Visual requirements of automobile drivers. *Journal of the American Medical Association, 81*(19), 1628.

Classen, S., Eby, D. W., Molnar, L. J., Dobbs, B., & Winter, S. (2011). Transportation and aging: Evaluating stakeholders' perspective on advancing safe mobility. *South African Journal of Occupational Therapy, 41*(3), 18–24.

Clements, C. (1906). Errors of vision as a factor in motor car accidents. *The British Medical Journal, 2*, 1636.

DeSilva, H. R. (1938). Age and highway accidents. *The Scientific Monthly, 47*(6), 536–545.

DeSilva, H. R. (1939). Normal versus accident drivers. *The Journal of Psychology, 7*, 337–342.

DeSilva, H. R., & Forbes T. W. (1937). *Testing results*. Project no. 6S46-18S59. Boston, MA: Harvard Traffic Bureau and W. P. A. of Massachusetts.

Dickerson, A. E., Molnar, L. J., Eby, D. W., Adler, G., Bédard, M., Berg-Weger, M., ... Trujillo, L. (2007). Transportation and aging: A research agenda for advancing safe mobility. *The Gerontologist, 47*, 578–590.

Eby, D. W., Molnar, L. J., & Kartje, P. S. (2009). *Maintaining safe mobility in an aging society*. New York, NY: CRC Press.

Foner, E., & Garraty, J. A. (1991). *The Reader's companion to American history*. Boston, MA: Houghton Mifflin Harcourt Publishing Company.

Forbes, T. W. (1938). Age performance relationships among accident-repeater automobile drivers. *Journal of Consulting Psychology, 2*(5), 143–148.

Gwyther, H., & Holland, C. (2012). The effect of age, gender and attitudes on self-regulation in driving. *Accident Analysis and Prevention, 45*, 19–28.

Kessler, H. H. (1924). Physical standards for drivers of motor vehicles. *Journal of the American Medical Association, 84*(4), 305.

Melosi, M. V. (2010). *The automobile and the environment in american history*. Dearborn, MI: Automobile in American Life and Society. ⟨http://www.autolife.umd.umich.edu/Environment/E_Overview/E_Overview6.htm⟩. Accessed March, 2018.

Molnar, L. J., & Eby, D. W. (2008). The relationship between self regulation and driving-related abilities in older drivers: An exploratory study. *Traffic Injury Prevention, 9*, 314–319.

Molnar, L. J., Eby, D. W., & Dobbs, B. M. (2005). Policy recommendations to the White House Conference on Aging Solutions Forum. *Public Policy & Aging Report, 15*(2), 24–27.

Molnar, L. J., Eby, D. W., Zhang, L., Zanier, N., St. Louis, R. M., & Kostyniuk, L. P. (2015). *Self-regulation of driving by older adults: A synthesis of the literature and framework for future research*. Washington, DC: AAA Foundation for Traffic Safety.

Solsson, P. W. (2012). *Social Impact of the Automobile From a 1920's perspective*. ⟨http://saltofamerica.com/contents/displayArticle.aspx?17_156⟩ Accessed March, 2018.

UShistory.org. (2015). *The age of the automobile*. Philadelphia, PA: Independence Hall Association. ⟨http://www.ushistory.org/us/46a.asp⟩ Accessed March, 2018.

Wong, I. Y., Smith, S. S., & Sullivan, K. A. (2012). The relationship between cognitive ability, insight and self-regulatory behaviors: Findings from the older driver population. *Accident Analysis & Prevention, 49*, 316–321.

# Acknowledgments

Several individuals helped in the development of this book. We thank Brian Romer from Elsevier Publishing for approaching us about the opportunity to write a book on aging and transportation, and for providing advice on the structure and organization of the book. Charlotte Rowley and Gabriela D. Capille, also from Elsevier, helped keep the book moving forward and handled the technical aspects of the process. We thank Gregory Kostyniuk for taking several of the photographs in the book. Several members of the University of Michigan Transportation Research Institute (UMTRI) Behavioral Sciences Group helped to gather literature, offer feedback on issues discussed in the book, and provide technical and editorial comments on chapter drafts. We are indebted to them for this assistance. Alphabetically, these people are Dana Demchak, Lidia P. Kostyniuk, Emeka Nriagu, Sergiu C. Stanciu, Jennifer S. Zakrajsek, and Nicole Zanier.

Development of this book was supported by the Center for Advancing Transportation Leadership and Safety (ATLAS Center). The ATLAS Center is supported by a grant from the US Department of Transportation, Office of the Assistant Secretary for Research and Transportation, University Transportation Centers Program (DTRT13-G-UTC54). The ATLAS Center is a collaboration between UMTRI and the Texas A&M Transportation Institute (TTI). The contents of this book reflect the views of the authors, who are responsible for the facts and the accuracy of the information presented. The US Department of Transportation's University Transportation Centers Program and the US Government assume no liability for the contents or use thereof.

# Part I

# Background

# The challenges

**1**

*The key to the future in an aging society is not found in increasing just our life span; we need to increase our health span at the same time.*

***Chuck Norris***

## The growing and aging world

Just as the introduction of the automobile in the early 1900s transformed societies around the world, medical and public health improvements have also had profound effects. Advancements in medicine and access to health care, educational and employment opportunities, and reproductive health improvements have reduced birth rates and infant mortality while also increasing life expectancy (United Nations, 2015). For example, according to World Bank (2017a) data, global life expectancy at birth increased from 52.5 years in 1960 to 71.7 years in 2015, an increase of nearly 19 years. Collectively, these improvements led to a progressive increase in population, with the world's population surpassing 7 billion in 2012, and a development of a global society that is older today than at any other time in history (He, Goodkind, & Kowal, 2016).

Fig. 1.1 shows the annual world population numbers for all ages combined and for those age 65 or older (Organisation for Economic Co-operation and Development, OECD, 2017). This figure shows that the world's population has grown steadily in the past three-quarters of a century. The figure also shows that the number of people age 65 and older has increased steadily during this time period and currently stands at slightly less than 1 billion. What this figure does not show is the proportional distribution of the age groups that comprise these population totals.

Figs. 1.2–1.5 display data from the United Nations (2017) in the form of "population pyramids." Each of these figures shows the percentages of males (left side of the figure, dotted) and females (right side of the figure, solid) in 5-year age group increments, except for the oldest age group that includes all people age 80 and older. Two of the figures show data for the United States (US) in 1950 (Fig. 1.2) and in 2016 (Fig. 1.3), while the other two figures show data for the world for the same 2 years (1950: Fig. 1.4; 2016: Fig. 1.5). Comparing years for both the US and the world shows that in 1950, the distribution by age was skewed toward the youngest segment of the population, leading to graphs that appear to be pyramid shaped. However, a similar comparison for 2016 shows that both the US and world graphs are considerably less pyramid shaped, with much less difference between

**Perspectives and Strategies for Promoting Safe Transportation among Older Adults.**
**DOI: https://doi.org/10.1016/B978-0-12-812153-5.00001-7**

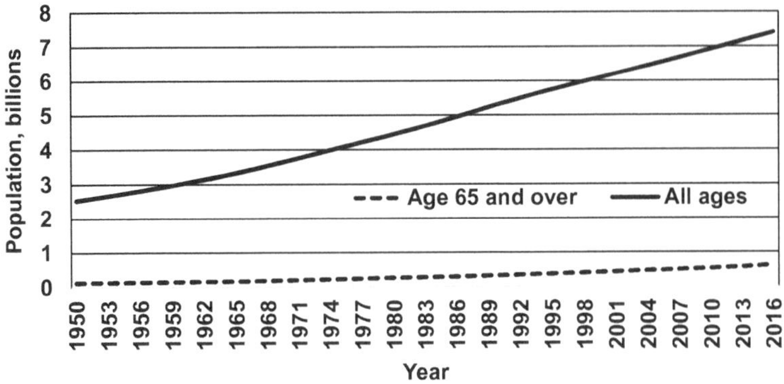


**Figure 1.1** Annual world population overall and for adults age 65 and older (1950–2016).

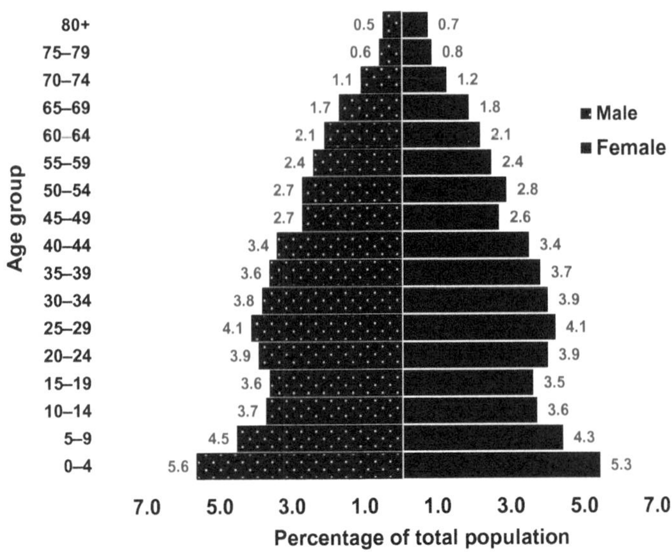


**Figure 1.2** Population pyramid: USA 1950.

younger- and middle-age groups. Indeed, the US graph for 2016 looks more like a rectangle. These graphs show that the age distribution of the US and the world is shifting toward older ages; that is, the world's population is aging.

The aging of the population is not uniform across countries for a variety of reasons. Changes in access to health care and increases in life expectancy vary by country (United Nations, 2015; World Bank, 2017a). Population aging is also being influenced by the sharp increase in births that occurred in many countries after World War II from about 1946 to 1964. This cohort, known as the "Baby Boomers," started turning age 65 in 2011, and all will be older adults by 2029 (Molnar & Eby, 2009). For example, according to United States Census Bureau

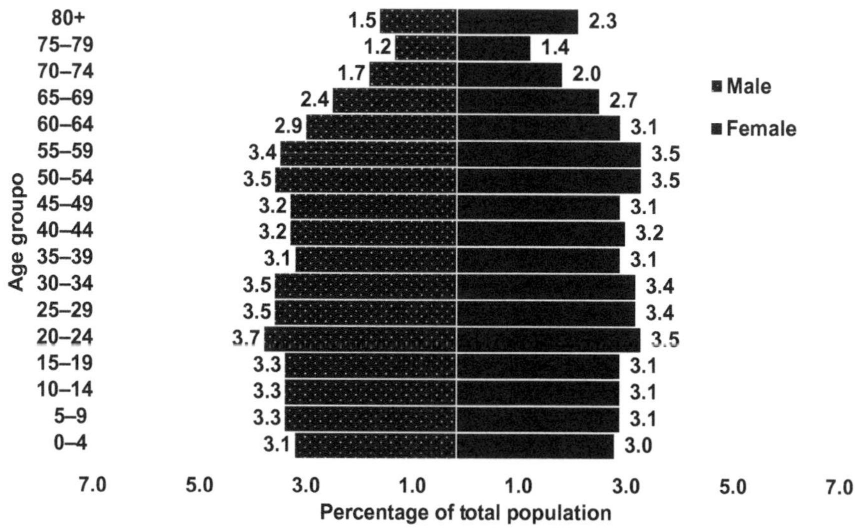


**Figure 1.3** Population pyramid: USA 2016.

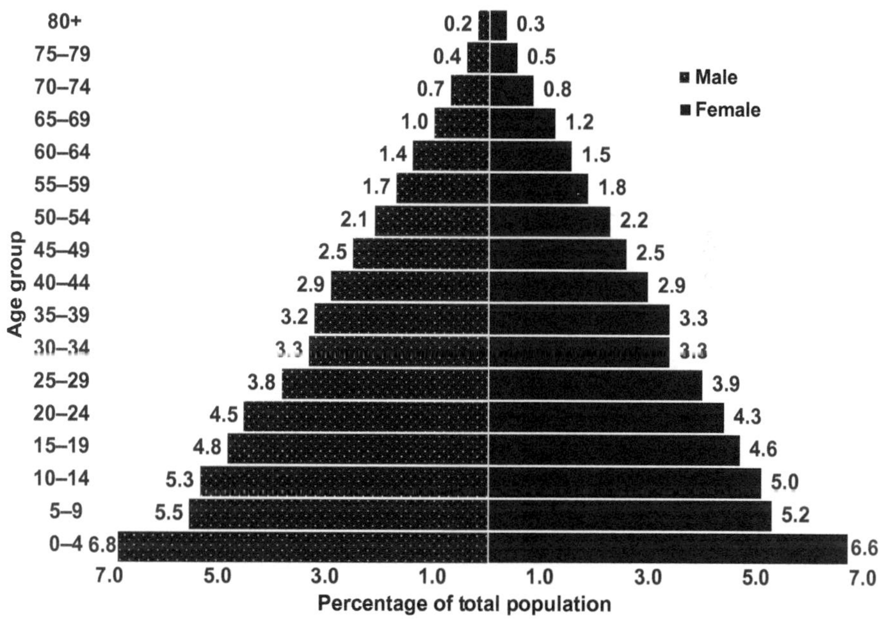


**Figure 1.4** Population pyramid: world 1950.

data and projections (West, Cole, Goodkind, & He, 2014), the percentage of older adults in the US population was 4.1% in 1900, 8.1% in 1950, and 12.4% in 2000 and is projected to be 20.9% in 2050. In other words, more than one in five people in the US will be an older adult in the next few decades.

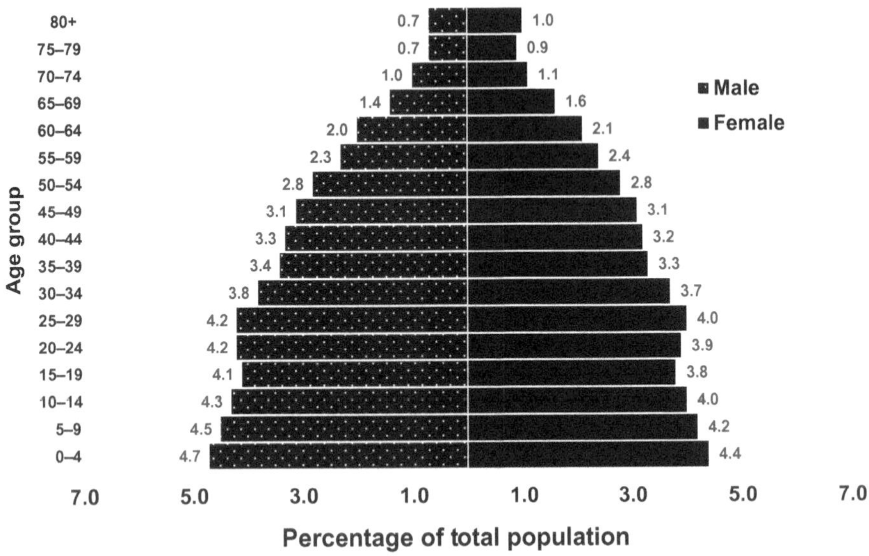


**Figure 1.5** Population pyramid: world 2016.

Not all countries are aging at the same rate or have a similar proportion of older adults. Fig. 1.6 uses data from the World Bank (2017b) and shows for a sample of countries the percentage of that country's population that is age 65 or older in 2016. There is clearly great variability among countries. The United Arab Emirates is the youngest country with just 1.1% of its population being age 65 or older, while the oldest country is Japan with more than one-quarter of the population age 65 or older. Despite these individual differences by country, the Europe Union is the region with the oldest population (19% older adults), followed by Central Europe and the Baltics (17%), North America (15%), East Asia and Pacific (10%), Latin America and Caribbean (8%), South Asia (6%), Middle East and North Africa (5%), Arab World (4%), and Sub-Saharan Africa (3%) (World Bank, 2017b). It is predicted by the United States Census Bureau that population aging over the next several decades will be greatest among Asian and Latin American countries (He et al., 2016).

## Older driver licensing

Not only is the world's population aging but people are also retaining their driver licenses well into older adulthood, and over the past few decades until recently, this trend accelerated. One study compared the percentage of people within age groups across the lifespan that were licensed for 15 countries (Sivak & Schoettle, 2012). These data were considered at two points in time which varied by the availability of data for each country but spanned 1983–2007 for the starting point and

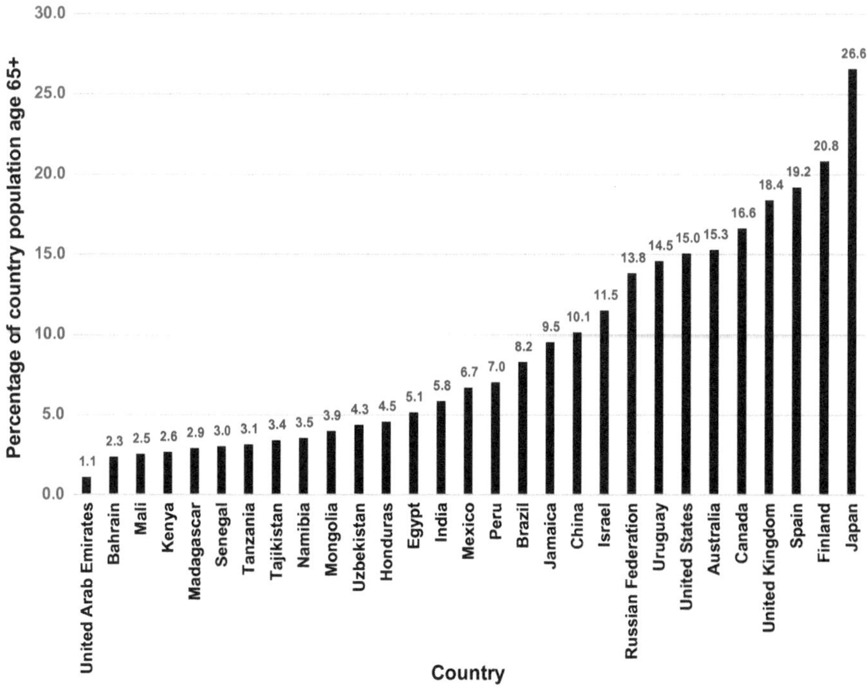


**Figure 1.6** Percentage of total population age 65 and older for 30 example countries in 2016.

2005–10 for the ending point. The results showed that for each country, there were large increases in the percentages of older adults who held driver licenses. In some countries, the percentages increased by more than double. For example, in Switzerland, about 36% of adults age 65–69 held driver licenses in 1984, while in 2005, this percentage increased to about 80%.

It is not known if this trend of increasing proportions of older people having driver licenses has continued past 2010, but evidence from the US suggests that things may be changing. Fig. 1.7 shows the percentages of people in five older adult age groups who were licensed in the US in 2000, 2005, 2010, and 2015 (Federal Highway Administration, FHWA, 2000, 2005, 2010, 2015), with men and women shown separately. These data show several interesting trends. First, in all older age groups, a greater proportion of men hold driver licenses than women, with a large difference for the oldest age group. Second, for both men and women, the proportion of licensed drivers decreases with increasing age group and decreases significantly in the 85 + group, particularly for women. Third, an examination of each grouping of the four bars in this graph show that in nearly all age groups, the percentage of people holding licenses increased between the years 2000 and 2010. However, for both sexes in all age groups, the percentages of people holding licenses decreased between 2010 and 2015. It is unknown why this trend reversed

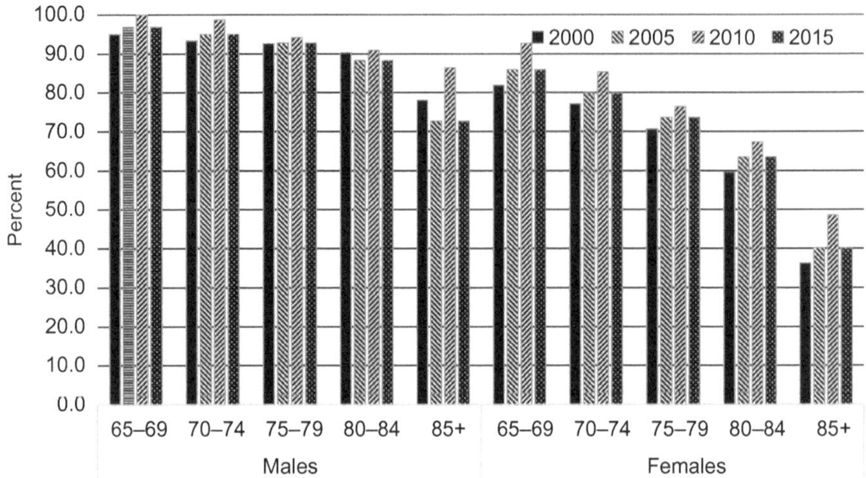


**Figure 1.7** Percentage of age group with a driver license by year for males and females.

over the past several years, but there are some possible explanations. These include older adults are starting to meet their mobility needs in ways other than driving, such as using ride-sharing services, community mobility options, and/or Internet connectivity with shopping, entertainment, and/or family/friends; the economic recession that occurred during his time period prompted more older drivers to opt out of renewing licenses to avoid vehicle ownership and license costs; public perceptions are changing about the stigma of losing one's license and more older adults are giving up their license; or interventions designed to keep only those older adults who are fit to drive on the road are starting to become more widespread and are influencing older adults to give up licenses. Whatever the reason, more research and more years of data are needed to understand this trend and to confirm that the trend is real and continuing.

## Age-related declines in abilities needed for safe driving

Driving is a complex activity that requires the coordination and integration of three categories of functional abilities. Broadly defined, these categories are psychomotor (movement), perception (mainly visual perception), and thinking (cognition). As people age into older adulthood, they generally begin to experience declines in their functional abilities due in part to the normal process of aging and in part because of certain medical conditions that are more common in old age, as well as the variety of medications (both prescription and over-the-counter) that people use to treat these conditions. Safe driving can be negatively impacted by declines in any of these three categories of functional abilities. Also associated with aging are the related conditions of frailty and fragility, which are important to consider within the context of driving because they can increase the seriousness of an injury for a given crash and make it more difficult to recover from injuries. Here, we briefly address how functional abilities can decline with age and touch on some of the common medical conditions that can lead to declines. There are several in-depth discussions on this topic in relation to driving in the literature (e.g., Charlton et al., 2010; Dobbs, 2005; Eby, Molnar, & Kartje, 2009; Owsley, 2011).

## Psychomotor

Psychomotor functioning involves all aspects of a person's ability to move and encompasses a number of aspects including strength, coordination, reaction time, flexibility, gait, and stamina. Along with general age–related declines, several medical conditions can impact psychomotor abilities and decrease driving safety: stroke that includes paralysis, arthritis, Parkinson's disease, and multiple sclerosis (Charlton et al., 2010; Dobbs, 2005; Eby et al., 2009). Loss of muscle strength is common with advancing age and can include declines in strength of up to 25% (Adams, O'Shea, & O'Shea, 1999; Petrofsky & Lind, 1975; Shepard, 1998). Declines in upper body strength can make steering more difficult and may affect a driver's ability to properly use the brake and throttle (Staplin, Lococo, Stewart, & Decina, 1999). An Australian study of 270 older drivers found that drivers judged as being unsafe on a professional driving assessment had significantly lower scores on quadriceps, ankle, and hand grip strength (Lacherez, Wood, Anstey, & Lord, 2014). Loss of strength can lead to difficulties with getting in and out of a vehicle, using the cargo area, use of foot pedals (throttle and brake), and steering (Staplin et al., 1999). Loss of muscle strength can also lead to more rapid driver fatigue. Good coordination is also important for safe driving (Wheatley, Pellerito, & Redpenning, 2006) and tends to decline with age (Marshall, Elias, & Wright, 1985; Woytowicz, Whitall, & Westlake, 2016). Declines in coordination can make it difficult for a driver to manipulate dashboard controls, operate manual transmissions, and have effective operational control of the vehicle, such as lane keeping.

Good reaction time and flexibility are also important for safe driving. It is well documented that various measures of reaction time show increases with increasing age (see, e.g., Der & Deary, 2006; Fozard, Vercruyssen, Reynolds, Hancock, & Quilter, 1994; Klavora & Heslegrave, 2002). Brake reaction time is a function of both psychomotor and cognitive abilities and can be slowed by declines in either of these areas (Alonso et al., 2016). In addition to braking, slowed reaction time can impact a driver's ability to respond quickly to changing traffic conditions, particularly to immediate threats. Flexibility has also been shown to decline with age (Adams et al., 1999) by up to 30% between age 30 and 70 (Chapman, deVries, & Swezey, 1972; Smith, 1989). Declines in flexibility can make several aspects of driving more difficult, including using a seat belt, starting the car, using vehicle controls, backing up, checking blind spots, and getting into and out of the vehicle (e.g., Jones, McCann, & Lassere, 1991; Malfetti, 1985; Marottoli et al., 1998; Staplin et al., 1999).

## *Visual perception*

Visual abilities are crucial for safe driving. Many visual abilities are known to decline with age either through the normal aging process or through the presence of medical conditions that are more common in older adulthood. These conditions include cataracts, diabetic retinopathy, glaucoma, age-related macular degeneration, and visual field loss (Charlton et al., 2010; Dobbs, 2005; Eby et al., 2009; Owsley, 2011). The literature on aging and visual abilities is large (see Owsley, 2011 for an excellent review); collectively, this research shows that a number of abilities decline with age. It is well established that visual acuity, or the ability to resolve details, declines with age (Burg, 1966; Burg & Hurlbert, 1961; Heron & Chown, 1967; Long & Crambert, 1989; Owsley & Sloane, 1990). Poor visual acuity can make it difficult to read street signs and pavement markings, interact with in-vehicle displays, and perceive traffic control device information. The relationship between declining visual acuity and traffic safety outcomes is not clear. Some studies have found associations between poor visual acuity and crash risk (e.g., Ivers, Mitchell, & Cumming, 1999; Marottoli et al., 1998), while others have not (e.g., Cross et al., 2009; Rubin et al., 2007). This discrepancy may be related to the fact that people with poor visual acuity drive less and avoid driving in demanding driving conditions (Owsley & McGwin, 2010). As people age, most will progressively have difficulty seeing at night due to declines in contrast sensitivity (the ability to see in low light conditions) and slowed recovery from glare (Owsley, 2011; Owsley, Sekuler, & Siemsen, 1983; Wolf, 1960). Research has found that glare recovery (also called glare disability) and poor contrast sensitivity are not significantly associated with increased crash risk but do seem to adversely affect driving performance (see, e.g., Owsley & McGwin, 2010; Owsley, Stalvey, Wells, Sloane, & McGwin, 2001; Rubin et al., 2007). These results may be explained in part by driver self-regulation; that is, research has found that older drivers who report having difficulty seeing at night also avoid driving at night (Molnar et al., 2013).

Visual processing speed can also deteriorate in some people as they age (e.g., Kline & Birren, 1975). Slowed visual processing can make it difficult to drive in heavy traffic, see pedestrians and other vulnerable road users, and slow reaction times to critical driving events. This ability has typically been measured in a laboratory by a divided attention task known as the useful field of view (UFOV) task that requires a person to attend to a central stimulus while also detecting stimuli to the periphery (e.g., Ball, Beard, Roenker, Miller, & Griggs, 1988; Wood & Owsley, 2014). There is strong evidence that poor performance on the UFOV test is associated with increased crash risk (e.g., Ball et al., 2005; Rubin et al., 2007). In their review of research on UFOV scores and crash risk among older drivers, Wood and Owsley (2014, pg. 317) concluded "A growing body of evidence gathered by many research groups suggests that reduced performance on the useful field of view, expressed either in terms of extent or speed of visual processing, is a strong predictor of a range of measures of driving ability and safety...."

Both stereoscopic space perception and sensitivity to motion are also known to exhibit declines with aging (e.g., Ball & Sekuler, 1986; Hofstetter & Bertsch,

1976). Deficits in these abilities can lead to problems with accurately judging the relative positions of vehicles in relation to the driver's vehicle, seeing dashboard controls, judging gaps in traffic, parking, and moving through intersections. Although the research on these abilities in relation to older driver crash risk is limited, studies show no association with crashes among those with poor stereoacuity (Owsley et al., 1998; Rubin et al., 2007) and a weak association for motion sensitivity (Shinar, 1977). Further research on the association between measures of motion perception and crash risk is warranted.

## Cognition

Safe driving is highly dependent on good cognitive abilities. Certain medical conditions and normal aging can lead to declines that impact the complex task of driving. The most common are dementia (including Alzheimer's disease), mild cognitive impairment, and Parkinson's disease (Charlton et al., 2010; Eby et al., 2009). Although there is considerable individual difference in cognitive functioning, even among those without a cognitive-related disease, several cognitive abilities are known to decline as people age (e.g., Harada, Love, & Triebel, 2013; Mather, 2010). Three types of attention tend to decline with age (Eby et al., 2009; Drag & Bieliauskas, 2010; Harada et al., 2013): sustained (ability to attend to relevant information for a period of time), selective (ability to keep your mind on important information and ignore irrelevant information), and divided attention (the ability to attend to multiple tasks simultaneously). Declining attentional abilities can make it more difficult for older adults to drive in heavy traffic, negotiate intersections, and navigate to destinations along with being more easily distracted (Staplin et al., 1999).

Studies have found that cognitive information processing speed becomes slower as people age (see Salthouse, 2010 for a review). Slowed processing speed can make it more difficult for a driver to respond appropriately and quickly to changing traffic conditions. Reductions in processing speed are associated with driving cessation (Anstey, Windsor, Luszcz, & Andrews, 2006; Edwards et al., 2008) and avoidance of certain challenging driving situations (Ball et al., 1998). However, recent work has suggested that speed of processing can be improved through training and can improve driving outcomes (e.g., Ross et al., 2016).

Spatial cognition refers to a person's ability to perceive and process the location and movement of objects in space (Klencklen, Després, & Dufour, 2012). This ability is used for wayfinding, navigating traffic, and predicting where vehicles will be in the near future. Several studies have found that spatial cognition declines with age (Bryden, Charlton, Oxley, & Lowndes, 2013; Head & Isom, 2010; Jansen, Schmelter, & Heil, 2010; Rodgers, Sindone, & Moffat, 2012; Salthouse, 1987). While having clear effects on mobility, the effects of decrements in spatial cognition on driving safety and performance have not been established.

Executive functioning has been defined as "... a higher order cognitive construct that is involved in the self-regulation of goal directed behavior and the effective organization and use of large amounts of information" (Drag & Bieliauskas, 2010, pg. 80). Research shows that performance on tasks requiring executive function declines with age (e.g., van Hooren et al., 2007; Mayr, Spieler, & Kliegl, 2001; Zelazo, Craik, & Booth, 2004). Poor executive function ability among drivers can lead to unsafe decisions that decrease driving safety, a lack of insight into driving abilities, and inappropriate self-regulation of driving (Wagner, Müri, Nef, & Mosimann, 2011). Indeed, research has established that declining executive function is associated with several adverse driving outcomes including increased crash risk, increase driving errors, and driving avoidance (see, e.g., Emerson et al., 2012; Dawson, Uc, Anderson, Johnson, & Rizzo, 2010; Ott et al., 2013; Rapoport et al., 2013).

### *Fragility/Frailty*

Aging into older adulthood can also result in fragility and frailty. According to Kent, Trowbridge, Lopez-Valdes, Ordoyo, and Segui-Gomez (2009), older vehicle occupants tend to sustain a greater level of injury in crashes (fragility) and have worse outcomes for a given injury (frailty). Studies have found that fragility plays a significant role in the elevated fatal crash rates of older drivers in both the US and Australia (e.g., Kent et al., 2009; Li, Braver, & Chen, 2003; Meuleners, Narding, Lee, & Legge, 2006). The causes underpinning fragility are largely due to age-related changes in internal morphology such as decreased bone density and changes in bone geometry (see, e.g., Kent, 2010). Such changes make bones more likely to be injured during a crash. The mechanisms underlying frailty, on the other hand, are not consistently agreed upon (see, e.g., Chen, Mao, & Leng, 2014; Fillit & Butler, 2009; Heppenstall, Wilkinson, Hanger, & Keeling, 2009; Szanton, Seplaki, Thorpe, Allen, & Fried, 2010; Yunkyung, Gruenewald, Seeman, & Sarkisian, 2010). Chen et al. (2014) describe frailty within the context of an older adult at increased vulnerability to stressors from age-related declines in physiologic reserve and multiple organ functions. According to the frailty phenotype definition (Fried et al., 2001), frailty is characterized by weakness, slowness, a low level of physical activity, exhaustion and/or poor endurance, and weight loss. Results from studies that have estimated the prevalence of frailty among older adults are mixed (e.g., Rockwood, Song, & Mitnitski, 2011; Syddall et al., 2010). A systematic review of 20 studies on the prevalence of frailty among community-dwelling older adults found the following results: prevalence varied between 4% and 59%; the average prevalence based on the physical frailty phenotype was 9.9%; and prevalence increased with age and was higher among women (Collard, Boter, Schoevers, & Voshaar, 2012).

## Fatal crashes and older drivers

One of the main concerns with aging is that declines in abilities needed for safe driving can lead to a higher likelihood of a motor vehicle crash. In 2015, there were

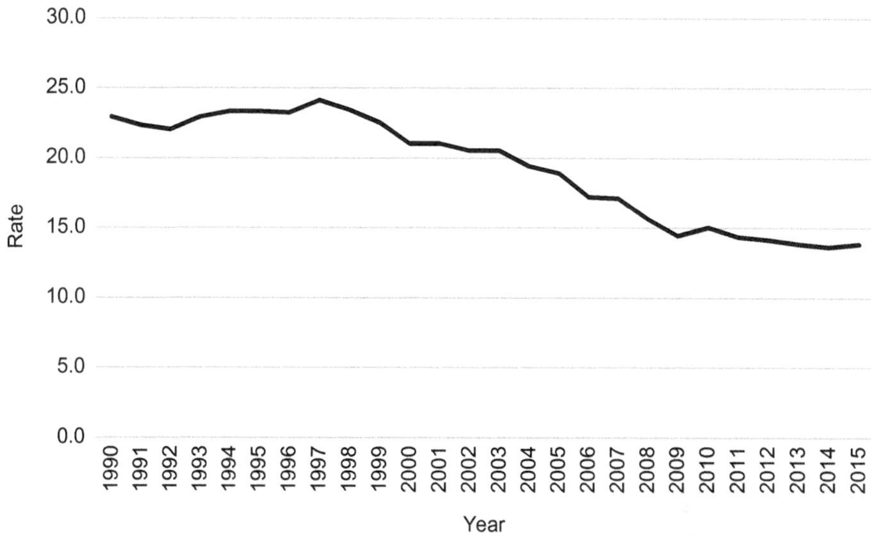


**Figure 1.8** United States driver age 70 + fatal crash rates per 100,000 population (1990–2015).

6165 older adults in the US killed in traffic crashes, which accounted for about 18% of all fatal crashes that year (National Highway Traffic Safety Administration, NHTSA, 2017). In that same year, there were 240,000 older adults injured in crashes. Data from the Insurance Institute for Highway Safety (2017) show that the motor vehicle crash rates for US drivers age 70 and older (calculated using population data) have declined over the past 25 years but may be leveling off. Fig. 1.8 plots these rates since 1990 and shows a relatively consistent decline up to about 2011, with rates then leveling off and possibly starting to increase.

Fatal crash rates, particularly for older drivers, can be difficult to interpret and there is much discussion in the literature about whether older adults are at a higher risk of being in a fatal crash (see, e.g., Alvarez & Fierro, 2008; Antin et al., 2017; Hakamies-Blomqvist, Raitanen, & O'Neill, 2002; Hanson & Hildebrand, 2011; Langford, Methorst, & Hakamies-Blomqvist, 2006; Langford et al., 2013; Staplin, Gish, & Joyce, 2008). Some of the issues are illustrated in Fig. 1.9. Shown in this figure are fatal crash rates for 2008 calculated in three ways: by population (the number of people in each age group in the US; Insurance Institute for Highway Safety, 2017), by licensed drivers (the number of people in each age group who hold a valid driver license; NHTSA, 2017; FHWA, 2017), and by miles driven (the number of annual miles driven by people in each age group; Insurance Institute for Highway Safety, 2017). The rates have been scaled so that the three functions fit on the same graph. The function displaying rates by population (solid line) shows higher rates for drivers under age 25 and drivers over age 69, but there is little variability in general. One issue with using population as the basis for calculating rates is that it is well known that not all people hold driver licenses which can bias the rates

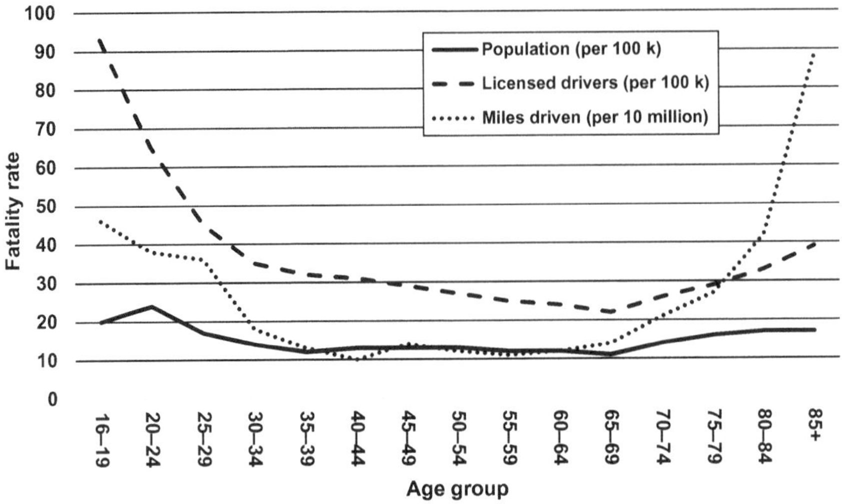


**Figure 1.9** United States motor vehicle fatality rates 2008 based on different denominators.

particularly for older drivers (see Fig. 1.7) and younger drivers (see, e.g., Sivak & Schoettle, 2012). Fatality rates calculated by licensed drivers (dashed line) show a very different picture. In this case, the youngest drivers have significantly higher rates, which decline rapidly up to about age 30. There is also an increase in rates that starts at about age 70 and consistently increases into older adulthood. However, not all people who have licenses drive the same number of miles or under the same driving conditions, leading to variations in the exposure that different drivers have to risk of a fatal crash. Ideally, rates should be calculated based on miles driven under various conditions that increase crash risk, such as bad weather, but these data do not exist by age group across a country. Instead, Fig. 1.9 also plots age group fatality rates as simply a function of total miles driven (dotted line). Plotted this way, fatal crash rates for drivers age 80 and older are the highest for any age group. While each of these lines shows increases in fatality rates in the older age groups, the age at which increases start and the steepness of these increases vary. Similar functions have been found for data in Japan (Ichikawa, Nakahara, & Taniguchi, 2015). To further complicate this discussion, there is building evidence that the fatality rates for older adults may be biased by the higher prevalence of fragility and frailty among the older population; that is, older people are more likely to die than younger drivers when they are involved in a crash (Langford & Koppel, 2006; Li et al., 2003; OECD, 2001; Koppel, Bohensky, Langford, & Taranto, 2011).

Data used to create Fig. 1.9 are from 2008. This year was chosen because more recent data for US miles driven by age group are not available and we wanted to show rates calculated in different ways using the same year. More recent evidence from 2015 suggests that fatal crash rates for older adults may be starting to decline at least for some countries. Fig. 1.10 shows fatal crashes by population for three age groups for 12 representative countries (data are from the International Transport Forum, 2017). This figure shows that in most countries, the fatal crash rates for drivers age 65 and older are higher than for drivers in the middle age group, suggesting that increased fatal crash risk for older drivers may be a global phenomenon. However, data for Sweden, the United Kingdom, and the US show

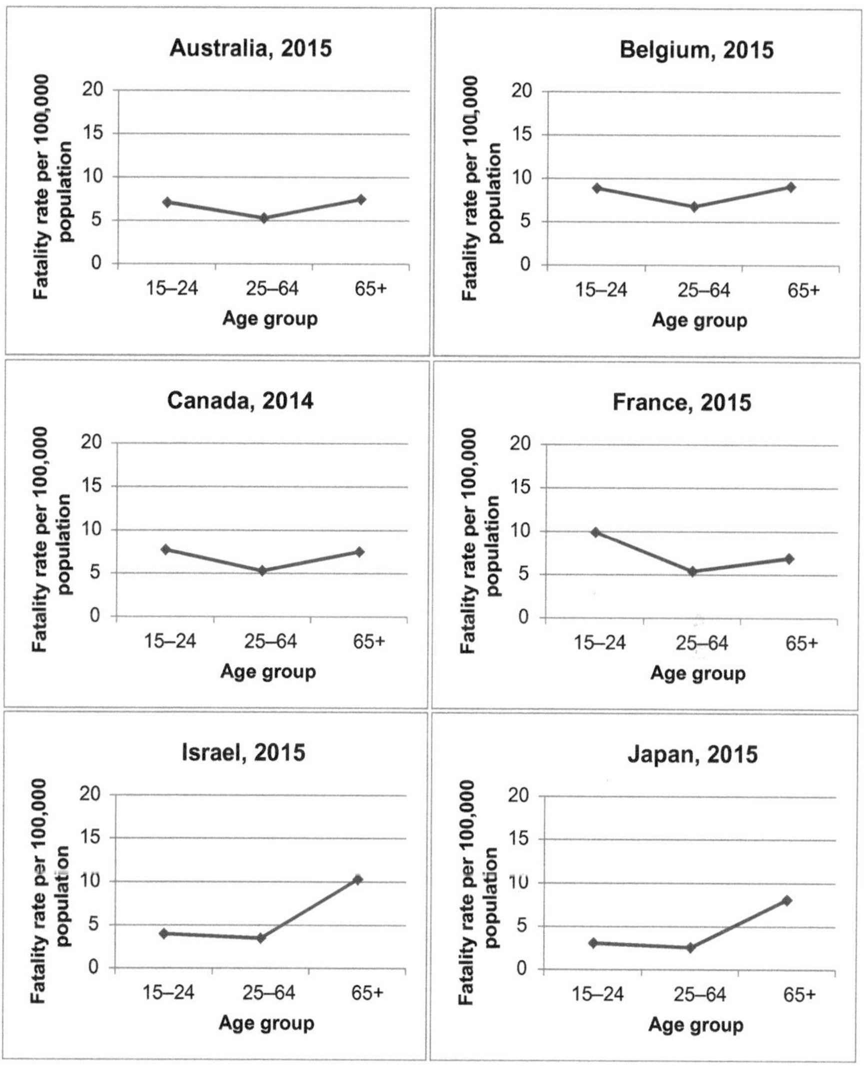


**Figure 1.10** Fatal crash rates by age group in 12 countries
Source: Data are from International Transport Forum. (2017). *Casualties by age and road user*. ITF Transport Statistics (database). <http://dx.doi.org/10.1787/3c6c57b0-en> Accessed October, 2017).

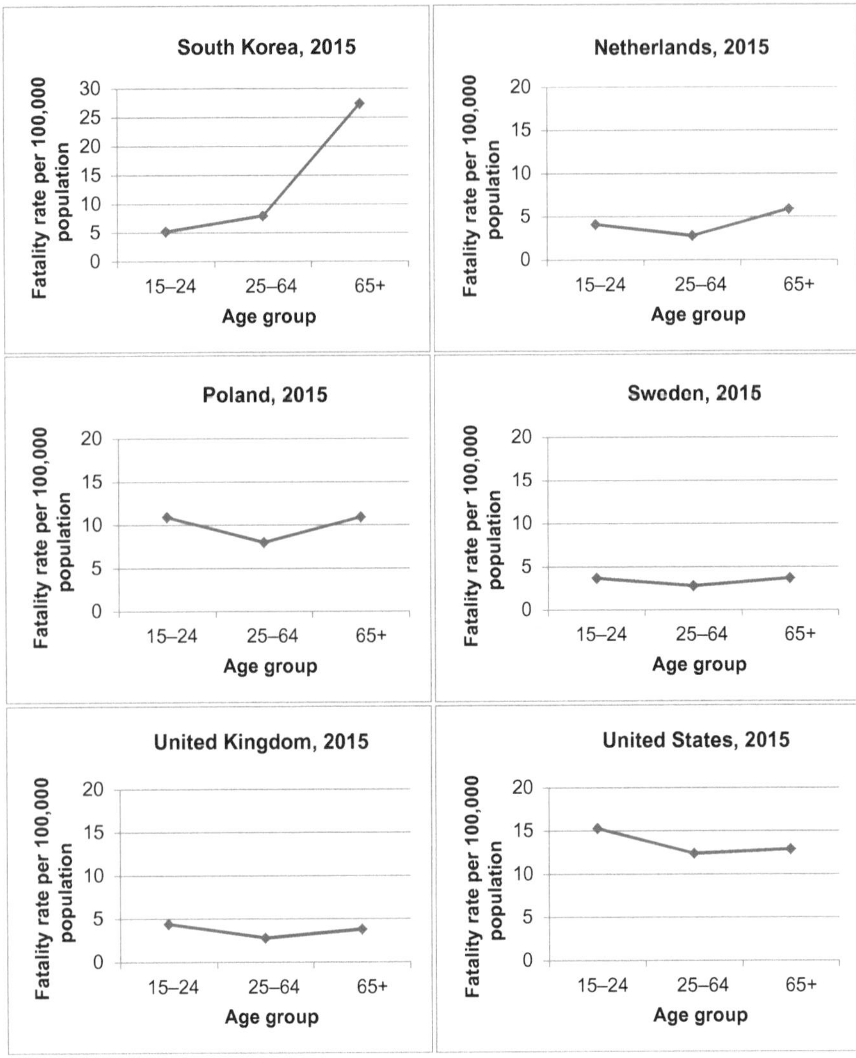


**Figure 1.10** (*Continued*)

little difference in fatal crash rates between the middle and older age groups. Thus, it appears that in some countries, progress has been made in improving safe transportation for older adults (Cheung & McCartt, 2011; Cicchino, 2015).

## Crash trends among older drivers

When crashes of all types are considered, it is clear that older driver crash involvement differs from that of drivers of other ages. One clear trend is that older drivers are overinvolved in intersection crashes as compared to younger drivers (see, e.g., Abdel-Aty & Radwan, 2000; Cicchino & McCartt, 2014; Clarke, Ward, Bartle, & Truman, 2010; Hakamies-Blomqvist, 1993; Koppel et al., 2011; Langford & Koppel, 2006; Larsen & Kines, 2002; McGwin & Brown, 1999; OECD, 2001; Oxley, Fildes, Corben, & Langford, 2006; Rakotonirainy, Steinhardt, Delhomme, Darvell, & Schramm, 2012; Skyving, Berg, & Laflamme, 2009; Staplin, Lococo, McKnight, McKnight, & Odenheimer, 1998). For example, a US study using police-reported crash data for the state of Alabama in 1996 compared driver actions in at-fault crashes among drivers age 16–34, 35–54, and 55 and older (McGwin & Brown, 1999). The study found that the oldest age group was more likely to be involved in turning-related crashes and failure-to-yield crashes, actions that occur at intersections. An Australian study analyzed the circumstances of 6084 fatal crashes in light vehicles during 1996–99 among three age groups—40–55, 65–74, and 75+ years (Langford & Koppel, 2006). Analyses of crash locations showed that the percentage of intersection crashes increased with age group (21%, 35%, and 50%, respectively), while the percentage of mid-block crashes decreased with age (78%, 65%, and 49%, respectively). The study also found that the percentage of crashes involving more than one vehicle also increased with age group (60%, 65%, and 74%, respectively), as would be expected given the higher percentage of intersection-related crashes. Another study using Australian police–reported crash data from Queensland, Australia during 2000–08 found that for crossroad and T-junction intersections (the two most common intersections), the proportion of crashes within an age group generally increased with age (Rakotonirainy et al., 2012). For roundabouts, the proportion was higher only for drivers age 80 and older. An analysis of fatal crash data in the US also supports the finding that older drivers are overinvolved in intersection-related crashes (Sifrit, Stutts, Martell, & Staplin, 2011). This study calculated crash-involvement ratios which represented a comparison of at-fault vs not-at-fault crashes such that values below 1.0 indicated that an age group was underrepresented in at-fault crashes and values greater than 1.0 showed overrepresentation. The study found that across all intersection types, drivers under age 20 had a ratio of about 1.5, drivers age 20–69 had ratios around 0.5–1.0, and at age 70, ratios increased steeply, with drivers age 80+ having a ratio of more than 5. Thus, across different countries, using different types of crash data and different types of analyses, study results show that older drivers are more likely to crash at intersections than their younger counterparts.

There are several other crash-related trends for older drivers. Table 1.1 lists these trends and representative references. Many of these trends (e.g., related to dry roads, good visibility, and daytime trends) can be explained by driving exposure; that is, these are the times when and conditions under which older drivers choose to be on the road. The driving patterns of older adults relative to younger drivers will be discussed in the next chapter. The trends related to crash types, however, can most likely be attributed to declines in abilities needed for safe driving that are more common in older adulthood.

**Table 1.1** Crash trends among older drivers compared to other drivers

| Crash trend | Reference(s) |
|---|---|
| More likely to be at-fault in crashes | Cooper (1990), Hakaimes-Blomqvist (1993), Henriksson and Sagberg (2010), Ichikawa et al. (2015), and Rakotonirainy et al. (2012) |
| More likely to be injured or killed in crash | Rakotonirainy et al. (2012) |
| More likely to be in left (right for Australia and Japan) turn crashes | Henriksson and Sagberg (2010) and Koppel et al. (2011) |
| More likely to crash on dry roads | Hakamies-Blomqvist (1993) and Henriksson and Sagberg (2010) |
| More likely to crash when visibility is good | Henriksson and Sagberg (2010) |
| More likely to crash during daylight hours | Clarke et al. (2010), Hakamies-Blomqvist (1993), Henriksson and Sagberg (2010), Langford and Koppel (2006), and McGwin and Brown (1999) |
| More likely to be in failure-to-yield right of way crashes | Braitman, Kirley, Ferguson, and Chaudhary (2007), Henriksson and Sagberg (2010), Langford and Koppel (2006), McGwin and Brown (1999), and Rakotonirainy et al. (2012) |
| More likely to be in unintended acceleration/spontaneous acceleration crashes | Clarke et al. (2010) |
| More likely to be in fatigue-related crashes | Clarke et al. (2010) |
| Less likely to be impaired by alcohol in crash | Eby (1995), Hakamies-Blomqvist (1993), Henriksson and Sagberg (2010), Langford and Koppel (2006), McGwin and Brown (1999), and Rakotonirainy et al. (2012) |
| Less likely to be in high speed–related crash | Langford and Koppel (2006), McGwin and Brown (1999), and Rakotonirainy et al. (2012) |
| Less likely to be unbelted in a crash | Langford and Koppel (2006) |

## Driving cessation

According to data from the FHWA (2015), there were 10,428,001 people of age 65 and older in the US without a license in 2015, equating to more than one in every five older adults in the US who needed to satisfy their mobility needs through non-driving means. It has been estimated that about 600,000 older drivers (age 70+) in the US give up driving each year (Kochera, Straight, & Guterbock, 2005), and this number has likely increased significantly since this estimate was made.

It is not surprising that many older drivers are reluctant to consider driving cessation (see, e.g., Adler & Rottunda, 2006; Kostyniuk & Shope, 2003; Yassuda, Wilson, & von Mering, 1997) given the challenges of meeting transportation needs when driving is not an option (Dickerson, Molnar, Bédard, Eby, Berg-Weger, et al., 2017). As discussed by Molnar and Eby (2009), in many countries, transportation is closely associated with being able to drive and driving is the preferred mode for meeting mobility needs. In part, this is due to preference for driving automobiles, and in part, this is due to the lack of acceptable non-driving transportation alternatives, particularly in rural areas (Dickerson, Molnar, Bédard, Eby, Berg-Weger, et al., 2017).

Driving cessation among older adults has been associated with a number of negative consequences. These include reduced activity outside the home (Harrison & Ragland, 2003; Marottoli et al., 2000), decreased life satisfaction (Harrison & Ragland, 2003; Liddle, Gustafsson, Bartlett, & McKenna, 2012), reduced productive engagement such as paid and/or volunteer work (Curl, Stowe, Cooney, & Proulx, 2013), increased depressive symptoms (Chihuri et al., 2016; Marottoli et al., 1997; Ragland, Satariano, & MacLeod, 2005), reduced network of friends and social activity (Bryanton, Weeks, & Lees, 2010; Mezuk & Rebok, 2008), reduced access to health care (Owsley et al., 2006), accelerated declines in cognitive abilities (Choi, Lohman, & Mezuk, 2014), declines in physical performance measures (Edwards, Lunsman, Perkins, Rebok, & Roth, 2009), and declines in subjective social and physical health (Edwards et al., 2009). While some of these negative consequences undoubtedly result in part from the declining abilities that can lead to cessation of driving, many of these studies attempted to account for this. More recent work suggests that the magnitude of some of these consequences may be less severe among people who live in cities where non-driving transportation options are more prevalent (Lee, Steinman, & Tan, 2011) and among older adults who are frequent and varied users of the Internet, particularly social media (Challands, Lacherez, & Obst, 2017).

## The changing transportation landscape

Underlying all the challenges for promoting safe transportation among older adults is, of course, the transportation system itself. While the transportation system is continually changing, some are predicting that the transportation system will undergo dramatic changes in the next 25 years (see, e.g., United States Department of Transportation, United States DOT, 2015). Some of the interrelated factors driving these changes will be advanced technology, shared mobility services, climate change, and urban development. A recent blog (Mäkinen, 2017) speculates about how advanced technology will lead to six changes in the future transportation system: gasoline powered cars will be replaced by electric vehicles; drivers will disappear and vehicles will be autonomous; people will no longer need to know where they are or where they are going because GPS-based systems will keep track; searching for parking will be eliminated; and everything will be connected (car, home, phone, etc.). While it remains to be seen the extent to which these speculations are borne out in the future, they do highlight several important technology developments that will influence how older adults of the future will meet mobility needs. Advanced in-vehicle technologies, including automated and connected vehicles, will be discussed in Chapter 12, In-Vehicle and Self-Driving Technologies, and other technological trends will be discussed in various other chapters.

Over the past decade, shared mobility services have developed rapidly (Chan & Shaheen, 2012; Parzen, Randall, & Feigon, 2015; Shaheen & Cohen, 2007). Shared mobility is the class of transportation services that are shared among users and not only includes traditional services such as public transit and taxis but also includes relatively new services such as car sharing, bike sharing, and ride sourcing (e.g., Uber, Lyft) (Parzen et al., 2015). For example, since Uber's launch in San Francisco, CA in 2011, it has grown to now operate in 632 cities across the globe (Uber, 2017). With shared mobility services, particularly with ride sourcing, people no longer need to own and operate a personal vehicle in order to get around. As these services become more widespread, as they are expected to do (Chan & Shaheen, 2012; Parzen et al., 2015; Shaheen & Cohen, 2007), there may be significant impacts and new challenges for promoting safe mobility for older adults. Share mobility services and other community mobility options will be discussed in more detail in Chapter 3, Use of Non-Driving Transportation Options.

The consensus of scientific opinion is that the global climate is warming and human activity is playing a large role in this change (National Academy of Sciences, Engineering, and Medicine, 2016). Climate change will have distinct impacts on the global transportation systems. These impacts include increase in severe weather events that disrupt transportation; more rapid deterioration of transportation infrastructures and higher costs for maintenance; an increase in the proportion hybrid and electric vehicles on roadways; and a trend toward less automobile driving or more use of alternative transportation modes (United States DOT, 2015). How climate change will specifically affect mobility for older adults is not clear, but weather will have an overarching influence on our future transportation system.

The transportation landscape is also transforming as the global population increases. Increasingly, people are moving into suburbs that are growing in size (United States DOT, 2015). In the US, these metropolitan areas have been termed megaregions that "... consist of interrelated population and employment centers that share common transportation networks, cultures, and environmental features" (Hagler, 2009, pg. 6). This clustering of people will impact transportation in several ways, including increased congestion; increased difficulty connecting older and low-income people to services and employment; and increased cost of living (United States DOT, 2015). On the other hand, with increased population density, non-driving modes of transportation will become more feasible and cost-effective.

## Conclusions

This chapter has addressed the primary issues and challenges for safe mobility among older adults that exist now and will likely extend into the future. The issue of safe transportation for older people is a global issue that will ultimately impact the societies of all nations in the coming decades. Several conclusions about the challenges for promoting safe transportation among older adults can be drawn from the research literature addressed in this chapter:

- The world's population is both growing in number and becoming older. In most countries, there will be significantly more older adults, and they will account for a larger proportion of the total population as compared to today.
- Older adults in most countries now prefer to meet their transportation needs through driving a personal motor vehicle, and large percentages of older adults hold licenses to drive well into older adulthood. It is not clear if this trend will continue.
- Despite advances being made in medical and rehabilitation sciences, older adulthood is characterized by declines in functional abilities and the presence of fragility and frailty, as will continue to be the case into the foreseeable future. These declines will not only impact the safe driving of older adults but they will also present challenges for meeting transportation needs in ways other than driving. For example, an older adult who has given up driving because of functional declines may also have difficulty being a pedestrian or using fixed-route public transportation.
- The rate of fatal crashes for older drivers will continue to be a concern in many countries, even though there is some evidence of lowered rates over the past several years in some countries.
- For all types of crashes, the greater likelihood of older adults being at-fault and several of the trends (such as a greater likelihood of being in intersection crashes) show that some older drivers may not be safe due to functional declines and society needs more and better ways to address this challenge.
- Most people who live long enough will eventually have to stop driving. Driving cessation is clearly associated with many negative consequences, largely due to the isolating effects of not being able to meet mobility needs.
- The global transportation system is transforming and there are several factors driving these changes. The future transportation system may be quite different than today's. Promoting safe transportation for older adults now and into the future will require transportation professionals to consider these trends as the transportation system continues to evolve.

In response to these challenges, researchers and practitioners in their field of transportation and aging often view transportation as occurring along a continuum with safe and independent driving at one end and driving cessation at the other (Dickerson et al., 2007; Dickerson, Molnar, Bédard, Eby, Berg-Weger, et al., 2017; Dickerson, Molnar, Bédard, Eby, Classen, et al., 2017; Eby et al., 2009). In between these ends is the process of transitioning from driving to non-driving. More on this framework and a new conceptualization of older adult safe transportation is discussed in Chapter 4, A Framework for Promoting Older Adult Safe Transportation.

## References

Abdel-Aty, M. A., & Radwan, A. E. (2000). Modeling traffic accident occurrence and involvement. *Accident Analysis & Prevention*, *32*, 633–642.

Adams, K., O'Shea, P., & O'Shea, K. L. (1999). Aging: Its effects on strength, power, flexibility, and bone density. *Strength and Conditioning Journal*, *21*(2), 65–77.

Adler, G., & Rottunda, S. (2006). Older adults' perspectives on driving cessation. *Journal of Aging Studies*, *20*, 227–235.

Alonso, A. C., Petersen, M. D., Busse, A. L., Jacob-Filho, W., Borges, M. T. A., Serra, M. M., … Greve, J. M. D. A. (2016). Muscle strength, postural balance, and cognition are associated with braking time during driving in older adults. *Experimental Gerontology*, *85*, 13–17.

Alvarez, F. J., & Fierro, I. (2008). Older drivers, medical conditions, medical impairment and crash risk. *Accident Analysis & Prevention*, *40*, 55–60.

Anstey, K. J., Windsor, T. D., Luszcz, M. A., & Andrews, G. R. (2006). Predicting driving cessation over 5 years in older adults: Psychological well-being and cognitive competence are stronger predictors than physical health. *Journal of the American Geriatrics Society*, *54*, 121–126.

Antin, J. F., Guo, F., Fang, Y., Dingus, T. A., Perez, M. A., & Hankey, J. M. (2017). A validation of the low mileage bias using naturalistic driving study data. *Journal of Safety Research*, *63*, 115–120.

Ball, K., Owsley, C., Stalvey, B., Roenker, D. L., Sloane, M. E., & Graves, M. (1998). Driving avoidance and functional impairment in older drivers. *Accident Analysis & Prevention*, *30*, 313–322.

Ball, K., & Sekuler, R. (1986). Improving visual perception in older observers. *Journal of Gerontology*, *41*, 176–182.

Ball, K. K., Beard, B. L., Roenker, D. L., Miller, R. L., & Griggs, D. S. (1988). Age and visual search: Expanding the useful field of view. *Journal of the Optical Society of America*, *5*, 2210–2219.

Ball, K. K., Roenker, D. L., Wadley, V. G., Edwards, J. D., Roth, D. L., McGwin, G., Jr., … Dube, T. (2005). Can high-risk older drivers be identified through performance-based measures in a Department of Motor Vehicles setting? *Journal of the American Geriatrics Society*, *54*, 77–84.

Braitman, K. A., Kirley, B. B., Ferguson, S., & Chaudhary, N. K. (2007). Factors leading to older drivers' intersection crashes. *Traffic Injury Prevention*, *8*(3), 267–274.

Bryanton, O., Weeks, L. E., & Lees, J. M. (2010). Supporting older women in the transition to driving cessation. *Activities, Adaptation & Aging*, *34*, 181–195.

Bryden, K. J., Charlton, J. L., Oxley, J. A., & Lowndes, G. J. (2013). Self-reported wayfinding ability of older drivers. *Accident Analysis & Prevention*, *59*, 277–282.

Burg, A. (1966). Visual acuity as measured by dynamic and static tests. *Journal of Applied Psychology*, *50*, 460–466.

Burg, A., & Hurlbert, S. (1961). Dynamic visual acuity as related to age, sex, and static acuity. *Journal of Applied Psychology*, *45*, 111–116.

Chan, N. D., & Shaheen, S. A. (2012). Ridesharing in North America: Past, present, and future. *Transport Reviews*, *31*(1), 93–112.

Chapman, E. A., deVries, H. A., & Swezey, R. (1972). Joint stiffness: Effects of exercise on young and old men. *Journal of Gerontology*, *27*(2), 218–221.

Challands, K. G., Lacherez, P., & Obst, P. L. (2017). Does online social connectedness buffer risk of depression following driving cessation? An analysis of older drivers and ex-drivers. *Cyberpsychology, Behavior, and Social Networking*, *20*(4), 232–237.

Charlton, J., Koppel, S., Odell, M., Devlin, A., Langford, J., O'Hare, M., … Scully, M. (2010). *Influence of chronic illness on crash involvement of motor vehicle drivers* (2nd ed.). Clayton, VIC, Australia: Monash University Accident Research Centre, Report No. 300.

Chen, X., Mao, G., & Leng, S. X. (2014). Frailty syndrome: An overview. *Clinical Investigations in Aging*, *9*, 433–441.

Cheung, I., & McCartt, A. T. (2011). Declines in fatal crashes of older drivers: Changes in crash risk and survivability. *Accident Analysis & Prevention, 43*, 666–674.

Chihuri, S., Mielenz, T. J., DiMaggio, C. J., Betz, M. E., DiGuiseppi, C., Jones, V. C., & Li, G. (2016). Driving cessation and health outcomes in older adults. *Journal of the American Geriatrics Society, 64*, 332–341.

Choi, M., Lohman, M. C., & Mezuk, B. (2014). Trajectories of cognitive decline by driving mobility: Evidence from the Health and Retirement Study. *International Journal of Geriatric Psychiatry, 29*, 447–453.

Cicchino, J. B. (2015). Why have fatality rates among older drivers declined? The relative contributions of changes in survivability and crash involvement. *Accident Analysis & Prevention, 83*, 67–73.

Cicchino, J. B., & McCartt, A. T. (2014). Trends in older driver crash involvement rates and survivability in the United States: An update. *Accident Analysis & Prevention, 72*, 44–54.

Clarke, D. D., Ward, P., Bartle, C., & Truman, W. (2010). Older drivers' road traffic crashes in the UK. *Accident Analysis & Prevention, 42*, 1018–1024.

Collard, R. M., Boter, H., Schoevers, R. A., & Voshaar, R. C. O. (2012). Prevalence of frailty in community-dwelling older persons: A systematic review. *Journal of the American Geriatric Society, 60*, 1487–1492.

Cooper, P. (1990). Differences in accident characteristics among elderly drivers and between elderly and middle-aged drivers. *Accident Analysis & Prevention, 5*, 499–508.

Cross, J. M., McGwin, G., Jr., Rubin, G. S., Ball, K. K., West, S. K., Roenker, D. L., & Owsley, C. (2009). Visual and medical risk factors for motor vehicle collision involvement among older drivers. *British Journal of Ophthalmology, 93*(3), 400–404.

Curl, A. L., Stowe, J. D., Cooney, T. M., & Proulx, C. M. (2013). Giving up the keys: How driving cessation affects engagement in later life. *The Gerontologist, 54*(3), 423–433.

Dawson, J. D., Uc, E. Y., Anderson, S. W., Johnson, A. M., & Rizzo, M. (2010). Neuropsychological predictors of driving errors in older adults. *Journal of the American Geriatrics Society, 58*, 1090–1096.

Der, G., & Deary, I. J. (2006). Age and sex differences in reaction time in adulthood: Results from the United Kingdom Health and Lifestyle Survey. *Psychology and Aging, 21*(1), 62–73.

Dickerson, A. E., Molnar, L. J., Bédard, M., Eby, D. W., Berg-Weger, M., Choi, M., ... Silverstein, N. M. (2017). Transportation and aging: An updated research agenda for advancing safe mobility among older adults transitioning from driving to non-driving. *The Gerontologist*. Available from https://doi.org/10.1093/geront/gnx120.

Dickerson, A. E., Molnar, L. J., Bédard, M., Eby, D. W., Classen, S., & Polgar, J. M. (2017). Transportation and aging: An updated research agenda for advancing safe mobility. *Journal of Applied Gerontology*. Available from https://doi.org/10.1177/0733464817739154.

Dickerson, A. E., Molnar, L. J., Eby, D. W., Adler, G., Bédard, M., Berg-Weger, M., ... Trujillo, L. (2007). Transportation and aging: A research agenda for advancing safe mobility. *The Gerontologist, 47*, 578–590.

Dobbs, B. (2005). Medical conditions and driving: A review of the scientific literature (1960–2000). Report no. DOT HS 809 690. Washington, DC: National Highway Traffic Safety Administration.

Drag, L. L., & Bieliauskas, L. A. (2010). Contemporary review 2009: Cognitive aging. *Journal of Geriatric Psychiatry, 23*(2), 75–93.

Eby, D. W. (1995). The convicted drunk driver in Michigan: A profile of offenders. *UMTRI Research Review*, *25*(5), 1–11.

Eby, D. W., Molnar, L. J., & Kartje, P. S. (2009). *Maintaining safe mobility in an aging society*. New York, NY: CRC Press.

Edwards, J. D., Lunsman, M., Perkins, M., Rebok, G. W., & Roth, D. L. (2009). Driving cessation and health trajectories in older adults. *The Journals of Gerontology Series A: Biological Sciences and Medical Sciences*, *64*, 1290–1295.

Edwards, J. D., Ross, L. A., Ackerman, M. L., Small, B. J., Ball, K. K., Bradley, S., & Dodson, J. E. (2008). Longitudinal predictors of driving cessation among older adults from the ACTIVE clinical trial. *Journal of Gerontology: Psychological Sciences*, *63B* (1), P6–P12.

Emerson, J. L., Johnson, A. M., Dawson, J. D., Uc, E. Y., Anderson, S. W., & Rizzo, M. (2012). Predictors of driving outcomes in advancing age. *Psychology and Aging*, *27*(3), 550–559.

Federal Highway Administration. (2000). *Highway statistics: 2000*. Washington, DC: Federal Highway Administration. https://www.fhwa.dot.gov/ohim/hs00/ Accessed October, 2017.

Federal Highway Administration. (2005). *Highway statistics: 2005*. Washington, DC: Federal Highway Administration. https://www.fhwa.dot.gov/policy/ohim/hs05/ Accessed October, 2017.

Federal Highway Administration. (2010). *Highway statistics: 2010*. Washington, DC: Federal Highway Administration. https://www.fhwa.dot.gov/policyinformation/statistics/2010/ Accessed October, 2017.

Federal Highway Administration. (2015). *Highway statistics: 2015. Distribution of licensed drivers—2015 by sex and percentage in each age group and relation to population*. Washington, DC: Federal Highway Administration. https://www.fhwa.dot.gov/policyinformation/statistics/2015/ Accessed October, 2017.

Federal Highway Administration. (2017). *Licensed drivers by age and sex*. Washington, DC: Federal Highway Administration. https://www.fhwa.dot.gov/ohim/onh00/bar7.htm Accessed October, 2017.

Fillit, H., & Butler, R. N. (2009). The frailty identity crisis. *Journal of the American Geriatrics Society*, *57*, 348–352.

Fozard, J. L., Vercruyssen, M., Reynolds, S. L., Hancock, P. A., & Quilter, R. E. (1994). Age differences and changes in reaction time: The Baltimore Longitudinal Study of Aging. *Journal of Gerontology, Psychological Sciences*, *49*(4), P179–P189.

Fried, L. P., Tangen, C. M., Walston, J., Newman, A. B., Hirsch, C., Gottdiener, J., … for the Cardiovascular Health Study Collaborative Research Group. (2001). Frailty in older adults: Evidence for a phenotype. *Journal of Gerontology: Medical Sciences*, *56A*(3), M146–M156.

Hakamies-Blomqvist, L. E. (1993). Fatal accidents of older drivers. *Accident Analysis & Prevention*, *25*, 19–27.

Hakamies-Blomqvist, L., Raitanen, T., & O'Neill, D. (2002). Driver ageing does not cause higher accident rates per km. *Transportation Research Part F*, *5*, 271–274.

Hagler, Y. (2009). *Defining United States megaregions*. New York, NY: Regional Plan Association, America 2050.

Hanson, T. R., & Hildebrand, E. D. (2011). Can rural older drivers meet their needs without a car? Stated adaptation responses from a GPS travel diary survey. *Transportation*, *38* (6), 975–992.

Harada, C. N., Love, M. C. N., & Triebel, K. (2013). Normal cognitive aging. *Clinical Geriatric Medicine, 29*(4), 737–752.
Harrison, A., & Ragland, D. R. (2003). Consequences of driving reduction or cessation for older adults. *Transportation Research Record, 1843*, 96–104.
He, W., Goodkind, D., & Kowal, P. (2016). *An aging world: 2015*. International population reports P95/16-1. Washington, DC: United States Census Bureau.
Head, D., & Isom, M. (2010). Age effects on wayfinding and route learning skills. *Behavioural Brain Research, 209*, 49–58.
Henriksson, P., & Sagberg, F. (2010). Elderly drivers' accidents in Norway. In *Paper presented at the 12th international conference on mobility and transport for elderly and disabled persons (TRANSED 2010)*. Hong Kong, 2–4 June, 2010.
Heppenstall, C. P., Wilkinson, T. J., Hanger, H. C., & Keeling, S. (2009). Frailty: Dominos or deliberation? *The New Zealand Medical Journal, 122*(1299), 42–52.
Heron, A., & Chown, S. M. (1967). *Age and function*. London, UK: Churchill.
Hofstetter, H. W., & Bertsch, J. D. (1976). Does stereopsis change with age? *American Journal of Ophthalmology & Physiological Optics, 53*, 664–667.
Ichikawa, M., Nakahara, S., & Taniguchi, A. (2015). Older drivers' risks of at-fault motor vehicle collisions. *Accident Analysis & Prevention, 81*, 120–123.
Insurance Institute for Highway Safety. *Older drivers: Trends*. (2017). <http://www.iihs.org/iihs/topics/t/older-drivers/fatalityfacts/older-people> Accessed October, 2017.
International Transport Forum (2017). Casualties by age and road user. *ITF Transport Statistics (database)*. <https://doi.org/10.1787/3c6c57b0-en> Accessed October, 2017.
Ivers, R. Q., Mitchell, P., & Cumming, R. G. (1999). Sensory impairment and driving: The Blue Mountains Eye Study. *American Journal of Public Health, 89*, 85–87.
Jansen, P., Schmelter, A., & Heil, M. (2010). Spatial knowledge acquisition in younger and elderly adults: A study in a virtual environment. *Experimental Psychology, 57*, 54–60.
Jones, J. G., McCann, J., & Lassere, M. N. (1991). Driving and arthritis. *British Journal of Rheumatology, 30*, 361–364.
Kent, R. (2010). *The biomechanics of aging. NTSB forum on safety, mobility, and aging drivers*. Washington, DC: Transportation Research Board.
Kent, R., Trowbridge, M., Lopez-Valdes, F. J., Ordoyo, R. H., & Segui-Gomez, M. (2009). How many people are injured and killed as a result of aging? Frailty, fragility, and the elderly risk-exposure tradeoff assessed via a risk saturation model. *Annals of Advances in Automotive Medicine, 53*, 41–50.
Klavora, P., & Heslegrave, R. J. (2002). Senior drivers: An overview of problems and intervention strategies. *Journal of Aging and Physical Activity, 10*, 322–335.
Klencklen, G., Després, O., & Dufour, A. (2012). What do we know about aging and spatial cognition? Reviews and perspectives. *Ageing Research Reviews, 11*, 123–135.
Kline, D. W., & Birren, J. E. (1975). Age differences in backwards dichoptic masking. *Experimental Aging Research, 1*, 17–25.
Kochera, A., Straight, A., & Guterbock, T. (2005). *Beyond 50.05: A report to the nation on livable communities: Creating environments for successful aging*. Washington, DC: AARP.
Koppel, S., Bohensky, M., Langford, J., & Taranto, D. (2011). Older drivers, crashes, and injuries. *Traffic Injury Prevention, 12*(5), 459–467.
Kostyniuk, L. P., & Shope, J. T. (2003). Driving and alternatives: Older drivers in Michigan. *Journal of Safety Research, 34*, 407–414.
Lacherez, P., Wood, J. M., Anstey, K. J., & Lord, S. R. (2014). Sensorimotor and postural control factors associated with driving safety in a community-dwelling older driver population. *Journals of Gerontology: Medical Sciences, 69*(2), 240–244.

Langford, J., Charlton, J. L., Koppel, S., Myers, A., Tuokko, H., Marshall, S., . . . Macdonald, W. (2013). Findings from the Candrive/Ozcandrive study: Low mileage older drivers, crash risk and reduced fitness to drive. *Accident Analysis & Prevention, 61*, 304–310.

Langford, J., & Koppel, S. (2006). Epidemiology of older driver crashes—Identifying older driver risk factors and exposure patterns. *Transportation Research Part F, 9*, 309–321.

Langford, J., Methorst, R., & Hakamies-Blomqvist, L. (2006). Older drivers do not have a high crash risk—A replication of low mileage bias. *Accident Analysis & Prevention, 38*, 574–578.

Larsen, L., & Kines, P. (2002). Multi-disciplinary in-depth investigations of head on and left turn road collisions. *Accident Analysis & Prevention, 34*, 367–380.

Lee, S. J., Steinman, M. A., & Tan, E. J. (2011). Volunteering, driving status, and mortality in United States retirees. *Journal of the American Geriatrics Society, 59*, 274–280.

Li, G., Braver, E., & Chen, L. (2003). Fragility vs excessive crash involvement as determinants of high death rates per vehicle-mile of travel among older drivers. *Accident Analyses & Prevention, 35*, 227–235.

Liddle, J., Gustafsson, L., Bartlett, H., & McKenna, K. (2012). Time use, role participation, and life satisfaction of older people: Impact of driving status. *Australian Occupational Therapy Journal, 59*, 384–392.

Long, G. M., & Crambert, R. F. (1989). The nature and basis of age-related changes in dynamic visual acuity. *Psychology of Aging, 5*, 138–143.

Mäkinen, A.-K. *6 Ways technology will change transportation in the future.* (2017). <http://blog.parkman.io/technology-transportation-future> Accessed November, 2017.

Malfetti, J. W. (1985). *Needs and problems of older drivers: Survey results and recommendations.* Falls Church, VA: AAA Foundation for Traffic Safety.

Marottoli, R. A., Mendes de Leon, C. F., Glass, T. A., Williams, C. S., Cooney, L. M., Jr., & Berkman, L. F. (2000). Consequences of driving cessation: Decreased out-of-home activity levels. *Journal of Gerontology: Social Science, 55B*, S334–S340.

Marottoli, R. A., Mendes de Leon, C. F., Glass, T. A., Williams, C. S., Cooney, L. M., Jr., Berkman, L. F., & Tinetti, M. E. (1997). Driving cessation and increased depressive symptoms: Prospective evidence from the New Haven EPESE. Established populations for epidemiologic studies of the elderly. *Journal of the American Geriatrics Society, 45*, 202–206.

Marottoli, R. A., Richardson, E. D., Stowe, M. H., Miller, E. G., Brass, L. M., Cooney, L. M., Jr., & Tinetti, M. E. (1998). Development of a test battery to identify older drivers at risk for self-reported adverse driving events. *Journal of the American Geriatrics Society, 46*, 562–568.

Marshall, P. H., Elias, J. W., & Wright, J. (1985). Age related factors in motor error detection and correction. *Experimental Aging Research, 11*, 201–206.

Mather, M. (2010). Aging and cognition. *Wiley Interdisciplinary Reviews: Cognitive Science, 1*, 346–362.

Mayr, U., Spieler, D. H., & Kliegl, R. (2001). *Aging and executive control.* New York, NY: Routledge.

McGwin, G., Jr., & Brown, D. B. (1999). Characteristics of traffic crashes among young, middle-aged, and older drivers. *Accident Analysis & Prevention, 31*, 181–198.

Meuleners, L. B., Narding, A., Lee, A. H., & Legge, M. (2006). Fragility and crash over-representation among older drivers in Western Australia. *Accident Analysis & Prevention, 38*, 1006–1010.

Mezuk, B., & Rebok, G. W. (2008). Social isolation and social support among older adults following driving cessation. *Journal of Gerontology: Social Sciences, 63B*(5), S298–S303.

Molnar, L. J., Charlton, J. L., Eby, D. W., Bogard, S. E., Langford, J., Koppel, S., ... Man-Son-Hing, M. (2013). Self-regulation of driving by older adults: Comparison of self-report and objective driving data. *Transportation Research Part F*, *20*, 29–38.

Molnar, L. J., & Eby, D. W. (2009). Getting around: Meeting the boomers' mobility needs. In R. Houston (Ed.), *Boomer bust? Economic and political issues of the graying society*. Praeger Publishing.

National Academy of Sciences, Engineering, and Medicine. (2016). *Attribution of extreme weather events in the context of climate change*. Washington, DC: National Academy of Sciences, Engineering, and Medicine.

National Highway Traffic Safety Administration. (2017). Traffic safety facts: older population. Report no. DOT HS 812 372. Washington, DC: United States Department of Transportation.

Organisation for Economic Co-operation and Development. (2001). *Ageing and transport. Mobility needs and safety issues*. Paris, France: OECD Publications.

Organisation for Economic Co-operation and Development. *Historical population data and projections (1950–2050)*. (2017). <http://stats.oecd.org/index.aspx?DatasetCode = POP_PROJ> Accessed October, 2017.

Ott, B. R., Davis, J. D., Papandonatos, G. D., Hewitt, S., Festa, E. K., Heindel, W. C., ... Carr, D. B. (2013). Assessment of driving-related skills prediction of unsafe driving in older adults in the office setting. *Journal of the American Geriatrics Society*, *61*, 1164–1169.

Owsley, C. (2011). Vision and aging. *Vision Research*, *51*, 1610–1622.

Owsley, C., Ball, K., McGwin, G., Jr., Sloane, M. E., Roenker, D. L., White, M. F., & Overley, T. E. (1998). Visual processing impairment and risk of motor vehicle crash among older adults. *Journal of the American Medical Association*, *279*, 1083–1088.

Owsley, C., & McGwin, G., Jr. (2010). Vision and driving. *Vision Research*, *50*, 2348–2361.

Owsley, C., McGwin, G., Scilley, K., Girkin, C. A., Phillips, J. M., & Searcey, K. (2006). Perceived barriers to care and attitudes about vision and eye care: Focus groups with older African Americans and eye care providers. *Investigative Ophthalmology & Visual Science*, *47*, 2797–2802.

Owsley, C., Sekuler, R., & Siemsen, D. (1983). Contrast sensitivity throughout adulthood. *Vision Research*, *23*, 689–699.

Owsley, C., Stalvey, B., Wells, J., Sloane, M. E., & McGwin, G., Jr. (2001). Visual risk factors for crash involvement in older drivers with cataract. *Archives of Ophthalmology*, *119*, 881–887.

Owsley, C., & Sloane, M. E. (1990). Vision and aging. In F. Bolter, & J. Grafman (Eds.), *Handbook of neuropsychology: Vol. 4*. Amsterdam, The Netherlands: Elsevier.

Oxley, J., Fildes, B., Corben, B., & Langford, J. (2006). Intersection design for older drivers. *Transportation Research Part F*, *9*, 335–346.

Parzen, J., Randall, C., & Feigon, S. (2015). *Shared-use mobility*. Chicago, IL: Shared-Use Mobility Center.

Petrofsky, J. S., & Lind, A. R. (1975). Aging, isometric strength and endurance, and cardiovascular responses to static effort. *Journal of Applied Psychology*, *1*, 91–95.

Ragland, D. R., Satariano, W. A., & MacLeod, K. E. (2005). Driving cessation and depressive symptoms. *Journal of Gerontology: Medical Sciences*, *60A*, 399–403.

Rakotonirainy, A., Steinhardt, D., Delhomme, P., Darvell, M., & Schramm, A. (2012). Older drivers' crashes in Queensland, Australia. *Accident Analysis & Prevention*, *48*, 423–429.

Rapoport, M. J., Naglie, G., Weegar, K., Myers, A., Cameron, D., Crizzle, A., ... Marshall, S. (2013). The relationship between cognitive performance, perceptions of driving comfort and abilities, and self-reported driving restrictions among healthy older drivers. *Accident Analysis & Prevention*, *61*, 288–295.

Rockwood, K., Song, X., & Mitnitski, A. (2011). Changes in relative fitness and frailty across the adult lifespan: Evidence from the Canadian National Population Health Survey. *Canadian Medical Association Journal*, *183*(8), E487–E494.

Rodgers, M. K., Sindone, J. A., & Moffat, S. D. (2012). Effects of age on navigation strategy. *Neurobiology of Aging*, *33*, 202.e15–202.e22.

Ross, L. A., Edwards, J. D., O'Connor, M. L., Ball, K. K., Wadley, V. G., & Vance, D. E. (2016). The transfer of cognitive speed of processing training to older adults' driving mobility across 5 years. *Journals of Gerontology: Psychological Sciences*, *71*(1), 87–97.

Rubin, G. S., Ng, E. S. W., Bandeen-Roche, E., Keyl, P. M., Freeman, E. E., West, S. K., & the SEE Project Team. (2007). *Investigative Ophthalmology & Visual Science*, *48*(4), 1483–1491.

Salthouse, T. A. (1987). Adult age differences in integrative spatial ability. *Psychology & Aging*, *2*, 254–260.

Salthouse, T. A. (2010). Selective review of cognitive aging. *Journal of the Neuropsychological Society*, *16*, 754–760.

Shaheen, S. A., & Cohen, A. P. (2007). Growth in worldwide carsharing. *Transportation Research Record*, *1992*, 81–89.

Sifrit, K.J., Stutts, J., Martell, C., & Staplin, L. (2011). Intersection crashes among drivers in their 60s, 70s, and 80s. Report no. DOT HS 811 495. Washington, DC: National Highway Traffic Safety Administration.

Sivak, M., & Schoettle, B. (2012). Recent changes in the age composition of drivers in 15 countries. *Traffic Injury Prevention*, *13*(2), 126–132.

Skyving, M., Berg, H.-Y., & Laflamme, L. (2009). A pattern analysis of traffic crashes fatal to older drivers. *Accident Analysis & Prevention*, *41*, 253–258.

Smith, E. L. (1989). Exercise in the elderly to prolong and improve the quality of life. In J. S. Skinner, C. B. Corbin, D. M. Landers, P. E. Martin, & C. L. Wells (Eds.), *Future directions in exercise and sport science research*. Champaign, IL: Human Kinetics.

Staplin, L., Gish, K. W., & Joyce, J. (2008). "Low mileage bias" and related policy implications—A cautionary note. *Accident Analysis & Prevention*, *40*, 1249–1252.

Staplin, L., Lococo, K.H., McKnight, A.J., McKnight, A.S., & Odenheimer, G.L. (1998). Intersection negotiation problems of older drivers, vol. II: Background synthesis on age and intersection driving difficulties. Report no. DOT HS 808 850. Washington, DC: United States Department of Transportation.

Staplin, L., Lococo, K.H., Stewart, J., & Decina, L. (1999). Safe mobility for older people: Notebook. Report no. DOT HS 808 853. Washington, DC: National Highway Traffic Safety Administration.

Shepard, R.J. (1998). Aging and exercise. In T. D. Fahey (Ed.), *Encyclopedia of sport medicine and science*. <http:\\sportsci.org> Accessed November, 2017.

Shinar, D. (1977). Driver visual limitations: Diagnosis and treatment. Report no. DOT-HS-803–260. Washington, DC: National Highway Traffic Safety Administration.

Syddall, H., Roberts, H. C., Evandrou, M., Cooper, C., Bergman, H., & Sayer, A. A. (2010). Prevalence and correlates of frailty among community-dwelling older men and women: Findings from the Hertfordshire Cohort Study. *Age and Ageing*, *39*, 197–203.

Szanton, S. L., Seplaki, C. L., Thorpe, R. J., Allen, J. K., & Fried, L. P. (2010). Socioeconomic status is associated with frailty: The women's health and aging studies. *Journal of Epidemiology and Community Health*, *64*, 63–67.

Uber. *The Uber story*. (2017). <https://www.uber.com/our-story/> Accessed November, 2017.

United Nations. (2015). *World population aging 2015*. New York, NY: United Nations, Report no. ST/ESA/SER.A/390.

United Nations. (2017). *World population prospects: The 2017 revision*. New York, NY: United Nations. <https://esa.un.org/unpd/wpp/Download/Standard/Population/> Accessed October, 2017.

United States Department of Transportation. (2015). *Beyond traffic 2045: Trends and choices*. Washington, DC: United States Department of Transportation.

van Hooren, S., Valentijn, A., Bosma, H., Ponds, R. W., van Boxtel, M. P., & Jolles, J. (2007). Cognitive functioning in health older adults aged 64–81: A cohort study into the effects of age, sex, and education. *Aging, Neuropsychology, and Cognition*, *14*(1), 40–54.

Wagner, J. T., Müri, R. M., Nef, T., & Mosimann, U. P. (2011). Cognition and driving in older persons. *Swiss Medical Weekly*, *104*, w13136.

West, L. A., Cole, S., Goodkind, D., & He, W. (2014). *65 + in the United States: 2010*. Washington, DC: United States Census Bureau, Report number P23–212.

Wheatley, C. J., Pellerito, J. M., Jr., & Redpenning, S. (2006). The clinical evaluation. In J. M. Pellerito (Ed.), *Driver rehabilitation and community mobility: Principles and practice*. St. Louis, MO: Elsevier Mosby.

Wolf, E. (1960). Glare and age. *Archives of Ophthalmology*, *64*, 502–514.

Wood, J. M., & Owsley, C. (2014). Gerontology viewpoint: Useful field of view test. *Gerontology*, *60*(4), 315–318.

World Bank. *Life expectancy at birth, total (years)*. (2017a). <https://data.worldbank.org/indicator/SP.DYN.LE00.IN?end = 2015&start = 2015> Accessed October, 2017.

World Bank. (2017b). Population ages 65 and above (% of total). Washington, DC: The World Bank. http://data.worldbank.org/indicator/SP.POP.65UP.TO.ZS. Accessed October, 2017.

Woytowicz, W., Whitall, J., & Westlake, K. P. (2016). Age-related changes in bilateral upper extremity coordination. *Current Geriatric Reports*, *5*, 191–199.

Yassuda, M. S., Wilson, J. J., & von Mering, O. (1997). Driving cessation: The perspective of senior drivers. *Educational Gerontology*, *23*(6), 525–538.

Yunkyung, J., Gruenewald, T. L., Seeman, T. E., & Sarkisian, C. A. (2010). Productive activities and development of frailty in older adults. *Journal of Gerontology: Biological Sciences and Social Sciences*, *65B*(2), 256–261.

Zelazo, P. D., Craik, F. I. M., & Booth, L. (2004). Executive function across the life span. *Acta Psychologica*, *115*(2–3), 167–183.

# Driving patterns and behaviors among older adults

# 2

*You just have to keep driving down the road. It's going to bend and curve and you'll speed up and slow down, but the road keeps going.*

*Ellen DeGeneres*

## Introduction

Thirty years ago, the Transportation Research Board (1988) released a seminal report on the transportation needs and problems of older Americans, authored by several experts in the field. In the report, Sandra Rosenbloom noted that despite the recognized importance of transportation to older adults, "... myths and misconceptions persist about the transportation patterns and problems of the elderly and how their mobility needs can be met" (p. 21, Rosenbloom, 1988). She challenged the widespread view in both the popular and scholarly literature at the time that older adults tended to live in high-density areas, were largely dependent on walking or using public transit, and lacked social support or resources. Rather, her analysis showed that large proportions lived in single-family homes and rural areas, drove their own cars, and made most of their trips in personal automobiles whether or not they drove themselves. She identified three major trends in driving patterns: people of all ages traveled more in 1983 than they did in 1977, women traveled fewer miles than men at all ages, and people drove fewer miles as they aged, especially after age 60. She also noted that older drivers made shorter, more frequent trips than drivers of other ages, especially when work-related trips were excluded.

How have the travel patterns, especially the driving patterns of older adults, changed in the past 30 years and what can we expect in the future? This chapter attempts to answer this question within the context of three sets of comparisons. First, we explore whether the travel and driving patterns of current older adults as a group are different from those of older drivers in the past. Second, we look at differences between today's older drivers and younger drivers, and changes that have occurred over time. Finally, we examine differences in driving patterns among the older driver cohort itself. This last consideration is important as we know that older adults are the most heterogeneous of all segments of the population in terms of health and functioning, as well as changing life course needs (e.g., Alsnih & Hensher, 2003; Newbold & Scott, 2017); so, we would expect to see variation in their driving patterns as well. Thus, while it is important to understand older drivers as a group, it is just as important to understand how they differ from one another in their driving and what factors might account for these differences.

Perspectives and Strategies for Promoting Safe Transportation among Older Adults.
DOI: https://doi.org/10.1016/B978-0-12-812153-5.00002-9

## Differences in travel and driving patterns between older drivers today and in the past

One clear trend over time in the United States (US) has been an increased reliance on the personal vehicle for getting around (e.g., Eberhard, 2008; Rosenbloom, 2001; Santos, McGuckin, Nakamoto, Gray, & Liss, 2011). For example, Rosenbloom (2001) found that between 1983 and 1995, adults age 65 or older increased the number of trips they made in a personal automobile by 13%, their average trip length by 11%, their average time spent driving (in minutes) by 40%, and their average miles traveled per driver by 98%.

More recently, Santos et al. (2011) examined US trends in driving patterns by gender, using the US Department of Transportation's travel survey series (referred to as the *National Household Travel Survey*, NHTS, in 2009 and 2001, and *Nationwide Personal Transportation Survey*, in previous surveys). The average annual miles driven by licensed drivers age 65 or older are shown in Table 2.1. Average annual miles increased by 53.2% between 1983 and 2009. During that same period, older men's annual miles driven increased by 43.4% and older women's by 76.1%. Thus, the growth in annual miles of driving was sizable for the 65 or older population of drivers.

Santos et al. (2011) also found that the average vehicle trip length of older drivers increased between 1983 and 2009, from 5.9 to 7.5 mi, although the 2009 level remained about the same as the 2001 level after taking into account the margin of error. By contrast, although the average time spent driving (in minutes) showed an overall increase from the 1990 level of 30.8 minutes (data not available prior to 1990), the 2009 level of 46.4 actually represented a decrease from 49.1 in 2001. Average trip length and time spent driving were not reported by gender.

The long-term increase in automobile use among older adults has also been seen in industrialized countries outside the US including Australia (e.g., Rosenbloom, 2001), Canada (e.g., Newbold, Scott, Spinney, Kanaroglou, & Páez, 2005; Scott et al., 2009), Denmark (e.g., Magelund, 2001), Germany (e.g., Brög, Erl, & Glorius, 2000; Buehler & Nobis, 2010), New Zealand (e.g., O'Fallon & Sullivan, 2009), Norway (Hjorthol & Sagberg, 2000; Hjorthol, 2004), Sweden (Dillén, 2005), and the United Kingdom (e.g., Oxley, 2000), although the use of the personal

**Table 2.1** Average annual miles driven by licensed driver age 65 + by year

| Year | Men age 65 + | Women age 65 + | Total age 65 + |
|---|---|---|---|
| 1983 | 7198 | 3308 | 5386 |
| 1990 | 9162 | 4750 | 7084 |
| 1995 | 10,304 | 4785 | 7646 |
| 2001 | 10,163 | 4803 | 7684 |
| 2009 | 10,322 | 5824 | 8250 |

Source: Adapted from Santos, A., McGuckin, N., Nakamoto, H. Y., Gray, D., & Liss, S. (2011). *Summary of travel trends: 2009 National Household Travel Survey*. Washington, DC: US Department of Transportation.

automobile in absolute terms remains higher among US older drivers. Some illustrative examples of the increased trend in automobile travel are provided below.

Scott et al. (2009) compared changes in travel behavior among Canadians from 1992 and 2005, using Canada's *General Social Surveys* (GSS). They found that older drivers not only became more dependent on the personal automobile but also were more likely to be the driver of that vehicle. Newbold et al. (2005) conducted a cohort analysis using data from three cycles of the GSS in Canada. Comparing the travel behavior of older Canadians and younger cohorts, along with changes with age, they found continued dependence on the private automobile, with the number of trips as a driver increasing over the 12 years of data. Trips per day by older drivers increased from 2.7 in 1986 to 3.3 in 1998 even as the cohort aged and both trip count and trip duration decreased, suggesting increased reliance on the personal automobile for those trips. At the same time, older adults made fewer trips of shorter duration with fewer trips as the driver of a personal automobile and traveled for different reasons than younger cohorts.

Hjorthol, Levin, and Sirén (2010) analyzed data from the national travel surveys over a 20-year period from 1985 to 2005 for Denmark, Norway, and Sweden and found a significant increase in automobile use among older adults, especially women. They also found a significant and strong increase in the number of automobile trips as a driver among all age groups in Denmark and Norway, including the older age groups. Looking just at travel surveys in Norway, Hjorthol and Sagberg (1998) reported that older adults traveled further in 1991/92 compared to 1984/85 and made more trips by automobile, although the latter increase was more pronounced among older men than women.

O'Fallon and Sullivan (2009) used the *New Zealand Household Travel Survey* dataset to compare older adults between 1997/87 and 2004/07. They found that as a group, older adults (age 60 or older) in New Zealand increased their volume of travel, especially driver trips and distance driven, at a much higher rate than their population increase would imply. However, this older age group continued to travel less than younger adults (age 25–59) in terms of the number of daily trip segments, typical distance per trip segment, mean distance per day, and mean distance per day driving.

While the cited studies from outside the US identify trends similar to those found for US older drivers, they also point to the need to disentangle age effects from cohort effects when examining changes over time. For example, findings from a study comparing older drivers in the US and Germany (Buehler & Nobis, 2010) suggested that in both countries, the travel behavior of 45–64-year olds in the early 1980s was a good predictor of travel behavior of drivers age 65 or older in 2001. The authors concluded that once a travel behavior is adopted, it seems to carry on into older age. However, their study focused on overall travel behavior rather than on driving-specific behavior and thus, their conclusions need to be understood within that context.

Research by Frändberg and Vilhelmson (2011) found declines among young people age 15–24 in Sweden between 1978 and 2006 in terms of everyday travel, long-distance domestic trips, and dependence on and use of the personal automobile, as well as postponement of licensure. They questioned whether these trends suggest a departure from the dependence on the personal automobile for community mobility, thus representing a cohort change that will characterize this generation as it ages.

Newbold and Scott (2017) specifically examined cohort effects in Canada, focusing on differences in driving over the life course by generational cohort (Millennial, Generation X, Baby Boomer, and the Greatest Generation). Using Canadian national travel survey data, they found that approximately three quarters of all trips made by Boomers (both early and late) were as automobile drivers, with relatively little change between 1992 and 2010. By comparison, only 52% of trips made by Millennials and 60% of the Greatest Generation were as automobile drivers in 2010. However, according to the authors, while Millennials were slower to obtain a driver's license than earlier generations, they ultimately achieved similar rates of licensure. They also exhibited an increasing number of trips as an automobile driver. While trip duration generally increased for all automobile drivers between 1992 and 2010, the greatest increase was among early Boomers (increasing by 6.8 minutes). Based on their analysis, the authors concluded that Canadians will continue to depend on the personal automobile as the primary mode for personal transportation barring major changes in policy, pricing, or accessibility of alternative modes.

## Differences in travel and driving patterns between younger and older adults

The analysis by Santos et al. (2011) highlighted earlier also looked at differences between older and younger drivers with respect to annual miles driven per licensed driver. In every survey year, the number of average miles driven among drivers age 65 or older was less than each of the other age groups except 16–19-year olds. The number of annual miles driven per licensed driver increased for each age group between 1983 and 2009. Although this number appeared to decrease for all but the oldest age groups between 2001 and 2009, the decrease in annual miles achieved statistical significance for only the youngest two age groups.

Shen, Koech, Feng, Rice, and Zhu (2017) used more recent data from the 2015 *American Time Use Survey* to compare the travel patterns of older drivers (age 65–74 and 75 or older) and younger drivers (age 25–64). They found that, based on results of "time-use diaries," 77.6% of all daily trips by 25–64-year olds were as drivers of a personal automobile, compared to 72.9% of 65–74-year olds and 68.9% of people age 75 or older. The average daily driving time (in minutes) among automobile drivers decreased with age (55.7 minutes for 25–64-year olds, 38.6 minutes for 65–74-year olds, and 28.4 minutes for those age 75 or older). In every age group, men drove more minutes than women, with the greatest difference between men and women among the oldest age group. In terms of when people drove, drivers age 65–74 and 75 or older took more trips in the morning and early afternoon than other times of day, while the younger age group took more trips in the late afternoon and early evening.

The age-related differences in driving found by Santos et al. (2011) and Shen et al. (2017) are consistent with other studies both within and outside the US (e.g., Boschmann & Brady, 2013; Collia, Sharp, & Giesbrecht, 2003; Mercado & Páez, 2009; Metz, 2010). For example, Collia et al. (2003) examined data from the 2001 NHTS in the US and found that older adults (age 65 or older) tended to be less mobile in that they took fewer trips, traveled shorter distances, and had shorter travel times than their younger counterparts (age 19–64). This pattern was more pronounced among older women.

Mercado and Páez (2009) found declines in distance traveled with increasing age among Canadian automobile drivers (total distance traveled over total number of trips), with an average reduction of about 5 km at the age of 65. There was no difference in the magnitude of travel reduction between the young old (age 65–79) and the oldest old (age 80 or older). In addition, neighborhoods with high commercial and residential mix were associated with shorter distances traveled.

Until recently, much of the available information on the driving patterns of drivers of various ages came from survey data that relied on self-reports of drivers. Advances in sensor, computer, and telecommunication technologies now make it possible to automatically collect detailed, objective information about individuals' driving patterns (e.g., LeBlanc, Sayer, Winkler, & Bogard, 2007; LeBlanc et al., 2006). This technology, placed unobtrusively in a driver's vehicle, can be used to study the driving behavior of individual drivers under naturalistic conditions, that is, as part of their everyday driving (SWOV Institute for Road Safety Research, 2010).

Findings from the few studies of this type confirm that driving patterns often differ across age groups. For example, Molnar et al. (2018) compared driving exposure and patterns among three age groups of drivers (20–30, 40–50, 60–70), using data from a naturalistic driving study conducted as part of the *Integrated Vehicle-Based Safety System* program (see Sayer et al., 2010). As described in Molnar, Charlton, et al. (2013), travel patterns were determined primarily based on global positioning system (GPS) measurements that included location, time of day, vehicle speed, heading, and GPS quality indicators. When looking at age independent of gender, drivers in the older age group (age 60–70) took fewer trips, drove fewer minutes, and were less likely to drive at night than the youngest age group (20–30). They were also less likely to drive during peak period morning traffic and on high-speed roads than their middle age counterparts (40–50).

Across all age groups, there were few differences by gender, with the exception that females drove fewer miles and fewer minutes. Results by combined age and gender groups provided insights into what was contributing to the independent age and gender differences. When both age and gender were taken into account, it was often the group of females age 60–70 that appeared to account for many of the age and gender differences found in driving exposure and patterns. An important research question raised by the investigators was whether these patterns will persist as younger cohorts age, given that women who have grown up with the automobile may drive differently than the current cohort of older women. The results of this study suggested that the younger and middle-aged female age groups were more dissimilar than similar to the older female age group.

## Differences in travel and driving patterns among today's older drivers

As noted earlier, older drivers do not represent a single homogeneous group, and this is evident in terms of their driving patterns. We know from travel surveys that driving patterns often differ by age and gender (e.g., Collia et al., 2003; Rosenbloom, 2006; Rosenbloom & Herbel, 2009; Santos et al., 2011; Truong & Somenahalli, 2011). For example, Santos et al. (2011) found that the percentage of drivers decreased with increasing age within the older driver cohort; that is, 91.4% of 60–69-year olds were drivers in 2009, compared to 83% of 70–79-year olds and 61.7% of those 80 or older. Similarly, the number of vehicle miles per driver decreased from 27.6 among 60–69-year olds to 18.8 among 70–79-year olds to 12.0 among those 80 or older. Truong and Somenahalli (2011) examined travel survey data for metropolitan Adelaide in Australia for people age 65 or older and found a decrease in the number of daily trips with increasing age (3.9, 3.0, and 2.4 for 65–74, 75–84, and 85 + year olds, respectively) and average distance traveled in kilometers (24.9, 15.8, and 12.5, respectively).

With regard to gender, Collia et al. (2003) examined data from the 2001 NHTS in the US and found that older women (age 65 or older) consistently took the least number of trips per day, had the lowest driving rates, and traveled shorter distances than their male counterparts. Rosenbloom (2006) also found significant differences in travel patterns between older men and women. Women drove less often and for fewer miles than men of comparable ages, with these differences more pronounced at older ages. She cautioned that the drop in trip making among women as they age may be the result of cohort and income effects and that as women increasingly come to resemble men (e.g., in terms of driving experience, education, professional accomplishments), they may display the same demand for travel now seen among men. This conclusion is consistent with other study findings that driving cessation among women with an active driving history was more similar to men's driving cessation, suggesting that personal driving history rather than gender per se is important in decisions to reduce or stop driving (Hakamies-Blomqvist & Sirén, 2003).

Findings from naturalistic driving studies have also provided evidence of decreased travel with increasing age, as well as differences by gender. For example, Molnar et al. (in press) recently examined objective measures of driving exposure and patterns among a large sample ($n = 2131$) of older drivers. Data were obtained from participants in the *Longitudinal Research on Aging Drivers* (LongROAD) study, a multisite prospective cohort study of drivers age 65–79, using GPS-derived driving measures averaged over 12 months following baseline (see Li et al.,

2017 for full detail on study methods). Three age groups were examined: 65–69, 70–74, and 75–79. Results indicated that in general, the oldest drivers (75–79-year olds) had the lowest overall driving exposure. They drove fewer miles, miles per trip, and minutes than either of the younger age groups. They also had fewer trips per month than the youngest age group. In terms of driving patterns, they had a lower percentage of trips on high-speed roads and a higher percentage of trips within 15 mi of home than either of the younger age groups. They also had a lower percentage of trips at night and in PM peak period traffic than the youngest age group. Women had lower overall driving exposure than men, driving fewer trips, miles, miles per trip, and minutes. They also had a lower percentage of trips at night, in AM peak traffic times, and on high-speed roads, as well as a higher percentage of trips within 15 mi of home than men.

Much of the research focusing on the driving patterns of older drivers has been done within the context of "self-regulation" of driving. Self-regulation is commonly thought of as the process by which individuals modify or adjust their driving patterns by driving less or intentionally avoiding situations considered challenging (e.g., driving at night, during rush hour traffic, in unfamiliar areas, on the freeway, and so forth; e.g., Baldock, Mathias, McLean, & Berndt, 2006; Ball et al., 1998; D'Ambrosio, Donorfio, Coughlin, Mohyde, & Meyer, 2008; Molnar & Eby, 2008; Stalvey & Owsley, 2000). Further, self-regulation has increasingly come to be seen as a strategy for compensating for declining health or loss of functional abilities that can compromise driving (e.g., Hakamies-Blomqvist & Wahlström, 1998; Jones, Cho, Abendschoen-Milani, & Gielen, 2011; Sullivan, Smith, Horswill, & Lurie-Beck, 2011). The idea behind this latter conceptualization is that drivers have some insight into and awareness of their declining abilities and self-regulate their driving to continue driving in some capacity.

Molnar et al. (2015) conducted an extensive synthesis of the literature on self-regulation of driving among older adults. The synthesis built upon earlier reviews of the literature by the authors (e.g., Molnar & Eby, 2008), as well as extended literature findings on specific aspects of self-regulation (e.g., Molnar, Eby, Charlton, et al., 2013; Molnar, Eby, Langford, et al., 2013, 2014). Given the timeliness and comprehensiveness of that review, we highlight some of its major findings here with regard to differences in self-regulation among older drivers.

The review found considerable variation in the extent and type of self-regulation engaged in by older drivers. That is, while many older drivers appeared to self-regulate by reducing their overall driving exposure (e.g., Benekohal, Michaels, Shim, & Resende, 1994; Charlton et al., 2006; Klavora & Heslegrave, 2002; Marottoli et al., 1993; Raitanen, Tormakangas, Mollenkopf, & Marcellini, 2003; Ruechel & Mann, 2005), or avoiding specific driving situations such as driving at night, in bad weather, in heavy traffic, and making left turns (e.g., Baldock et al., 2006; Ball et al., 1998; Benekohal et al., 1994; Charlton et al., 2006; Choi, Adams, & Kahana, 2013; Hakamies-Blomqvist & Wahlström, 1998; Klavora & Heslegrave, 2002; Kostyniuk & Molnar, 2008; Molnar, Eby, Charlton et al., 2013; Molnar, Eby, Langford et al., 2013; Molnar, Charlton et al., 2013; Ruechel & Mann, 2005; Sirén & Meng, 2013; Stalvey & Owsley, 2000), specific rates varied greatly across studies, making it difficult to reach meaningful conclusions on just how widespread self-regulation is.

The review also examined various factors affecting self-regulation. Study findings on the effect of age were mixed; some studies showed increased self-regulation with increasing age (e.g., Charlton et al., 2006; Donorfio, D'Ambrosio, Coughlin, & Mohyde, 2008; Gwyther & Holland, 2012; Sargent-Cox, Windsor, Walker, & Anstey, 2011; Unsworth, Wells, Browning, Thoman, & Kendig, 2007), and others did not (e.g., Blanchard & Myers, 2010; Molnar, Eby, Roberts, St. Louis, & Langford, 2009; Molnar et al., 2014). According to Molnar et al. (2015), this could have been due to differences in study design or to mediating effects of factors such as health and functioning status, or driving experience (e.g., Donorfio, Mohyde, Coughlin, & D'Ambrosio, 2008; Gwyther & Holland, 2012).

The review found growing evidence that older women self-regulate their driving more than their male counterparts (e.g., Charlton et al., 2006; Choi et al., 2013; Classen, Wang, Crizzle, Winter, & Lanford, 2013; D'Ambrosio et al., 2008; Hakamies-Blomqvist & Wahlström, 1998; Kostyniuk & Molnar, 2008; Naumann, Dellinger, & Kresnow, 2011; Rosenbloom & Herbel, 2009; Rosenbloom & Santos, 2014; Sengupta et al., 2014; West et al., 2003). However, several reviewed studies did not find greater self-regulation among women (e.g., Blanchard & Myers, 2010; Gwyther & Holland, 2012; Molnar et al., 2009; Ross et al., 2009; Unsworth et al., 2007). One explanation offered for these mixed findings was the mediating role that perceived confidence may play in various driving situations (Kostyniuk & Molnar, 2008). This conclusion is supported by studies that found reduced effects of gender and age on driving avoidance when some type of confidence variable was added in the analyses (e.g., Charlton et al., 2006).

In fact, the relationship between perceptions of confidence or comfort in specific driving situations and self-regulation in terms of avoiding those situations is one of the most consistent findings in the literature (e.g., Baldock et al., 2006; Blanchard & Myers, 2010; Charlton et al., 2006; MacDonald, Myers, & Blanchard, 2008; Molnar & Eby, 2008; Molnar, Eby, Charlton, et al., 2013, 2014; Rudman, Friedland, Chipman, & Sciortino, 2006; Sirén & Meng, 2013). This finding has persisted regardless of how confidence or comfort is measured. In turn, driving comfort appears to be mediated by other factors, although there is limited research in this area (Carmel, Rechavi, & Ben-Moshe, 2014). Among the findings from studies that have been conducted are that driving confidence may be associated with cognitive performance (Anstey & Smith, 2003) and perceived health status (overall health and health symptoms such as pain, stiffness, limited strength in five body areas particularly relevant to driving, Tuokko et al., 2013).

Overall health and functioning clearly plays a role in self-regulation. Given the complexity of the relationship between medical conditions and driving (e.g., the myriad combinations of diseases with associated varying severity, and variability in treatment and medication effects; Marshall & Man-Son-Hing, 2011), many studies on self-regulation have focused on the effects of specific functional impairments rather than medical conditions per se. Visual impairment has been among the most frequently studied functional decline with regard to self-regulation. Findings from a number of studies provide evidence of an association between visual impairment and increased self-regulation (e.g., Ball et al., 1998; Charlton et al., 2006; Choi et al., 2013; Fraser, Meuleners, Ng, & Morlet, 2013; Lotfipour et al., 2010; Sengupta et al., 2014; Unsworth et al., 2007; West et al., 2003).

The effects of psychomotor impairments on self-regulation have been less studied than other areas of functioning and findings are less conclusive, with some studies finding only modest or no associations (e.g., Braitman & Williams, 2011; Vance et al., 2006). While there has been increased research attention on cognitive impairment and self-regulation in recent years, findings have been mixed. Results of several studies showed that many drivers with cognitive impairment such as dementia restricted their driving or stopped driving completely within a few years (e.g., Adler, 2010; Drachman & Swearer, 1993; Festa, Ott, Manning, Davis, & Heindel, 2013; Ross et al., 2009; Talbot et al., 2005; Vance et al., 2006). However, other studies found either weak associations between cognitive function and self-regulation or no evidence that older drivers with cognitive impairment restricted their driving (e.g., Baldock, Thompson, & Mathias, 2008; Betz & Lowenstein, 2010; Braitman & Williams, 2011; Charlton et al., 2006; Kowalski et al., 2012; O'Connor, Edwards, & Bannon, 2013; Ragland, Satariano, & MacLeod, 2004; Rapoport et al., 2013; Sandlin, McGwinn, & Owsley, 2014; Wong, Smith, & Sullivan, 2012). It appears that awareness of and insight into declining functional abilities may be an important precursor to self-regulation (e.g., Ball et al., 1998; Betz & Lowenstein, 2010; Carr, Meuser, & Morris, 2006; Cotrell & Wild, 1999; Freund, Colgrove, Burke, & McLeod, 2005; Gil et al., 2001; Holland & Rabbit, 1992; Owsley et al., 2004; Owsley, Stalvey, & Phillips, 2003; Stalvey & Owsley, 2003) and may be more important than actual driving ability (Anstey, Wood, Lord, & Walker, 2005). Thus, individual differences in recognizing one's cognitive limitations may help explain the lack of consistent findings with regard to cognitive impairment and self-regulation.

Results from more recent studies conducted since the review by Molnar et al. (2015) are generally consistent with the review's overall conclusions. Of particular interest, given the increasing value ascribed to objective measures of driving, are studies that used naturalistic driving methods to study self-regulation. Coxon et al. (2015) found that self-reported driving confidence was independently associated with several naturalistic measures of driving among a sample of drivers age 75 or older including farthest distance traveled from home, average trip distance, and night driving. Specifically, they found that older drivers with lower confidence took shorter trips, stayed closer to home, and were less likely to drive at night. Confidence, in terms of lower body balance, was found to be associated with worse contrast sensitivity and more reported driving avoidance in a study of drivers with Parkinson's disease (Crizzle, Myers, Roy, & Almeida, 2015). Keay et al. (2018) compared subjective and objective measures of driving and found no gender differences in objective measures of distance traveled, distance from home, and driving at night despite men being more likely to report that they drove further from home and did not avoid driving at night. The authors questioned the role of gender in self-regulation and suggested that it may be that women self-report differently than men but that actual driving practices are quite similar among both men and women.

Some recent studies have investigated the role that self-awareness and cognitive functioning play in self-regulation. For example, Choi and Feng (2018) explored the relationship between self-awareness of declines in driving-related cognitive abilities and self-regulatory practices among older adults, noting the importance of such self-awareness in adopting self-regulation. They found that self-awareness of declines in driving cognition but not in everyday cognition was significantly correlated with the number of self-regulatory practices adopted by older drivers. They concluded that older drivers may be likely to self-regulate their driving when they become aware of age-related functional declines. Another study examined the role of self-awareness and insight in self-regulation through interviews with older drivers and passengers, with the latter acting as informants (Devlin & McGillivray, 2016). Although drivers with cognitive impairment reported self-regulating in more driving situations than drivers without cognitive impairment, the greatest discrepancy between driver and informant reports of self-regulation was for drivers with cognitive impairment. According to the authors, results might reflect a reduced awareness of self-regulatory practices in this subgroup of older drivers, with other external factors contributing to self-regulation in older drivers with cognitive impairment.

Finally, Conlon, Rahaley, and Davis (2017) examined the influence of age-related health difficulties and attitudes toward driving on driving self-regulation among 399 Australian drivers age 48–91. Results indicated that different mechanisms explained self-regulation among men compared to women, based on self-reports. Self-regulation among men was predicted by visual and cognitive difficulties and poor driving confidence. Among women, negative attitudes toward driving mediated the associations found between health-related difficulties and self-regulation. As a group, women reported lower driving confidence, greater driving difficulty, and more driving self-regulation than men. Poorer driving confidence was associated with increased self-regulation among both men and women, after controlling for all other variables. The authors concluded that age-related and disease-related difficulties are related to increasing driving self-regulation in older men and women; however, men and women appear to use different cognitive and affective processes when making decisions about self-regulation and different pathways are needed in models of self-regulation for men and women. According to the authors, effects were independent of generational grouping of the sample, with results showing that women, regardless of age, reported significantly greater driving self-regulation, driving difficulty, and lower driving confidence than men.

There are several limitations in the literature on self-regulation that make it difficult to reach firm conclusions about current and expected self-regulatory practices among older drivers. First, while most researchers conceptualize self-regulation as a process that occurs as a direct or indirect response to declining functioning abilities, most measures of self-regulation focus solely on whether individuals avoid certain driving situations without examining the motivations for such avoidance. It is clear from a number of studies that driving avoidance is often due to changes in lifestyle or preferences rather than awareness of age-related declines or more general driving discomfort (e.g., Ball et al., 1998; Blanchard & Myers, 2010; Charlton et al., 2006;

Hassan, King, & Watt, 2017; Kowalski et al., 2012; Kowalski, Jeznach, & Tuokko, 2014; Molnar, Eby, Charlton, et al., 2013; Moták, Gabaude, Bougeant, & Huet, 2014; Oxley, Charlton, Scully, & Koppel, 2010).

A second limitation in the self-regulation literature is the narrow set of driving situations examined by most studies, making it difficult to understand the full extent to which older drivers might actually be self-regulating their driving. Most studies to date are also limited to cross-sectional designs that rely on convenience samples, making it difficult to generalize study findings to the general population of older drivers. In addition, until recently, most studies relied on self-reports from drivers about their self-regulatory practices rather than collecting objective measures of driving, leading to concerns about the validity and accuracy of the data (e.g., Huebner, Porter, & Marshall, 2006; Staplin, Gish, & Joyce, 2008; Staplin, Gish, & Wagner, 2003). Finally, although the increased attention on self-regulation has resulted largely from the promise that it holds for extending the safe driving of older adults, there has been little research on the actual safety outcomes of self-regulation and results have been mixed (e.g., Ball et al., 1998, 2006; Charlton et al., 2006; De Raedt & Kristofferson, 2000; Owsley et al., 2004; Raitanen et al., 2003; Ross et al., 2009).

To overcome many of these limitations, Molnar et al. (2015) proposed that continuing research in this area should: (1) expand the scope of self-regulatory practices examined by focusing on not only pre-trip decisions such as whether to drive at night or on freeway (termed strategic self-regulation) but also decisions made while driving such as whether to engage in secondary tasks inside the vehicle, the speed at which to drive, and the distance at which to follow another vehicle (termed tactical self-regulation), and broader "life-goal" decisions such as moving to a new location to be closer to desired destinations or moving into a retirement community that provides transportation; (2) move beyond simply asking older drivers about avoidance behaviors to take into account the motivations for driving modification so that self-regulators can be distinguished from people who choose to modify their driving for reasons unrelated to declining driving abilities or feelings of discomfort; (3) use objective driving data but in conjunction with self-reported data to better understand the context for self-regulatory behavior and examine important factors such as self-perceptions about health and functioning, confidence and comfort, and so forth that cannot be derived from objective data collected within a vehicle; (4) improve the study designs employed in self-regulation research by conducting more prospective, longitudinal studies and move away from the reliance on cross-sectional analyses to reduce the potential confounding effects of uncontrolled group differences; and (5) investigate how self-regulation actually affects safety and crash risk.

## Conclusions

Over the past three decades, older drivers in the US and elsewhere have increased their reliance on the personal automobile, with data generally showing increased trip taking, time spent driving, and annual average miles driven. At the same time, older drivers generally drive less as a group, when compared to younger age groups. Within the older age group itself, there are differences in driving patterns by various individual characteristics—most commonly, age and gender. Self-regulation is often the context within which driving patterns among older drivers are examined. An extensive and growing literature on self-regulation shows considerable variation in the extent and type of self-regulation engaged in by older drivers. In terms of factors affecting self-regulation, the most consistent finding is the relationship between perceptions of confidence or comfort in specific driving situations and self-regulation in terms of avoiding those situations. There are several limitations of studies on self-regulation that could be overcome by several recommendations highlighted in this chapter.

## References

Adler, G. (2010). Driving decision-making in older adults with dementia. *Dementia*, *9*, 45–60.

Alsnih, R., & Hensher, D. A. (2003). The mobility and accessibility expectations of seniors in an aging population. *Transportation Research Part A: Policy and Practice*, *37*(10), 903–916.

Anstey, K. J., & Smith, G. A. (2003). Associations of biomarkers, cognition and self-reports of sensory function with self-reported driving behavior and confidence. *Gerontology*, *49*, 196–202.

Anstey, K. J., Wood, J., Lord, S., & Walker, J. G. (2005). Cognitive, sensory and physical factors enabling driving safety in older adults. *Clinical Psychology Review*, *25*, 45–65.

Baldock, M. R. J., Mathias, J. L., McLean, A. J., & Berndt, A. (2006). Self-regulation of driving and its relationship to driving ability among older adults. *Accident Analysis & Prevention*, *38*, 1038–1045.

Baldock, M. R. J., Thompson, J. P., & Mathias, J. L. (2008). Self-regulation of driving behavior among older drivers: Findings from a five year follow up. In *Proceedings of 2008 Australasian road safety research, policing and education conference* (pp. 470–478).

Ball, K., Roenker, D., Wadley, V., Edwards, J., Roth, D., McGwin, G., Jr., … Dube, T. (2006). Can high risk older drivers be identified through performance 30 based measures in a Department of Motor Vehicles setting? *Journal of the American Geriatrics Society*, *54*(77–84).

Ball, K. K., Owsley, C., Stalvey, B., Roenker, D. L., Sloane, M. E., & Graves, M. (1998). Driving avoidance and functional impairment in older drivers. *Accident Analysis & Prevention*, *30*, 313–322.

Benekohal, R. F., Michaels, R. M., Shim, E., & Resende, P. T. V. (1994). Effects of aging on older drivers' travel characteristics. *Transportation Research Record*, *1438*, 91–98.

Betz, M. E., & Lowenstein, S. R. (2010). Driving patterns of older adults: Results from the Second Injury Control and Risk Survey. *Journal of the American Geriatrics Society*, *58*, 1931–1935.

Blanchard, R. A., & Myers, A. (2010). Examination of driving comfort and self-regulatory practices in older adults using in-vehicle devices to assess natural driving patterns. *Accident Analysis & Prevention*, *42*, 1213–1219.

Boschmann, E. E., & Brady, S. A. (2013). Travel behaviors, sustainable mobility, and transit-oriented developments: A travel counts analysis of older adults in the Denver, Colorado metropolitan area. *Journal of Transport Geography*, *33*, 1–11.

Braitman, K. A., & Williams, A. F. (2011). Changes in self-regulatory driving among older drivers over time. *Traffic Injury Prevention*, *12*, 568–575.

Brög, W., Erl, E., & Glorius, B. (2000). Introductory reports: Germany. Transport and the ageing of the population. Round table, 112.

Buehler, R., & Nobis, C. (2010). Travel behavior in aging societies. *Transportation Research Record*, *2182*, 62–70.

Carmel, S., Rechavi, T. B., & Ben-Moshe, Y. (2014). Antecedents of self-regulation in driving among older drivers. *Ageing and Society*, *34*, 1097–1117.

Carr, D. B., Meuser, T. M., & Morris, J. C. (2006). Driving retirement: The role of the physician. *Canadian Medical Association Journal*, *175*, 601–602.

Charlton, J. L., Oxley, J., Fildes, B., Oxley, P., Newstead, S., Koppel, S., & O'Hare, M. (2006). Characteristics of older drivers who adopt self-regulatory driving behaviors. *Transportation Research Part F: Traffic Psychology and Behaviour*, *9*, 363–373.

Choi, H. & Feng, J. (2018). Older drivers' compensatory driving behaviors and self-awareness of functional declines. In *The proceedings of the 2018 transportation research board meeting*. Washington, DC.

Choi, M., Adams, K. B., & Kahana, E. (2013). Self-regulatory driving behaviors: Gender and transportation support effects. *Journal of Women and Aging*, *25*, 104–118.

Classen, S., Wang, Y., Crizzle, A. M., Winter, S. M., & Lanford, D. N. (2013). Gender differences among older drivers in a comprehensive driving evaluation. *Accident Analysis & Prevention*, *61*, 146–152.

Collia, D. V., Sharp, J., & Giesbrecht, L. (2003). The 2001 National Household Travel Survey: A look into the travel patterns of older Americans. *Journal of Safety Research*, *34*(4), 461–470.

Conlon, E. G., Rahaley, N., & Davis, J. (2017). The influence of age-related health difficulties and attitudes toward driving on driving self-regulation in the baby boomer and older adult generations. *Accident Analysis & Prevention*, *102*, 12–22.

Cotrell, V., & Wild, K. (1999). Longitudinal study of self-imposed driving restrictions and deficit awareness in patients with Alzheimer disease. *Alzheimer Disease and Associated Disorders*, *13*, 151–156.

Coxon, K., Chevalier, A., Lo, S., Ivers, R., Brown, J., & Keay, L. (2015). Behind the Wheel. *Transportation Research Record*, *2516*, 35–43.

Crizzle, A. M., Myers, A. M., Roy, E. A., & Almeida, Q. J. (2015). Associations between falls, balance, confidence, driving speed, braking, and other driving practices in Parkinson's disease. *Physical & Occupational Therapy in Geriatrics*, *33*(1), 72–86.

D'Ambrosio, L. A., Donorfio, L. K. M., Coughlin, J. F., Mohyde, M., & Meyer, J. (2008). Gender differences in self-regulation patterns and attitudes toward driving among older adults. *Journal of Women and Aging*, *20*, 265–282.

De Raedt, R., & Ponjaert-Kristoffersen, I. (2000). Can strategic and tactical compensation reduce crash risk in older drivers. *Age and Ageing*, *29*, 517–521.

Devlin, A., & McGillivray, J. (2016). Self-regulatory driving behaviours amongst older drivers according to cognitive status. *Transportation Research Part F: Traffic Psychology and Behaviour*, *39*, 1–9.

Dillén, J. (2005). *Äldre personers resvanor och aktiviteter. Resultat från undersökningar med personer i åldern 65 år och äldre*. Stockholm: Transek AB.

Donorfio, L. K. M., D'Ambrosio, L. A., Coughlin, J. F., & Mohyde, M. (2008). Health, safety, self-regulation and the older driver: It's not just a matter of age. *Journal of Safety Research*, *39*, 555–561.

Donorfio, L. K. M., Mohyde, M., Coughlin, J. F., & D'Ambrosio, L. A. (2008). A qualitative exploration of self-regulation behaviors among older drivers. *Journal of Aging & Social Policy*, *20*, 323–339.

Drachman, D. A., & Swearer, J. M. (1993). Driving and Alzheimer's disease: The risk of crashes. *Neurology*, *43*(12), 2448–2456.

Eberhard, J. (2008). Older drivers' "high per-mile crash involvement": The implications for licensing authorities. *Traffic Injury Prevention*, *9*(4), 284–290.

Festa, E. K., Ott, B. R., Manning, K. J., Davis, J. D., & Heindel, W. C. (2013). Effects of cognitive status on self-regulatory driving behavior in older adults: An assessment of naturalistic driving using in-car video recordings. *Journal of Geriatric Psychiatry and Neurology*, *26*, 10–18.

Frändberg, L., & Vilhelmson, B. (2011). More or less travel: Personal mobility trends in the Swedish population focusing gender and cohort. *Journal of Transport Geography*, *19*(6), 1235–1244.

Fraser, M. L., Meuleners, L. B., Ng, J. Q., & Morlet, N. (2013). Driver self-regulation and depressive symptoms in cataract patients awaiting surgery: A cross sectional study. *BMC Ophthalmology*, *13*, 1–7.

Freund, B., Colgrove, L. A., Burke, B. L., & McLeod, R. (2005). Self-rated driving performance among elderly drivers referred for driving evaluation. *Accident Analysis & Prevention*, *37*, 613–618.

Gil, R., Arroyo-Anllo, E. M., Ingrand, P., Gil, M., Neau, J. P., Ornon, C., & Bonnaud, V. (2001). Self-consciousness and Alzheimer's disease. *Acta Neurologica Scandinavia*, *104*, 296–300.

Gwyther, H., & Holland, C. (2012). The effect of age, gender and attitudes on self-regulation in driving. *Accident Analysis & Prevention*, *45*, 19–28.

Hakamies-Blomqvist, L., & Sirén, A. (2003). Deconstructing a gender difference: Driving cessation and personal driving history of older women. *Journal of Safety Research*, *34*, 383–388.

Hakamies-Blomqvist, L., & Wahlström, B. (1998). Why do older drivers give up driving? *Accident Analysis & Prevention*, *30*, 305–312.

Hassan, H., King, M., & Watt, K. (2017). Examination of the precaution adoption process model in understanding older drivers' behaviour: An explanatory study. *Transportation Research Part F: Traffic Psychology and Behaviour*, *46*, 111–123.

Hjorthol, R., & Sagberg, F. (1998). *Changes in elderly persons' modes of travel*. Report no. TOI-1105/1998. Etterstad Oslo, Norway: Norwegian Institute of Transport Economics.

Hjorthol, R., & Sagberg, F. (2000). Introductory report: Norway. In S. Rosenbloom (Ed.), *Transport and ageing of the population* (pp. 177–2010). Paris, France: Economic Research Centre.

Hjorthol, R. J. (2004). Kan utviklingen i mobilitet og reisevanor fortelle noe om likestilling? *Kvinder, Køn & Forskning*, *13*(1), 18–30.

Hjorthol, R. J., Levin, L., & Sirén, A. (2010). Mobility in different generations of older persons: The development of daily travel in different cohorts in Denmark, Norway and Sweden. *Journal of Transport Geography*, *18*(5), 624–633.

Holland, C. A., & Rabbit, P. M. A. (1992). People's awareness of their age-related sensory and cognitive deficits and the implications for road safety. *Applied Cognitive Psychology*, *6*, 217–231.

Huebner, K. D., Porter, M. M., & Marshall, S. C. (2006). Validation of an electronic device for measuring driving exposure. *Traffic Injury Prevention, 7*, 76–80.

Jones, V. C., Cho, J., Abendschoen-Milani, J., & Gielen, A. (2011). Driving habits and risk exposure in older drivers: Lessons learned from the implementation of a self-regulation curriculum. *Traffic Injury Prevention, 12*, 468–474.

Keay, L., Coxon, K., Chevalier, A., Brown, J., Rogers, K., Clarke, E., & Ivers, R. Q. (2018). Sex differences evident in self-reported but not objective measures of driving. *Accident Analysis & Prevention, 111*, 155–160.

Klavora, P., & Heslegrave, R. J. (2002). Senior drivers: An overview of problems and intervention strategies. *Journal of Aging and Physical Activity, 10*, 322–335.

Kostyniuk, L. P., & Molnar, L. J. (2008). Driving self-restriction among older adults: Health, age, and sex effects. *Accident Analysis & Prevention, 40*, 1576–1580.

Kowalski, K., Jeznach, A., & Tuokko, H. A. (2014). Stages of driving behavior change with the Transtheoretical Model (TM). *Journal of Safety Research, 50*, 17–25.

Kowalski, K., Love, J., Tuokko, H., MacDonald, S., Hultsch, D., & Strauss, E. (2012). The influence of cognitive impairment with no dementia on driving restriction and cessation in older adults. *Accident Analysis & Prevention, 49*, 308–315.

LeBlanc, D., Sayer, J., Winkler, C., & Bogard, S. (2007). Field test results of a road departure crash warning system: Driver utilization and safety implications. In *Proceedings of the fourth international driving symposium on human factors in driver assessment, training, and vehicle design.*

LeBlanc, D., Sayer, J., Winkler, C., Ervin, R., Bogard, S., Devonshire, J., ... Gordon, T. (2006). *Road departure crash warning system field operational test: Methodology and results*. Report no. UMTRI-2006-9-1. Ann Arbor, MI: University of Michigan Transportation Research Institute.

Li, G., Eby, D. W., Santos, R., Mielenz, T. J., Molnar, L. J., Strogatz, D., ... for the LongROAD Research Team. (2017). Longitudinal Research on Aging Drivers (LongROAD): Study design and methods. *Injury Epidemiology, 4*, 22.

Lotfipour, S., Patel, B. H., Grotsky, T. A., Anderson, C. L., Carr, E. M., & Ahmed, S. S. (2010). Comparison of the Visual Function Index to the Snellen Visual Acuity Test in predicting older adult self-restricted driving. *Traffic Injury Prevention, 11*, 503–507.

MacDonald, L. M., Myers, A. M., & Blanchard, R. A. (2008). Correspondence among older drivers' perceptions, abilities, and behaviors. *Topics of Geriatric Rehabilitation, 24*, 239–252.

Magelund, L. (2001). Eldres Automobilitet. *Transportrådets Nyhetsbrev, 4*.

Marottoli, R. A., Ostfeld, A. M., Merrill, S. S., Perlman, G. D., Foley, D. J., & Cooney, L. M., Jr. (1993). Driving cessation and changes in mileage driven among elderly individuals. *Journal of Gerontology: Social Science, 48*, S255–S260.

Marshall, S., & Man-Son-Hing, M. (2011). Multiple medical conditions and associated driving risk: A systematic review. *Traffic Injury Prevention, 12*, 142–148.

Mercado, R., & Páez, A. (2009). Determinants of distance traveled with a focus on the elderly: A multilevel analysis in the Hamilton CMA, Canada. *Journal of Transport Geography, 17*(1), 65–76.

Metz, D. (2010). Saturation of demand for daily travel. *Transport Reviews, 30*(5), 659–674.

Molnar, L. J., Charlton, J. L., Eby, D. W., Bogard, S. E., Langford, J., Koppel, S., ... Man-Son-Hing, M. (2013). Self-regulation of driving by older adults: Comparison of self-report and objective driving data. *Transportation Research Part F: Traffic Psychology and Behaviour, 20*, 29–38.

Molnar, L. J., Charlton, J. L., Eby, D. W., Langford, J., Koppel, S., Kolenic, G. E., & Marshall, S. (2014). Factors affecting self-regulatory driving practices among older adults. *Traffic Injury Prevention, 15*, 262–272.

Molnar, L. J., & Eby, D. W. (2008). The relationship between self-regulation and driving related abilities in older drivers: An exploratory study. *Traffic Injury Prevention, 9*(4), 314–319.

Molnar, L.J., Eby, D.W., Bogard, S.E., Kostyniuk, L.P., Zakrajsek, J., St. Louis, R.M., . . ., and the LongROAD Research Team. (in press). *Objective measures of driving exposure and patterns among a large cohort of older drivers. Research brief.* Washington, DC: AAA Foundation for Traffic Safety.

Molnar, L. J., Eby, D. W., Bogard, S. E., LeBlanc, D. J., & Zakrajsek, J. S. (2018). Using naturalistic driving data to better understand the driving exposure and patterns of older drivers. *Traffic Injury Prevention, 19*(s1), S83–S88.

Molnar, L. J., Eby, D. W., Charlton, J. L., Langford, J., Koppel, S., Marshall, S., & Man-Son Hing, M. (2013). Driving avoidance by older adults: Is it always self-regulation? *Accident Analysis & Prevention, 57*, 96–104.

Molnar, L. J., Eby, D. W., Langford, J., Charlton, J. L., St. Louis, R., & Roberts, J. S. (2013). Tactical, strategic, and life-goal self-regulation of driving by older adults: Development and testing of a questionnaire. *Journal of Safety Research, 46*, 107–117.

Molnar, L.J., Eby, D.W., Roberts, J.S., St. Louis, R., & Langford, J. (2009). *A new approach to assessing self-regulation by older drivers: Development and testing of a questionnaire instrument.* Report no. M-CASTL-2009-04. Ann Arbor, MI: University of Michigan Transportation Research Institute.

Molnar, L. J., Eby, D. W., Zhang, L., Zanier, N., St. Louis, R. M., & Kostyniuk, L. P. (2015). *Self-regulation of driving by older adults: A synthesis of the literature and framework for future research.* Washington, DC: AAA Foundation for Traffic Safety.

Moták, L., Gabaude, C., Bougeant, J. C., & Huet, N. (2014). Comparison of driving avoidance and self-regulatory patterns in younger and older drivers. *Transportation Research Part F: Traffic Psychology and Behaviour, 26*, 18–27.

Naumann, R. B., Dellinger, A. M., & Kresnow, M. J. (2011). Driving self-restriction in high-risk conditions: How do older drivers compare to others? *Journal of Safety Research, 42*, 67–71.

Newbold, K. B., & Scott, D. M. (2017). Driving over the life course: The automobility of Canada's Millennial, Generation X, Baby Boomer and Greatest Generations. *Travel Behaviour and Society, 6*, 57–63.

Newbold, K. B., Scott, D. M., Spinney, J. E. L., Kanaroglou, P., & Páez, A. (2005). Travel behavior within Canada's older population: A cohort analysis. *Journal of Transport Geography, 13*(4), 340–351.

O'Connor, M. L., Edwards, J. D., & Bannon, Y. (2013). Self-rated driving habits among older adults with clinically-defined mild cognitive impairment, clinically-defined dementia, and normal cognition. *Accident Analysis & Prevention, 61*, 197–202.

O'Fallon, C. & Sullivan, C. (2009). Trends in older New Zealanders' travel patterns. In *Presented at the Australasian Transport Research Forum* (Vol. 32). Auckland, New Zealand.

Owsley, C., McGwin, G., Jr., Phillips, J. M., McNeal, S. F., & Stalvey, B. T. (2004). Impact of an educational program on the safety of high-risk, visually impaired, older drivers. *American Journal of Preventive Medicine, 26*, 222–229.

Owsley, C., Stalvey, B. T., & Phillips, J. M. (2003). The efficacy of an educational intervention in promoting self-regulation among high-risk older drivers. *Accident Analysis & Prevention, 35*, 393–400.

Oxley, J., Charlton, J., Scully, J., & Koppel, S. (2010). Older female drivers: An emerging transport safety and mobility issue in Australia. *Accident Analysis & Prevention, 42*(2), 515–522.

Oxley, P. (2000). Introductory report: Great Britain. In S. Rosenbloom (Ed.), *Transport and aging of the population*. Paris, France: Economic Research Centre.
Ragland, D., Satariano, W. A., & MacLeod, K. E. (2004). Reasons given by older people for limitation or avoidance of driving. *The Gerontologist, 44*, 237–244.
Raitanen, T., Tormakangas, T., Mollenkopf, H., & Marcellini, F. (2003). Why do older drivers reduce driving? Findings from three European countries. *Transportation Research Part F: Traffic Psychology and Behaviour, 6*, 81–95.
Rapoport, M. J., Naglie, G., Weegar, K., Myers, A., Cameron, D., Crizzle, A., ... Marshall, S. (2013). The relationship between cognitive performance, perceptions of driving comfort and abilities, and self-reported driving restrictions among healthy older drivers. *Accident Analysis & Prevention, 61*, 288–295.
Rosenbloom, S. (1988). *The mobility needs of the elderly, . Special report 218: Transportation in an aging society: Improving mobility and safety for older persons* (Vol. 2)). Washington, DC: Transportation Research Board, National Research Council.
Rosenbloom, S. (2001). Sustainability and automobility among the elderly: An international assessment. *Transportation, 28*(4), 375–408.
Rosenbloom, S. (2006). Is the driving experience of older women changing? Safety and mobility consequences over time. *Transportation Research Record, 1956*, 127–132.
Rosenbloom, S., & Herbel, S. (2009). The safety and mobility patterns of older women: Do current patterns foretell the future? *Public Works Management & Policy, 13*(4), 338–353.
Rosenbloom, S., & Santos, R. (2014). *Understanding older drivers: An examination of medical conditions, medication use, and travel behavior*. Washington, DC: AAA Foundation for Traffic Safety.
Ross, L. A., Clay, O. J., Edwards, J. D., Ball, K. K., Wadley, V. G., Vance, D. E., ... Joyce, J. J. (2009). Do older drivers at-risk for crashes modify their driving over time? *Journal of Gerontology B: Psychological Sciences Social Sciences, 64B*, 163–170.
Rudman, D. L., Friedland, J., Chipman, M., & Sciortino, P. (2006). Holding on and letting go: The perspectives of pre-seniors and seniors on driving self-regulation in later life. *Canadian Journal on Aging, 25*, 65–76.
Ruechel, S., & Mann, W. C. (2005). Self-regulation of driving by older persons. *Physical & Occupational Therapy in Geriatrics, 23*, 91–101.
Sandlin, D., McGwinn, G., & Owsley, C. (2014). Association between vision impairment and driving exposure in older adults aged 70 years and over: A population-based examination. *ACTA Ophthalmologica, 92*, e207–e212.
Santos, A., McGuckin, N., Nakamoto, H. Y., Gray, D., & Liss, S. (2011). *Summary of travel trends: 2009 National Household Travel Survey*. Washington, DC: US Department of Transportation.
Sargent-Cox, K. A., Windsor, T., Walker, J., & Anstey, K. J. (2011). Health literacy of older drivers and the importance of health experience for self-regulation of driving behaviour. *Accident Analysis & Prevention, 43*, 898–905.
Sayer, J.R., Buonarosa, M.L., Bao, S., Bogard, S., LeBlanc, D.J., Blankespoor, A.D., ... Winkler, C.B. (2010). *Integrated vehicle-based safety systems light-vehicle field operational test methodology and results*. Report no. UMTRI-2010-19. Ann Arbor, MI: University of Michigan Transportation Research Institute.
Scott, D. M., Newbold, K. B., Spinney, J. E. L., Mercado, R., Páez, A., & Kanaroglou, P. S. (2009). New insights into senior travel behavior: The Canadian experience. *Growth and Change, 40*(1), 140–168.

Sengupta, S., van Landingham, S. W., Solomon, S. D., Do, D. V., Friedman, D. S., & Ramulu, P. Y. (2014). Driving habits in older patients with central vision loss. *Ophthalmology*, *121*, 727–732.

Shen, S., Koech, W., Feng, J., Rice, T. M., & Zhu, M. (2017). A cross-sectional study of travel patterns of older adults in the USA during 2015: Implications for mobility and traffic safety. *BMJ Open*, *7*(8), e015780.

Sirén, A., & Meng, A. (2013). Older drivers' self-assessed driving skills, driving-related stress and self-regulation in traffic. *Transportation Research Part F: Traffic Psychology and Behaviour*, *17*, 88–97.

Stalvey, B. T., & Owsley, C. (2000). Self-perceptions and current practices of high-risk older drivers: Implications for driver safety interventions. *Journal of Health Psychology*, *5*, 441–456.

Stalvey, B. T., & Owsley, C. (2003). The development and efficacy of a theory-based educational curriculum to promote self-regulation among high-risk older drivers. *Health Promotion Practice*, *4*, 109–119.

Staplin, L., Gish, K., & Wagner, E. (2003). Mary PODS revisited: Updated crash analysis and implications for screening program implementation. *Journal of Safety Research*, *34*, 389–397.

Staplin, L., Gish, K. W., & Joyce, J. (2008). 'Low mileage bias' and related policy implications—A cautionary note. *Accident Analysis & Prevention*, *40*, 1249–1252.

Sullivan, K. A., Smith, S. S., Horswill, M. S., & Lurie-Beck, J. K. (2011). Older adults' safety perceptions of driving situations: Toward a new driving self-regulation scale. *Accident Analysis & Prevention*, *43*, 1003–1009.

SWOV Institute for Road Safety Research. (2010). *SWOV fact sheet: Naturalistic driving: Observing everyday driving behaviour*. Leidschendam, The Netherlands: SWOV.

Talbot, A., Bruce, I., Cunningham, C. J., Coen, R. F., Lawlor, B. A., Coakley, D., ... O'Neill, D. (2005). Driving cessation in patients attending a memory clinic. *Age and Ageing*, *34*, 363–368.

Transportation Research Board. (1988). *Special report 218. Transportation in an aging society: Improving mobility and safety for older persons* (Vol. 2). Washington, DC: Transportation Research Board.

Truong, L.T. & Somenahalli, S. (2011). Exploring mobility of older people: A case study. In *Presented at 34th Australasian transport research forum*. Adelaide, South Australia.

Tuokko, H., Myers, A., Jouk, A., Marshall, S., Man-Son-Hing, M., Porter, M. M., ... Vrkljan, B. (2013). Associations between age, gender, psychosocial and health characteristics in the Candrive II study cohort. *Accident Analysis & Prevention*, *61*, 267–271.

Unsworth, C. A., Wells, Y., Browning, C., Thoman, S. A., & Kendig, H. (2007). To continue, modify or relinquish driving: Findings from a longitudinal study of healthy ageing. *Gerontology*, *53*, 423–431.

Vance, D. E., Roenker, D. L., Cissell, G. M., Edwards, J. D., Wadley, V. G., & Ball, K. K. (2006). Predictors of driving exposure and avoidance in a field study of older drivers from the state of Maryland. *Accident Analysis & Prevention*, *38*, 823–831.

West, C. G., Gildengorin, G., Haegerstrom-Portnoy, G., Lott, L., Schneck, M. E., & Brabyn, J. A. (2003). Vision and driving self-restriction in older adults. *Journal of the American Geriatrics Society*, *51*, 1348–1355.

Wong, I. Y., Smith, S. S., & Sullivan, K. A. (2012). The relationship between cognitive ability, insight and self-regulatory behaviors: Findings from the older driver population. *Accident Analysis & Prevention*, *49*, 316–321.

# Use of nondriving transportation options

# 3

*Nothing compares to the simple pleasure of a bike ride.*

*John F. Kennedy*

## Introduction

Nearly 20 years ago, Burkhardt, McGavock, Nelson, and Mitchell (2002) introduced American audiences to the concept of "family of services," which recognizes that there is no single solution to the mobility needs of the older adult population, especially for those individuals who are unable or choose not to drive. Initially developed in Sweden (Ståhl, 1992), the family of services concept in the United States (US) was described by Burkhardt et al. (2002) as follows: "... services that provide for larger sectors of the population can provide wider coverage, higher frequency, and lower cost, but they will not be usable by some groups. Services that become more specialized to meet the needs of small groups will be less flexible to use and more expensive to supply. The objective of the family of services is to provide mobility for all at the lowest cost and with the greatest potential for spontaneous travel by encouraging people to use the tier of service that offers greatest flexibility and costs least to provide" (p. 162).

Suen and Sen (2004) further delineated this concept, noting that the mobility needs of older adults are complex, with no single mobility option meeting the needs or preferences of every individual in every geographical area or even of one individual in one geographical area. They observed that the availability and appropriateness of mobility options for meeting the needs of older adults depend on where an individual lives and his or her abilities. For example, activities that are reachable by foot or transit in dense urban areas may not be reachable in suburban areas where destinations and activities are farther apart. In addition, physical impairments may limit the distance that individuals can walk without a rest or prevent them from climbing the steps of the bus or standing when the bus is in motion; therefore, they may be unable to use public transit even when it is available.

Suen and Sen (2004) identified a range of nondriving mobility options for older adults emerging in Europe at the time of their writing that they considered to be part of the family of services concept. As described by the authors, these included "... transit services, that are easy for everybody to use, including older people; people who find walking or climbing steps difficult; people with briefcases, carts, baby strollers, luggage, or mobility devices; shoppers; and people in wheelchairs. Other options include routes for people who can use transit if walking distances are

**Perspectives and Strategies for Promoting Safe Transportation among Older Adults.**
**DOI: https://doi.org/10.1016/B978-0-12-812153-5.00003-0**

reduced and more time is provided for boarding, paying the fare, and finding a seat; subsidized taxis; dial-a-ride for people who need assistance while traveling; and an accessible and safe infrastructure for pedestrians and people in wheelchairs" (p. 109).

In other work by Kim and Ulfarsson (2004) using travel survey data from the state of Washington, the choice of mobility options by older adults was associated with neighborhood and trip characteristics, as well as personal and household characteristics. Like Burkhardt et al. (2002) and Suen and Sen (2004), the authors emphasized the diversity of needs of the older adult population in terms of transportation modes and travel options. They concluded that transportation strategies must move beyond the personal automobile if society is to prepare effectively for the increasing number of older adults in the population and their mobility needs.

In the ensuing 15 years or so, there have been dramatic changes in the transportation landscape in the US and elsewhere due to advances in mobile technology, an influx of new urban mobility options, and changes in travel behavior (Shared-Use Mobility Center, 2015a). Many of these changes have important implications for how older adults get around in their communities and beyond. This chapter discusses traditional nondriving mobility options for older adults as well as introduces and highlights many of the new and emerging mobility options and services. We also discuss the implications of these services for travel by older adults, as well as the potential transformative effects of these new services on traditional transportation more generally.

## Traditional mobility options

### *Fixed-route transit*

As described by Suen and Sen (2004), traditional public transit generally operates on a schedule with predetermined stops along a specified route. Specific forms of fixed-route transit include buses, subways, light rail, and commuter rail. The literature shows that older adults' use of fixed-route transit is relatively low. For example, data from the American Community Survey indicated that adults age 65 or older accounted for 17% of the population but only 7% of public bus ridership (Clark, Basinger, Maloney, & Whiteman, 2017). The majority of transit users were in the 25–54-year-old age group; this group accounted for 50% of the population but 63% of transit users.

Suen and Sen (2004) also reported infrequent use of fixed-route transportation by older adults in the US, accounting for only about 1%–2% of all their trips. The authors offered several potential reasons for such low use including a mismatch between this transportation mode and the needs of older adults, the physical difficulties of using buses, and psychological factors that might predispose older adults against public transportation. In Chapter 10, Transportation Service Providers, we discuss more fully the barriers that older adults face in using public transportation and strategies for making public transportation more age-friendly.

In recent work, Shen, Koech, Feng, Rice, and Zhu (2017) examined travel patterns of older adults in the US using the 2015 *American Time Use Survey* dataset, an annual, nationally representative survey by the US Census Bureau. They reported the distribution of daily trips by mode of transit for three age groups—those age 25–64, 65–74, and 75 or older. They found that regardless of age, more than 90% of trips taken were in personal automobiles. By comparison, the percentages of daily bus trips among all trips across the three age groups were 1% or less.

In a nationwide survey conducted by Adams-Price (2013), 1200 adults age 60 or older were asked about their driving and riding habits, as well as perceptions of several potential alternative transportation options. Results indicated that most respondents had never used fixed-route transportation and were not very familiar with such options, and 40% reported that they would not consider using public transportation even if it were more convenient. There has been much attention on identifying barriers to the use of public transit among older adults and developing strategies for overcoming these barriers. As noted earlier, these issues are discussed in detail in Chapter 10, Transportation Service Providers.

## Paratransit

According to Suen and Sen (2004), paratransit, which translates as "alongside transit," encompasses all public and private mass transportation options that fall between the personal automobile and conventional transit (Suen & Sen, 2004). This broad definition is based on their perspective that paratransit includes not only those mobility options in compliance with the US Americans with Disabilities Act (ADA) of 1990, collectively referred to as ADA complementary paratransit, but also all other demand-responsive services (Suen & Mitchell, 2000). Taken together, paratransit options represent demand-responsive services that can range from curb-to-curb, door-to-door, or door-through-door (Suen & Sen, 2004).

Feigon, Murphy, and McAdam (2018) also discussed the varying ways of thinking about paratransit. They argued that, since the passage of ADA, the idea of paratransit has moved from encompassing the entire spectrum of flexible transit services to take on a more narrow meaning of publicly provided, demand-responsive services (e.g., dial-a-ride). In any case, paratransit has generally been characterized as a flexible-routing mobility option, in which individuals request services between certain locations at a certain time, usually requiring a reservation (Eby, Molnar, & Kartje, 2009).

Estimating ridership demand for overall paratransit or demand-responsive services is challenging, especially given a lack of data for demand-response service characteristics and geographic coverage (Mattson, 2016). There have been several efforts to estimate such demand using modeling techniques. Mattson (2016) reported on the development of a model that extends earlier models by specifically taking into account service characteristics (e.g., number of days per week and hours per day that service is provided, advance reservation requirements, and fares) in addition to population characteristics. He found that ridership increased when the proportion of the older adult population or individuals without access to a personal automobile increased, agencies served smaller geographic areas with more concentrated demand and shorter trip lengths, fares were lower, more days of service were provided, and agencies allowed users to reserve rides on a shorter notice. Ridership was lower when agencies also offered a fixed-rate service or if the service area overlapped with that of another transit agency.

## *Private transit*

For many years, when people thought of private transit, they generally thought of taxis. According to the former National Center on Senior Transportation (2011), taxis offer older adults an opportunity for independence and personalized service; however, barriers to their widespread use include their limited availability and costs. Other reported barriers to the increased use of taxis by older adults as private transit included attitudes of drivers, older adult concerns about personal safety, and accessibility.

Results from a US nationwide survey of older adult perceptions about and preferences for five transportation alternatives (volunteer drivers, shuttle buses, senior-center-based shuttle buses, prepaid taxi services, and specially coordinated bus/rail service to distant medical centers) indicated that the prepaid taxi option was the least preferred transportation alternative by respondents (Rahman, Strawderman, Adams-Price, & Turner, 2016). The authors concluded that limitations in the distance covered and number of rides provided, combined with the requirement for a prepaid monthly contract, made this option less attractive to respondents.

The challenges associated with the use of taxis by older adults may help explain why rates of taxi use by this population are relatively low. In the work cited earlier by Shen et al. (2017), the percentage of daily taxi trips among all trips for both younger (age 25–64) and older adults (age 65–74 and 75 or older) was found to be 1% or less.

While often thought of only as private transit, taxis can also be considered a form of paratransit providing demand-response services to older adults. In fact, Ellis (2016) noted that while older adults and people with disabilities who are able to ride in a sedan have used taxis for as long as taxis have existed, public transportation agencies are now using specially equipped taxis to serve these populations, including people who cannot transfer to a sedan seat. Also new is technology that allows riders to pay with a swipe card, automatically verifying each trip and processing the trip data for oversight, monitoring, and payment. Because of these advancements, in Ellis's view, public transportation agencies are viewing taxis as a potentially cost-efficient and responsive resource for serving people with disabilities and older adults.

Ellis (2016) reported on the way that taxis are used by public transit agencies, based on results of a survey of 39 public transportation agencies. She found that 13 of the 39 agencies used taxis for their ADA paratransit service, 11 used taxis only for same-day service (not required by the ADA), and 15 used taxis for both ADA paratransit and same-day service. For taxis used for ADA paratransit, services were mainly on a non-dedicated basis, with a combination of transit-subsidized trips,

trips for private-pay, and general-public trips. She concluded that taxis serve multiple operational roles for ADA paratransit trips, most frequently providing same-day services that do not fit on the schedules of dedicated vehicles, and often at a lower cost. One reported barrier to the use of taxis was the lack of accessible vehicles and accessible service; however, 35 of the agencies surveyed noted that at least one of the taxi companies used had accessible taxis. At the same time, an inadequate number of accessible vehicles were reported to compromise the scheduling of trips by taxi.

## Supplemental transportation services

As described by Kerschner and Harris (2007), supplemental transportation services (STPs) add to the traditional array of transportation services to meet the needs of nondriving older adults better. For many years, the Beverly Foundation monitored and gave awards to winning STP programs across the US. Although the Beverly Foundation is no longer in existence, past reports suggest that STPs vary considerably in terms of services provided, budget, number of rides given, service area, number of drivers, number of riders, and number of collisions (Kerschner & Harris, 2007). As described by the authors, an STP is a supplemental community option that can be built within a community; needs to be linked with local transit, aging, and human services; can be designed to limit exposure and potential liability; can involve "volunteer vehicles" as well as purchased vehicles; can use volunteers as well as paid drivers; can be organized so as to secure insurance; can provide transportation in urban, suburban, and rural areas; can be started with limited funds; and can be supported and sustained without having to charge fees.

Door-through-door transportation represents one type of STP intended to meet the needs of older adults with greater mobility limitations. These services were described by Burkhardt (2007) as "the high-intensity end of the service spectrum" in a multimodal family of services transportation network; thus targeting a relatively small group of people, but one with great need for such services. Burkhardt noted that door-through-door services can be distinguished from other transportation programs by the personal hands-on support provided to users. He identified several levels of assistance including

- Gentle support (opening doors and providing verbal guidance),
- Physical support (assisting riders with balancing, climbing steps, or performing similar functions),
- Activity support (staying with riders and helping with activities at the destination),
- Personal support (helping riders with activities in the rider's home such as putting on coats, shoes or boots, or putting away groceries).

He concluded that unfortunately, regardless of level of assistance, door-through-door services are too often overlooked in standard community transportation planning efforts.

Another important component of many STPs is volunteer drivers. Volunteer drivers are used in more than half of STPs, based on surveys conducted by the Beverly Foundation and the AAA Foundation for Traffic Safety (see Kerschner & Harris, 2007). The authors reported that, among the STPs using volunteer drivers, budgets varied widely, 74% were in rural areas, 84% used the vehicles of the volunteer drivers, 97% provided door-to-door services, 13% charged fees, 71% received grant support, 62% used rider donations, 18% used tax revenues for some of their support, and most mentioned that their drivers acted as escorts.

In the survey on older adults' preferences for various transportation alternatives discussed earlier (Rahman et al., 2016), the volunteer drivers option was found to be the most preferred transportation alternative by both drivers and nondrivers. The authors suggested that the attractiveness of this option may have been due to its convenience and respondents' personal connection to the volunteer drivers.

One of the most notable programs using volunteer drivers is ITNAmerica, a network of over 20 ride-service programs in 21 states in the US offering on-demand, door-through-door transportation services for any ride purpose for older adults (either 60 + or 65 + depending on location) and adults of any age with visual impairments (Bird et al., 2017). The ITNAmerica model is designed to replicate the feelings of independence and choice that characterize private automobile ownership, using both paid and volunteer drivers (Kerschner & Harris, 2007). In a recent exploratory study of how adults age 65 or older used ITNAmerica from 2010 to 2014, it was found that, of 2661 total participants, 77% were women; 81% were age 75 or older; 64% lived alone; 60% reported getting around at the time of enrollment by riding with a friend or family member; half used an assistive device to support their mobility; 567 took no rides during the study period, while the remaining 2094 took a total of 67,883 rides (translating into 16.2 rides per year; Bird et al., 2017).

## Walking and bicycling

Walking and bicycling represent additional mobility options for older adults, especially those individuals who are relatively fit and free of serious physical and cognitive impairment (Eby et al., 2009). Given these caveats, however, as well as community designs that are often unresponsive to the needs of older adults, it is not surprising that the prevalence of walking and bicycling among this age group is less than that of other segments of the population (Alliance for Biking & Walking, 2016).

Rates of walking and bicycling in the US are also considerably lower than many other industrialized countries, although there is a great deal of variation across countries (e.g., Buehler & Pucher, 2012; Kuzmyak & Dill, 2012; Pucher, Buehler, Bassett, & Dannenberg, 2010). For example, Pucher et al. (2010) reported that walking and bicycling's shares of trips in some European countries were three to five times as high as the shares in any state in the US. In other work based on a comparison of travel surveys in individual countries, Buehler and Pucher (2012) found that walking and bicycling trips ranged from a low of one-tenth of all daily trips in the US, Australia, and Canada to about a quarter of all daily trips in the United Kingdom, Belgium, France, Austria, and Norway, to about one-third of all daily trips in Finland, Sweden, Germany, and Denmark, to a high of more than one-half of all daily trips in the Netherlands. The authors also reported that walking and bicycling had generally declined in the US and Western Europe over the past four decades.

In trying to explain the lower rates of walking and bicycling in the US, Kuzmyak and Dill (2012) cited the design of modern US cities and neighborhoods, lack of facilities to ensure safe and efficient travel by foot or bicycle, and incentives for driving (e.g., low fuel prices, free parking, and large road capacity) as possible barriers in the US. More generally, variations in walking and bicycling in different geographic locations have been attributed to differences in the built environment, such as infrastructure for walking and bicycling, availability of public transit, street connectivity, housing density, and mixed land use (e.g., Saelens & Handy, 2008).

Given the benefits that walking and bicycling can potentially bestow to individuals and society in the form of improved health, fitness, and longevity (Pucher et al., 2010), reductions in noise and air pollution and less demand for nonrenewable resources (Buehler & Pucher, 2012), and greater efficiencies in the transportation system by providing connections between modes, destinations, and activities (Litman, 2010), efforts to support increased walking and bicycling among older adults, when appropriate, are warranted. At the same time, such efforts must take into account the increased risk of death and serious injury associated with being a pedestrian or bicyclist (e.g., Oxley, Charlton, & Fildes, 2005) and include strategies to mitigate this risk.

## New and emerging mobility paradigms

As noted earlier, the past 15 years or so has seen the introduction and growth of a wide array of new mobility options—collectively, these have been termed innovative mobility services (Spulber, Brugeman, Dennis, & Fard, 2017). As described by Spulber et al. (2017), "... innovative mobility services are transportation solutions enabled by emerging technologies and wireless connectivity that allow for more convenient, efficient, and flexible travel. Carsharing, ridehailing, ridesharing, microtransit, bikesharing, and mobility-as-a-service are among the most noteworthy innovative mobility services currently in development" (p. 3). Because of the rapid growth of these services and the complexity of the industry overall (Shared-Use Mobility Center, 2015a), it is not surprising that definitions of some services are still evolving and terms can be defined differently by different individuals (e.g., services like Uber and Lyft have been alternatively termed ridehailing, ridesharing, and ridesourcing). Here, we provide brief, general descriptions of the services, based on Spulber et al. (2017). Estimates of use are also provided when available;

however, given the novelty of many of these services and the proprietary nature of much of the data, research on use is sparse, particularly for older adults, and often limited to a single program (Rayle, Dai, Chan, Cervero, & Shaheen, 2016). Later in the chapter, we discuss studies that have examined these services specifically with regard to older adults.

### Carsharing

Carsharing services provide members with access to an automobile for short-term use, generally by the hour. In the past, carsharing was considered distinct from traditional car rental services because of its electronic systems that allowed customers direct access to vehicles, and the inclusion of fuel and insurance costs. However, distinctions have become increasingly blurred as the two services have become more similar. Carsharing vehicles can be owned by a company (e.g., Zipcar or car2go) or by private individuals, and services can be provided on a round-trip or one-way basis. Carsharing services are currently offered in more than 50 US cities and regions. Worldwide, carsharing has been estimated to be available in about 600 cities and 18 countries, with about 348,000 individuals sharing nearly 11,700 vehicles as part of organized carsharing services globally and 117,656 individuals sharing 3337 vehicles in North America (Shaheen & Cohen, 2007).

### Ridehailing

Ridehailing services connect passengers with drivers who offer rides in their own vehicles for a fee. These connections are made primarily through smartphone applications using online platforms designed and operated by transportation network companies (TNCs). Drivers are self-employed and include individuals with both commercial and standard drivers' licenses. The two largest ridehailing services in the US are operated by Uber (established in 2009 and available in 200 urban areas) and Lyft (established in 2012 and available in 300 urban areas). As noted earlier, Uber and Lyft are also commonly referred to as ridesharing services. Use of ridehailing is still relatively low. It has been estimated that only 15% of all US adults have ever used a ridehailing service and only 4% of adults age 65 or older (Smith, 2016).

### Ridesharing

Ridesharing is a type of carpooling service that allows travelers with either a common origin or destination to arrange shared short- or long-distance rides on a short notice using personal vehicles. Trip costs are shared by travelers through ridesharing platforms that require a fee for making the connection. Real-time ridesharing started in the mid-2000s and has been successful in densely populated areas (e.g., in the San Francisco Bay area currently served by Waze Carpool, one of the prominent ridesharing services), but more challenging in lower density areas. While ridematching programs have easy success connecting passengers in densely populated areas with insufficient transportation options, areas with lower population densities represent a challenge. One challenge to the expansion of ridesharing is how to match rides and meetings at centralized locations that are not always convenient, such shopping malls, grocery stores, or carpool lots. A ridesharing program piloted in California (Lyft Carpool) in 2016 was discontinued in the same year because of low overall match rates (Shaheen & Cohen, 2018).

## *Microtransit*

Microtransit services encompass a variety of private transit services using vans or small buses that develop flexible routes and schedules based on user demand. These services are similar to city-operated paratransit or flexible route services, but unique in their use of wireless connectivity and data analytics. Thus, they offer a way for communities to be more responsive to travel demand when and where it is needed, without large investments in material or transportation infrastructure. Microtransit services were established around 2012 in the US and are provided in several cities by companies such as Via and Chariot. Data on users of microtransit are limited; however, Shaheen, Stocker, Lazarus, and Bhattacharyya (2016) surveyed users and registered riders of a microtransit pilot program in Kansas City (RideKC:Bridj) and found that most respondents who reported using the service were under age 54 (94%), only 6% of reported users were age 60–64, and none were age 65 or older.

## *Bikesharing*

Bikesharing programs provide free or affordable access to bicycles for short-distance trips, mostly in urban areas. These programs can be created and managed by local community groups or nonprofit organizations, or by public–private partnerships involving municipalities or transit agencies. Bikesharing programs, available in more than 120 US cities, are experiencing significant growth and are considered to play a vital role in complementing other modes of shared mobility (Shared-Use Mobility Center, 2015b). As defined by Shaheen, Chan, Bansal, and Cohen (2015), shared mobility refers to the shared use of a vehicle, bicycle, or other low-speed mode that provides users with short-term access to transportation modes on an as-needed basis; included are carsharing, personal vehicle sharing, bikesharing, shuttle services, carpooling and vanpooling, and on-demand ride services (ridesourcing/TNCs). Use of bikesharing varies considerably across the cities in which it is available; for example, trips per bikeshare bicycle per day ranged from 0.6 in Seattle to 3.6 in New York City, based on data from 2015 to 2016 (Priceonomics Data Studio, 2018). Data were not available by age. A survey of bikesharing use in Vancouver, Canada found that use of bikesharing decreased with age, and those age 65 or older used this service less than all other age groups (Therrien et al., 2014).

## Mobility-as-a-service

Mobility-as-a-service (MaaS) refers to how individuals satisfy their transportation needs over a single interface that bundles together multiple transportation options (e.g., mass transit, carsharing, and ridehailing) in an integrated solution presented to users through a smartphone app which is paid for via a single account. The aim of MaaS is to provide end-to-end transportation by linking various transportation modes and make better use of the existing transportation options in a given geographical area. As such, MaaS can be especially beneficial in urban regions with at least two to three nondriving transportation modes and strong local and regional cooperation between public agencies and private providers. MaaS is highly data-driven, powered by information technology improvements including precise Global Positioning Systems, and relies on widespread penetration of smartphones on high-speed cellular networks, a high level of connectivity, real-time travel option schedules, and cashless payment systems. Companies operating in the US include TransLoc, Xerox, and moovel N.A. While MaaS has the potential to help meet the mobility needs of older adults who are unable or choose not to drive, thus far, its audience has been made up largely of the younger population (Mulley, Nelson, & Wright, 2018).

An increasing number of studies have focused on the impact of these new and emerging mobility paradigms on the overall transportation system (e.g., Feigon & Murphy, 2016; Feigon et al., 2018; Shaheen et al., 2015). Collectively, findings suggest that these services have the potential to reduce vehicle use, ownership, and vehicle miles traveled; lead to cost savings and increased convenience; and extend the catchment area of public transit, thereby helping to bridge gaps in existing transportation networks by addressing the "first and last mile" issue in public transit, as well as expand transportation access in underserved or hard-to-serve communities by adding to existing options or by providing the only viable option for some types of trips.

What has been less studied are the potential impacts of new and emerging mobility paradigms on the older adult population and their mobility needs and preferences. However, a research literature addressing these issues, is beginning to be established. Results from a few of the studies that have focused specifically on what these services might mean for the older adult population are discussed here.

Use of ridehailing services among older adults appear to be low. A study in seven large US cities found that only about 4% of older adults have used ridehailing services compared to about 36% for people age 18–29 (Clewlow & Mishra, 2017). Vivoda, Harmon, Babulal, and Zikmund-Fisher (2018) examined older adults' knowledge and use of, reliance on, and future expectations for ridehailing (e.g., Uber and Lyft) through a survey of 712 adults age 65 or older. Of those surveyed, about three-quarters reported knowing about ridehailing but only 1.7% had used ridehailing to arrange rides and 3.3% relied on it for any of their transportation needs. The authors noted that these rates were consistent with national estimates of ridehailing use by older adults (Smith, 2016) and suggested that this low use could be related to a lack of access to the service (due to low rates of smartphone and

Internet use), rather than lack of desire to use it. They concluded that for services such as ridehailing to become more feasible for older adults, efforts are needed to make these services more accessible and provide education and training about their use as an alternative form of transportation.

Leistner and Steiner (2017) examined the implications of ridesharing as a viable transportation option for older adults. They studied 40 older adults enrolled over a 9-month period in a dynamic ridesharing (i.e., scheduling in real time) program in Gainesville, Florida in which trips were subsidized based on income. They found that 83% of participants in the program were women, more than 35% of all enrollees completed more than five trips per month, women were less likely than men to discontinue participation, and about 15% of all participants did not have a smartphone at enrollment. They concluded that dynamic ridesharing has the potential to increase mobility and accessibility of older adults, but lack of familiarity with smartphone and dynamic ridesharing technology may after the rate of system use. Like Vivoda et al. (2018), they called for increased outreach and training for older adults.

Carsharing services among older adults may have a market in older adult communities. A study in California examined the possibility of an electric carsharing option for mobility among residents of a senior adult community (Shaheen, Cano, & Camel, 2016). The study found that 66% of older adults reported being interested or possibly interested in participating in the program. A larger percentage (71%) of older adults reported that they were or might be interested in the service if both electric and nonelectric vehicle were utilized.

As part of a report on shaping the relationship between public transport and innovative mobility, Crist (2017) addressed the important question of what it will take to make innovative mobility services accessible, acceptable, and usable for older adults and people with physical, sensory, and cognitive impairments The report highlights findings from a workshop sponsored by the International Transport Forum (ITF) in 2016 in San Francisco. The author identified several issues relative to older adults that will need to be considered, including low levels of access to, use of, and comfort with smartphones and the Internet; preferences for human contact and interaction; privacy and personal safety concerns; physical access to vehicles; and availability of vehicles for spontaneous travel. He concluded that mobility services will need to be responsive to these issues to make them accessible and acceptable to, and usable by, older adults; to that end, he discussed several past initiatives by the ITF.

Finally, a white paper by Broderick (2018) examined the future of rural transportation and mobility for older adults, focusing specifically on current trends and future directions in technology-enabled solutions. Based on a review of the literature and interviews with more than 30 experts, he identified several themes related to the potential role of technology in advancing mobility for older adults in rural areas, including the following: awareness of rural older adults' transportation needs is lacking in the technology community; awareness of the opportunities afforded by technology is lacking in rural communities; transportation solutions for older adults need to start with identifying user preferences, local resources, and potential partners; more mobility options lead to potentially greater resilience of the community transportation networks; community-wide coalitions with shared goals are important for pooling resources and bring varying perspectives to the table; transportation impacts not only health but also quality-of-life by enabling individuals to fully engage in community life; transportation services that serve the entire community are potentially more sustainable than more specialized services; matching service options to individuals' personal mobility needs is an emerging trend across aging services; and balancing the use of technology with human-centered support is important for older adults.

## Conclusions

This chapter identified a number of community mobility options for older adults who are unable or choose not to drive. Central to the discussion was the recognition by a number of researchers that there is no single solution to the mobility needs of the older adult population. This led to the development of the family of services concept introduced in the US almost 20 years ago, in which different levels of mobility options are needed for different levels of older adult capabilities and functioning. What is clear is that this concept is just as applicable today as it was 20 years ago. The main difference is that the portfolio of mobility options within the family of services has evolved considerably and new mobility services continue to emerge. While these new and emerging services must still be responsive to the same challenges faced by more traditional services, in terms of being available, accessible, acceptable, affordable, and adaptable, they have also introduced new challenges, such as the need to have access to and be familiar with smartphone technology and the Internet. Research on the implications of these new and emerging services specifically for older adults is arguably still in its infancy. There is undoubtedly a need for more studies on how older adults use these services and what improvements are needed to help these services better meet the mobility needs of this population. Based on the relatively few studies that have been done, efforts to make these services more accessible to older adults and providing them with better information and training about the services are clearly warranted. In addition, addressing the limitations of technology reliance on smartphones and access to the Internet will help expand the market of potential older adult users.

## References

Adams-Price, C. E. (2013). *Aging in place: Intermodal transportation and options for meeting the unmet transportation needs of nonmetropolitan older adults*. Starkville, MS: National Center for Intermodal Transportation for Economic Competitiveness, NCITEC Project No. 2012_01.

Alliance for Biking & Walking. *Bicycling and walking in the United States: Benchmarking report.* (2016). ⟨https://www.aarp.org/livable-communities/getting-around/info-2016/bike-walk-alliance-2016-benchmark-report.html⟩ Accessed July, 2018.

Bird, D. C., Freund, K., Fortinsky, R. H., Staplin, L., West, B. A., Bergen, G., & Downs, J. (2017). Driving self-regulation and ride service utilization in a multicommunity, multi-state sample of U.S. older adults. *Traffic Injury Prevention, 18*(3), 267–272.

Broderick, A. (2018). *The future of rural transportation and mobility for older adults: Current trends and future directions in technology-enabled solutions.* Arlington, VA: Grantmakers in Aging.

Buehler, R., & Pucher, J. (2012). Walking and cycling in Western Europe and the United States trends, policies, and lessons. *TR News, 280*, 34–42.

Burkhardt, J. E. (2007). High-quality transportation services for seniors. In *11th International conference on mobility and transport for elderly and disabled persons (TRANSED) transport Canada transportation research board.*

Burkhardt, J. E., McGavock, A. T., Nelson, C. A., & Mitchell, C. G. B. (2002). *Improving public transit options for older persons. Vol. 2: Final report.* TCRP report 82. Washington, DC: Federal Transit Administration.

Clark, H. M., Basinger, K., Maloney, K., & Whiteman, C. (2017). *Who rides public transportation.* Washington, DC: American PublicTransportation Association.

Clewlow, R. R. & Mishra, G. S. (2017). *Disruptive transportation: The adoption, utilization, and impacts of ride-hailing in the United States.* Report No. UCD-ITS-RR-17-07. Davis, CA: Institute for Transportation Studies.

Crist, P. (2017). *Shaping the relationship between public transport and innovative mobility.* Paris, France: International Transport Forum.

Eby, D. W., Molnar, L. J., & Kartje, P. S. (2009). *Maintaining Safe Mobility in an Aging Society.* New York, NY: CRC Press.

Ellis, E. H. (2016). *Use of taxis in public transportation for people with disabilities and older adults.* Washington, DC: Transportation Research Board, Transit Cooperative Research Program, TCRP Synthesis 119.

Feigon, S. & Murphy, C. (2016). *Shared mobility and the transformation of public transit.* TCRP research report 188. Washington, DC: Transportation Research Board.

Feigon, S., Murphy, C., & McAdam, T. (2018). *Private transit: Existing services and emerging directions.* TCRP research report 196. Washington, DC: Transportation Research Board.

Kerschner, H., & Harris, J. (2007). Better options for older adults. *Public Roads, 70*(5), 16–23.

Kim, S., & Ulfarsson, G. (2004). Travel mode choice of the elderly: Effects of personal, household, neighborhood, and trip characteristics. *Transportation Research Record, 1894*, 117–126.

Kuzmyak, J. R., & Dill, J. (2012). Walking and bicycling in the United States: The who, what, where, and why. *TR News, 280*, 4–7.

Leistner, D. L., & Steiner, R. L. (2017). Uber for seniors? Exploring transportation options for the future. *Transportation Research Record, 2660*, 22–29.

Litman, T. (2010). *Quantifying the benefits of nonmotorized transportation for achieving mobility management objectives.* Victoria, BC, Canada: Victoria Transport Policy Institute.

Mattson, J. (2016). Estimating ridership of rural demand–response transit services for the general public. *Transportation Research Record, 2647*, 127–133.

Mulley, C., Nelson, J. D., & Wright, S. (2018). Community transport meets mobility as a service: On the road to a new flexible future. *Research Transportation Economics*. Available from https://doi.org/10.1016/j.retrec.2018.02.004.

National Center on Senior Transportation. *Taxis for senior transportation*. (2011). ⟨https://www.aarp.org/content/dam/aarp/livable-communities/learn/transportation/taxis-for-senior-transportation-aarp.pdf⟩ Accessed July, 2018.

Oxley, J., Charlton, J., & Fildes, B. (2005). *The effect of cognitive impairment on older pedestrian behaviour and crash risk*. Victoria, Australia: Monash University Accident Research Centre.

Priceonomics Data Studio. *Public bike sharing: Analyzing the usage data in US cities*. (2018). https://priceonomics.com/public-bike-sharing-analyzing-the-usage-data-in-us/ Accessed July, 2018.

Pucher, J., Buehler, R., Bassett, D. R., & Dannenberg, A. L. (2010). Walking and cycling to health: A comparative analysis of city, state, and international data. *American Journal of Public Health*, *100*(10), 1986–1992.

Rahman, M. M., Strawderman, L., Adams-Price, C., & Turner, J. J. (2016). Transportation alternative preferences of the aging population. *Travel Behaviour and Society*, *4*, 22–28.

Rayle, L., Dai, D., Chan, N., Cervero, R., & Shaheen, S. (2016). Just a better taxi? A survey-based comparison of taxis, transit, and ridesourcing services in San Francisco. *Transport Policy*, *45*, 168–178.

Saelens, B. E., & Handy, S. L. (2008). Built environment correlates of walking: A review. *Medical Science Sports Exercise*, *40*(7 Suppl), S550–S566.

Shaheen, S., Cano, L., & Camel, M. (2016). Exploring electric vehicle carsharing as a mobility option for older adults: A case study of a senior adult community in the San Francisco Bay Area. *International Journal of Sustainable Transportation*, *10*(5), 406–417.

Shaheen, S., Chan, N., Bansal, A., & Cohen, A. (2015). *Shared mobility—A sustainability and technologies workshop. Definitions, industry developments, and early understanding*. Berkeley, CA: Transportation Sustainability Research Center.

Shaheen, S., & Cohen, A. (2018). Shared ride services in North America: Definitions, impacts, and the future of pooling. *Transportation Reviews*. Available from https://doi.org/10.1080/01441647.2018.1497728.

Shaheen, S., Stocker, A., Lazarus, J., & Bhattacharyya. (2016). Ridekc: Bridj pilot evaluation: Impact, operational, and institutional analysis. Berkley, CA: Transportation Sustainability Research Center.

Shaheen, S. A., & Cohen, A. P. (2007). Growth in worldwide carsharing: An international comparison. *Transportation Research Record*, *1992*(1), 81–89.

Shared-Use Mobility Center. *Shared-use mobility reference guide*. (2015a). ⟨http://sharedusemobilitycenter.org/wp-content/uploads/2016/10/Reference-Guide-Editsweb-version-10.24.2016.pdf⟩ Accessed July, 2018.

Shared-Use Mobility Center. *What bikesharing's growth means for shared mobility*. (2015b). ⟨http://sharedusemobilitycenter.org/news/what-bikesharings-growth-means-for-shared-mobility/⟩ Accessed July, 2018.

Shen, S., Koech, W., Feng, J., Rice, T. M., & Zhu, M. (2017). A cross-sectional study of travel patterns of older adults in the USA during 2015: Implications for mobility and traffic safety. *BMJ Open*, *7*(8), e015780.

Smith, A. (2016). *On-demand: Ride-hailing apps*. Pew Research Center Internet & Technology. http://www.pewinternet.org/2016/05/19/on-demand-ride-hailing-apps/. Accessed July, 2018.

Spulber, A., Brugeman, V. S., Dennis, E. P., & Fard, Z. B. (2017). *Future cities: Navigating the new era of mobility*. Ann Arbor, MI: Center for Automotive Research.

Ståhl, A. (1992). The provision of community responsive public transportation in urban areas. In *Sixth international conference on mobility and transport for elderly and disabled persons*. Lyon, sponsored by the Institut National de Recherche sur les Transports et leur Sécurité, Arcueil, France.

Suen, S. L., & Mitchell, C. G. B. (2000). *Accessible transportation and mobility. Transportation in the New Millennium*. Washington, DC: Transportation Research Board. National Research Council.

Suen, S. L., & Sen, L. (2004). Mobility options for seniors. Transportation in an aging society: A decade of experience. *Conference* Proceedings, *27*. Washington, DC: Transportation Research Board.

Therrien, S., Brauer, M., Fuller, D., Gauvin, L., Teschke, K., & Winters, M. (2014). Applying diffusion of innovation theory to use of a public bikesharing system in Vancouver, Canada. *Transportation Research Record, 2468*, 740−783.

Vivoda, J. M., Harmon, A. C., Babulal, G. M., & Zikmund-Fisher, B. J. (2018). E-hail (rideshare) knowledge, use, reliance, and future expectations among older adults. *Transportation Research Part F, 55*, 426−434.

# A framework for promoting older adult safe transportation

# 4

*Language is not simply a reporting device for experience but a defining framework for it.*

*Benjamin Whorf*

## Introduction

Transportation and mobility are central to society, playing important roles in many aspects of people's lives from economics, to health, to quality of life. For aging adults in particular, there is general agreement on the importance of maintaining safe transportation into older adulthood. There is also considerable agreement that the issues, perspectives, and fields related to aging and transportation are complex and multifaceted (Classen, Eby, Molnar, Dobbs, & Winter, 2011; Dickerson, Molnar, Bédard, Eby, Berg-Weger, et al., 2017; Dickerson, Molnar, Bédard, Eby, Classen, et al., 2017; Dickerson et al., 2007; Eby, Molnar, & Kartje, 2009; Lindstrom-Forneri, Tuokko, Garrett, & Molnar, 2010; Webber, Porter, & Menec, 2010; Wong, Smith, Sullivan, & Allan, 2016). To better understand and visualize the relationships among the various factors involved in older adult safe transportation and to develop strategies that better facilitate safe transportation, it is useful to consider models or frameworks for older adult transportation.

In recent years, several researchers have developed frameworks specifically for conceptualizing the transportation issues among older adults, all with a slightly different focus. For example, Dickerson and other investigators (Dickerson, Molnar, Bédard, Eby, Classen, et al., 2017; Dickerson et al., 2007; Eby et al., 2009; Eby, Molnar, Kostyniuk, Zanier, & St. Louis, 2016) conceptualized older adult transportation as a continuum with fully capable older adults who are safe drivers at one end and older adults who are no longer able or have chosen not to drive at the other end. Between these two ends are older adults who are in the process of transitioning to driving cessation. This framework also shows the main focus of research and programs, with crash prevention being of prime importance for those who are independent drivers, maintaining safe mobility being the main goal for older adults who have ceased driving, and both of these factors being important for those who are transitioning. Finally, the framework categorizes research and programs as falling into three areas: driver/person-based, vehicle-based, and environment/roadway-based. This framework allowed these researchers to depict graphically where countermeasures and topics for promoting older adult mobility fit within the transportation continuum.

**Perspectives and Strategies for Promoting Safe Transportation among Older Adults.**
**DOI: https://doi.org/10.1016/B978-0-12-812153-5.00004-2**

Taking a different and more comprehensive approach, Canadian researchers (Lindstrom-Forneri et al., 2010) applied an existing model of everyday competence (Willis, 1991) to aging and driving, called the driving as an everyday competence (DEC) model. According to the researchers, the model was developed to help explain the interactions among older adults' driving level of competence (what they are capable of doing), their level of performance (what they actually do), and social and environmental factors. The DEC posits that an older driver's level of competence is constantly in flux, influenced by changes in individual and environmental factors. Individual factors include a variety of issues including a driver's health, functioning, experience, emotions, and attitudes, while environmental factors include weather, lighting, roadway conditions, laws, and social influences. Driving competence is also influenced by four moderators: beliefs, awareness, self-monitoring, and self-efficacy. According to the model, driving performance is the outcome of these multiple interactions and involves decisions made at the three levels of driving as described by Michon (1985): strategic, tactical, and operational.

In an effort to more comprehensively conceptualize older adult mobility as linked to both driving and other forms of transportation, other Canadian researchers proposed a holistic framework for understanding older adult mobility (Webber et al., 2010). The framework utilizes the concept of life-space levels (May, Nayak, & Isaacs, 1985; Peel et al., 2005) conceptualized as a series of concentric areas radiating out from the older adult's bedroom, with each subsequent area having increasing requirements for independent mobility in any form, not just driving. The framework includes the following life-space levels: room, home, outdoors, neighborhood, service community (e.g., shops, churches, banks), surrounding areas (within the country), and the world. The framework can be visualized as an upside down cone (the mobility cone) sliced horizontally in seven sections with lower levels of life space at the bottom and life space increasing as an individual moves up vertically. Further, the model posits that each life-space slice is divided into five categories of "mobility determinants" that affect older adult mobility in some way: financial, psychosocial, environmental, physical, and cognitive. There can be interactions among some or all of the mobility determinants. The larger cross-sectional areas associated with large life spaces imply that there are a greater number of mobility determinants with increasing life space. Surrounding the entire mobility cone are three moderators that influence all mobility determinants: gender, culture, and biography. One implication of this model is that individuals can move from one section of the mobility cone to another (in both directions), and when this happens, the options for influencing mobility change in type, function, and number.

## An ecological framework for promoting and understanding older adult safe transportation

While each of these frameworks have strengths and served the purposes of the researchers who developed and supported them, they do not well capture the various perspectives of groups, namely, the people and organizations that are integral components in maintaining safe transportation among older adults. Central to our thinking are three complementary goals for older adult mobility discussed by a number of researchers and practitioners (see, e.g., Dickerson, Molnar, Bédard, Eby, Classen, et al., 2017; Dickerson et al., 2007; Eby et al., 2009, 2016). As presented by Eby et al. (2016), these goals are to (1) help older adults who are able to drive safely continue to do so; (2) facilitate the transitioning process from driving to non-driving for those who are unable or choose not to drive; and (3) support the use of non-driving community mobility options for those who no longer drive.

Fig. 4.1 presents our framework for older adult transportation. This framework is partially based on the Social Ecological Approach (McLeroy, Bibeau, Steckler, & Glanz, 1988) commonly used in public health research that recognizes that solutions for maintaining safe transportation happen at multiple levels. Central in the model are the older adults themselves, who are influenced by a myriad of factors that impact transportation, including functional abilities, resources, beliefs, preferences, gender, experiences, emotions, and attitudes. Many of these factors are reviewed in Chapters 1, 2, 3, and 5 of this book. Interacting with or otherwise influencing older adults are six groups of stakeholders, each of whom has a unique and important perspective related to older adult transportation. The first group comprises family members, friends, and other informal caregivers who are well positioned to be able to assess transportation issues and needs, as well as to understand the individual factors that are interacting with these influences and needs.

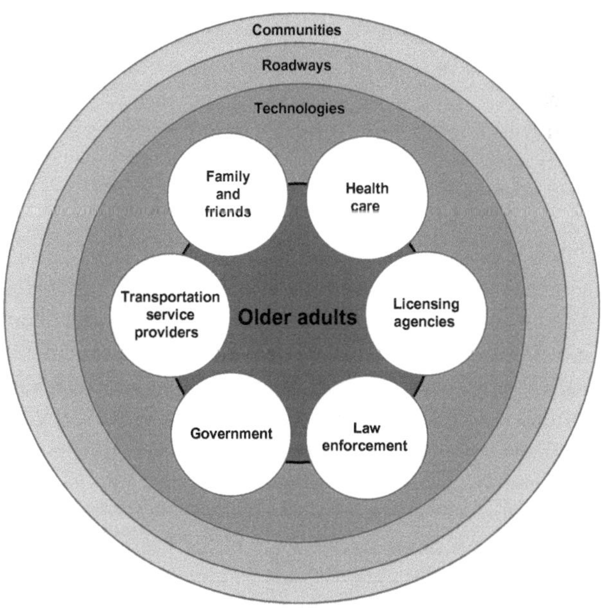


**Figure 4.1** An ecological framework for promoting and understanding older adult safe transportation.

Chapter 6, Family Members, Friends, and Other Informal Caregivers discusses these factors from the perspective of informal caregivers. The second group is made up of physicians and other health-care professionals who are best able to assess functional capacities and abilities and recommend treatments and/or remediation. Chapter 7, Physicians and Other Health Professionals discusses the issues facing health-care professionals and their role in older adult transportation. Another group consists of licensing agencies. Nearly all jurisdictions require drivers to be licensed, and usually the licensing agency has sole authority for restricting or revoking a driver license. Thus, licensing agencies are on the front line for older adult transportation, at least where driving is considered. Chapter 8, Licensing Agencies discusses policies, procedures, and other issues related to licensing agencies and older drivers.

Law enforcement also plays an integral role in older adult transportation, as patrol officers are present when adverse outcomes involving older adults happen on the roadway, such as crashes. Chapter 9, Law Enforcement discusses this important role of law enforcement and reviews several educational materials and programs to help law enforcement be more effective in helping maintain safe transportation among older adults. Fifth, transportation service providers have a significant role, particularly for those older adults who are transitioning from or have ceased driving. Chapter 10, Transportation Service Providers reviews a number of issues relevant to transportation service providers and discusses some of the larger initiatives to promote better services for older adults. Finally, local, state, and federal government are also integral to safe older adult transportation by not only defining the rules and regulations that govern transportation behaviors but also by setting agendas and organizing jurisdiction-wide strategies that promote safe transportation. These issues are discussed in Chapter 11, Federal, State, and Local Government. In the framework, these six groups of stakeholders do not act independently; rather they all can and should interact with the objective of maintaining safe mobility for the individual older adult.

The framework also includes three overarching influences that can affect older adults directly but also are beneficial to all members of society. Technological advances have always been at the forefront of improving people's lives. The continuing development of in-vehicle technology and self-driving vehicles is increasingly making driving easier, safer, and more convenient. The development of these technologies, specifically related to older adults, is discussed in Chapter 12, In-Vehicle and Self-Driving Technologies. Nearly all surface transportation options, from walking, to buses, to driving, takes place on the roadways. As such, the roadway infrastructure not only enables most transportation options but also is intimately linked with safety. The issues of roadway design and infrastructure, as they relate to older adults, are reviewed in Chapter 13, Roadway Design and Infrastructure. The final overarching influence in the framework is the community. Whether large or small, communities share common traits, ideals, and resources that ultimately impact the existence and quality of transportation options, connectivity, senior-based facilities, and access to the places that are necessary for daily living and a high quality of life. Chapter 14, Age-Friendly Communities examines the research on developing age-friendly communities and reviews the relatively new concept of smart and connected communities, within which community members can be increasingly connected to each other and to certain services through developing technologies.

## Conclusions

While there are several frameworks for facilitating understanding of the multiple factors that are interacting and underlying safe transportation for older adults, previous frameworks did not highlight or address the multiple groups of stakeholders who interact with older adults to promote safe transportation. Here, we present a new framework that includes not only these groups but also three important fundamental influences. The framework is not intended as an improvement over previous frameworks and models, but rather as a way to describe visually the interplay among the factors and groups of people involved in older adult safe transportation as discussed in this book.

## References

Classen, S., Eby, D. W., Molnar, L. J., Dobbs, B., & Winter, S. (2011). Transportation and aging: Evaluating stakeholders' perspectives on advancing safe mobility. *South African Journal of Occupational Therapy*, *41*(3), 18–24.

Dickerson, A. E., Molnar, L. J., Eby, D. W., Adler, G., Bédard, M., Berg-Weger, M., ... Trujillo, L. (2007). Transportation and aging: A research agenda for advancing safe mobility. *The Gerontologist*, *47*, 578–590.

Dickerson, A. E., Molnar, L. J., Bédard, M., Eby, D. W., Berg-Weger, M., Choi, M., ... Silverstein, N. M. (2017). Transportation and aging: An updated research agenda for advancing safe mobility among older adults transitioning from driving to non-driving. *The Gerontologist*. Available from https://doi.org/10.1093/geront/gnx120.

Dickerson, A. E., Molnar, L. J., Bédard, M., Eby, D. W., Classen, S., & Polgar, J. M. (2017). Transportation and aging: An updated research agenda for advancing safe mobility. *Journal of Applied Gerontology*. Available from https://doi.org/10.1177/0733464817739154.

Eby, D. W., Molnar, L. J., & Kartje, P. S. (2009). *Maintaining safe mobility in an aging society*. New York, NY: CRC Press.

Eby, D. W., Molnar, L. J., Kostyniuk, L. P., Zanier, N., & St. Louis, R. M. (2016). *Safe drivers smart options, keys to lifelong mobility: Final report*. Report no. UMTRI-2016-18. Ann Arbor, MI: University of Michigan Transportation Research Institute.

Lindstrom-Forneri, W., Tuokko, H. A., Garrett, D., & Molnar, F. (2010). Driving as an everyday competence: A model of driving competence and behavior. *Clinical Gerontologist*, *33*(4), 283–297.

May, D., Nayak, U. S. L., & Isaacs, B. (1985). The life-space diary: A measure of mobility in old people at home. *International Rehabilitation Medicine*, *7*(4), 182–186.

McLeroy, K. R., Bibeau, D., Steckler, A., & Glanz, K. (1988). An ecological perspective on health promotion programs. *Health Education Quarterly*, *15*, 351–377.

Michon, J. A. (1985). A critical view of driver behavior models: What do we know, what should we do? In R. Schwing, & L. Evans (Eds.), *Human behavior and traffic safety* (pp. 487–525). New York, NY: Plenum Press.

Peel, C., Baker, P. S., Roth, D. L., Brown, C. J., Bodner, E. V., & Allman, R. M. (2005). Assessing mobility in older adults: The UAB study of aging life space assessment. *Physical Therapy*, *85*(10), 1008–1019.

Webber, S. C., Porter, M. M., & Menec, V. H. (2010). Mobility in older adults: A comprehensive framework. *The Gerontologist*, *50*(4), 443–450.

Willis, S. L. (1991). Cognition and everyday competence. *Annual Review of Gerontology and Geriatrics*, *11*, 80–109.

Wong, I. Y., Smith, S. S., Sullivan, K. A., & Allan, A. C. (2016). Toward the multilevel older person's transportation and road safety model: A new perspective on the role of demographics, functional, and psychophysical factors. *Journals of Gerontology: Psychological Sciences*, *71*(1), 71–86.

# Part II

# Perspectives

# Older adults

# 5

*The longer I live, the more beautiful life becomes.*

*Frank Lloyd Wright*

## Introduction

Like people of all ages, older adults want to be able to travel safely to destinations of their choosing and to do so when it is best for them. The focus of this book is on promoting safe transportation for older adults, and we have argued that this endeavor is multidisciplinary, with efforts from many fields contributing to the improvement of transportation for this age group. Stakeholders from health professionals, to families, to transportation service providers, to vehicle manufacturers, and to road builders are all working to improve older adult transportation. Older adults themselves also play a key role in their own safe transportation. This chapter reviews activities that older adults can engage in to improve their ability to meet their mobility needs. Most of these areas are related to keeping older adults driving for as long as they can safely do so, but some of the activities will also help drivers transition from driving to non-driving and help them stay mobile after they have stopped driving. The following areas are covered in this chapter: education and training, exercise and fitness, vehicles, and planning for future mobility.

## Education and training

Numerous educational materials and programs for helping older drivers have been developed in the past 20 years, most of which have not been formally evaluated. Many governmental agencies and organizations related to traffic safety and aging have produced informational brochures and fact sheets and include them on their websites. Table 5.1 presents a few illustrative examples targeted at least in part to older adults. These materials address a variety of topics and are generally designed to be quick-references and/or guidelines for behavior. Despite the fact that most educational brochures have not been formally evaluated, they serve several important purposes: they can provide additional cues or red-flags that, when combined with all of the other information older drivers are receiving, can help older adults think more critically about their driving; they can refresh older drivers' memories of driving-related issues they may have forgotten; and they can provide a "safe"

**Perspectives and Strategies for Promoting Safe Transportation among Older Adults.**
**DOI: https://doi.org/10.1016/B978-0-12-812153-5.00005-4**

**Table 5.1** Sample informational materials for older drivers

| Resource (URL) | Organization (country) | Description |
|---|---|---|
| *At the Crossroads: Family Conversations and Alzheimer's Disease, Dementia & Driving* (http://www.thehartford.com/sites/thehartford/files/at-the-crossroads-2012.pdf) | The Hartford Center for Mature Market Excellence and the MIT AgeLab (US) | Brochure targeted at both older drivers and their families/caregivers that includes information on several aspects of driving and dementia, including transitioning from driving to non-driving |
| *Driving Safely as you Age* (https://www.caot.ca/document/5628/Older_Adults_EN.pdf) | Canadian Association of Occupational Therapists (Canada) | Brochure that discusses how aging can impact driving, the warning signs of unsafe driving, strategies for safe driving, and where to go for help with driving |
| *Information on Driving with Medical Conditions* (https://www.nhtsa.gov/road-safety/older-drivers#topic-medical-conditions) | NHTSA (US) | Brief fact sheets about how medical conditions can affect driving and what drivers with the following conditions can do to continue driving safely: Alzheimer's disease, arthritis, cataracts, diabetes, glaucoma, macular degeneration, Parkinson's disease, sleep apnea, and stroke |
| *Mobility Beyond Driving: Transport Options for Seniors* (https://www.racv.com.au/content/dam/racv/images/public-policy/pdfs/publictransport/RACV-transport-options-for-seniors.pdf) | RACV (Australia) | A brochure that provides information about transportation options available to older adults, tips on how to use these options, and contact information |
| *Older Drivers License Renewal* (https://nzta.govt.nz/assets/resources/factsheets/57/docs/57-older-drivers.pdf) | NZ Transport Agency (New Zealand) | A fact sheet that describes the license renewal process for drivers age 75 or older |

(*Continued*)

**Table 5.1** (Continued)

| Resource (URL) | Organization (country) | Description |
|---|---|---|
| *Older Drivers: Safe Driving Tips* (http://www.olderdrivers.org.uk/keep-driving/safe-driving/) | The Royal Society for the Prevention of Accidents (UK) | Informational webpage that includes guidelines in 13 areas for improving the safety of older drivers |
| *Safe Driving Tips for Seniors* (https://www.aota.org/~/media/Corporate/Files/Practice/Aging/Driving/Safe-Driving-Tips-Seniors.pdf) | American Occupational Therapy Association (US) | Brochure that offers five tips for older drivers to be able to drive more safely |
| *Senior Drivers: Safe Driving* (https://www.qld.gov.au/seniors/transport/safe-driving) | Queensland Government (Australia) | A webpage offering general advice on how older drivers can maintain their license after age 75 and information on how aging can impact driving |
| *Straight Talk for Mature Drivers: Rx for Safe Driving* (http://exchange.aaa.com/wp-content/uploads/2012/08/Straight-Talk-For-Mature-Drivers-Rx-for-Safe-Driving.pdf) | AAA (US) | Brochure about prescription medications and driving among older drivers, including guidelines for taking medications and driving safely |
| *There's No Safe or Unsafe Age for a Driver* (https://www.theaa.com/driving-advice/safety/older-drivers) | Automobile Association (UK) | Webpage that provides facts about older drivers and tips for older drivers to continue driving safely |

*NHTSA*, National Highway Traffic Safety Administration; *US*, United States; *UK*, United Kingdom; *RACV*, Royal Automobile Club of Victoria.

first step for an older adult to begin addressing problems that they may be experiencing when driving. In addition, because these materials are often brief and noninteractive, they can be widely distributed to a global audience.

Older driver education and training programs are also abundant and vary widely in terms of purpose, format, and content. Educational programs are designed to increase knowledge and awareness, while training programs generally are designed to improve driving-related skills. Some older driver programs include both education and training. Despite the fact that programs are increasingly being formally evaluated, most have not been evaluated in terms of the outcome measures most important for older drivers: changes in knowledge/awareness, changes in behaviors, and changes in crash risk. Two systematic reviews of older driver retraining programs (Korner-Bitensky, Kua, von Zweck, & van Benthem, 2009; Kua, Korner-Bitensky, Desrosiers, Man-Son-Hing, & Marshall, 2007) critically analyzed evaluation results of 12 programs. These authors reached the following conclusions about older driver retraining programs: programs that included education and on-road training improve driving performance and knowledge; physical retraining alone can improve driving performance; physical retraining programs and visual perception training programs do not seem to improve driving-related skills; and educational programs alone are not effective in reducing crashes but can improve awareness. Another systematic review considered the effectiveness of 16 older driver rehabilitation programs in improving on-road fitness-to-drive (Unsworth & Baker, 2014). The study found that the most common program approach was driving simulator training, followed in frequency by off-road skill-specific training and off-road education. The authors concluded that there was moderate evidence that off-road skill-specific training, off-road educational training, and driving simulator training can improve older driver fitness. A recent literature review of interventions to maintain mobility among older adults included sections on cognitive and educational interventions and older drivers (Ross, Schmidt, & Ball, 2013). The authors concluded that cognitive training interventions (namely speed-of-processing training) can improve older driver on-road driving performance, improve reaction time to driving-critical events, may reduce older driver at-fault crashes, and may delay driving cessation. They also concluded that educational interventions can be beneficial under some circumstances, can improve knowledge, and can improve driving performance when combined with an on-road training component.

Table 5.2 shows a list of older driver education and training programs that we consider promising approaches. As discussed by Molnar, Eby, St. Louis, and Neumeyer (2007), a program can be considered promising if formal evaluations have shown its effectiveness, or in the absence of evaluation data, the program was developed with the capabilities of older adults in mind and program components can be logically linked to positive driving outcomes.

## *Self-screening*

As discussed in Chapter 2, Driving Patterns and Behaviors Among Older Adults, older drivers who are experiencing declines in functional abilities will often engage in self-regulatory practices (see also, Molnar et al., 2015, for a review). Appropriate self-regulation and other compensatory actions can best be implemented when one has accurate knowledge of the types and level of functional impairment being experienced. To this end, several researchers have developed and evaluated self-screening tools for older driver use. As described by Eby and Molnar (2010), self-screening refers to screening or testing for functional ability declines or potential problems with driving that an older driver engages in himself or herself to increase self-awareness of declines. Early work described these tools as "self-assessment," but recent discussions have clarified the terminology and many researchers in older adult mobility advocate making a distinction between the terms "screening" and "assessment" (Lang, Parkes, & Medina, 2013; Transportation Research Board, 2016).

**Table 5.2** Example promising approaches for older driver education and training

| Name (reference) | Description |
|---|---|
| *55 Alive/Mature Driving Program Plus On-Road Training* (Bédard et al., 2008) | Classroom and on-road training course that consists of two 4-h classroom sessions (using content from the original AARP program) and two 30 min on-road training sessions in which participants receive constructive feedback on driving. This is an experimental course that adds on-road driving instruction to a well-established educational course that had previously been shown to have little effect on driving outcomes (Bédard, Isherwood, Moore, Gibbons, & Lindstrom, 2004) |
| *AAA's Roadwise Driver* (AAA, 2018) | Classroom or Internet educational course available to the public at nominal cost. As described by AAA (2018), the course covers: ways to extend a safe driving career; issues related to distractions, drowsiness, aggressive driving, and road rage; how to manage visibility, time, and space while driving; impaired (alcohol and medications) driving; and comfort and safety tips |
| *AARP Smart* Driver *Course* (AARP, 2018) | Classroom or Internet educational course available at nominal cost to the public and targeted at drivers age 50 and older. Covers state-specific traffic laws, strategies and techniques to improve driving safety, and methods for dealing with hazardous driving situations |
| *DriveWell: Promoting Older Driver Safety and Mobility in Your Community* (National Highway Traffic Safety Administration, 2007a) | Classroom presentation that encourages older drivers to change when and how they drive and prompts older adults to use alternative forms of transportation. Taught by experts who conduct information sessions about older driver wellness, safety, and mobility. DriveWell was developed by the American Society on Aging |
| *DriveWise: Seniors Program* (DriveWise Canada, 2018) | Classroom, simulator, and on-road education training course that is instructor-led and designed to help older drivers in Ontario, Canada, prepare for the mandatory license renewal assessment. The course is tailored to the individual needs of older drivers |

(*Continued*)

**Table 5.2** (Continued)

| Name (reference) | Description |
|---|---|
| *Education Program to Enhance Older Driver Performance* (Marottoli, Van Hess, et al., 2007) | Classroom and on-road training program designed to enhance driving performance. The course consists of two 4-h classroom sessions and two 1-h on-road sessions focused on the common problem areas for older drivers. This was an experimental program |
| *Knowledge Enhances Your Safety (KEYS)* (Stalvey & Owsley, 2003) | An one-on-one educational program designed to increase self-awareness of a driver's visual impairments, how they affect driving, and how to self-regulate driving to better compensate for the impairment |
| *Mature Driver Course (Senior Driver Refresher Course)* (Alberta Motor Association, 2018) | Six-hour classroom educational course that covers traffic laws, driver impairments and how to recognize impairments, vehicle safety and driving habits, effects of aging on driving, and tips on sharing the road and physical fitness |
| *Metec Driver Refresher Course for Seniors* (Metec, 2018) | Classroom and on-road training course that covers traffic laws, education, and practical advice to improve driving performance |
| *Seniors Driving Longer, Smarter, Safer: An Older Driver Training Program* (Scully, Devlin, Oxley, & Charlton, 2010) | Classroom course that consists of two 5-h sessions that included instruction, guided discussions, and small workgroups. Content includes risk situations, crash types, functional assessments, alternative transportation and mobility options, and strategies for managing/decreasing risk |
| *Tailored On-Road Driving Lessons* (Anstey, Eramudugolla, Kiely, & Price, 2018) | Classroom and on-road training course designed to improve older driver safety. The course consists of one 2-h classroom refresher session on traffic laws and two 1-h on-road driving lessons tailored to improve individual poor driving skills and habits. This is an experimental program |
| *Years Ahead: Senior Driving Program* (RACV, 2018) | Classroom educational presentation that covers information and advice for safe driving |

According to the Transportation Research Board (2016, p. 9), assessment is defined as "use of specific measurements, tools, or instruments during the evaluation process," whereas self-screening is defined in the context that "an individual obtains and reviews his or her own data to determine the need for evaluation." In other words, screening is the first step in the process to determine older driver fitness and may lead to assessment, but screening results themselves are not the sole basis for making decisions about fitness to drive.

Self-screening tools have several benefits, including they are nonthreatening to use because the older adult has complete control over how the screening data are used; due to its nonthreatening nature, older adults may be more likely to engage in self-screening at an earlier stage when declines are just starting to occur, allowing for better opportunities for getting help prior to the occurrence of significant declines; and self-screening tools are easy and cost-effective to disseminate, providing access to these tools among a wide audience (Eby, Molnar, Shope, Vivoda, & Fordyce, 2003). In the past two decades, several self-screening tools have been developed that range in format from paper-and-pencil tests to computer-assisted testing (Eby et al., 2003; Classen et al., 2010; Levasseur et al., 2015; Molnar, Eby, Kartje, & St. Louis, 2010; Staplin & Dinh-Zarr, 2006; Vardaki & Yannis, 2012). Here, we review the research on several of the more recent self-screening tools.

Perhaps the most recognizable self-screening tool is the *Roadwise Review* (Staplin & Dinh-Zarr, 2006), developed based on the *DrivingHealth Inventory* (DHI, Ball et al., 2006; Staplin, Lococo, Gish, & Decina, 2003a, 2003b). The *Roadwise Review* is a computer-based tool that assesses several functional abilities using brief tests including leg strength, general mobility, neck flexibility, low and high contrast visual acuity, working memory, visualization of missing information, visual search, and information processing speed. Some of the testing require someone else to assist with administration, making this tool not strictly a self-screening tool. Summary results are given to the older driver, along with advice on what can be done about the declining abilities. Two studies have addressed the efficacy of the DHI as a screening tool to identify potential high-risk drivers in a licensing agency setting (see, e.g., Edwards et al., 2008; Scialfa, Ference, Boone, Tay, & Hudson, 2010). In both studies, a tester administered the screening tool and several other driving outcome measures were also gathered. The results were mixed. Edwards et al. (2008) found that older drivers with a history of crashes performed worse than older drivers without such a history, and a majority of participants supported the use of similar screening tests like the DHI at licensure. Scialfa et al. (2010) reported that some of the tests exhibited ceiling effects limiting the usefulness of the tests, there was a high failure rate for the neck flexibility test, and the DHI scores did not predict self-reported driving problems or crash risk. Evaluation results for the *Roadwise Review* have also shown mixed results.

Myers, Blanchard, MacDonald, and Porter (2008) conducted an external process-evaluation of the *Roadwise Review*, using a small convenience sample of paired older drivers. Outcome measures were derived from data collected by experimenters unobtrusively observing the older adults working through the testing procedures, and focus groups with these older adults. The authors reported that the older drivers' impressions of the *Roadwise Review* were generally favorable, but several areas of concern or improvement were noted. Many participants had difficulty using the mouse even after completing a practice session. This was noted for both the person being screened and his or her partner. The investigators noted that the scores for some tests were inaccurate because of difficulty selecting the intended buttons with the mouse. In addition, the partners influenced the results both intentionally and unintentionally by assisting the drivers in tasks and encouraging second tries. With regard to the actual test battery in the *Roadwise Review*, most of the tasks were judged as enjoyable by the participants. There was difficulty understanding the instructions for one task, and another task that required sustained attention over a large number of trials was judged as frustrating, with 12% of participants refusing to complete the test. Finally, the *Roadwise Review* uses cut points to determine levels of impairment on certain tasks. Some participants were reportedly upset about being told that they had "severe impairment" on some tasks.

A study in Canada (Porter & Tuokko, 2011) investigated the *Roadwise Review* among 96 older drivers at two sites. Participants completed the *Roadwise Review* following the instructions included in the tool, with some additional instructions included based on the results of the Myers et al. (2008) study. Results showed that very few participants had impairment in visual acuity or leg strength, more than 60% were classified as having serious impairment in neck flexibility, and about 75% had some level of impairment in visual search. Only four participants had zero impairments. Regression models showed that participant characteristics had low predictive value for any of the test scores. Qualitative results were positive with 91% reporting that the testing made them more aware of changes that can affect driving, 98% reporting that they would recommend the testing to others, 95% thought the information would be useful for family conversations about driving, and 81% reporting that they would be willing to pay for the testing. The authors concluded that the *Roadwise Review* offers promise as a self-screening tool, but modifications are needed.

Another Canadian study evaluated the *Roadwise Review* in relation to on-road driving performance and standard tests of visual-cognitive processing speed among older drivers (Bédard, Riendeau, Weaver, & Clarkson, 2011). A convenience sample of 51 drivers aged 51–86 completed the *Roadwise Review*, the standard tests, and an on-road evaluation with a licensed examiner who scored driving errors using a demerit point system (errors were given 5 or 10 demerit points depending on the severity and 50 demerit points overall was considered failing the examination). Correlations between scores on the *Roadwise Review* tests and other standardized tests ranged from 0.46 to 0.61, indicating a low level of association. Correlations between *Roadwise Review* scores and demerit point scores ranged from −0.40 to 0.50, indicating poor associations. Finally, an analysis using a "pass/fail" approach also failed to show a relationship with the number of problems found by the *Roadwise Review*. The authors concluded that these results indicated a low convergence between findings of functional declines as measured by the *Roadwise Review* and actual performance using several standardized approaches. In a similar study, 65 healthy older drivers (mean age = 74 years) completed the *Roadwise Review* and an on-road evaluation scored by demerit points (Jones, Cordazzo, & Scialfa, 2014). The results showed that raw scores on the *Roadwise Review* did not predict total demerit points, or automatic disqualifications, but did predict who would pass or fail the on-road evaluation. The total number of problems identified in *Roadwise Review* was significant in predicting automatic disqualifications.

Collectively, these results suggest that at least in its current form, the *Roadwise Review* may be best suited for use by licensing agency or health-care personnel as a screening tool that may point to further evaluation, rather than a self-screening tool to raise an individual's awareness of his or her own declines and what he or she can do about them in order to keep driving safely. The high failure rate for neck flexibility, the ceiling effect for the visual acuity measures, the difficulty people have completing the visual processing speed test, and the need for a partner to complete some of the tests all point to the need for modifications to this instrument to improve its efficacy as a self-screening tool. Perhaps because of these research results, AAA no longer distributes the *Roadwise Review* on its website or in field offices.

Researchers at the University of Michigan Transportation Research Institute have developed and evaluated two self-screening tools with sponsorship from National Highway Traffic Safety Administration (NHTSA). The first, called the *Driving Decisions Workbook*, is a paper-and-pencil workbook that allows older drivers to answer questions about themselves and, depending on how they answer, gives them individualized feedback on functional declines, driving problems they may be experiencing, general knowledge about how declines affect driving, and recommendations for further evaluation (Eby, Molnar, & Shope, 2000; Eby et al., 2003). The *Driving Decisions Workbook* was developed based on a critical review of the literature, focus groups with older drivers, an expert panel, and pilot testing. The instrument includes three broad areas of screening: health (medical conditions, medications), driving abilities (vision, cognition, psychomotor), and experiences/attitudes/behaviors. The second is called *SAFER Driving: The Enhanced Driving Decisions Workbook*, standing for Self-Awareness and Feedback for Responsible Driving (Eby et al., 2008; Molnar et al., 2010). This tool is contained on a website (http://www.um-saferdriving.org/) and was developed using similar background information and expert and qualitative feedback. Unlike the first instrument, *SAFER Driving* is organized around 27 health concerns (i.e., the symptoms caused by health conditions and medications such as neuropathy or reduced visual acuity) and 15 critical driving skills (skills required for safe driving such as turning and gap acceptance). Health conditions are assessed in this tool under the assumption that the wide range of possible health conditions and effects of medication produce a relatively small number of health concerns allowing the tool to be more comprehensive than previous self-screening instruments. *SAFER Driving* asks three to four questions regarding the severity level of each health concern and links these algorithmically to the critical driving skills that they impact and gives tailored feedback to the older driver in four ways: general awareness, self-awareness, compensation strategies, and suggestions for further evaluation.

Both self-screening instruments have been evaluated with older drivers: 99 and 68 older drivers for the *Driving Decisions Workbook* and *SAFER Driving*, respectively (Eby et al., 2003; Molnar et al., 2010). In both studies, scores on the self-screening were compared to on-road driving performance. Data on what participants thought about the instruments were also collected. For *SAFER Driving*, comprehensive data on visual, cognitive, and psychomotor functioning were also collected. Correlations between on-road driving scores and the three broad categories and overall were 0.15 (health), 0.35 (abilities), 0.21 (experiences), and 0.30 (overall), with only health not being statistically significant. These correlations showed that problems found in the *Driving Decisions Workbook* were at least modestly associated with problems in on-road driving, except for the health category. For *SAFER Driving*, scores were significantly correlated with on-road driving scores (−0.26) and clinical evaluation scores (0.25). When only drivers age 75 and above were considered, these correlations were −0.44 and 0.54 for on-road and clinical evaluation, respectively. Again, these results showed that problems identified by *SAFER Driving* were modestly associated with problems identified through both on-road and clinical evaluation, with a much stronger association for drivers age 75 or older. Subjective data from participants in each study are shown in Table 5.3 as the percentages of older drivers in each study agreeing with statements about the self-screening instrument. These results strongly support the conclusion that the instruments increase self-awareness and general knowledge among older drivers.

Several other self-screening instruments have been introduced recently. Researchers in Greece (Vardaki & Yannis, 2012) have developed a self-screening tool called the *Handbook for Safe Driving at an Older Age*. The *Handbook* was developed based on the *Driving Decisions Workbook* and includes sections on safety within the car, safety in traffic, safe practices on freeways, driving and emotions, driving in good conditions, driving problems and age-related changes, indication of serious concern about driving ability, and general information. The instrument was evaluated with 64 older drivers who were given the *Handbook* to read and then the next day were asked to complete a questionnaire. The results showed that older drivers reported very positive impressions of the *Handbook*, with more than 80% responding that the *Handbook* informed them about changes that come with aging that affect driving; was a useful reminder of things they already knew; was worth reading even if the content was already known; would be useful to read again in the future; would be recommended to friends; and was an opportunity for discussions with family or friends.

Researchers in Florida have developed the *Safe Driving Behavior Measure* instrument (Classen et al., 2010; Winter et al., 2011). This instrument includes questions on driving patterns, habits, and ability. Respondents rate the difficulty they have had with driving behaviors over the past 3 months, using a 5-level scale along with a "not-applicable" response category for behaviors and situations that they did not encounter. Evaluation results on the *Safe Driving Behavior Measure* have not been reported, but developmental research reports that the instrument has good face and scale content validity (Classen et al., 2010).

**Table 5.3** Reported older drivers' thoughts about the driving decisions workbook and SAFER driving

| Statement[a] | Driving decisions workbook (%, $n = 99$) | SAFER driving (%, $n = 68$) |
|---|---|---|
| Did the workbook make you more aware of changes that can affect your driving? | 76.5 | 76.2 |
| Did you discover changes in yourself that you had not been aware of before? | 14.1 | 37.7 |
| Did the feedback serve as a useful reminder of things I already knew? | 93.8 | 96.9 |
| Now that you have completed the (self-screening instrument), are you planning to make changes in the way you drive? | 23.7 | 41.9 |
| Did completing the (self-screening instrument) make you think more about the possibility of taking a driver refresher course? | 41.4 | 33.3 |
| Now that you have completed (self-screening instrument), do you think you will be more likely to have a doctor to check functioning or discuss health concerns? | 35.7 | 52.5 |
| If available, would you use the (self-screening instrument) in the future? | 72.4 | 76.6 |
| Would you recommend the (self-screening instrument) to older adult friends or family members? | 96.9 | 92.2 |
| Do you think the (self-screening instrument) could be useful for helping older adults talk about driving concerns with their families? | 100 | 93.7 |
| Overall, how would you rate the usefulness of the (self-screening instrument)? | | |
| Very useful | 53.5 | 36.5 |
| Somewhat useful | 40.4 | 47.6 |
| A little useful | 6.1 | 12.7 |
| Not at all useful | 0.0 | 3.2 |

[a]Note that the wording of the statements has been modified for this table in order to compare participant responses across the two studies. The original articles should be consulted for exact wording (Eby et al., 2003; Molnar et al., 2010).

A group of Canadian researchers have developed and evaluated a self-screening instrument called *OSCAR* (In French: *Outil de Sensibilisation des conducteurs âgés aux capacités requises pour une Conduite Automobile sécuritaire et Responsible*) (Levasseur et al., 2014, 2015). *OSCAR* was developed based on a systematic review of the literature and expert consultation and is based on theoretical models. *OSCAR* includes 15 questions and 15 tips related to aging and driving. As described by the developers, the purpose of the tool is to foster and maintain the mobility of older drivers through safe driving. Levasseur et al. (2014) conducted an evaluation of

*OSCAR* with 15 older adults (mean age = 69.7 years), who completed the instrument and then participated in a structured interview. The results showed that *OSCAR* was easily understandable, interesting, and increased self-awareness. For example, 58% found the instrument "very useful;" 33% reported that the instrument served as a useful reminder for things they already knew; 25% reported being more aware of the linkage between driving safety records and problems with driving; 83% reported that the instrument helped them to better monitor changes in functioning; 75% said that they would recommend *OSCAR* to friends and family members; and the majority reported that the instrument would help them discuss driving problems with family and health-care professionals. Another study by the same researchers (Levasseur et al., 2015) evaluated *OSCAR* with 48 older drivers, using a pre- and post-test design to determine changes in interest, openness, and knowledge 8–10 weeks after completing *OSCAR*. The study found that *OSCAR* increased interest, openness, and knowledge about declining abilities and strategies that can be used for continued safe driving. Further, more than one-half of the drivers reported having started six or more compensatory strategies during the 2-month follow-up period.

## Exercise and fitness

It is generally agreed that exercise and physical activity is a critical component of healthy aging (see, e.g., Chodzko-Zajko, 2014). Indeed, research has found that exercise can slow or improve functional declines in older adults, including improved measures of walking, balance, and falls in frail older adults (de Labra, Guimaraes-Pinheiro, Maseda, Lorenzo, & Millán-Calenti, 2015; Giné-Garriga, Roqué-Fíguls, Coll-Planas, Sitjà-Rabert, & Salvà, 2014); cognitive functioning (Kelly et al., 2014); and overall quality of life (Awick et al., 2015). Research has also investigated the effects of exercise and fitness programs on driving abilities. Fig. 5.1 shows an older adult exercise class held in Ann Arbor, Michigan.

In one in the earliest investigations into the effects of an exercise program on older adult driving performance, researchers from the US studied the effects of an exercise and flexibility program on measures of driving performance among 38 older drivers age 60–85 (Ostrow, Shaffron, & McPherson, 1992). The program included upper-body stretching exercises performed by the older adult in a home setting. The older adult logged both the exercise sessions and their amount of driving. The older driver met weekly with a clinician who reviewed compliance with the program and introduced new exercises to keep the program fresh. A control group of older drivers received information about their vehicle along with instruction but did not engage in the exercise program. Study outcome measures were range of motion tests and an on-road driving performance test. On-road driving was assessed through a 6.8-mi course on actual roadways that was driven by participants and scored on several measures by a professional examiner who rode with the participant. The results showed that the experimental group exhibited increased

**Figure 5.1** Older adults participating in an exercise class.
Source: Photography by Gregory Kostyniuk.

shoulder flexibility and a greater range of trunk motion, while these same measures decreased in the control group. Analysis of the on-road driving skills showed that the exercise group had significantly better performance as compared to controls on driving skills that required upper body flexibility (checking mirrors, turning the body to check blind spots, and parallel parking). There were no differences between the groups on driving skills that did not require good upper-body flexibility.

A study by Marottoli, Allore, et al. (2007) investigated the effects of a 3-month fitness program conducted by an occupational therapist in the participant's own home. This intensive, graduated fitness program focused on exercises to improve stamina, flexibility, coordination, and speed of movement. The participants were 178 older drivers (age 70 + ) without substantial visual or cognitive impairment, assigned randomly to the exercise group or to the control group (the latter receiving in-home safety education but no physical fitness training). Driving performance for all participants was measured through an on-road assessment with a professional evaluator. Driving performance was rated on a 36-item scale that addressed performance on several driving maneuvers and traffic situations. Performance measures also included an overall score from the evaluator and the number of critical errors during the driving test. Performance was assessed for both groups of participants before and after completion of the program. Results showed that driving performance decreased for the control group, while performance did not decline for the fitness group. The authors concluded that although the fitness program did not improve driving abilities, it did seem to prevent the loss of skills over the 3 months of the program.

Researchers from Portugal have conducted two studies investigating the effects of exercise programs on driving-related abilities among older drivers (Marmeleira, Godinho, & Fernandes, 2009; Marmeleira, Melo, Tlemcani, & Godinho, 2011). The first of these studies examined the effects of an exercise program on several abilities related to driving performance among 32 older drivers age 60–82 (Marmeleira et al., 2009). The 3-month, supervised exercise program consisted of three 1-hour sessions each week that focused on not only aerobic fitness but also perceptual and cognitive training. In many exercises, the types of training were combined, such as keeping several balloons in the air or walking in one direction while moving the arms in a different direction. A battery of perceptual, cognitive, and psychomotor tests was administered to the exercise group and to a control group that received no exercise activities before and after the program. The results showed that, compared to the control group, those in the exercise program showed greater improvement in reaction time, movement time, response time, visual attention, speed of processing, divided attention, and lower limb mobility. The authors concluded that these improved abilities should translate into better driving performance but did not address this directly in their study.

The second study (Marmeleira et al., 2011) investigated the effects of a 2-month exercise program on the speed of behavior during on-road driving among 26 older adults (age 55–78). The activities in the exercise program were similar to those used in the previous study (Marmeleira et al., 2009) and the control group continued with their normal activity without participating in the exercise program. On-road driving was measured in both groups at baseline and the program used an instrumented vehicle on rural roadways that followed a lead vehicle driven by an experimenter. During the drive, the participant engaged in a number of scripted activities such as braking as quickly as possible when the lead vehicle braked (brake reaction time). As compared to the control group, older drivers who participated in the exercise program showed significantly improved performance in brake reaction time, brake response time, peripheral reaction time, and choice reaction time. Analysis of composite driving scores showed that the control group did not change between baseline and the 8-week program while these scores significantly improved after the program for the exercise group. The authors concluded that exercise can improve movement times for driving-related behaviors among older adults and recommends that training interventions for older drivers should include exercise programs.

A study in the United States investigated the effects of an exercise program on tactical and strategic driving performance as assessed on the road by a trained evaluator and by performance in a driving simulator among 40 older drivers (20 in an exercise group and 20 in a control group, Staplin, Lococo, Brooks, & Srinivasan, 2013). These outcome measures were obtained before the program, immediately after the program, and during a 3-month follow-up. The exercise program consisted of 8 hours of supervised exercise, divided into four 2-hour group sessions. The program focused on flexibility, strength, coordination, and several perceptual-cognitive, dual-task activities, similar to the studies in Portugal previously discussed. When compared to a control group, the participants in the exercise group did not show improved driving performance on either the on-road or simulated driving measures. The authors noted that the small sample sizes and the high functioning of the older adults at baseline may have limited the outcomes in the study.

Finally, another US study investigated the effectiveness of Tai Chi exercise on cognitive and physical functions related to driving performance among 58 older drivers (Miller & Taylor-Piliae, 2018). Tai Chi is a low-to-moderate form of aerobic, low-impact exercise that also includes mental concentration, balance, and breath control as shown in Fig. 5.2. Participants all were attending a supervised Tai Chi class and completed a battery of assessment instruments including cognitive and physical measures and self-reported measures. The study results found that the Tai Chi older drivers' performance on most of the cognitive and physical measures was significantly better than normative reference values that have been previously shown to be related to safe driving. The authors concluded that Tai Chi exercise has the potential to improve functions related to safe driving but recognize that the study findings could be limited by a self-selection bias and the lack of a control group.

**Figure 5.2** Older adult practicing Tai Chi.
Source: Photography by Gregory Kostyniuk.

Collectively, the evidence suggests that exercise classes can be beneficial for maintaining older adult mobility. To realize these benefits, however, it appears that the exercise program needs to be frequent, moderately intense, and sustained over the long term. The research indicates that programs that focus on flexibility, strength, balance, and coordination may be the most appropriate for maintaining driving skills, but dual-task activities that incorporate physical fitness activities with activities that provide an opportunity to practice perceptual and/or cognitive skills may also be beneficial.

## Vehicles

In addition to seeking out education, training, and fitness opportunities, older adults can also improve their safety while traveling in an automobile as a driver or passenger in a number of ways. These include use of seat belts, proper use of aftermarket vehicle adaptations, and personalized training about adjusting a vehicle to fit a specific driver. Here, we review research related to these areas.

### *Seat belt use*

Use of seat belts is the single most effective way to protect a vehicle occupant during a crash (see Vivoda & Eby, 2011 for a discussion). Despite the fact that seat belt use for older adults is among the highest of any age group, belt use in certain circumstances, such as the back seat, is significantly lower. For example, a 2016 nationally representative direct observation survey of belt use in the US found that front seat belt use for occupants age 70 and older was 91.9%, but only 74.9% for the same age group when they were passengers in the back seat (Li & Pickrell, 2018). Other work in the US and Australia investigating factors contributing to nonuse of seat belts among older adults concluded that a major factor was the comfort and convenience of using belts (Brown, Coxon, Fong, Clarke, & Keay, 2013; Fong, Keay, Coxon, Clarke, & Brown, 2016; Levi & De Leonardis, 2008). These studies noted the following issues related to belt use comfort and convenience among older adults, particularly those who were overweight or small in stature:

- Difficulty reaching for shoulder belt and pulling it across the body;
- Shoulder belt cuts across neck or chokes occupant;
- Belt tightening over time;
- Belt touching neck when they turn their head;
- Seat belt puts pressure on skin and chest;
- Difficulty inserting latch plate into buckle;
- Belt buckle and stock are too hard to locate;
- Confusion with how to unbuckle;
- Discomfort or difficulty using belt because of girth or height; and
- Desire not to wrinkle clothes.

The authors suggested that some of these issues could be ameliorated through better vehicle design and the use of aftermarket devices such as shoulder belt pads, seat cushions, pivoting seats, ribbon or a plastic loop to permit easier reaching for the belt, seat belt adjusters, and seat belt extenders. Indeed, recent work shows that some of these adaptations, particularly seat cushions and shoulder belt padding, are being utilized by older drivers (Zanier et al., 2018).

## Aftermarket vehicle adaptation

An aftermarket vehicle adaptation (modification) is "... any mechanical or structural change to a passenger car, van, truck, or other motor vehicle that permit an individual with a disability and/or aging-related concern to safely drive or ride as a passenger" (Pellerito & Blanc, 2006, pg. 57). Several types of vehicle adaptations are available for older adults who are experiencing difficulties with seating and positioning, steering, using the accelerator and/or brakes, and using auxiliary systems (dashboard controls) as shown in Table 5.4 (Bouman & Pellerito, 2006).

There are clearly many vehicle adaptation options not only to help older adults with declining abilities drive more safely but also to increase the comfort and convenience of riding in a vehicle. Despite these advantages, a study in the US has found that at least among a relatively healthy cohort of 2900 older drivers in five cities, only 9% utilized an aftermarket vehicle adaptation (Eby et al., 2018). Of the 268 vehicles of older drivers that reported having a vehicle adaptation, 45% reported a seat cushion, 39% reported special mirrors, 6% reported seat belt adaptations, and other adaptations were reported at a frequency of less than 5%. Such results suggest that aftermarket vehicle adaptations may be an underutilized strategy for maintaining safe mobility for older adults.

How does one determine if he or she could benefit from a vehicle adaptation and if so, make the adaptation? In a report from the US titled *Adapting Motor Vehicles for Older Drivers*, a sensible seven-part process is described as follows (National Highway Traffic Safety Administration, 2007b):

- *Investigate Cost-Saving Opportunities.* Adapting a vehicle can be expensive and the ways to help cover costs should be considered, including nonprofits that provide funding for disabilities, vehicle insurance, worker's compensation, rebates from vehicle manufacturers, state tax waivers, and tax deductions.
- *Investigate Licensing Opportunities.* Some states may require restricted licenses for certain adaptations.
- *Evaluate Your Needs.* It is recommended that older adults work with certified driver rehabilitation specialists (CDRSs) who are occupational therapists with special training on driving issues. The CDRS can professionally evaluate abilities for both driving and riding in a car and suggest appropriate adaptations.

**Table 5.4** Examples of possible vehicle adaptations for overcoming aging-related declines

| Category | Equipment | Description |
|---|---|---|
| **Seating and positioning** | Seat cushion | Helps with seeing out of the vehicle, comfort, and postural support |
| | Custom armrests | Helps with upper extremity support, comfort, and steering |
| | Seat belt modification | A number of devices can help with reaching, buckling, and comfort |
| | Airbags | Airbags can be deactivated if occupant needs to sit closer to airbag than is safe |
| | Upper body support with Velcro closures | Helps maintain posture for those with impaired upper body strength |
| **Steering** | Steering knob | Helps driver steer when holding the wheel is difficult |
| | Spin pin | Helps driver steer when holding the wheel is difficult |
| | V-grip | Helps driver steer when hand strength is impaired |
| | Palm grip | Helps driver steer when hand strength is impaired |
| | Tri pin | Helps driver steer when hand strength is impaired |
| | Steering splint | Helps driver steer when hand strength is impaired |
| | Amputee ring | Allows the driver to steer using a prosthetic hook |
| **Accelerator and brake controls** | Left foot accelerator | Helps with driving for people with impaired strength or movement in the right foot/leg |
| | Gas pedal extension | Helps with driving for people with impaired foot/leg strength or movement or those who cannot reach the accelerator |
| | Pedal extensions | Helps with driving for people with impaired foot/leg strength or movement or those who cannot reach the pedals |
| | Hand controls | Allows people with lower body strength or movement impairments operate the throttle and brake using the hands |
| | Parking brake extension | Allows the parking brake to be set using the hands |
| | Modification of steering column controls | Depending on the specific functional decline, horn, headlights, wipers, turn signal, and cruise control can all be modified to fit the functional abilities of the driver |
| **Auxiliary systems** | Push button ignition | Helps with starting the vehicle for those with hand strength and/or movement impairment |
| | Convex/ Multifaceted mirrors | Helps with seeing around the vehicle for those who have difficulty moving the neck or upper body |

List adapted from Bouman, J., & Pellerito, J. M., Jr. (2006). Preparing for the on-road evaluation. In J. M. Pellerito (Ed.), *Driver rehabilitation and community mobility*. St. Louis, MO: Elsevier Mosby.

- *Select the Right Vehicle.* Working with the CDRS or other professional, a vehicle should be selected that can reasonably be adapted in the way that is necessary for the individual driver.
- *Choose a Qualified Mobility Dealer to Modify Your Vehicle.* It is recommended that older adults work with companies that have experience making vehicle adaptations. The report noted that some US states require the use of certain dealers to qualify for credits/rebates.
- *Obtain Training on the Use of New Equipment.* It is recommended that in addition to basic instruction of the operation of the adaptive equipment, older adults also receive on-road training.
- *Maintain Your Vehicle.* It is important not only to perform regular scheduled maintenance but also to perform special maintenance on some types of adaptive equipment.

A common theme through this report is the recommendation to work with a CDRS for each part of this process. Recent research shows that older drivers who have vehicle adaptations tend to not work with CDRSs or other professionals (Eby et al., 2018), even though they are readily available. In the United States, for example, CDRSs can be found on the websites of the Association for Driver Rehabilitation Specialists and the American Occupational Therapy Association, Inc. (AOTA).

## Vehicle maintenance

As previously discussed, one area that could potentially improve older driver safety has to do with vehicle maintenance. Logically, a vehicle with broken headlights, inappropriate tire pressures, and/or nonoperational windshield wipers should have a higher risk of being in a crash, yet very little research can be found on this topic. Zein and Navin (2003) include proper vehicle maintenance in their proposed systems approach to improving traffic safety. The US federal government has recognized the adverse safety consequences of underinflated tires and, as of 2003, has required new motor vehicles to have a tire pressure warning (Thiriez & Bondy, 2001). Informational pamphlets encouraging proper tire maintenance have also been published (see, e.g., National Highway Traffic Safety Administration, 2001). A study in Taiwan analyzed records of 65,095 people who used a certain insurance company and a certain vehicle manufacturer for service between 2001 and 2006 (Bair, Huang, & Wang, 2012). The study found a small but significant association between level of vehicle maintenance and the probability of a liability claim being filed; that is, properly maintained vehicles had a slightly lower probability of being in a property-damage-only or worse crash. An Australian study examined the effects of periodic vehicle safety inspections and tire pressure checks on the probability of a crash and found that vehicles without a current inspection and vehicles without a current tire pressure check were significantly more likely to have been in a crash as compared to controls (Blows, Ivers, Connor, Ameratunga, & Norton, 2003).

Collectively, this background information suggests that proper vehicle maintenance may be an important contributor to improved traffic safety for older drivers. Little research is available on the prevalence of various vehicle maintenance-related measures among older drivers. In 2001, NHTSA conducted the Tire Pressure Special Study in which they interviewed a nationally representative sample of more than 11,000 drivers and measured their vehicle's tire pressure (Thiriez & Bondy, 2001). The study found that among drivers age 70 or older, 89% were concerned about maintaining proper tire inflation, 86% were responsible for maintaining the vehicle they drove, 28% checked tire pressure monthly (4% never checked), and 33% asked another person about what the proper tire pressure for their vehicle should be. Another study in the US visually inspected the vehicles of nearly 3000 drivers age 65–79 and found that vehicles overall were well maintained and had little damage (Zanier et al., 2018). These authors also reported that for the maintenance metrics related to driving safety (tire tread depth, tire pressure, dents, scratches, and major damage), vehicles of older drivers in the lowest income group had scores indicating potentially lower vehicle safety than other income groups.

## CarFit

In an effort to improve older driver safety and comfort, an educational program, called *CarFit*, was developed by the American Society on Aging, the AAA, AARP, and the AOTA to help older drivers better "fit" their vehicles (AARP, AAA, & AOTA, 2018). *CarFit* is an educational program designed to promote optimal alignment of older drivers with their vehicle. To this end, the program offers older adults the opportunity to assess how well their personal vehicle is adjusted to fit their personal preferences and needs. The program also offers information and material on community-specific resources that have the potential to enhance driving safety and/or increase community mobility. *CarFit* instructors are trained on a standardized multi-item protocol that they execute individually with program participants. This protocol includes observation of and advice about seat belt use, steering wheel tilt/head restraint devices, distance to steering wheel, line of sight above steering wheel, positioning relative to throttle and brake, mirrors, neck mobility and blind spot, ignition, operation of vehicle controls, and a vehicle inspection. *CarFit* has been implemented in the US, Australia, New Zealand, and Canada (Craik, Stern, Lapointe, McCarthy, & Davis, 2015).

A few studies have evaluated the *CarFit* program. One evaluation investigated the self-reported effects of the program among 54 older drivers who participated in a *CarFit* event and later returned a questionnaire that was completed after the event (Stav, 2010). The study found that when asked about what helpful new thing they learned at the event regarding their vehicle, 46% reported mirror adjustment, 20% reported seat belt positioning, and 17% reported distance to airbag and seat positioning. Participants were asked about adjustments they had made to their vehicle based on recommendations from the event, and nearly all suggested recommendations were made by participants (ranging from 67% to 100%, depending on the specific recommendation). Other findings included the following: 74% of the respondents reported they discussed the program with family and friends; 67% reported *CarFit* was "very useful;" and many participants responded in an open-ended question about *CarFit* that they were grateful for the volunteers' attention to personal safety and welfare.

Another evaluation of *CarFit* utilized 570 drivers living in retirement communities who completed driving surveys and were asked to participate in the intervention. Of those, 195 consented and were randomly assigned to a *CarFit* intervention group ($n = 83$) or a comparison group ($n = 112$; Gaines, Burke, Marx, Wagner, & Parrish, 2011). Results indicated that 71% of participants assigned to the *CarFit* intervention actually attended a *CarFit* program and 86% of them received recommendations. At the 6-month follow-up, 60% reported following the recommendations, although there were no significant changes in driving behaviors at the follow-up. The authors concluded that the *CarFit* program was able to detect addressable opportunities that may contribute to driving safety, but stronger reinforcement of recommendations may be needed to ensure that they are followed.

While these evaluations show that older adults like and highly value *CarFit*, evaluations that objectively measure the adjustments made by older drivers in the months following the program are needed as well as research that addresses the safety implications of these adjustments. Nevertheless, *CarFit* events have great potential for keeping older drivers safely on the road for longer and are recommended as one of many activities that an older adult can seek out to help them be a safer, more comfortable driver.

## Planning for future mobility

Despite participating in education and training programs, maintaining good physical fitness, and adjusting a vehicle to optimize its use, many older adults will eventually need to transition from driving and find non-driving options for maintaining safe mobility. Here, we review some activities that older adults can engage in to both help ease the transition from driving and meet mobility needs after stopping driving. Clearly, one of the most pressing needs of older adults who have stopped driving is figuring out how to meet mobility needs. At least for the current cohort of older adults, most have not thought much about they will get around after they stop driving (e.g., Kostyniuk & Shope, 2003). A vast majority of non-driving older adults rely primarily on informal caregivers to provide transportation assistance. Indeed, in a statewide study of 268 caregivers of older adults in Michigan, 100%

reported providing transportation assistance of some sort (Eby, Molnar, Kostyniuk, Louis, & Zanier, 2017). While such transportation assistance will continue to be sought and necessary, older adults can lessen their reliance on friends and family by becoming more familiar with community mobility options. Chapter 3, Use of Non-driving Transportation Options provides an overview of the many mobility options that may be available in a community, including some that are new and possibly unfamiliar to today's older adults, such as *Uber* or *Lyft*.

Programs also exist to help older adults locate these services and learn how to use them. For example, several studies have documented that older adults tend to be unfamiliar with how to use fixed-route transit services (see, e.g., Babka, Cooper, & Ragland, 2009; Burkhardt, McGavock, & Nelson, 2002; Ling & Murray, 2010; Tuokko, McGee, Stepaniuk, & Benner, 2007; Wolf-Branigin, Wolf-Branigin, Culver, & Welch, 2012). Travel training programs have been designed to give older adults experience in using fixed-route transit, including providing information on entering and exiting the transit facility, paying fares, special passes, purchasing tickets, reading schedules, locating seating, planning trips, personal safety, and transferring. Studies show that travel training can provide several benefits to older adults (Burkhardt et al., 2014). These programs are discussed in more detail in Chapter 10, Transportation Service Providers.

Another type of service is known as mobility management. The service provides a unified approach to community mobility, allowing an older adult to contact a single person and receive one-on-one education and counseling about transportation options and alternatives to driving (National Center on Senior Transportation, 2014). Many jurisdictions in the US and elsewhere have developed mobility management programs, yet research on how well these programs improve mobility for older adults is still lacking. Chapter 10, Transportation Service Providers reviews this research.

Support groups are another potential way to help ease the transition from driving and maintain mobility after driving cessation. Researchers in Australia, for example, have developed an older driver group education and support program called *UQDRIVE*, with the goal of helping older adults meet their mobility needs after stopping driving (Liddle et al., 2013). These researchers evaluated the program in a randomized controlled trial with 13 participants age 60 or older who had ceased driving or were planning to stop driving in the next year. Participants recorded their community travel using a diary and also self-reported on a number of mobility issues. Data were recorded at baseline, 7 weeks after the program, and at a 3-month follow-up. The study found that the *UQDRIVE* program was significantly associated with more travel away from home in the first 7 weeks, but not at the 3-month follow-up. As compared to the control group, program participation was also associated with higher public transportation use, higher use of walking, increased community mobility self-efficacy, and higher satisfaction with transportation at the 3-month follow-up. Such results suggest that older adults can benefit from support programs, which may improve the quality-of-life of people who are in the process of stopping driving.

## Conclusions

While promoting the mobility of older adults is a multidisciplinary and multifaceted endeavor, older adults themselves play a critical role in their own mobility. As we have discussed, there are numerous education and training opportunities that have the ultimate goals of keeping older adults driving for as safely as they can, helping them transition to non-driving when it is appropriate, and keeping older adults safely mobile after driving cessation. This review has only touched on the many resources available to older adults, and it is recommended that an Internet search of local resources be conducted by older adults with assistance from friends and family members as appropriate. In addition, many jurisdictions have organizations that can provide this information, such as Area Agencies on Aging in the US.

It is evident from the research that many gains in traffic safety and driving comfort can be obtained through vehicle-based activities. Vehicle adaptations, proper maintenance, and appropriate adjustments of standard vehicle features have all been shown to help improve safety. Vehicle technology, too, can improve safety and comfort, and we refer the interested reader to Chapter 12, In-Vehicle and Self-Driving Technologies for a review of the research on advanced driving technologies and older drivers.

Finally, many older adults tend to avoid any serious planning for a future when they can no longer drive. We have briefly discussed some of the programs and services that can help older adults transition to driving cessation. Many of the current community mobility options available to older adults are only located in certain areas, usually in urban or suburban areas, and most older adults have little to no experience using these options. Even before they are experiencing declines in driving abilities, older adults can and should be thinking about where to live when driving is no longer possible. Older adults can also begin to gain experience using these options, even when they can still drive. Many of the negative effects of driving cessation could be diminished if cessation was expected and plans were in place for when it happened.

## References

AAA. (2018). *Driver improvement courses for seniors*. Heathrow, FL: AAA. <https://seniordriving.aaa.com/maintain-mobility-independence/driver-improvement-courses-seniors/> Accessed April, 2018.

AARP. (2018). *AARP Smart Driver course*. Washington, DC: AARP. <https://www.aarp.org/content/dam/aarp/auto/2016/05/AARP-Smart-Driver-course-flyer.pdf> Accessed April, 2018.

AARP, AAA, & AOTA. *CarFit: Helping mature driver find their safest seat*. (2018). <https://www.car-fit.org/> Accessed April, 2018.

Alberta Motor Association. (2018). *Mature driver course: Senior driver refresher course*. Alberta, Canada: AMA. <https://ama.ab.ca/auto-and-driving/driver-education/drivers-ed-courses/senior-driver-refresher-course> Accessed April, 2018.

Anstey, K. J., Eramudugolla, R., Kiely, K. M., & Price, J. (2018). Effect of tailored on-road driving lessons on driving safety in older adults: Randomised controlled trial. *Accident Analysis & Prevention, 115*, 1–10.

Awick, E. A., Wójcicki, T. R., Olsoon, E. A., Fanning, J., Chung, H. D., Zuniga, K., ... McAuley, E. (2015). Differential exercise effects on quality of life and health-related quality of life in older adults: A randomized control trial. *Quality of Life Research, 24*, 455–462.

Babka, R., Cooper, J. F., & Ragland, D. R. (2009). Evaluation of urban travel training for older adults. *Transportation Research Record, 2614*, 149–154.

Bair, S.-T., Huang, R. J., & Wang, K. C. (2012). Can vehicle maintenance records predict automobile accidents? *The Journal of Risk and Insurance, 79*(2), 567–584.

Ball, K. K., Roenker, D. L., Wadley, V. G., Edwards, J. D., Roth, D. L., McGwin, G., ... Dube, T. (2006). Can high-risk older drivers be identified through performance-based measures in a Department of Motor Vehicles setting? *Journal of the American Geriatrics Society, 54*, 77–84.

Bédard, M., Isherwood, I., Moore, I., Gibbons, C., & Lindstrom, W. (2004). Evaluation of a re-training program for older drivers. *Canadian Journal of Public Health, 95*, 295–298.

Bédard, M., Porter, M. M., Marshall, S., Isherwood, I., Riendeau, J., Weaver, B., ... Miller-Polgar, J. (2008). The combination of two training approaches to improve older adults' driving safety. *Traffic Injury Prevention, 9*(1), 70–76.

Bédard, M., Riendeau, J., Weaver, B., & Clarkson, A. (2011). Roadwise review has limited congruence with actual driving performance of aging drivers. *Accident Analysis & Prevention, 43*, 2209–2214.

Blows, S., Ivers, R. Q., Connor, J., Ameratunga, S., & Norton, R. (2003). Does periodic vehicle inspection reduce car crash injury? Evidence from the Auckland Car Crash study. *Australian and New Zealand Journal of Public Health, 27*(3), 323–327.

Bouman, J., & Pellerito, J. M., Jr. (2006). Preparing for the on-road evaluation. In J. M. Pellerito (Ed.), *Driver Rehabilitation and Community Mobility*. St. Louis, MO: Elsevier Mosby.

Brown, J., Coxon, K., Fong, C., Clarke, E., & Keay, L. (2013). *Seat belt wearing characteristics of drivers aged 75 years or older. Proceedings of the 23rd international technical conference on the enhanced safety of vehicles.* Washington, DC: United States Department of Transportation.

Burkhardt, J. E., Bernstein, D. J., Kulbicki, K., Eby, D. W., Molnar, L. J., Nelson, C. A., & McLary, J. M. (2014). *Travel training for older adults: A handbook. Volume 1: Handbook*. Washington, DC: Transportation Research Board.

Burkhardt, J. E., McGavock, A. T., & Nelson, C. A. (2002). *Improving public transit options for older persons. Volume 1: Handbook.* TCRP report 82. Washington, DC: Transportation Research Board.

Chodzko-Zajko, W. J. (2014). Exercise and physical activity for older adults. *Kinesiology Review, 3*, 101–106.

Classen, S., Winter, S. M., Velozo, C. A., Bédard, M., Lanford, D. N., Brumback, B., & Lutz, B. J. (2010). Item development and validity testing for a self- and proxy report: The *safe driving behavior measure. The American Journal of Occupational Therapy, 64* (2), 296–305.

Craik, J., Stern, E., Lapointe, J., McCarthy, N., & Davis, E. S. (2015). CarFit Canada: Lessons learned from an international collaboration. *World Federation of Occupational Therapists Bulletin, 71*(1), 22–25.

de Labra, C., Guimaraes-Pinheiro, C., Maseda, A., Lorenzo, T., & Millán-Calenti, J. C. (2015). Effect of physical exercise interventions in frail older adults: A systematic review of randomized controlled trials. *BMC Geriatrics*, *15*, 154.

DriveWise Canada. (2018). *DriveWise: Seniors program*. London, ON, Canada: DriveWise. <https://www.drivewisesafestart.com/seniors-driving> Accessed April, 2018.

Eby, D. W. & Molnar, L. J. (2010). *M-CASTL 2010 synthesis report—Volume 1: Older adult safety and mobility*. Report no. M-CASTL-2010-02. Ann Arbor, MI: Michigan Center for Advancing Safe Transportation Throughout the Lifespan.

Eby, D. W., Molnar, L. J., Kartje, P., St. Louis, R., Parow, J. E., ... & Neumeyer, A. (2008). *Older driver self screening based on health concerns. Volume I: Technical report*. Report no. DOT HS 811 046A. Washington, DC: NHTSA.

Eby, D. W., Molnar, L. J., Kostyniuk, L. P., St. Louis, R. M., & Zanier, N. (2017). Characteristics of informal caregivers who provide transportation assistance to older adults. *PLoS ONE*, *12*(9), e0184085.

Eby, D. W., Molnar, L. J., & Shope, J. T. (2000). *Driving decisions workbook*. Report no. UMTRI-2000-14. Ann Arbor, MI: University of Michigan Transportation Research Institute.

Eby, D. W., Molnar, L. J., Shope, J. T., Vivoda, J. M., & Fordyce, T. A. (2003). Improving older driver knowledge and awareness through self-assessment: The *Driving Decisions Workbook*. *Journal of Safety Research*, *34*, 371–381.

Eby, D. W., Molnar, L. J., Zakrajsek, J., Ryan, L., Zanier, N., St. Louis, R. M., ... on behalf of the LongROAD Research Team. (2018). Prevalence, attitudes, and knowledge of in-vehicle technologies and vehicle adaptations among older drivers. *Accident Analysis & Prevention*, *113*, 54–62.

Edwards, J. D., Leonard, K. M., Lunsman, M., Dodson, J., Bradley, S., Myers, C. A., & Hubble, B. (2008). Acceptability and validity of older driver screening with the *DrivingHealth® Inventory*. *Accident Analysis & Prevention*, *40*, 1157–1163.

Fong, C. K., Keay, L., Coxon, K., Clarke, E., & Brown, J. (2016). Seat belt use and fit among drivers aged 75 years and older in their own vehicles. *Traffic Injury Prevention*, *17*(2), 142–150.

Gaines, J. M., Burke, K. L., Marx, K. A., Wagner, M., & Parrish, J. M. (2011). Enhancing older driver safety: A driving survey and evaluation of the CarFit program. *Journal of Safety Research*, *42*, 351–358.

Giné-Garriga, M., Roqué-Fíguls, M., Coll-Planas, L., Sitjà-Rabert, M., & Salvà, A. (2014). Physical exercise interventions for improving performance-based measures of physical function in community-dwelling, frail older adults: A systematic review and meta-analysis. *Archives of Physical Medicine and Rehabilitation*, *95*, 753–769.

Jones, R. W. R., Cordazzo, S. T. D., & Scialfa, C. T. (2014). Predicting on-road driving performance and safety in healthy older adults. *Journal of Safety Research*, *51*, 73–80.

Korner-Bitensky, N., Kua, A., von Zweck, C., & van Benthem, K. (2009). Older driver retraining: An updated systematic review of evidence of effectiveness. *Journal of Safety Research*, *40*, 105–111.

Kostyniuk, L. P., & Shope, J. T. (2003). Driving alternatives: Older drivers in Michigan. *Journal of Safety Research*, *34*, 404–417.

Kelly, M. E., Loughrey, D., Lawlor, B. A., Robertson, I. H., Walsh, C., & Brennan, S. (2014). The impact of exercise on the cognitive functioning of health older adults: A systematic review and *meta*-analysis. *Ageing Research News*, *16*, 12–31.

Kua, A., Korner-Bitensky, N., Desrosiers, J., Man-Son-Hing, M., & Marshall, S. (2007). Older driver retraining: A systematic review of evidence of effectiveness. *Journal of Safety Research*, *38*, 81–90.

Lang, B., Parkes, A., & Medina, K. F. (2013). *Driving choices for the older motorist: The role of self-assessment tools*. London, England: RAC Foundation.

Levasseur, M., Audet, T., Gélinas, I., Bédard, M., Langlais, M.-E., Therrien, F.-H., ... D'Amours, M. (2014). Development and validation of an intervention to enhance or maintain the mobility of older drivers in the community: The awareness tool for safe and responsible driving (OSCAR). *Journal of Scientific Research and Reports*, *3*(18), 2422–2433.

Levasseur, M., Audet, T., Gélinas, I., Bédard, M., Langlais, M.-E., Therrien, F.-H., ... D'Amours, M. (2015). Awareness tool for safe and responsible driving (OSCAR): A potential educational intervention for increasing interest, openness and knowledge about abilities required and compensatory strategies among older drivers. *Traffic Injury Prevention*, *16*(6), 578–586.

Levi, S. & De Leonardis, D. (2008). *Occupant protection issues among older drivers and passengers: Volume 1 final report*. Report no. DOT HS 810 938. Washington, DC: United States Department of Transportation.

Li, H. & Pickrell, T. M. (2018). *Occupant restraint use in 2016: Results from the NOPUS Controlled Intersection Study*. Report no. DOT HS 812 463. Washington, DC: United States Department of Transportation.

Liddle, J., Haynes, M., Pachana, N. A., Mitchell, G., McKenna, K., & Gustafsson, L. (2013). Effect of group intervention to promote older adults' adjustment to driving cessation on community mobility: A randomized controlled trial. *The Gerontologist*, *54*(3), 409–422.

Ling, D. & Murray, S. (2010). Sustaining independent mobility for elder people in an ageing population: Managing the transition from car dependency to confident use of public transport. In *Paper presented at the 12th international conference on mobility and transport for elderly and disabled persons (TRANSED 2010)*. Held in Hong Kong, 2–4 June 2010.

Marmeleira, J. F., Melo, F. M. S., Tlemcani, M., & Godinho, M. A. B. (2011). Exercise can improve speed of behavior in older drivers. *Journal of Aging and Physical Activity*, *19*, 48–61.

Marmeleira, J. F., Godinho, M. B., & Fernandes, O. M. (2009). The effects of an exercise program on several abilities associated with driving performance in older adults. *Accident Analysis & Prevention*, *41*, 90–97.

Marottoli, R. A., Allore, H., Araujo, K. L., Iannone, L. P., Acampora, D., Gottschalk, M., ... Peduzzi, P. (2007). A randomized trial of a physical conditioning program to enhance the driving performance of older persons. *Journal of General Internal Medicine*, *22*, 590–597.

Marottoli, R. A., Van Hess, P. H., Araujo, K. L. B., Iannone, L. P., Acampora, D., Charpentier, P., & Peduzzi, P. (2007). A randomized trial of an educational program to enhance older driver performance. *Journal of Gerontology: Medical Sciences*, *62A*(10), 1113–1119.

Metec. (2018). *Senior safety session*. Victoria, Australia: Metec. <http://www.metec.com.au/safe-driving-training/driver-refresher-course-seniors/> Accessed April, 2018.

Miller, S., & Taylor-Piliae, R. E. (2018). The association between Tai Chi exercise and safe driving performance among older adults: An observational study. *Journal of Sport and Health Science*, *7*, 83–94.

Molnar, L. J., Eby, D. W., Kartje, P. S., & St. Louis, R. (2010). Increasing self-awareness among older drivers: The role of self-screening. *Journal of Safety Research*, *41*, 367–373.

Molnar, L. J., Eby, D. W., St. Louis, R. M., & Neumeyer, A. L. (2007). *Promising approaches for promoting lifelong community mobility*. Washington, DC: AARP.

Molnar, L. J., Eby, D. W., Zhang, L., Zanier, N., St. Louis, R. M., & Kostyniuk, L. P. (2015). *Self-regulation of driving by older adults: A synthesis of the literature and framework for future research*. Washington, DC: AAA Foundation for Traffic Safety.

Myers, A. M., Blanchard, R. A., MacDonald, L., & Porter, M. M. (2008). Process evaluation of the American Automobile Association *Roadwise Review* CD-ROM: Observed and reported experiences of older drivers. *Topics in Geriatric Rehabilitation*, *24*, 224–238.

National Center on Senior Transportation. *Mobility management*. (2014). ⟨http://ncst.madwolf.com/ResourcesPublications/MobilityManagement.aspx⟩ Accessed April, 2018.

National Highway Traffic Safety Administration. (2001). *Tire safety: Everything rides on it*. Report no. DOT HS 809 361. Washington, DC: United States Department of Transportation.

National Highway Traffic Safety Administration. (2007a). *DriveWell: Promoting older driver safety and mobility in your community*. Report no. DOT HS 809–838. Washington, DC: United States Department of Transportation.

National Highway Traffic Safety Administration (2007b). *Adapting Motor Vehicles for Older Drivers*. Report no. DOT HS 810 732. Washington, DC: United States Department of Transportation.

Ostrow, A. C., Shaffron, P., & McPherson, K. (1992). The effects of a joint range-of-motion physical fitness training program on the automobile driving skills of older adults. *Journal of Safety Research*, *23*, 207–219.

Pellerito, J. M., Jr., & Blanc, C. A. (2006). Service delivery models. In J. M. Pellerito (Ed.), *Driver rehabilitation and community mobility*. St. Louis, MO: Elsevier Mosby.

Porter, M., & Tuokko, H. A. (2011). An evaluation of the *Roadwise Review*: A mixed methods approach. *Traffic Injury Prevention*, *12b*, 451–458.

Ross, L. A., Schmidt, E. L., & Ball, K. (2013). Interventions to maintain mobility: What works? *Accident Analysis & Prevention*, *61*, 167–196.

Royal Automobile Club of Victoria. *Years ahead: Senior driving program*. (2018). <https://www.racv.com.au/on-the-road/driving-maintenance/road-safety/older-drivers.html> Accessed April, 2018.

Scialfa, C., Ference, J., Boone, J., Tay, R., & Hudson, C. (2010). Predicting older adults' driving difficulties using the *Roadwise Review*. *Journal of Gerontology: Psychological Sciences*, *65B*(4), 434–437.

Scully, M., Devlin, A., Oxley, J., & Charlton, J. (2010). *Seniors driving longer, smarter, safer: An older driver training program*. Report no. 303. Clayton, VIC, Australia: Monash University Accident Research Centre.

Stalvey, B. T., & Owsley, C. (2003). The development and efficacy of a theory-based educational curriculum to promote self-regulation among high-risk older drivers. *Health Promotion Practice*, *4*(2), 109–119.

Staplin, L., & Dinh-Zarr, T. B. (2006). Promoting rehabilitation of safe driving abilities through computer-based clinical and personal screening techniques. *Topics in Geriatric Rehabilitation*, *22*, 129–138.

Staplin, L., Lococo, K. H., Brooks, J. O., & Srinivasan, R. (2013). *Validation of rehabilitation training programs for older drivers*. Report no. DOT HS 811 749. Washington, DC: National Highway Traffic Safety Administration.

Staplin, L., Lococo, K. H., Gish, K. W., & Decina, L. E. (2003a). *Model driver screening and evaluation program, final technical report, Volume I: Project summary and model program recommendations*. Report no. DOT HS 809 582. Washington, DC: United States Department of Transportation.

Staplin, L., Lococo, K. H., Gish, K. W., & Decina, L. E. (2003b). *Model driver screening and evaluation program, final technical report, Volume II: Maryland pilot older driver study*. Report no. DOT HS 809 583. Washington, DC: United States Department of Transportation.

Stav, W. (2010). CarFit: An evaluation of behavior change and impact. *British Journal of Occupational Therapy*, *73*(12), 589–597.

Thiriez, K. & Bondy, N. (2001). *NHTSA's tire pressure special study, February, 2001*. Paper number 256. Washington, DC: National Highway Traffic Safety Administration.

Transportation Research Board (2016). *Taxonomy and terms for stakeholders in senior mobility*. Transportation Research Board Circular no. E-C211. Washington, DC: Transportation Research Board.

Tuokko, H., McGee, P., Stepaniuk, J., & Benner, E. (2007). *The older and wiser rider: An examination of transportation for older drivers*. Victoria, BC: University of Victoria Centre on Aging.

Unsworth, C. A., & Baker, A. (2014). Driver rehabilitation: A systematic review of the types and effectiveness of interventions used by occupational therapists to improve on-road fitness-to-drive. *Accident Analysis & Prevention*, *71*, 106–114.

Vardaki, S., & Yannis, G. (2012). Investigation of the acceptance of a handbook for safe driving at an older age. *International Journal of Injury Control and Safety*, *19*(1), 27–36.

Vivoda, J. M., & Eby, D. W. (2011). Factors influencing safety belt use. In B. Porter (Ed.), *The Handbook of traffic psychology* (pp. 215–229). San Diego, CA: Elsevier Inc.

Winter, S. M., Classen, S., Bédard, M., Lutz, B. J., Velozo, C. A., Lanford, D. N., & Brumback, B. A. (2011). Focus group findings for the self-report Safe Driving Behavior Measure. *Canadian Journal of Occupational Therapy*, *78*(2), 72–79.

Wolf-Branigin, K., Wolf-Branigin, M., Culver, J. D., & Welch, K. (2012, January-February). Can travel training services save public transportation agencies money? *TR News, 278*, 36–38.

Zanier, N., Molnar, L. J., Eby, D. W., Zakrajsek, J., Ryan, L., St. Louis, R. M., ... the LongROAD Research Team. (2018). Observed maintenance, damage, technologies, and adaptations among vehicles of older drivers: A LongROAD study. Research brief. Washington, DC: AAA Foundation for Traffic Safety.

Zein, S. R., & Navin, F. P. D. (2003). Improving traffic safety: A new systems approach. *Transportation Research Record*, *1830*, 1–9.

# Family members, friends, and other informal caregivers

# 6

*Family is the most important thing in the world.*

*Princess Diana*

## Caregivers and their role

As the world's population continues to age, the need for long-term care for older adults has escalated. Family members continue to be the primary source of support and assistance to older adults, both during times of illness and when they can no longer function independently (National Academies of Sciences, Engineering, and Medicine, 2016). Family members, and oftentimes close friends and neighbors, who provide assistance or care without financial compensation are referred to as informal caregivers (Burton-Chase, Kwak, Hennig, & Haley, 2017). The caregiving landscape has shifted quite dramatically in the recent past, with informal caregiving becoming more complex and longer lasting due to several reasons: medical advances, the shift in health-care practices that involve shorter hospital stays and the management of chronic illnesses in home settings, and increased longevity (Casado, van Vulpen, & Davis, 2011; National Academies of Sciences, Engineering, and Medicine, 2016). Informal caregivers are also managing difficult technical and medical procedures that would have historically been the responsibility of formal caregivers, such as home health nurses or health-care aides, who receive financial compensation to provide a service (Burton Chase et al., 2017). In this chapter, *caregiving* denotes care that is provided by a family member or friend rather than by a professional who is reimbursed for services.

Caregivers play a critical role in enabling older adults to maintain mobility during the transition from driving and following driving cessation. Several studies have found that when transitioning from driving to non-driving, older adults are more likely to seek transportation assistance from their informal networks, such as families or friends, rather than use public transportation (Adler & Rottunda, 2006; Choi, Adams, & Kahana, 2012; Hendrickson & Mann, 2005; Johnson, 2008; Kostyniuk & Shope, 1999; Rosenbloom, 2009; Taylor & Tripodes, 2001). As discussed in Chapter 3, Use of Non-Driving Transportation Options, alternative transportation options are oftentimes not available to older adults, and if they are, they may be unusable due to concerns about safety or personal security, or lack of flexibility,

**Perspectives and Strategies for Promoting Safe Transportation among Older Adults.**
**DOI: https://doi.org/10.1016/B978-0-12-812153-5.00006-6**

reliability, or comfort with public transit (Rosenbloom, 2009). In the absence of other viable options for getting around, coupled with the preference to travel by personal automobile (Coughlin, 2001), responsibility for providing transportation often falls to a caregiver. For example, a recent survey of former older drivers in North America found that 76% reported that they most often rely on family members to drive them, and 40% identified friends as another source of transportation (Home Instead, Inc., 2016).

Transportation continually ranks as one of the top services provided by caregivers in both the United States (US) and other developed countries [Australian Bureau of Statistics, 2016; National Alliance for Caregiving (NAC) & American Association of Retired Persons (AARP), 1997, 2004, 2009, 2015; Turner & Findlay, 2012]. This includes providing rides in the caregiver's own car as well as arranging for rides, and to a lesser extent, accompanying the care recipient on other forms of transit. The most recent study of caregivers by the NAC and AARP (2015) found that transportation is the most common instrumental activity of daily living (IADL) that caregivers provide, with 78% reporting that they provide rides or arrange for transportation for their care recipient. This finding was consistent with all previous publications of the caregiver study. An analysis conducted by AARP found that family and friends provided 1.4 billion trips per year for non-driving relatives over age 70, with adult children providing 33% of the trips (Feinberg, Reinhard, Houser, & Choula, 2011). A study by Kostyniuk and Shope (2003) found that 94.8% of former drivers met their transportation needs by relying on caregivers to drive them to various destinations. A study of more than 30,000 informal caregivers of older adults in Canada found that providing transportation was the most frequently cited type of assistance provided by caregivers, with 39% reporting this activity (Turner & Findlay, 2012). A study conducted in Michigan found that more than 90% of informal caregivers for older adults reported that they provide some form of transportation assistance (Eby, Molnar, Kostyniuk, St Louis, & Zanier, 2011), and of those providing transportation assistance, 98% reported that they gave rides in a car (Eby, Molnar, Kostyniuk, Louis, & Zanier, 2017). The same study found that caregivers reported providing transportation assistance for a variety of trip purposes including medical/dental (91%), shopping/errands (65%), family/personal business (62%), social or recreational activities (58%), and school/religious activities (33%).

Although transportation assistance is frequently provided by informal caregivers of older adults, there is little specific information about the characteristics of these caregivers, the types of transportation assistance they provide, the frequency with which they provide it, and where they seek information and/or services to help them provide such assistance. Due to the lack of more detailed information on this particular subgroup of caregivers, many of the statistics presented in this chapter are for caregivers more generally who assist a person with a disability, whether age-related or otherwise. Where possible, information is provided specifically on caregivers who assist older adults. Due to the high percentage of caregivers providing transportation assistance as outlined above, the general information presented for caregivers is likely to capture the majority in this subgroup.

According to Bauer and Sousa-Poza (2015), exact numbers on informal caregivers are unavailable due in part to the lack of an official definition of informal care. Studies differ in their designation of who qualifies as a caregiver and for measuring and confirming the types of assistance provided (Colombo, Llena-Nozal, Mercier, & Tjadens, 2011; Roth, Fredman, & Haley, 2015); therefore, it is difficult to make comparisons between studies. There are defining characteristics of an informal caregiver that are common among most studies. These include being a person who provides some type of unpaid assistance with activities of daily living (e.g., eating, bathing, or dressing) or IADLs (e.g., providing transportation, shopping, or preparing meals) to a person with chronic illness, functional limitation, or disability, including disability relating to old age.

Estimates of the prevalence of caregivers in different countries throughout the world have been formulated using population-based surveys and long-term care, disability, and health-care data. Estimates from a survey conducted across 20 countries in the European Union (EU) show that more than one-third of the countries' populations provide informal care to a person due to long-term physical or mental health issues or problems related to aging (Verbakel, Tamlagsrønning, Winstone, Fjær, & Eikemo, 2017), although there is considerable variability in the prevalence of informal care by country. According to a survey conducted by the NAC and AARP (2015) in the US, approximately 34.2 million people provide unpaid care to an adult age 50 or older. Although women shoulder the majority of caregiving responsibilities, the contribution of men is on the rise. For example, in 13 countries across the EU, men accounted for 39% of caregivers (Bettio & Verashchagina, 2010). Similarly, in the US, men accounted for 40% of caregivers (NAC & AARP, 2015); however, women tended to provide more hours of care and performed more intensive caregiving tasks (e.g., bathing, toileting, and dressing) than their male counterparts (Colombo et al., 2011; NAC & AARP, 2015).

In the US, the average age of a caregiver of someone over age 50 was 50.3 years (NAC & AARP, 2015). The average age of a care recipient was 74.4 years and more than half (55%) of caregivers of someone over age 50 cared for someone age 75 or older. A study of 17 Organization for Economic Co-operation and Development (OECD) countries found that providing care to a parent was most common (Colombo et al., 2011) and that this group of caregivers has increased in recent years. In fact, the percentage of adult children providing personal care or financial assistance to a parent in the US has more than tripled over the past 15 years (MetLife Mature Market Institute, 2011).

## Recognizing signs of driving problems

Family members of older adults are often well positioned to recognize the decline in abilities needed for safe driving. Changes in day-to-day behavior outside of a vehicle, such as slower or inappropriate reactions, difficulty with processing information, or inattentiveness may be noticeable to those who have interacted closely with the individual over time and may justify significant concern regarding driving ability. In addition, a family member may observe unsafe driving behaviors while riding as a passenger of the older driver, notice new dents or scrapes on the vehicle due to minor collisions with objects such as a mailbox, shopping cart, or garbage cans, or have knowledge of recent traffic citations the older adult received. In more severe circumstances, the older driver may also be involved in a serious crash resulting in harm to himself, herself, or others. It should also be noted that despite the fact that some family members have firsthand knowledge of an older driver's situation, research shows that it is difficult for a caregiver to assess accurately the older adult's driving capabilities. A study by Eby et al. (2009) found poor agreement between caregivers' subjective assessments of their care recipient's driving behaviors and objective driving measures of those same behaviors derived from in-vehicle monitoring equipment. Given the negative consequences associated with driving cessation discussed in Chapter 1, The Challenges, the impact that driving reduction and cessation can have on the family, and the difficulty in assessing an older drivers' capabilities, introducing the topic with an older adult can be highly emotional for both the family member and older adult.

Research shows that older adults who plan and gradually cease driving face far less negative impact than those who are told to stop driving or who must stop driving suddenly (Musselwhite & Haddad, 2010). Despite the benefits of planning for driving reduction and cessation, families are unsure about how best to approach this topic and tend to avoid discussions about the transition from driving to non-driving (Connell, Harmon, Janevic, & Kostyniuk, 2013; Home Instead, Inc., 2016; Kostyniuk & Shope, 2003; Rudman, Friedland, Chipman, & Sciortino, 2006; Silverstein, 2008). Adult children of older drivers play a key role in their parents' driving reduction and cessation process and often assume a caregiving role by providing transportation. To explore the role of adult children, Connell et al. (2013) conducted a study to examine family dynamics surrounding the driving reduction and cessation process with a specific focus on adult children of older drivers. Several adult children reported making plans and discussing anticipated changes in their parents' driving. These conversations reportedly helped prepare adult children and their parents for the transition to non-driving. Conversely, many other participants did not feel comfortable having these discussions with their parents and expressed concern about their parents' reactions to restricted mobility following driving cessation, discomfort in reversing established parent–child roles, and dealing with feelings of anger and resentment from their parent. Furthermore, even as abilities declined and stopping driving was seen as the safest option, some participants stated their apprehension to discuss driving cessation with their parent due to the responsibility and potential burden to them that would result if their parent stopped driving (Connell et al., 2013).

Focus groups and interviews with older drivers and nondrivers found that the greatest concern among all participants was feeling dependent on caregivers for transportation, imposing on others for rides, and feeling obligated as a result of accepting a ride from a family member or friend (Coughlin, 2001). Similarly, other studies have reported that older drivers do not want to rely on family and friends for transportation (Home Instead, Inc., 2016) and are fearful of becoming a burden to family and friends who fulfill their transportation needs (Adler & Rottunda, 2006). These feelings can delay the transition to non-driving, resulting in safety issues, as well as increase the potential of social isolation following driving cessation. This may be especially true if the older adult has always been independent and self-sufficient. Research by Davey (2007) also found that the level of discomfort in seeking assistance with transportation varied by trip purpose. For example, older adults felt more comfortable seeking transportation assistance for health or medical purposes ("serious" travel) than for other purposes such as visiting friends ("discretionary" travel). However, reducing trips for discretionary purposes may lead to a reduction in quality of life of the older adult (Davey, 2007).

The decision to stop driving is strongly influenced by the support and availability of others to provide transportation to the care recipient. Johnson (2008) found that older adults were more likely to cease driving if a potential caregiver was geographically proximate and committed to assisting the older adult with needed activities, including providing transportation. In addition, Choi et al. (2012) found that older adults with transportation support from their friends or neighbors were more likely to stop driving than those without such support. Similarly, a study in Japan by Ichikawa, Nakahara, and Takahashi (2016) found that older adults were far more likely to stop driving if they were sure there was someone available to drive them.

There is often a reluctance on the part of both older drivers and caregivers to communicate openly about the driving cessation process. In an effort to facilitate the process of broaching this topic with aging adults, in 2003, The Hartford developed a guidebook to help families and caregivers initiate productive conversations about driving safety with older adults. This guidebook is currently in its 14th revision with up-to-date statistics (The Hartford and MIT AgeLab, 2017). There is recognition that each situation is unique to the family involved, and emphasis is placed on the importance of continual conversations about driving safety that will positively influence the decision of the older adult to restrict or cease driving. Another booklet by the National Highway Traffic Safety Administration (NHTSA, 2013) also provides suggestions for how to start this conversation with an older adult. Several studies have found that older drivers are influenced by the conversations they have with others regarding their driving (Adler & Rottunda, 2006; Connell et al., 2013; Ichikawa et al., 2016; Johnson, 2008; The Hartford and MIT AgeLab, 2017). For example, a survey by The Hartford and MIT AgeLab (2017) found that, of older adults who reported that someone had talked with them about their driving, more than half said they followed the suggestions of others. A study in Japan also found that the strongest predictor of stopping driving was being advised by someone to do so (Ichikawa et al., 2016).

Alternatively, a study by Shope and Eby (1998) found mixed results from focus groups with older drivers and former drivers as well as focus groups with adult children of older drivers and former drivers. Many older drivers reported that they had not had a discussion with a relative or friend regarding their driving safety, but that their children or friends would tell them when they had concerns about their driving. However, many adult children said they had expressed their concerns to their parent and most were met with strong negative reactions, such as becoming defensive and stating their discomfort in the reversal of the parent–child roles (Shope & Eby, 1998). These results again highlight the complexity and emotional nature of these conversations.

Older drivers have preferences for these conversations that vary based on marital status, gender, health, and presence of other supportive individuals (The Hartford and MIT AgeLab, 2017). The Hartford and MIT AgeLab survey indicated that older adults with spouses preferred hearing about driving concerns first from their spouse, while older adults living alone preferred to have these conversations with their physician, adult children, or a close friend. Participants reported that having a third party involved, such as a physician or licensing agency, would be beneficial in persuading the older adult to stop driving (Connell et al., 2013). The Hartford and MIT AgeLab (2017) survey found that older adults often valued the opinions of physicians and 40% of those living alone preferred to discuss driving concerns with their physician. Family members are advised to share observations about driving behavior and health issues to help the older adult make his or her driving decision.

## Cost of caregiving

For many caregivers, providing transportation is the most trustworthy and cost-effective solution to meeting the transportation needs of their care recipient following driving cessation. However, Easter Seals (2003) reported that transportation problems are among the most troublesome issues for caregivers, and challenges are greater when the care recipient has mobility problems that require the use of an assistive device, such as a wheelchair or scooter, or being physically helped into and out of the vehicle. These difficulties may cause some caregivers to stop transporting their care recipient completely or to transport them only for the most essential appointments (Easter Seals, 2003), which, as mentioned earlier, can lead to a reduction in the quality of life for the older adult.

Given the critical role that caregivers play in the health and well-being of older adults, it is important to consider the effects that caregiving has on the health of caregivers, and what can be done to enable this population to continue to provide these important services. Caregivers' circumstances vary widely and in ways that affect their availability, capacity, and willingness to assume caregiving responsibilities. On average, a caregiver assumes this role for a duration of 4 years, with 30% of caregivers providing care for less than 1 year, and nearly 25% of caregivers providing care for more than 5 years (NAC & AARP, 2015). There is a wealth of literature examining the effects of short- and long-term caregiving on the caregiver, and while there are positive aspects of caregiving, the research overwhelmingly shows the negative impact that caregiving can have on the life of a caregiver in terms of finances, health, and well-being. Informal caregiving has been linked to economic hardship and poorer health among caregivers (e.g., Colombo et al., 2011; MetLife Mature Market Institute, 2006, 2011; NAC & AARP, 2009, 2015).

It is important to note that positive aspects of informal caregiving have been reported, such as companionship with and closeness to the care recipient, feelings of satisfaction and fulfillment, and enhanced self-esteem (Ashworth & Baker, 2000; Cohen, Colantonio, & Vernich, 2002). In addition, some caregivers experience a sense of competence and mastery in their role as caregiver, and one study showed that caregivers have more strongly developed coping strategies compared to non-caregivers (Trukeschitz, Schneider, Mühlmann, & Ponocny, 2013). Despite some of the known benefits to caregiving, providing care can also be a mentally and physically demanding task that often leads to unfavorable health outcomes in the caregiver, and several studies have documented the negative impact caregiving has on caregiver health and well-being. Studies have found that informal caregivers have poorer physical health than non-caregivers, measured by perceived health as well as objective health measures such as stress hormones, antibodies, and medication use (Ho, Chan, Woo, Chong, & Sham, 2009; Pinquart & Sörensen, 2003, 2007; Schulz & Monin, 2012; Schulz & Sherwood, 2008; Vitaliano, Zhang, & Scanlan, 2003).

These negative effects of caregiving are moderated by many factors, such as number of hours and type of care provided, cognitive status of the care recipient, financial resources, and social support available (Bauer & Sousa-Poza, 2015; Brodaty, Thomson, Thompson, & Fine, 2005; Pinquart & Sörensen, 2003; Verbakel, 2014). Many caregivers experience both positive experiences and strain simultaneously; Roth et al. (2015) argued that the positive experiences of caregiving could potentially buffer against some of the possible stress-related health consequences.

There are various ways of examining the economic cost of informal caregiving, and each method provides a different value. What remains clear, however, is the economic cost of providing this care is extraordinarily high. For instance, one study in the US found the total estimated aggregate lost wages, pension, and Social Security benefits for adult children providing care to aging parents is nearly $3 trillion (MetLife Mature Market Institute, 2011). Another study estimated the cost of informal caregiving in the US, including such things as lost wages, keeping an older adult out of a nursing home, and performing tasks that otherwise someone would have to be hired to do, to be $470 billion in 2013, up from $450 billion in 2009 (Reinhard, Feinberg, Choula, & Houser, 2015). In fact, the total estimated economic value of uncompensated care provided by family caregivers in 2013 surpassed total Medicaid spending ($449 billion). Other estimates of the value of caregiving from around the world, expressed in US dollars for comparison, are Australia: $47.3 billion; Canada: $25 billion; Ireland: $4.7 billion; Sweden: $23.9 billion; and the United Kingdom: $160.7 billion (International Alliance of Carer Organizations, 2016).

Across 18 OECD countries, caregivers were less likely to be employed, and when employed, more likely to be in a part-time position and to work 2 hours less per week on average relative their non-caregiver counterparts (Colombo et al., 2011). Data from Australia and the United Kingdom indicated that caregivers were 30% more likely to hold a temporary job (Colombo et al., 2011). For those providing 20 hours of care or more per week, the negative impact on employment was more pronounced. According to NAC and AARP (2015), 49% of caregivers in the US reported going into work late, leaving early, or taking time off to meet the needs of their care recipient. Another study found that 56% of employed caregivers experienced at least one work-related strain, including working different hours, working fewer as well as more hours, and taking time off work to provide care (Rainville, Skufca, & Mehegan, 2016). Caregivers who have to take time out of the work force to care for a family member may lose wages and fail to accrue savings and benefits, which may place them at economic risk over their lifetimes. The MetLife Mature Market Institute (1999) found that as a result of caregiving, caregivers in the US lost a lifetime-estimated average of $566,433 in pre-taxable wage wealth, $25,494 in Social Security wealth, and $67,202 in pension wealth. Combined, the result is a loss in total pre-taxable wealth of approximately $659,000 per person over a lifetime. In addition, Rainville et al. (2016) estimated that 78% of family caregivers in the US spend an average of $6954 per year on out-of-pocket costs related to caregiving, nearly 20% of their annual income. Approximately 9.7 million adult children over the age of 50 care for their parents, which suggests that family caregivers are themselves aging and yet are providing care at a time when they also need to plan and save for their own retirement (MetLife Mature Market Institute, 2011).

Caregiving duties can also affect the company at which the caregiver is employed. MetLife Mature Market Institute (2006) estimated that the costs of lost productivity in the US due to caregiver accommodations are $17.1 billion annually. A case study of a large corporate US employer (Albert, Schulz, & Colombi, 2010) found that employees providing care for others reported poorer physical and mental health than employees not providing care. The study estimated that health-care costs for those employees providing care was about 8% higher than for those not providing care. The researchers extrapolated these data to the general US business sector and estimated that unpaid caregiving costs employers about $13 billion annually.

## Identifying and making use of services

It is well documented that without some form of support, caregivers face substantial psychological, physical, and financial health risks. Studies have shown that programs that assist caregivers can reduce caregiver depression, anxiety, and stress and enable them to provide care longer, thereby avoiding or delaying the need for costly institutional care for the care recipient (Bookwala et al., 2004; Elliott, Burgio, & DeCoster, 2010; Schulz et al., 2002). The growing demand for care provided in the home has focused the attention of federal and state governments on efforts to expand programs that provide services and support to family caregivers. The extent to which these services are available varies by community. There is also considerable variation in how aware people are of the services, how difficult they are to use, and how much they cost.

While providing transportation is a very common form of assistance provided by caregivers, transportation is also one of the most frequently identified service gaps in caring for an older adult (e.g., Whittier, Scharlach, & Dal Santo, 2005; Innes, Blackstock, Mason, Smith, & Cox, 2005). The lack of available transportation serves as a barrier to accessing services for the caregiver as well as for those receiving care. This is especially a problem in suburban and rural areas, where services may be far apart and public transportation limited. Indeed, there is a dearth of transportation services available within rural communities to meet the needs of an older adult population (Dickerson et al., 2007; Hash, Jurkowski, & Krout, 2014), and providing public transportation in remote areas is especially complex and expensive (Kihl et al., 1997). Moreover, in both rural and urban communities, transportation can be a challenge for older adults as both driving and taking public transportation become increasingly difficult (Wachs, 2000). In addition, services that are available in heavily populated urban communities (e.g., respite care, home health care, rehabilitation, and transportation services) may not be available in remote and rural environments.

Home and community-based care services (HCBS) encompass a range of preventive and supportive health, and social services provided to older individuals so that they may remain independent in their own homes and communities (Neary, 1993). Some HCBS are funded by federal and state tax dollars. Many organizations also offer services on a private pay basis. Examples of home and community-based care are transportation services, homemaker services, adult day centers, and senior center activities. These services can assist caregivers indirectly by allowing them to continue working and directly by providing brief respite from caregiver responsibilities or helping to alleviate caregiver burden. Despite beneficial outcomes, the literature consistently indicates that few older adults and their caregivers use HCBS (Brodaty et al., 2005; Brown & Chen, 2008; Winslow, 2003). Data from a study by Casado et al. (2011) revealed that a vast majority of caregivers of older Americans had never used most types of HCBS, including 88.3% of caregivers who reported never having used transportation services. One-third of caregivers stated they were not aware of the service in their area, and nearly 25% said the service was not available to them. A study of caregivers in Australia found that 26% were unaware of the caregiver services available in their community (Australian Bureau of Statistics, 2014). Similarly, a study by Li (2006) showed that the HCBS to which caregivers most frequently reported access barriers were respite care, transportation, and homemaker services. The main barriers varied depending on individual services, but generally, they were unavailability, lack of awareness, and unaffordability (Li, 2006). Furthermore, a national survey of caregivers in the US found that only 23% of caregivers have utilized transportation services where available, and one-quarter said they had difficulty finding affordable support services in the community in which they provide care (NAC & AARP, 2015).

Policies that provide services for informal caregivers vary by country. A study by Verbakel (2014) aimed to increase knowledge about the effectiveness of national policies that potentially alleviate the negative consequences of informal caregiving. Results from over 20,000 participants across 18 European countries showed that the wellbeing gap between caregivers and non-caregivers was smallest in countries with strong national policies that provide generous resources for formal long-term care, such as those found in Scandinavian countries (Verbakel, 2014). While this result is encouraging, the author pointed out that the rising cost of long-term care would render this option unsustainable as the demand for this type of care increases with the aging population.

Across the EU, there are different policies and service initiatives aimed at supporting caregivers, but few have been independently evaluated for evidence of their effectiveness. Measures that appear to provide effective support for caregivers include packages of complementary interventions tailored to specific groups of caregivers and care recipients (Glendinning et al., 2009). Policies concerning paid or unpaid leave from work and flexible work arrangements facilitate the combination of caregiving and employment to alleviate the stress and restrictions placed on a caregiver's working life (e.g., Colombo et al., 2011; Deloitte Access Economics, 2015; Verbakel, 2014). However, apart from short-term or unpaid leave, policy measures to help caregivers stay in or return to work are scarce (Glendinning et al., 2009).

Financial support may alleviate the economic stress that can result from having to reduce work hours to perform one's role as informal caregiver (Verbakel, 2014). Several studies have found that caregivers prefer financial assistance for the hours of care they provide (Glendinning et al., 2009; NAC & AARP, 2015; World Health Organization, 2015). A study by NAC and AARP (2015) found that caregivers of those over age 50 most preferred compensation for hours of care and an income tax credit. In May, 2017, the Credit for Caring Act was introduced in the US House and Senate (Congress.gov, 2017). The Credit for Caring Act was developed to help address the financial challenges of family caregiving, primarily out of pocket expenditures, and to help family caregivers be more financially secure. It would give eligible family caregivers the opportunity to receive a federal tax credit of up to $3000 annually. The demand for such assistance may grow more pronounced, given the demographic changes coming in our aging society.

A large number of OECD countries provide financial support to caregivers through cash benefits either paid directly to caregivers through a caregiver allowance or paid to those in need of care, part of which may be used to compensate family caregivers (Colombo et al., 2011). For example, the Australian Government currently provides a range of support services to alleviate caregiver burdens, including selected payment programs such as the Carer Payment, Carer Allowance, and Carer Supplement (Australian Government Department of Social Services, 2017b).

In the US, the National Family Caregiver Support Program (NFCSP), established in 2000, provides grants to states and territories, based on the proportion of population age 70 or older, to fund a variety of programs that assist informal caregivers in providing care to their care recipients [Administration for Community Living (ACL), 2017]. The creation of this program was the mechanism by which Congress explicitly recognized the role that caregivers have in the nation's long-term services and supports system. Types of services the NFCSP provides include information to caregivers about available services; assistance to caregivers in gaining access to the services; individual counseling, organization of support groups, and caregiver training; respite care; and supplemental services (ACL, 2017). These services are intended to work in conjunction with other state- and community-based services to provide a coordinated set of supports. A national survey of caregivers showed that nearly 700,000 caregivers received services through the NFCSP in 2014 (ACL, 2017), and data from the ACL (2016) showed that nearly 49,000 individuals were assisted with transportation.

Area Agencies on Aging (AAAs) were established under the Older Americans Act in 1973 to respond to the needs of Americans age 60 or older in every local community [National Association of Area Agencies on Aging (n4a), 2016]. AAAs provide assistance to older adults and caregivers in need of information and resources and provide a range of HCBS that allow older adults to maintain their lifestyle outside of institutionalized care. While AAAs do not provide direct services, they are a link between service providers and older adults and caregivers. Examples of services include home delivered meals, chore services, respite care for caregivers, legal assistance, and transportation. The Eldercare Locator, a call center and website administered by n4a, connects users to local resources, programs and services related to aging and caregiving. Data gathered from over 308,000 inquires made to the Eldercare Locator from phone calls, online chats, and emails show that information regarding transportation was the top consumer service request for 2016 (n4a, 2017).

## Other caregiver resources for providing transportation or assisting in transitioning from driving to non-driving

There are many other resources available to caregivers for assisting in the transition process or providing transportation assistance following driving cessation. It is not always possible for caregivers to provide transportation when needed; therefore, The National Aging and Disability Transportation Center (NADTC) (2018) in the US, a program of the Federal Transit Administration administered by Easterseals and n4a, encourages caregivers to seek out transportation services to assist, provide, or arrange transportation for their care recipient. The National Aging and Disability Transportation Center (NADTC) website (www.nadtc.org) provides resources to a variety of audiences with the goal of promoting the availability and accessibility of transportation options for older adults, people with disabilities, and caregivers.

The *Clearinghouse for Older Road User Safety* (ChORUS) is another website (www.roadsafeseniors.org) that provides resources for caregivers of older adults making the transition to non-driving as well as for those that have already ceased driving (Roadway Safety Foundation, 2018). In addition to the NADTC and ChORUS websites, there are countless other websites on the internet that contain information about caregiving and allow access to resources that are available near the caregiver.

Along with the guidebooks mentioned earlier in this chapter, there are many more publications aimed at helping caregivers with the transportation aspect of their caregiving role. For example, the AAA Foundation for Traffic Safety (2000) published a guide for caregivers to assist in planning safe transportation tailored around an older driver's strengths and weaknesses. This publication encourages caregivers to communicate openly and respectfully with their care recipient and to plan early for the driving retirement of an older adult family member. In addition, Alzheimer's Australia Vic (2014) released a guide specifically targeting caregivers, family members, and friends of people with dementia that are still driving. This guide provides strategies to support caregivers as their care recipients transition to non-driving. The information in the guide is supplemented by five worksheets to help the caregiver: document observations of driving and support their care recipient to reduce and stop driving; start a conversation about driving safety with their care recipient; determine the types of trips their care recipient drives and how to reduce the need to drive without impinging upon the physical and social benefits of driving; explore alternative transportation options available to their care recipient; and identify other people that are able to offer support to the caregiver and care recipient during the transitioning process and following driving cessation.

## Caregiving gap and policy recommendations

Despite the growth in the number of adult child caregivers in recent years, Redfoot, Feinberg, and Houser (2013) project a sharp decline in the availability of potential family caregivers, particularly adult children, over the next 20 years. Reasons for this include declining family size, rising childlessness, fewer intergenerational households, delayed marriage and childbirth, rising divorce rates, increasing female participation in the workforce, greater geographic mobility, and potentially less willingness for informal caring (Feinberg et al., 2011; National Academies of Sciences, Engineering, and Medicine, 2016; Pickard, Wittenberg, Comas-Herrera, Davies, & Darton, 2000; Roth et al., 2015; Verbakel, 2014). In developed countries, there will be increasing numbers of older adults ceasing driving in the near future, and due to the anticipated changes in caregiver availability, it will become increasingly difficult to have a family member or friend available to provide a ride to an older adult (Deka, 2014; Ichikawa et al., 2016). Older drivers who cannot secure transportation assistance with informal caregivers might continue driving, even after it is no longer safe to do so. Ichikawa et al. (2016) recommended that authorities prepare alternative transportation systems that can satisfy the needs of people who cease driving, paying particular attention to the possible barriers to the use of existing transportation alternatives.

The World Health Organization (2015) asserted that the role of family caregivers is often neither supported nor properly acknowledged. Providing support for caregivers is a pressing social problem that demands broad policy action (The National Academies of Sciences, Medicine and Engineering, 2016). There are calls from researchers, health professionals, public policy experts, and advocacy groups around the world to bring more awareness of and recognition to the caregiving population in an effort to plan and implement programs and policies that will ease the burden of caregivers as the world undergoes a shift in demographics. A tangible example of increasing the recognition of caregivers is a piece of legislation passed in Australia in 2010 to acknowledge formally the role of caregivers. The *Carer Recognition Act 2010* (Australian Government Department of Social Services, 2016) aims to increase the consideration of caregivers and the role they play in providing support to people with disability or age-related issues. The Act provides a definition of a caregiver, 10 principles that articulate how caregivers should be treated and considered, and gives obligations and responsibilities for public service agencies with respect to the 10 principles. For example, one of the principles states: "Carers should be supported to enjoy optimum health and social well-being and to participate in family, social and community life." (Australian Government Department of Social Services, 2016, p. 3). The ultimate goal is to change the culture and attitudinal norms throughout Australian Public Service agencies and associated providers, and as a result, the community as a whole (Australian Government Department of Social Services, 2016). In addition, the Australian government recently developed an Integrated Plan for Carer Support Services. The plan was developed to reflect the Australian Government's priorities for carers and outlines actions to recognize, support, and sustain the vital work of unpaid carers (Australian Government Department of Social Services, 2017a).

The National Academies of Sciences, Engineering, and Medicine (2016) called upon the US Department of Health and Human Services, in collaboration with other federal agencies and private-sector organizations, to "... develop and execute a National Family Caregiver Strategy that, administratively or through new legislation, explicitly and systematically addresses and supports the essential role of family caregivers to older adults" (National Academies of Sciences, Engineering, and Medicine, 2016, p. 256). The recommendations provided in this report emphasize the importance of making caregiving a part of the nation's collective responsibility for caring for its older adult population rather than implicitly assuming that a family caregiver is available to provide necessary support for the continued health and well-being of the older adult.

Glendinning et al. (2009) provided policy recommendations for EU member states to make visible the role of caregivers and their contributions to the long-term care system. In particular, there is a recommendation that employers should take into account the caregiving responsibilities of working age people. The need for flexibility in the workplace and policies that would benefit working caregivers is likely to increase in importance as more working caregivers approach their own retirement, while still caring for an aging parent. Flexible work arrangements in the United Kingdom, Australia, and the US attenuate the risk of a reduction in working hours associated with caregiving (Colombo et al., 2011). Research in Scotland showed that flexible work hours and the ability to reduce working hours are each associated with about 13% more hours of informal care, with evidence that the effect comes more through enabling people to become caregivers rather than increasing hours of existing care (Bryan, 2012).

Shergold, Lyons, and Hubers (2015) argued that it is critical that transportation planners around the world begin to respond now to anticipate the mobility demands of the rapidly increasing older adult population. Due to the frequency with which transportation assistance is provided by informal caregivers, it is necessary that this group be considered when planning for the future transportation needs of older adults. In fact, growing evidence suggests that services that address social factors, such as transportation and caregiver support issues, must be integrated into new models of care for older adults and the long-term care system (Shier, Ginsburg, Howell, Volland, & Golden, 2013).

## Conclusions

This chapter discussed informal caregivers, one segment of the population that is integral to the continued health and well-being of older adults. As noted in Chapter 1, The Challenges, the greatest population growth will be among the oldest old, the group most in need of assistance because of its increased likelihood of physical, cognitive, and other functional limitations. Given the projected increase in the population of the oldest old, the percentage of caregivers providing transportation will also increase in the coming years. The negative consequences associated with caregiving, and the importance that this segment of the population continues to provide this service, suggest necessary improvements to the recognition and support that is offered to caregivers who provide transportation and other assistance to older adults. Caregivers provide a valuable service to their care recipients and, more broadly, to society. Without family-provided help, the economic cost to the US health and long-term services and supports systems would skyrocket (Reinhard et al., 2015). Efforts to bolster caregivers in their role as well as identify other ways to meet the transportation and mobility needs of the expanding older adult population will be important policy issues to consider throughout the world as we move into the future.

## References

AAA Foundation for Traffic Safety. *How to help an older driver.* (2000). <https://seniordriving.aaa.com/download/how-to-help-an-older-driver-brochure/?wpdmdl = 404> Accessed March, 2018.

Adler, G., & Rottunda, S. (2006). Older adults' perspectives on driving cessation. *Journal of Aging Studies, 20*(3), 227–235.

Administration for Community Living (ACL). *AGing Integrated Database (AGID): Profile of State OAA Programs: 50 States + DC & Territories, State Profiles.* (2016). <https://agid.acl.gov/StateProfiles/Profile/Pre/?id = 109&topic = 0> Accessed January, 2018.

Administration for Community Living (ACL). *National Family Caregiver Support Program.* (2017). <https://www.acl.gov/node/314> Accessed January, 2018.

Albert, S. M., Schulz, R., & Colombi, A. (2010). *The MetLife study of working caregivers and employer health care costs: New insights and innovations for reducing health care costs for employers*. Westport, CT: MetLife Mature Market Institute.

Alzheimer's Australia Vic. (2014). *Changed conditions ahead: Dementia and driving guide for families and carers*. Kingston, Australian Capital Territory: Alzheimer's Australia.

Ashworth, M., & Baker, A. H. (2000). Time and space: Carers' views about respite care. *Health & Social Care in the Community*, *8*(1), 50–56.

Australian Bureau of Statistics. (2014). *Caring in the community, Australia 2012: Summary of Findings-2012, cat. no. 4436.0.* Canberra, ACT: Australian Bureau of Statistics.

Australian Bureau of Statistics. (2016). *Australian Bureau of Statistics Survey of disability, ageing and carers, Australia: Summary of Findings-2015, cat. no. 4430.0.* Canberra, ACT: Australian Bureau of Statistics.

Australian Government Department of Social Services. *Carer Recognition Act 2010 Guidelines: A guide for Australian Public Service Agencies for the implementation of the Carer Recognition Act 2010.* (2016). <https://www.dss.gov.au/sites/default/files/documents/05_2016/carer_recognition_act_2010_guidelines_april_2016.pdf> Accessed January, 2018.

Australian Government Department of Social Services. *Integrated plan for carer support services.* (2017a). <https://www.dss.gov.au/disability-and-carers/programmes-services/for-carers/integrated-plan-for-carer-support-services> Accessed January, 2018.

Australian Government Department of Social Services. *Payments for carers.* (2017b). <https://www.humanservices.gov.au/individuals/subjects/payments-carers> Accessed February, 2018.

Bauer, J. M., & Sousa-Poza, A. (2015). Impacts of informal caregiving on caregiver employment, health, and family. *Journal of Population Ageing*, *8*(3), 113–145.

Bettio, F., & Verashchagina, A. (2010). *Long-term care for the elderly: Provisions and providers in 33 European countries*. Luxembourg: EU Expert Group on Gender and Employment.

Bookwala, J., Zdaniuk, B., Burton, L., Lind, B., Jackson, S., & Schulz, R. (2004). Concurrent and long-term predictors of older adults' use of community-based long-term care services. *Journal of Aging and Health*, *16*(1), 88–115.

Brodaty, H., Thomson, C., Thompson, C., & Fine, M. (2005). Why caregivers of people with dementia and memory loss don't use services. *International Journal of Geriatric Psychiatry*, *20*(6), 537–546.

Brown, J., & Chen, S. L. (2008). Help-seeking patterns of older spousal caregivers of older adults with dementia. *Issues in Mental Health Nursing*, *29*(8), 839–852.

Bryan, M. L. (2012). Access to flexible working and informal care. *Scottish Journal of Political Economy*, *59*(4), 361–389.

Burton-Chase, A. M., Kwak, J., Hennig, K., & Haley, W. E. (2017). Elder caregiving. *Reference Module in Neuroscience and Biobehavioral Psychology*. <https://doi.org/10.1016/B978-0-12-809324-5.05543-7> Accessed January, 2018.

Casado, B. L., van Vulpen, K. S., & Davis, S. L. (2011). Unmet needs for home and community-based services among frail older Americans and their caregivers. *Journal of Aging and Health*, *23*(3), 529–553.

Choi, M., Adams, K. B., & Kahana, E. (2012). The impact of transportation support on driving cessation among community-dwelling older adults. *The Journals of Gerontology, Series B: Psychological Sciences and Social Sciences*, *67*(3), 392–400.

Cohen, C. A., Colantonio, A., & Vernich, L. (2002). Positive aspects of caregiving: rounding out the caregiver experience. *International Journal of Geriatric Psychiatry*, *17*(2), 184–188.

Colombo, F., Llena-Nozal, A., Mercier, J., & Tjadens, F. (2011). *Help Wanted? Providing and paying for long-term care*. Paris, France: OECD Health Policy Studies, OECD Publishing.

Congress.gov. H.R.2505 – *Credit for Caring Act of 2017*. (2017). <https://www.congress.gov/bill/115th-congress/house-bill/2505> Accessed November, 2017.

Connell, C. M., Harmon, A., Janevic, M. R., & Kostyniuk, L. P. (2013). Older adults' driving reduction and cessation: Perspectives of adult children. *Journal of Applied Gerontology*, *32*(8), 975–996.

Coughlin, J. *Transportation and older persons: Perceptions and preferences: A report on focus groups*. (2001). <https://assets.aarp.org/rgcenter/il/2001_05_transport.pdf> Accessed November, 2017.

Davey, J. A. (2007). Older people and transport: Coping without a car. *Ageing & Society*, *27* (1), 49–65.

Deka, D. (2014). The role of household members in transporting adults with disabilities in the United States. *Transportation Research Part A: Policy and Practice*, *69*, 45–57.

Deloitte Access Economics. (2015). *The economic value of informal care in Australia in 2015*. Canberra, ACT: Carers Australia.

Dickerson, A. E., Molnar, L. J., Eby, D. W., Adler, G., Bédard, M., Berg-Weger, M., ... Trujillo, L. (2007). Transportation and aging: A research agenda for advancing safe mobility. *The Gerontologist*, *47*, 578–590.

Easter Seals. *Transportation Solutions for Caregivers: A Solutions Package for Volunteer Transportation Programs*. (2003). <http://es.easterseals.com/site/DocServer/Transportation_Solutions.pdf?docID = 2081> Accessed November, 2017.

Eby, D.W., Silverstein, N.M., Molnar, L.J., LeBlanc, D., Adler, G., Gottlieb, A., ... Way, J. (2009). *Fitness to drive in early stage dementia: An instrumented vehicle study*. Report No. M-CASTL-2009-03. Ann Arbor, MI: Michigan Center for Advancing Safe Transportation throughout the Lifespan.

Eby, D.W., Molnar, L.J., Kostyniuk, L.P., St Louis, R.M., & Zanier, N. (2011). *Recommendations for meeting the transportation needs of Michigan's aging population*. Report No. RC-1562. Lansing, MI: Michigan Department of Transportation.

Eby, D. W., Molnar, L. J., Kostyniuk, L. P., St. Louis, R. M., & Zanier, N. (2017). Characteristics of informal caregivers who provide transportation assistance to older adults. *PLoS ONE*, *12*(9), e0184085.

Elliott, A. F., Burgio, L. D., & DeCoster, J. (2010). Enhancing caregiver health: Findings from the resources for enhancing Alzheimer's caregiver health II intervention. *Journal of the American Geriatrics Society*, *58*(1), 30–37.

Feinberg, L., Reinhard, S. C., Houser, A., & Choula, R. (2011). Valuing the invaluable: 2011 update, the growing contributions and costs of family caregiving. Washington, DC: AARP Public Policy Institute.

Glendinning, C., Tjadens, F., Arksey, H., Morée, M., Moran, N., & Nies, H. (2009). *Care provision within families and its socio-economic impact on care providers*. New York, NY: Social Policy Research Unit, University of York.

Hash, K. M., Jurkowski, E. T., & Krout, J. (2014). *Aging in rural places: Programs, policies, and professional practice*. New York, NY: Springer Publishing Company.

Hendrickson, C. C., & Mann, W. C. (2005). Changes over time in community mobility of elders with disabilities. *Physical & Occupational Therapy in Geriatrics*, *23*(2–3), 75–89.

Ho, S. C., Chan, A., Woo, J., Chong, P., & Sham, A. (2009). Impact of caregiving on health and quality of life: A comparative population-based study of caregivers for elderly persons and noncaregivers. *Journals of Gerontology Series A: Biomedical Sciences and Medical Sciences*, *64*(8), 873–879.

Home Instead, Inc. *Let's talk about driving. North American Research Report*. (2016). <https://www.caregiverstress.com/wp-content/uploads/2016/04/HISC_Lets_Talk_about_Driving_Executive_Summary_US.pdf> Accessed January, 2018.

Ichikawa, M., Nakahara, S., & Takahashi, H. (2016). The impact of transportation alternatives on the decision to cease driving by older adults in Japan. *Transportation*, *43*(3), 443–453.

Innes, A., Blackstock, K., Mason, A., Smith, A., & Cox, S. (2005). Dementia care provision in rural Scotland: Service users' and carers' experiences. *Health & Social Care in the Community*, *13*(4), 354–365.

International Alliance of Carer Organizations. *Global carer facts*. (2016). <http://www.internationalcarers.org/carer-facts/global-carer-stats/#_ednref5> Accessed November, 2017.

Johnson, J. E. (2008). Informal social support networks and the maintenance of voluntary driving cessation by older rural women. *Journal of Community Health Nursing*, *25*(2), 65–72.

Kihl, M., Knox, J., Sanchez, T., Glennon, C. S., Hurd, B., Ross, T., ... Maletina, O. (1997). *Alternative approaches to providing passenger transportation in low density cities: The case of Council Bluffs, Iowa*. Lincoln, NE: Mid-America Transportation Center.

Kostyniuk L.P. & Shope J.T. (1999). *Choice of transportation mode among older drivers and former drivers*. Report No. UMTRI-99-45. Ann Arbor, MI: University of Michigan Transportation Research Institute.

Kostyniuk, L. P., & Shope, J. T. (2003). Driving alternatives: Older drivers in Michigan. *Journal of Safety Research*, *34*, 407–414.

Li, H. (2006). Rural older adults' access barriers to in-home and community-based services. *Social Work Research*, *30*(2), 109–118.

MetLife Mature Market Institute. (1999). *The MetLife juggling act study: Balancing caregiving with work and the costs involved*. Westport, CT: Mature Market Institute.

MetLife Mature Market Institute. (2006). *The MetLife caregiving cost study: Productivity losses to U.S. business*. Westport, CT: Mature Market Institute.

MetLife Mature Market Institute. (2011). *The MetLife study of caregiving costs to working caregivers: Double jeopardy for baby boomers caring for their parents*. Westport, CT: MetLife Mature Market Institute.

Musselwhite, C., & Haddad, H. (2010). Mobility, accessibility and quality of later life. *Quality in Ageing and Older Adults*, *11*(1), 25–37.

National Academies of Sciences, Engineering, and Medicine. (2016). *Families caring for an aging America*. Washington, DC: The National Academies Press.

National Aging and Disability Transportation Center (NADTC). *Resources and publications*. (2018). <http://www.nadtc.org/resources-publications/> Accessed March, 2018.

National Alliance for Caregiving (NAC) & American Association of Retired Persons (AARP). (1997). *Caregiving in the U.S. 1997*. Bethesda, MD and Washington, DC: National Alliance for Caregiving and AARP.

National Alliance for Caregiving (NAC) & American Association of Retired Persons (AARP). (2004). *Caregiving in the U.S. 2004*. Bethesda, MD and Washington, DC: National Alliance for Caregiving and AARP.

National Alliance for Caregiving (NAC) & American Association of Retired Persons (AARP). (2009). *Caregiving in the U.S. 2009*. Bethesda, MD and Washington, DC: National Alliance for Caregiving and AARP.

National Alliance for Caregiving (NAC) & American Association of Retired Persons (AARP). (2015). *Caregiving in the U.S. 2015 – A focused look at those caring for someone age 50 or older*. Bethesda, MD and Washington, DC: National Alliance for Caregiving and AARP.

National Association of Area Agencies on Aging (n4a). *AAAs & Title VI Aging Programs*. (2016). <https://www.n4a.org/aaastitlevi> Accessed January, 2018.

National Association of Area Agencies on Aging (n4a). (2017). *Making connections: Consumer needs in an aging America*. Washington, DC: National Association of Area Agencies on Aging.

National Highway Traffic Safety Administration (NHTSA). (2013). *How to understand and influence older drivers*. Report No. DOT HS 810 633. Washington, DC: US Department of Transportation.

Neary, M. A. (1993). Community services in the 1990s: Are they meeting the needs of caregivers? *Journal of Community Health Nursing*, *10*, 105–111.

Pickard, L., Wittenberg, R., Comas-Herrera, A., Davies, B., & Darton, R. (2000). Relying on informal care in the new century?: Informal care for elderly people in England to 2031. *Ageing and Society*, *20*(6), 745–772.

Pinquart, M., & Sörensen, S. (2003). Differences between caregivers and noncaregivers in psychological health and physical health: A meta-analysis. *Psychology and Aging*, *18*, 250–267.

Pinquart, M., & Sörensen, S. (2007). Correlates of physical health of informal caregivers: A meta-analysis. *Journal of Gerontology: Social Sciences*, *62*, 126–137.

Rainville, C., Skufca, L., & Mehegan, L. *Family caregiving and out-of-pocket costs: 2016 report*. (2016). <http://www.aarp.org/content/dam/aarp/research/surveys_statistics/ltc/2016/family-caregiving-cost-survey-res-ltc.pdf> Accessed December, 2017.

Redfoot, D., Feinberg, L., & Houser, A. N. (2013). *The aging of the baby boom and the growing care gap: A look at future declines in the availability of family caregivers*. Washington, DC: AARP Public Policy Institute.

Reinhard, S. C., Feinberg, L. F., Choula, R., & Houser, A. (2015). Valuing the invaluable: 2015 update. *Insight on the Issues*, *104*, 1–25.

Roadway Safety Foundation. *Family/caregiver resources and alternative transportation*. (2018). <https://www.roadsafeseniors.org/resources/family-caregiver-resources-and-alternative-transportation> Accessed March, 2018.

Rosenbloom, S. (2009). Meeting transportation needs in an aging-friendly community. *Generations*, *33*(2), 33–43.

Roth, D. L., Fredman, L., & Haley, W. E. (2015). Informal caregiving and its impact on health: A reappraisal from population-based studies. *The Gerontologist*, *55*(2), 309–319.

Rudman, D. L., Friedland, J., Chipman, M., & Sciortino, P. (2006). Holding on and letting go: The perspectives of pre-seniors and seniors on driving self-regulation in later life. *Canadian Journal on Aging/La Revue Canadienne du Vieillissement*, *25*(1), 65–76.

Schulz, R., & Monin, J. K. (2012). The costs and benefits of informal caregiving. In S. L. Brown, R. M. Brown, & L. A. Penner (Eds.), *Moving beyond self-interest: Perspectives from evolutionary biology, neuroscience, and the social sciences* (pp. 178–198). New York, NY: Oxford University Press.

Schulz, R., & Sherwood, P. (2008). Physical and mental health effects of family caregiving. *The American Journal of Nursing*, *108*(9 Suppl.), 23–27.

Schulz, R., O'Brien, A., Czaja, S., Ory, M., Norris, R., Martire, L. M., … Stevens, A. (2002). Dementia caregiver intervention research. *The Gerontologist*, *42*(5), 589–602.

Shergold, I., Lyons, G., & Hubers, C. (2015). Future mobility in an ageing society—Where are we heading? *Journal of Transport & Health*, *2*(1), 86–94.

Shier, G., Ginsburg, M., Howell, J., Volland, P., & Golden, R. (2013). Strong social support services, such as transportation and help for caregivers, can lead to lower health care use and costs. *Health Affairs*, *32*(3), 544–551.

Shope, J.T. & Eby, D.W. (1998). *Improvement of older driver safety through self-evaluation: Focus group results*. Report No. UMTRI-98-29. Ann Arbor, MI: University of Michigan Transportation Research Institute.

Silverstein, N. M. (2008). When life exceeds safe driving expectancy: Implications for gerontology and geriatrics education. *Gerontology & Geriatrics Education*, *29*(4), 305–309.

Taylor, B. D., & Tripodes, S. (2001). The effects of driving cessation on the elderly with dementia and their caregivers. *Accident Analysis & Prevention*, *33*(4), 519–528.

The Hartford and MIT AgeLab. *We need to talk: Family conversations with older drivers, 14th revision*. (2017). <https://s0.hfdstatic.com/sites/the_hartford/files/we-need-to-talk.pdf> Accessed November, 2017.

Trukeschitz, B., Schneider, U., Mühlmann, R., & Ponocny, I. (2013). Informal eldercare and work-related strain. *Journals of Gerontology Series B: Psychological Sciences and Social Sciences*, *68*(2), 257–267.

Turner, A., & Findlay, L. (2012). Informal caregiving for seniors. *Health Reports*, *23*(3), 33–36.

Verbakel, E. (2014). Informal caregiving and well-being in Europe: What can ease the negative consequences for caregivers? *Journal of European Social Policy*, *24*(5), 424–441.

Verbakel, E., Tamlagsrønning, S., Winstone, L., Fjær, E. L., & Eikemo, T. A. (2017). Informal care in Europe: Findings from the European Social Survey (2014) special module on the social determinants of health. *The European Journal of Public Health*, *27* (Suppl. 1), 90–95.

Vitaliano, P. P., Zhang, J., & Scanlan, J. M. (2003). Is caregiving hazardous for one's physical health? A meta-analysis. *Psychological Bulletin*, *129*, 946–972.

Wachs, M. (2000). *Mobility for California's aging population*. Berkeley, CA: University of California, California Policy Research Center.

Whittier, S., Scharlach, A., & Dal Santo, T. S. (2005). Availability of caregiver support services. *Journal of Aging & Social Policy*, *17*(1), 45–62.

Winslow, B. J. (2003). Family caregivers' experiences with community services: A qualitative approach. *Public Health Nursing*, *20*, 341–348.

World Health Organization. *Supporting informal caregivers of people with dementia*. (2015). <http://www.who.int/mental_health/neurology/dementia/dementia_thematicbrief_informal_care.pdf?ua = 1> Accessed December, 2017.

# Physicians and other health professionals 7

*The doctor of the future will give no medicine, but will interest his or her patients in the care of the human frame, proper diet, and in the cause and prevention of disease.*

*Thomas Edison*

## Introduction

As described in Chapter 1, The Challenges, adults become more susceptible to health and medical conditions as they age that can affect functioning, and, in turn, safe driving. Several meta-analyses and in-depth reviews of the literature on these conditions and their impacts on driving among older adults have been conducted (e.g., Charlton et al., 2010; Dobbs, 2005; Eby, Molnar, & Kartje, 2009; Eby, Trombley, Molnar, & Shope, 1998). A brief summary is presented here.

A number of age-related medical conditions have been found to be associated with impaired driving ability. They are commonly grouped into broader disease categories that include vision-related (e.g., cataracts, glaucoma, and macular degeneration), cardiovascular (e.g., implantable defibrillators, arrhythmias, and angina pectoris), respiratory (e.g., chronic obstructive pulmonary disease, and sleep apnea), neurologic diseases (e.g., mild cognitive impairment, dementia, and Parkinson's disease), psychiatric (e.g., psychosis, anxiety, and depression), metabolic (e.g., hyper or hypo glycemia), and musculoskeletal diseases (e.g., cervical arthritis with restrictive range of motion, Carr & O'Neill, 2015; Carr & Ott, 2010). Anstey, Eramudugolla, Ross, Lautenschlager, and Wood (2016) identified several medical conditions prevalent among the oldest old (age 85 or older) that reduce driving safety including dementia, stroke, and eye disease. They concluded that the progressive nature of dementia and macular degeneration, in particular, inevitably leads to the need to stop driving.

Many studies have focused specifically on dementia as a health condition affecting safe driving. This focus is justified for several reasons. First, because dementia is a progressive condition, the challenge is to determine which individuals are safe to drive and at what point driving cessation is necessary (Cameron et al., 2017). Second, as dementia progresses, individuals are likely to lose insight into their cognitive declines and how these declines are affecting their driving, thus adding to the challenge of deciding when it is time to stop driving and accepting that decision (Allan, Behrman, Baruch, & Ebmeier, 2016). Adding further complication to the effects of dementia on driving is the issue of comorbidities. For example, Carr and

**Perspectives and Strategies for Promoting Safe Transportation among Older Adults.**
**DOI: https://doi.org/10.1016/B978-0-12-812153-5.00007-8**

O'Neill (2015) argued that the effects of multiple medical conditions should be considered when assessing fitness to drive of individuals with dementia, but they also noted that such comorbidities have not been well studied.

The effects of multiple health conditions on driving pose challenges for older adults beyond just those individuals with dementia. For example, Marshall and Man-Son-Hing (2011) reviewed the literature on multiple medical conditions and driving. They concluded that "... the myriad combinations of diseases with associated varying severity present a level of complexity that currently prevents distillation of clear and relevant information to assist administrators, health-care professionals, or the consumer in making informed decisions about driving with multiple chronic medical conditions" (p. 147). The medications used to treat these medical conditions can also adversely affect driving, although it is often difficult to disentangle the effects of medications from the effects of the conditions being treated. In addition, medications not only have a primary effect (therapeutic) on health conditions, but also side effects that can directly affect driving abilities (e.g., Devlin, Odell, Charlton, & Koppel, 2012; Eby & Molnar, 2009; Eby et al., 2009). Nevertheless, several efforts in different countries have been undertaken to categorize the effects of medications on driving (e.g., see Álvarez, 2016).

Given the complex relationship between medical conditions, medications, and driving, much of the work on aging and driving has focused on functional impairments in vision, cognition, and psychomotor functioning that can result from medical conditions and medications, rather than on medical conditions or medications per se, as noted in earlier chapters. However, health professionals, especially physicians, are responsible for attending to both functional impairments and medical conditions among their aging patients and therefore have a unique opportunity to address driving-related issues with their patients. This chapter discusses the role of health professionals in addressing driving issues with their older patients and highlights the barriers and challenges associated with this role. The chapter also identifies education and training approaches that have been used to overcome these challenges and describes some of the specific resources that have been developed.

## The role of health professionals in older driver safety

The central role that health professionals play in older driver safety is widely recognized and is related to several factors. One of the most salient factors is that physicians and other health-care professionals regularly care for patients with newly acquired impairments or diseases that may affect their ability to drive (Marshall & Gilbert, 1999). Physicians, in particular, are judged to be leaders in the "frontline of health care," playing an important role in decision-making about driving and advising patients and their families about driving safety (Adler & Rottunda, 2011, p. 61). Expanding on this theme, Anstey et al. (2016) argued that given "... the accessibility of family physicians and their capacity to screen for a range of medical conditions that potentially impact driving safety, primary care is the logical first point of contact in the process of evaluating fitness to drive" (p. 349). The role of other health professionals such as nurse practitioners in older driver safety in the primary care setting has also been recognized (e.g., Arms, 2016).

A second factor is that health professionals are generally considered to be trusted figures of respect and authority (e.g., Adler & Rottunda, 2011; Betz, Scott, Jones, & DiGuiseppi, 2016). With regard to cognitive impairment, Carr and Ott (2010) noted that the opinion of the primary care physician or subspecialist may be the only one that is acceptable to the patient, his or her family, and the larger community. Finally, health professionals have an obligation to balance the individual needs of their patients with the need to protect the larger public or society. To this end, Arms (2016) pointed to driving safety as both a public and personal safety issue and noted that nurse practitioners have a duty to routinely assess and intervene when appropriate.

Despite the compelling reasons why health professionals often take on the role of decision maker with respect to older driver safety, there are significant barriers to their ability to do so. Physicians are often reluctant to discuss driving issues with their patients for many reasons. First, many physicians are concerned that assessing the fitness to drive of their patients will negatively affect their relationships with them (e.g., Álvarez, 2016; Cameron et al., 2017; Classen et al., 2016; Jang et al., 2007; Marshall & Gilbert, 1999). As importantly, a number of studies have found that many physicians do not feel confident making such assessments of fitness to drive (e.g., Anstey et al., 2016; Cameron et al., 2017; Classen et al., 2016; Jang et al., 2007; Marshall, Demmings, Woolnough, Salim, & Man-Son-Hing, 2012; Sims, Rouse-Watson, Schattner, Beveridge, & Jones, 2012). For example, Jang et al. (2007) surveyed Canadian physicians about their attitudes and practices regarding fitness to drive. Forty-five percent reported that they were not confident in assessing fitness to drive and did not consider themselves the most qualified professionals to make those judgments. Classen et al. (2016) conducted semi-structured interviews with health professionals in Canada and identified a perceived lack of training, education, and resources for assessing fitness to drive as an important barrier to their initiating such actions.

Other barriers identified in the literature include physician concerns about the consequences on the quality of life of their patients, and perceived communication barriers between caregivers, physicians, and other stakeholders such as licensing agencies (Cameron et al., 2017). In addition, several characteristics of health professionals themselves have been identified as influencing whether they engage with their aging patients about driving safety. For example, Huseth-Zosel, Sanders, O'Connor, Fuller-Iglesias, and Langley (2016) examined rural and urban differences in the perceptions, attitudes, and practices of health-care providers with regard to their provision of guidance about driving safety to their aging patients through surveys of 256 health-care providers in several north-central states in the United States (US). They found that rural health professionals were less likely than their urban counterparts to provide such guidance to patients age 75 or older. Rural health professionals were also less likely to refer patients for a driving fitness evaluation if they had questions related to driving issues and were less likely to believe that adequate resources for helping with driving issues were available. In related work using the same sample, Huseth-Zosel, Sanders, and O'Connor (2016) examined the predictors of providing driving-related guidance more broadly. They found that predictors differed by patient age. For patients age 65–74, significant predictors of providing guidance included the health professional having had a personal experience involving a motor vehicle crash (consistent with Abramson, Stein, Schaufele, Frates, and Rogan, 2000; Brunero, Smith, Bates, & Fairbrother, 2008; Weiss, O'Neil, Shope, O'Connor, & Levin, 2012). For patients age 75 or older, significant predictors included the health professional being in an urban practice (consistent with Andrus, Kelley, Murphey, & Herndon, 2004; Kemper, Uren, Moseley, & Clark, 2006), being older himself or herself, and having a higher percentage of patients who were older adults.

## Physician assessment of fitness to drive

Health professionals', particularly physicians', lack of confidence relative to assessing fitness to drive is not surprising, given the lack of strong and consistent evidence for valid and reliable tests or batteries of tests to identify at-risk drivers (Anstey et al., 2016; Bédard, Weaver, Dārzin, & Porter, 2008; Ferreira, Simões, & Marôco, 2013). For example, Bédard et al. (2008) argued that despite numerous studies of tests or batteries of tests for potentially identifying at-risk drivers, the predictive value of currently available instruments is unclear at best. Other investigators have also called attention to this issue, noting that receiver operating characteristics curves and test characteristics such as positive and negative predictive values and likelihood ratios are now considered the statistical benchmark for evidence-based research (Dickerson, Meuel, Ridenour, & Cooper, 2014).

Unfortunately, few studies have examined how health professionals, especially physicians, actually go about making decisions about driving fitness in daily practice (Meuser, Berg-Weger, Carr, Shi, & Stewart, 2016). Meuser et al. (2016) examined the clinical ratings of 652 adults age 60 or older by physicians, using data from Missouri physician statements submitted to Missouri licensing agencies. They found three main influences on ratings of driving capability: judgments of disease severity, decrements in driver insight, and older age of the patient. In addition, they found imperfect associations between physicians' ratings and on-road testing, which, according to the authors, speaks to the fundamental challenge of equating clinical judgments with actual performance. Allan et al. (2016) reviewed the relatively few studies that examined the accuracy of clinicians, particularly dementia specialists, in predicting fitness to drive for patients with dementia. Results were mixed, with most showing modest or limited agreement between clinicians' predictions and outcomes from on-road testing. They concluded that clinicians "... are generally unable to predict driving ability accurately and reliably and that clinical assessment alone should not be used as a basis for decision-making" (p. 111).

Despite these limitations, Lee and Molnar (2017) argued that the lack of a single office-based test for reliably identifying at-risk drivers does not mean that in-office tests are of no use to frontline health professionals. They noted that physicians and other health professionals still need to make decisions about their patients' fitness to drive, especially those with cognitive impairment. In making these decisions, they cautioned that because safe driving relies on multiple cognitive and functional skills, health professionals should carefully weigh a number of factors when deciding if cognitive deficits may be affecting driving safety. Other studies also support the use of multiple measures of driving fitness (e.g., Dickerson et al., 2014). For example, Ross, Scialfa, and Cordazzo (2015) evaluated the ability of several measures to predict on-road driving in cognitively impaired drivers and found that the best prediction of passing or failing an on-road test was a combination of several tests (with a model sensitivity of 71% and specificity of 75%). According to the authors, the need for a battery of tests to measure different abilities to predict driving outcomes is not surprising, given the complexity of the driving task. Similarly, a systematic review by Bennett, Chekaluk, and Batchelor (2016) found that composite batteries, rather than individual cognitive tests, were a better predictor of driving performance.

## In-depth evaluation of fitness to drive

Regardless of whether individual or composite measures are used to examine fitness to drive, many researchers have maintained that the process undertaken by physicians should be more appropriately termed screening than assessment. For example, Korner-Bitensky, Menon, von Zweck, and Van Benthem (2010) argued that the purpose of screening is to distinguish those individuals who need further evaluation of driving safety from those who are most likely safe drivers, on the basis of a quick examination of their driving-specific skills (Korner-Bitensky, Gelinas, Man-Son-Hing, & Marshall, 2005). On the other hand, they described assessment as involving a more detailed evaluation of an individual's driving-specific skills and safety in domains identified as potential concerns during the screening process. They noted that this assessment may be done in a generalized occupational therapy (OT) practice or conducted by an OT who is specifically trained in driving assessment. The latter evaluation is interchangeably termed a comprehensive driving evaluation, driving assessment, or functional driving evaluation (Carr, Schwartzberg, Manning, & Sempek, 2010). A driving assessment can also be conducted in a licensing agency.

Carr and O'Neill (2015) also addressed this issue, noting that in the absence of a gold standard or consensus for determining driving fitness, physicians sometimes refer their patients to an occupational therapist or a driver rehabilitation specialist (DRS) to conduct an in-depth evaluation of driving fitness. As described by Carr and O'Neill, DRSs in the US are often OTs with additional training in driver evaluation, vehicle modifications, and rehabilitation. The in-depth or comprehensive evaluation generally includes a clinical assessment component (including a medical and driving history and assessment of physical, cognitive, and visual abilities) and an on-road assessment to measure actual driving (Dickerson, 2013a). This on-road or behind-the-wheel evaluation is considered by many to be the most clinically useful method for evaluating driving performance, especially when combined with results from the off-road assessment (Manning & Schultheis, 2013).

Nevertheless, concerns have been raised about the lack of standardization across in-depth evaluations of fitness to drive, and solid evidence of their validity and reliability (Brenner, Homaifar, & Schultheis, 2008; Dickerson, 2013b). For example, Korner-Bitensky, Bitensky, Sofer, Man-Son-Hing, and Gelinas (2006) point out that although there are OT practice guidelines for in-depth evaluations of driving fitness, there is considerable variability in how such assessments are conducted, and many do not use standardized tools. Vrkljan, Myers, Crizzle, Blanchard, and Marshall (2013) surveyed professionals (mainly OTs) who assessed fitness to drive in Canada and found considerable variation in terms of the length of the evaluation, the use of cognitive measures, the duration and type of on-road assessment, and criteria used for determining if it was needed. They concluded that, given these inconsistencies in practice, evidence-based guidelines for training and assessment are needed.

Korner-Bitensky et al. (2005) have argued that addressing the competency gaps of OTs relative to managing older driver safety requires capacity building at three levels. These include: (1) general training to identify individuals who need to be referred for in-depth assessment or who could benefit from a driving refresher course; (2) more advanced training to evaluate driving-related skills, using in-depth and on-road assessments, as well as provide targeted interventions aimed at driver retraining; and (3) advanced specialization, including assessment, training, and retraining of driving skills, vehicle adaptations, and use of assistive technology for those with health conditions beyond the effects of normal aging.

Collectively, the information introduced in this chapter supports the need for a multitiered and multifaceted approach to screening and assessment of older drivers. To this end, Molnar, Byszewski, Marshall, and Man-Son-Hing (2005) have argued that "... the issue is not who can best assess fitness to drive but rather what complementary role can each profession play to improve road safety and decrease morbidity and mortality" (p. 375). At the same time, the results of the studies discussed here suggest that physicians and other professionals could benefit from education and training related to aging adults and driving, especially those adults with dementia, and multiple studies have found that health professionals would welcome such efforts (e.g., Jang et al., 2007). Numerous resources have been developed. While it is beyond the scope of this chapter, some of the more promising resources are highlighted here.

## Education and training for health professionals

As discussed earlier, health and medical professionals are often expected to address concerns about older driver safety and mobility in the course of providing care to their patients, but few have received specialized training on driving issues. To address the challenges discussed in this chapter, several initiatives have been undertaken to educate physicians and other health professionals. Briefly highlighted here are some of the more promising initiatives. One of the best known resources for health professionals involved in the care of older drivers is the *Physicians' Guide to Assessing and Counseling Older Drivers*, which came out of the American Medical Association's (AMA) *Older Driver Project,* aimed at helping older drivers continue to drive safely to preserve their mobility and independence (Wang & Carr, 2004). The most current version of the guide was produced by the American Geriatrics Society, in collaboration with the National Highway Traffic Safety Administration (Dattoma, 2017). The purpose of the guide is to assist physicians in planning for older driver safety; it provides information on how to informally and formally assess older drivers, interpret the resulting scores, and help manage and treat patients (Carr et al., 2010). The guide also provides information about referring patients to a DRS for further evaluation, how to counsel patients, legal and ethical responsibilities of physicians, state licensing policies and reporting laws, and medical conditions that may affect driving.

Based on the guide, the AMA developed a curriculum to train health professionals on how to examine the driving fitness of their patients; determine whether they are at increased risk due to a medical or functional problem; and develop a plan for further evaluation and/or transitioning to non-driving when necessary (Meuser, Carr, Irmiter, Schwartzberg, & Ulfarsson, 2010). The curriculum is made up of five modules in a multimedia format, with slides, video case segments, and handouts. It is delivered in-person to physicians and other health professionals by trained teaching teams consisting of a physician, rehabilitation specialist, and other driving specialist.

Meuser et al. (2010) evaluated the curriculum by examining changes in the attitudes and behaviors of participants in 22 training sessions held in 2006–2007. Of 693 participants in the sessions, 235 completed both pre- and posttests. Results indicated improvements in attitudes and knowledge for the following: comfort with personal knowledge of topic, familiarity with driver rehabilitation options, comfort in counseling at-risk patients, familiarity with state laws and procedures, and regularly discussing driving with patients. There were also improvements in practice as measured by incorporating driving questions into regular assessment, discussing driving as a clinical concern with any patient, specifically documenting driving abilities in chart, working with patient/family on driving retirement plans, and referring patients for other driving evaluation. The authors concluded that an evidence-based, resource-oriented continuing education intervention can enhance health-care practice relative to the evaluation of older driver fitness and safety.

The AMA curriculum has been expanded into a 2-hour multimedia workshop delivered by a multidisciplinary team, with added focus on several dementia-related topics (e.g., dementia diagnosis, screening, and staging of impairment; Meuser, Carr, Berg-Weger, Niewoehner, & Morris, 2006). The curriculum was evaluated by comparing participants' knowledge, confidence, attitudes, and practice behaviors before and at three points following a series of workshops (Meuser et al., 2006).

Modest gains in knowledge and confidence, and significant increases in the frequency of driving-related practices were found (e.g., incorporating driving-related questions into clinical evaluation, reporting impaired drivers).

Despite promising evaluation results of the AMA curriculum with regard to participant knowledge and confidence, one limitation of the *Physician's Guide to Assessing and Counseling Older Drivers* is that evidence of the effectiveness of its recommended assessment battery for identifying at-risk drivers is inconclusive. Eby et al. (2009) reviewed several studies on the assessment battery, referred to as the assessment of driving-related skills (ADReS). They found evidence of high interrater reliability among various practitioners administering the battery (e.g., Posse, McCarthy, & Mann, 2006). However, results from an evaluation of the battery's specificity (the probability that the screen is negative given that the person does not have a problem) and sensitivity (the probability that the screen is positive given that the person does have a problem) by McCarthy and Mann (2006) were less promising. They found that although the battery successfully identified all participants who failed, it also identified 70% of the sample as needing intervention when in fact they were not at risk. These results are consistent with another study by Fender, Wilber, Stiffler, and Blanda (2007) in which only one of 50 participants assessed by ADReS did not end up with at least one "red flag" based on outcomes of the assessment. More recently, Woolnough et al. (2013) found that scores from ADReS did not correlate with motor vehicle crashes in a large sample of older drivers.

Another curriculum for health professionals in the US was developed, based on AMA guidelines, and evaluated in California (Hill, Rybar, & Styer, 2012). The purpose of the curriculum is to improve the ability of participants to: understand the safety risks associated with older drivers; identify conditions that may place patients at risk for unsafe driving; and select appropriate screening tests to evaluate patients' level of function for driving fitness. The curriculum specifically focuses on increasing awareness of referral and treatment options for patients determined unfit to drive, as well as California's driver licensing methods and requirements. It was delivered to participants by physicians through 47, 1-hour sessions from 2009 to 2011. Results of pre and post testing conducted with 641 of the participants indicated that the curriculum increased both confidence and ability to screen patients, as well as intent to screen.

In Canada, a continuing medical education program was developed to improve health professionals' understanding of older driver safety (Dow, 2009; Dow & Jacques, 2012). The program consists of a 90-minute workshop combining presentation and discussion methods and centering on five case studies. In an evaluation of the program, 824 participants in the program reported high levels of satisfaction with the workshop and results suggested an increase in the number of reports submitted by physicians, and improvements in the quality of the reports. Dow and Jacques (2012) concluded that the positive outcomes of the program were due primarily to the clinical rather than administrative orientation of the program, the use of physicians to deliver the workshop, and formal recognition of the program by the authorities responsible for licensing physicians.

More recently, Casey, Salinas, and Eckstrom (2015) reported on the development and testing of an electronic health record–based *Driving Clinical Support Tool* for primary care physicians to assess fitness to drive. According to the authors, the tool relies on a driving evaluation algorithm based on a literature review of evidence-based practice for evaluating at-risk drivers, as well as a patient-visit-note template focused on driving. A sample of 86 providers, trained on how to use the tool, completed pre- and post-surveys about it. Improvements were found in self-reported preparedness and knowledge of how to evaluate at-risk older drivers, as well as documentation of driving-related issues and access to interdisciplinary care coordination.

## Physician reporting

Physicians who treat patients they consider to be medically at risk for safe driving can, and in some states are required to, report them to the licensing agency in their jurisdiction. Physician reporting laws vary from state to state within the US; however, no state prohibits reporting by physicians. A recent review of such laws conducted by Hill, Rajasekar, and Parsons (2018) found that most states allow and often encourage physicians to voluntarily report patients they consider to be medically unfit to drive but do not explicitly require such reporting. Seven states in the US (California, Delaware, Maine, Nevada, New Jersey, Oregon, and Pennsylvania) mandate or require physicians to report patients for specific medical conditions such as dementia or epilepsy (AAA Foundation for Traffic Safety, 2018). Hill et al. (2018) noted that in these states, physicians generally cannot be sued for reporting their patients. They also identified 10 states that have no reporting requirements. Based on findings from another review by Dugan, Barton, Coyle, and Lee (2013), most states (36) provide physicians with immunity from civil liability, but only a few states allow physicians to report their patients anonymously.

The reporting of medically at-risk patients to the licensing agency can result in several actions by the licensing agency. These include the requirement of a specialized on-road driving test; suspension or revocation of the individual's license; or increased monitoring or restriction (Dugan et al., 2013; Rapoport et al., 2014; Winston & Jaiser, 2012).

A study of older drivers reported as medically impaired in Missouri from 2001 to 2005 provides some evidence that reporting of at-risk drivers is effective (Meuser, Carr, & Ulfarsson, 2009). Physicians were responsible for 20% of reports to the licensing agency in this study. The authors found that crash involvement among all reported drivers was significantly higher than among controls—four times as high in 2001. The crash involvement of all reported drivers decreased significantly after reporting. The authors attributed these outcomes to the impact of license revocation and to a lesser extent mortality.

However, there are a number of barriers to physician reporting, many of which have been previously discussed in relation to the more general challenges that physicians and other health professionals face in terms of addressing driving safety with their patients. First, physicians face the challenge of having to "... balance their legal and ethical responsibilities to protect their patients' health and confidentiality with their duty to protect the general public from unsafe drivers" (Goodwin et al., 2013, ch. 7, p. 15). Other barriers to physician reporting include the emotional demands of a lengthy review process; the negative effect on the physician–patient relationship; the challenging and lengthy process of license reinstatement in the event that a reported patient's condition improves over time or abilities improve with training; and overestimation by the licensing agency or general public of physicians' ability to predict whether patients will be involved in a crash (Molnar et al., 2005). With regard to this last barrier, Molnar et al. (2005) noted several reasons why these predictions are challenging. First, a patient's driving-related abilities may vary and his or her presentation in the office may not be representative of all driving experiences. Second, all drivers are at some baseline risk for crashing. Third, physicians primarily assess operational skills; yet there are many tactical skills that are amenable to compensation. Fourth, standard physical examinations were designed to identify the presence or absence of disease and not to assess function. Finally, as discussed earlier, reliable, clinically sensible, and valid tools to assist screening and assessment of driving do not exist.

## Dementia-specific resources

Given the special challenges associated with dementia and driving, it is not surprising that there has been increasing attention to developing resources for health professionals who treat this segment of the older driver population. For example, Carter et al. (2014) recently reported on a clinical pathway for patients with dementia developed in the United Kingdom. The pathway provides a decision-making framework for health professionals across a range of disciplines who deal with patients with dementia who drive. Developed, based on multidisciplinary expert input, its purpose is to help overcome reluctance of health professionals to deal with the issue of driving and dementia by providing specific guidance. The authors concluded the pathway is something that can be easily adapted for use internationally.

Cameron et al. (2017) reported on the development of a decision-making tool for reporting drivers in Ontario, Canada with mild dementia and mild cognitive impairment to licensing agencies in Canada. The driving in dementia decision tool was developed as an online user-friendly tool to help physicians decide when to report older drivers with either mild dementia or mild cognitive impairment. Development of the tool was based on review of literature, guidelines, a Delphi survey and qualitative interviews, and focus groups with physicians, caregivers of former drivers with dementia, and transport administrators. The authors noted that limitations of the approach included a dearth of high-quality evidence guiding physicians to make reporting decisions.

Finally, various guidelines for dealing with dementia and driving have been developed to provide direction to physicians and other health professionals who treat this segment of the population. For example, Selway (2018) reviewed evidence-based guidelines developed by the American Academy of Neurology regarding driving risk among individuals with dementia. Recommendations included the use of the Clinical Dementia Rating scale to determine whether a person's driving is marginal or unsafe.

## Transitioning counseling

When older adults are deemed unsafe to drive or choose not to drive, efforts to facilitate the process of transitioning to non-driving can have a significant influence on continued mobility and quality of life. One noteworthy initiative is referred to as mobility transition counseling (MTC), a collaborative, professional intervention to bring about a planned transition for optimal personal mobility. Led by researchers at the University of Missouri (e.g., Meuser, Berg-Weger, Chibnall, Harmon, & Stowe, 2011), MTC is built on the assumption that strategies such as mobility management and transportation plans are most effective when tailored to fit the attitudes, beliefs, and needs of individual older drivers. Underlying the MTC approach is a person-specific assessment tool called the *Assessment* of *Readiness* for *Mobility Transition* (ARMT; Meuser et al., 2011), an evidence-based tool intended to increase awareness about mobility loss and assess attitudes that might support or hinder productive planning. Its developers recommend that MTC be integrated into a comprehensive assessment and intervention process to help older adults maintain their mobility.

ARMT was validated as a screening tool, using a sample of 297 older adults whose mean age was 71 years (Meuser et al., 2012). Results of the validation yielded sound internal validity and reliability. According to the authors, results confirm the usefulness of ARMT as a clinical practice tool that can be used by social service, health, and transportation professionals to assess older adults on measures of emotional and attitudinal readiness and engage in individualized planning for the transition to non-driving.

## Conclusions

Physicians and other health professionals are positioned to play a central role in older adult mobility, in particular, screening and assessment of fitness to drive among their patients. However, studies show that these professionals face significant barriers in carrying out this role, especially a lack of confidence in, and availability of, reliable tests for assessing fitness to drive. Study results discussed in this chapter suggest that continuing efforts are needed to help health professionals in decision-making. Older drivers with dementia pose a special challenge, because of the progressive nature of their condition, and targeted resources for this population are needed. Collectively, efforts to assist physicians and other health professionals should focus on identifying and developing resources and strategies that are evidence based and can be implemented practically in health-care settings. In addition, better standardizations in the processes used to screen and assess fitness to drive are needed. Finally, physicians and other health professionals will benefit by continuing to be part of a multitiered and multifaceted approach for screening and assessing older drivers and their fitness to drive. Efforts to strengthen such an approach are warranted.

## References

AAA Foundation for Traffic Safety. *Driver licensing policies and practices database*. (2018). Available from http://lpp.seniordrivers.org/index.cfm?selection = visionreqs. Accessed June, 2018.

Abramson, S., Stein, J., Schaufele, M., Frates, E., & Rogan, S. (2000). Personal exercise habits and counseling practices of primary care physicians: A national survey. *Clinical Journal of Sport Medicine*, *10*(1), 40–48.

Adler, G., & Rottunda, S. J. (2011). The driver with dementia: A survey of physician attitudes, knowledge, and practice. *American Journal of Alzheimer's Disease & Other Dementias*, *26*(1), 58–64.

Allan, C. L., Behrman, S., Baruch, N., & Ebmeier, K. P. (2016). Driving and dementia: A clinical update for mental health professionals. *Evidence-Based Mental Health*, *19*(4), 110–113.

Álvarez, F. J. (2016). Parkinson's disease, anti-Parkinson medicines, and driving. *Expert Review of Neurotherapeutics*, *16*(9), 1023–1032.

Andrus, M. R., Kelley, K. W., Murphey, L. M., & Herndon, K. C. (2004). A comparison of diabetes care in rural and urban medical clinics in Alabama. *Journal of Community Health*, *29*(1), 29–44.

Anstey, K. J., Eramudugolla, R., Ross, L. A., Lautenschlager, N. T., & Wood, J. (2016). Road safety in an aging population: Risk factors, assessment, interventions, and future directions. *International Psychogeriatrics*, *28*(3), 349–356.

Arms, T. (2016). The NPs role of assessing and intervening with older adult drivers. *Nursing Research and Practice*, *2016*, 3254857.

Bédard, M., Weaver, B., Dārzin, P., & Porter, M. M. (2008). Predicting driving performance in older adults: We are not there yet!. *Traffic Injury Prevention*, *9*(4), 336–341.

Bennett, J. M., Chekaluk, E., & Batchelor, J. (2016). Cognitive tests and determining fitness to drive in dementia: A systematic review. *Journal of the American Geriatrics Society*, *16*, 1904–1917.

Betz, M. E., Scott, K., Jones, J., & DiGuiseppi, C. (2016). "Are you still driving?" Metasynthesis of patient preferences for communication with health care providers. *Traffic Injury Prevention*, *17*(4), 367–373.

Brenner, L. A., Homaifar, B. Y., & Schultheis, M. T. (2008). Driving, aging, and traumatic brain injury: Integrating findings from the literature. *Rehabilitation Psychology*, *53*(1), 18–27.

Brunero, S., Smith, J., Bates, E., & Fairbrother, G. (2008). Health professionals' attitudes towards suicide prevention initiatives. *Journal of Psychiatric and Mental Health Nursing*, *15*(7), 588–594.

Cameron, D. H., Sarracini, C. Z., Rozmovits, L., Naglie, G., Herrmann, N., Molnar, F., ... Rapoport, M. (2017). Development of a decision-making tool for reporting drivers with mild dementia and mild cognitive impairment to transportation administrators. *International Psychogeriatrics*, *29*(9), 1551–1563.

Carr, D. B., & O'Neill, D. (2015). Mobility and safety issues in drivers with dementia. *International Psychogeriatrics*, *27*(10), 1613–1622.

Carr, D. B., & Ott, B. R. (2010). The older adult driver with cognitive impairment: "It's a very frustrating life.". *Journal of the American Medical Association*, *303*(16), 1632 1641.

Carr, D. B., Schwartzberg, J. G., Manning, L., & Sempek, J. (2010). *Physician's guide to assessing and counseling older drivers* (*2nd ed.*). Washington, DC: NHTSA.

Carter, K., Monaghan, S., O'Brien, J., Teodorczuk, A., Mosimann, U., & Taylor, J. P. (2014). Driving and dementia: A clinical decision pathway. *International Journal of Geriatric Psychiatry*, *30*(2), 210–216.

Casey, C. M., Salinas, K., & Eckstrom, E. (2015). Electronic health record tools to care for at-risk older drivers: A quality improvement project. *The Gerontologist*, *55*(Suppl_1), S128–S139.

Charlton, J.L., Koppel, S., Odell, M., Devlin, A., Langford, J., O'Hare, M., ... & Scully, M. (2010). *Influence of chronic illness on crash involvement of motor vehicle drivers.* 2nd ed. Report no. 300. Clayton, Australia: Monash University Accident Research Centre.

Classen, S., Alvarez, L., Ferreira, P. J. M., Chen, C. H., Meyer, C. K., & Nywening, A. G. (2016). Developing a Canadian-specific version of the Fitness-to-Drive Screening Measure©. *OTJR: Occupation, Participation and Health*, *36*(2), 82–91.

Dattoma, L. L. (2017). Evaluation of the older driver. *Primary Care: Clinics in Office Practice*, *44*(3), 457–467.

Devlin, A. L., Odell, M., Charlton, J. L., & Koppel, S. (2012). Epilepsy and driving: Current status of research. *Epilepsy Research*, *102*(3), 135–152.

Dickerson, A. E. (2013a). Driving assessment tools used by driver rehabilitation specialists: Survey of use and implications for practice. *The American Journal of Occupational Therapy*, *67*(5), 564–573.

Dickerson, A. E. (2013b). Driving with dementia: Evaluation, referral, and resources. *Occupational Therapy in Health Care*, *28*(1), 62–76.

Dickerson, A. E., Meuel, D. B., Ridenour, C. D., & Cooper, K. (2014). Assessment tools predicting fitness to drive in older adults: A systematic review. *The American Journal of Occupational Therapy*, *68*(6), 670–680.

Dobbs, B.M. (2005). *Medical conditions and driving: A review of the scientific literature (1960–2000).* Report no. DOT HS 809 690. Washington, DC: National Highway Traffic Safety Administration.

Dow, J. (2009). Commentary: Evaluation of driver fitness—The role of continuing medical education. *Traffic Injury Prevention*, *10*(4), 309–311.

Dow, J., & Jacques, A. (2012). Educating doctors on evaluation of fitness to drive: Impact of a case-based workshop. *Journal of Continuing Education in the Health Professions*, *32* (1), 68–73.

Dugan, E., Barton, K. N., Coyle, C., & Lee, C. M. (2013). U.S. policies to enhance older driver safety: A systematic review of the literature. *Journal of Aging & Social Policy*, *25*(4), 335–352.

Eby, D. W., & Molnar, L. J. (2009). Older adult safety and mobility: Issues and research needs. *Public Works Management & Policy*, *13*(4), 288–300.

Eby, D.W., Trombley, D., Molnar, L.J., & Shope, J.T. (1998). *The assessment of older driver's capabilities: A review of the literature*. Report no. UMTRI-98-24. Ann Arbor, MI: University of Michigan Transportation Research Institute.

Eby, D. W., Molnar, L. J., & Kartje, P. S. (2009). *Maintaining safe mobility in an aging society*. New York, NY: CRC Press.

Fender, T., Wilber, S. T., Stiffler, K. A., & Blanda, M. (2007). Use of ADReS screening tool in an ED population of older drivers. *Annals of Emergency Medicine*, *50*, S94.

Ferreira, I. S., Simões, M. R., & Marôco, J. (2013). Cognitive and psychomotor tests as predictors of on-road driving ability in older primary care patients. *Transportation Research Part F: Traffic Psychology and Behaviour*, *21*, 146–158.

Goodwin, A., Kirley, B., Sandt, L., Hall, W., Thomas, L., O'Brien, N., & Summerlin, D. (2013). *Countermeasures that work: A highway safety countermeasure guide for state highway safety offices*. 7th ed. Report no. DOT HS 811 727. Washington, DC: National Highway Traffic Safety Administration.

Hill, L., Rajasekar, G., & Parsons, S. (2018). Physician reporting requirements in the US. In *Presented at the transportation research board 97th annual meeting*. Washington, DC: Transportation Research Board.

Hill, L. L., Rybar, J., & Styer, T. (2012). Evaluation of curriculum to improve health professionals' ability to manage age-related driving impairments. *Accident Analysis & Prevention*, *61*, 222–232.

Huseth-Zosel, A. L., Sanders, G., & O'Connor, M. (2016). Predictors of health care provider anticipatory guidance provision for older drivers. *Traffic Injury Prevention*, *17*(8), 815–820.

Huseth-Zosel, A. L., Sanders, G., O'Connor, M., Fuller-Iglesias, H., & Langley, L. (2016). Health care provider mobility counseling provision to older adults: A rural/urban comparison. *Journal of Community Health: The Publication for Health Promotion and Disease Prevention*, *41*(1), 1–10.

Jang, R. W., Man-Son-Hing, M., Molnar, F. J., Hogan, D. B., Marshall, S. C., Auger, J., ... Naglie, G. (2007). Family physicians' attitudes and practices regarding assessments of medical fitness to drive in older persons. *Journal of General Internal Medicine*, *22*, 531–543.

Kemper, A. R., Uren, R. L., Moseley, K. L., & Clark, S. J. (2006). Primary care physicians' attitudes regarding follow-up care for children with positive newborn screening results. *Pediatrics*, *118*(5), 1836–1841.

Korner-Bitensky, N., Gelinas, I., Man-Son-Hing, M., & Marshall, S. (2005). Recommendations of the Canadian Consensus Conference on driving evaluation in older drivers. *Physical and Occupational Therapy in Geriatrics*, *23*(2–3), 123–144.

Korner-Bitensky, N., Bitensky, J., Sofer, S., Man-Son-Hing, M., & Gelinas, I. (2006). Driving evaluation practices of clinicians working in the United States and Canada. *The American Journal of Occupational Therapy*, *60*, 428–434.

Korner-Bitensky, N., Menon, A., von Zweck, C., & Van Benthem, K. (2010). Occupational therapists' capacity-building needs related to older driver screening, assessment, and intervention: A Canadawide survey. *The American Journal of Occupational Therapy*, *64* (2), 316–324.

Lee, L., & Molnar, F. (2017). Driving and dementia: Efficient approach to driving safety concerns in family practice. *Canadian Family Physician*, *63*(1), 27–31.

Manning, K. J., & Schultheis, M. T. (2013). *Driving evaluation in older adults. Handbook on the neuropsychology of aging and dementia* (pp. 135–152). New York, NY: Springer.

Marshall, S., Demmings, E. M., Woolnough, A., Salim, D., & Man-Son-Hing, M. (2012). Determining fitness to drive in older persons: A survey of medical and surgical specialists. *Canadian Geriatrics Journal, 15*, 101.

Marshall, S. C., & Gilbert, N. (1999). Saskatchewan physicians' attitudes and knowledge regarding assessment of medical fitness to drive. *Canadian Medical Association Journal, 160*, 1701–1704.

Marshall, S. C., & Man-Son-Hing, M. (2011). Multiple chronic medical conditions and associated driving risk: A systematic review. *Traffic Injury Prevention, 12*(2), 142–148.

McCarthy, D., & Mann, W. (2006). Sensitivity and specificity of the assessment of driving-related skills older driver screening tool. *Topics in Geriatric Rehabilitation, 22*, 138–152.

Meuser, T. M., Carr, D. B., Berg-Weger, M., Niewoehner, P., & Morris, J. C. (2006). Driving and dementia in older adults: Implementation and evaluation of a continuing education project. *The Gerontologist, 46*(5), 680–687.

Meuser, T. M., Carr, D. B., & Ulfarsson, G. F. (2009). Motor-vehicle crash history and licensing outcomes for older drivers reported as medically impaired in Missouri. *Accident Analysis & Prevention, 41*, 246–252.

Meuser, T. M., Carr, D. B., Irmiter, C., Schwartzberg, J. G., & Ulfarsson, G. F. (2010). The American Medical Association older driver curriculum for health professionals: Changes in trainee confidence, attitudes, and practice behavior. *Gerontology & Geriatrics Education, 31*(4), 290–309.

Meuser, T. M., Berg-Weger, M., Chibnall, J. T., Harmon, A. C., & Stowe, J. D. (2011). Assessment of readiness for mobility transition (ARMT): A tool for mobility transition counseling with older adults. *Journal of Applied Gerontology, 32*, 484–507.

Meuser, T. M., Berg-Weger, M., Niewoehner, P. M., Harmon, A. C., Kuenzie, J. C., Carr, D. B., & Barco, P. P. (2012). Physician input and licensing of at-risk drivers: A review of all-inclusive medical evaluation forms in the US and Canada. *Accident Analysis & Prevention, 46*, 8–17.

Meuser, T. M., Berg-Weger, M., Carr, D. B., Shi, S., & Stewart, D. (2016). Clinician effectiveness in assessing fitness to drive of medically at-risk older adults. *Journal of the American Geriatrics Society, 64*(4), 849–854.

Molnar, F. J., Byszewski, A. M., Marshall, S. C., & Man-Son-Hing, M. (2005). In-office evaluation of medical fitness to drive: Practical approaches for assessing older people. *Canadian Family Physician, 51*, 372–379.

Posse, C., McCarthy, D. P., & Mann, W. C. (2006). A pilot study of interrater reliability of the Assessment of Driving-Related Skills: Older driver screening tool. *Topics in Geriatric Rehabilitation, 22*, 113–120.

Rapoport, M. J., Naglie, G., Herrmann, N., Sarracini, C. Z., Mulsant, B. H., Frank, C., … Molnar, F. (2014). Developing physician consensus on the reporting of patients with mild cognitive impairment and mild dementia to transportation authorities in a region with mandatory reporting legislation. *The American Journal of Geriatric Psychiatry, 22* (12), 1530–1543.

Ross, R. J., Scialfa, C., & Cordazzo, S. T. D. (2015). Predicting on-road driving performance and safety in cognitively impaired older adults. *Journal of the American Geriatrics Society, 63*(11), 2365–2369.

Selway, J. S. (2018). To drive or not to drive: When there is dementia. *The Journal for Nurse Practitioners, 14*(3), 202–209.e1.

Sims, J., Rouse-Watson, S., Schattner, P., Beveridge, A., & Jones, K. (2012). To drive or not to drive: Assessment dilemmas for GPs. *International Journal of Family Medicine, 2012*, 417512.

Vrkljan, B. H., Myers, A. M., Crizzle, A. M., Blanchard, R. A., & Marshall, S. C. (2013). Evaluating medically at-risk drivers: A survey of assessment practices in Canada. *Canadian Journal of Occupational Therapy, 80*(5), 295–303.

Wang, C. C., & Carr, D. B. (2004). Older driver safety: A report from the older drivers project. *Journal of American Geriatrics Society, 52*, 143–149.

Weiss, J. C., O'Neil, J., Shope, J. T., O'Connor, K. G., & Levin, R. A. (2012). Paediatrician knowledge, attitudes, and counselling patterns on teen driving. *Injury Prevention, 18*(1), 10–15.

Winston, G. P., & Jaiser, S. R. (2012). Western driving regulations for unprovoked first seizures and epilepsy. *Seizure, 21*(5), 371–376.

Woolnough, A., Salim, D., Marshall, S. C., Weegar, K., Porter, M. M., Rapoport, M. J., ... Vrkljan, B. (2013). Determining the validity of the AMA guide: A historical cohort analysis of the Assessment of Driving Related Skills and crash rate among older drivers. *Accident Analysis & Prevention, 61*, 311–316.

# Licensing agencies

# 8

*I made my own assessment of my life, and I began to live it. That was freedom.*
*Fernando Flores*

## Introduction

Licensing agencies play a pivotal role in setting appropriate standards for responsible driving and riding and in maintaining a safe environment for all road users. The responsibility for issuing, renewing, suspending, refusing, canceling, or reinstating a person's driver's license rests in the hands of the licensing agency (Austroads, 2017). In addition, the licensing agency is responsible for identifying, assessing, and rendering licensing decisions on medically or functionally at-risk drivers (Lococo, Stutts, Sifrit, & Staplin, 2017).

Licensing agencies are well positioned to identify at-risk drivers during the license renewal process. As the aging driver population grows, there is a higher probability of both physical and cognitive issues affecting capabilities needed for safe driving. However, as discussed in other chapters, driving cessation is associated with many negative health outcomes. Indeed, the loss of the privilege to drive has been described as a "major stressful life event" (Davey, 2007, p. 54) which can have detrimental effects on an older adult. For many older adults, the ability to drive allows them to maintain a sense of autonomy and provides freedom to travel to the places they want to go. As licensing decisions are made for older drivers, it is important to understand this important connection between a driver's license and an older adult's sense of independence. In this respect, licensing agencies have the difficult task of balancing the mandate to protect public safety with the objective of allowing older drivers to continue to drive as long as they can safely do so. However, as this chapter will show, the ability to detect at-risk or impaired older drivers is not an easy task due to the variability both within individuals in the older driver population as well as within the policies and procedures in effect at licensing agencies in different jurisdictions.

This chapter focuses on current licensing policies for older drivers in the United States (US) and abroad and discusses research regarding the effectiveness of such policies. It also includes discussion of the different types of assessments older drivers are required to undergo for licensure, and the various ways in which an older driver can be referred to the licensing agency for reexamination if there is concern regarding their ability to operate a motor vehicle safely.

**Perspectives and Strategies for Promoting Safe Transportation among Older Adults.**
**DOI: https://doi.org/10.1016/B978-0-12-812153-5.00008-X**

## Policies

In many countries, including the US, driver licensing is regulated at the state level. In others, it is controlled at either the federal or the local level. Licensing policies vary widely depending on the jurisdiction in which an older driver resides. While some jurisdictions have no additional requirements for older drivers to maintain their license relative to the general driving population, others have age-based laws that go into effect as a driver ages. Age-based mandatory testing of older drivers is a policy that requires older drivers to undergo additional testing measures, such as medical examinations or on-road assessments, in order to maintain their license upon reaching a certain age. In addition, older drivers are often subject to shortened license renewal cycles as well as the requirement to renew their license in-person, rather than by mail or online as may be available to the general population. Accelerated renewal is intended to provide the licensing authority more opportunities to detect major functional declines, and the rationale of in-person renewal is that those who are too impaired to go to the licensing agency to renew the license are too impaired to continue to drive (Dugan, Barton, Coyle, & Lee, 2013).

Screening policies based on chronological age are used extensively in the US, Japan, Australia, and Europe [see, e.g., AAA Foundation for Traffic Safety (AAAFTS), 2016; Ichikawa, Nakahara, & Inada, 2015; Langford, Fitzharris, Koppel, & Newstead, 2004; White & O'Neill, 2000]. The age at which these laws commence differs. For example, in Maine, the renewal cycle decreases from 6 to 4 years at 62 years. Comparatively, in Texas, the renewal cycle decreases from 6 to 2 years at 85 years [Insurance Institute for Highway Safety (IIHS), 2018]. In New South Wales, Australia, at 75 years of age, all drivers are required to have a vision test and a medical examination each year, and at age 85, drivers are also required to pass an on-road assessment every second year (Austroads, 2017). In the Northern Territory, Australia, a medical assessment and road test are only required when the licensing authority is notified of a condition that may affect driving and when recommended by a health professional (Austroads, 2017).

As illustrated above, in populous countries such as the US and Australia, each state and/or territory can have differing laws governing the licensing process for older adults. Currently, 33 US states and the District of Columbia have various policies in place that specifically affect older drivers (Governors Highway Safety Association, 2017). Licensing agencies also have the authority to impose measures beyond the standard procedure if there is concern over a person's fitness to drive [Insurance Institute for Highway Safety (IIHS), 2018]. These can include physical or cognitive exams, or requiring the person to retake vision, written, or road tests. There may also be restrictions placed on an individual's license, such as limiting the time of day or geographic area in which he or she can legally drive. Additional restrictions include requiring the driver to wear corrective lenses or hearing aids, as well as installing aftermarket equipment on the vehicle such as supplementary external mirrors (Lococo et al., 2017).

European countries employ a wide range of licensing policies (see, e.g., Siren et al., 2013; Siren & Haustein, 2015). For example, countries such as Germany and France issue unlimited licenses; that is, individuals do not ever need to renew their license and are not required to undergo additional assessments to determine fitness to drive. Other countries have accelerated renewal periods, as well as physical and cognitive assessments and medical statements required from a general practitioner for license renewal. The age at which these laws take effect ranges from 50 years in Italy to the age of 70 years in many other countries (Siren & Haustein, 2015).

In the past decade, Japan has introduced new age-based licensing laws targeted at older drivers. Current licensing policy in Japan requires drivers age 70 or older to attend a driving lesson, consisting of a 30-minute lecture, a 1-hour driver aptitude test which includes a driving simulator task and vision test, a 1-hour on-road driving assessment, and a 30-minute discussion section as part of the license renewal process (Ichikawa et al., 2015). In addition, all drivers age 75 or older must complete a cognitive impairment screening test prior to the driving lesson (National Police Agency, 2018). If the screening test indicates an issue with cognition, the older adult can renew his or her license only if he or she has not been ticketed for a traffic violation in the previous year. Those who have been ticketed must undergo an examination by a physician specializing in dementia. If the doctor diagnoses the older adult with dementia, his or her license is revoked (Ichikawa et al., 2015). Older drivers in Japan are also required by law to display signs at the front and rear of their vehicles indicating to others that they are older drivers (Kosuge, Okamura, Kihira, Nakano, & Fujita, 2017).

The following section discusses the breadth of research on the effectiveness of age-based licensing policies and whether the additional requirements are providing the intended outcome of lowering crashes, injuries, and fatalities among older drivers.

## Effectiveness of age-based mandatory licensing assessments

Age-based licensing assessments are controversial because of the wide recognition that it is not chronological age itself that affects safe driving, but rather the decline in abilities needed for safe driving that older adults experience as they age. Researchers around the world have examined the effectiveness of age-based licensing assessments for older adults for more than two decades. In the mid-1990s, Hakamies-Blomqvist, Johansson, and Lundberg (1996) compared crash rates in Sweden, where there is no age-based mandatory licensing assessments, and Finland, where drivers age 70 or older have to undergo a medical review of their general health and vision to renew their license. In addition, Finnish older drivers must present a document signed by two people declaring that they drive regularly, and after the age of 80, license renewal periods are usually shortened to less than 5 years. Rates of crashes and fatalities were analyzed, and the results did not show any safety benefits resulting from the more stringent Finnish licensing policies. In fact, Finland had a higher pedestrian fatality rate for those age 70 or older. The authors argued that a modal shift from driver to vulnerable road user (pedestrian, cyclist, and moped rider) had occurred, and the licensing policy indirectly caused an increase in the number of fatalities among these road users.

A study by Mitchell (2008) compared licensing renewal practices in seven countries across Europe, including France, the Netherlands, the United Kingdom, Denmark, Finland, Norway, and Sweden. The countries were compared on car ownership, overall road safety, license holding statistics, and fatality rates for middle-aged drivers, older drivers, and pedestrians. Results showed that the countries with the least stringent licensing procedures (France, the United Kingdom, the Netherlands, and Sweden) had the lowest fatality rates for drivers age 65 or older. Mitchell concluded that there was no evidence that any license renewal procedure or requirement for medical assessment had any effect on the overall road safety of people age 65 or older.

A recent study in Denmark compared the number of fatalities before and after the implementation of an age-based screening program for cognitive impairment for older drivers (Siren & Meng, 2012). The number of fatalities and per capita crash rates were analyzed for drivers age 18–69 and 70 years or older from 2002 to 2008, with implementation of the cognitive screening occurring in 2006. Results showed no significant difference in the number of drivers age 70 or older involved in fatal crashes in the periods before and after the cognitive screening program was implemented. In addition, there was a statistically significant increase in the rate of older people killed as unprotected road users, reflecting the findings of Hakamies-Blomqvist et al. (1996) nearly 20 years prior.

Siren and Haustein (2015) conducted a systematic review of evaluation studies to examine evidence for and against age-based driver screening policies. The authors then reviewed age-based driver screening policies throughout 27 countries in the European Union (EU) to explore the extent to which the European policies are evidence-based and the implications of the policies. Based on the studies in the literature review, many of which are also reviewed in this section, there were no positive safety effects of age-based licensing policies, and some policies may actually lead to negative safety outcomes for older adults. Thus, the authors concluded that policymaking in this area is not evidence based and recommended shifting the focus of current licensing policies and practices to one in which the main goal is to prolong an older adults' safe driving career rather than limiting mobility.

Several studies in the US have examined crash rates in different states with different age-based licensing policies. The following three studies employed different methods of study design and data analysis techniques but reached similar conclusions. Using data from the Fatality Analysis Reporting System from 1990 to 2000, Grabowski, Campbell, and Morrisey (2004) examined the effectiveness of state laws requiring in-person license renewal, vision tests, road tests, and frequency of license renewal on the fatality rate of older drivers. They found that states with in-person license renewal policies were associated with a lower driver fatality rate for those age 85 or older. However, vision tests, on-road tests, more frequent renewal periods, and in-person renewal policies for those age 65–84 were not associated with a lower fatality rate.

A more recent study by Tefft (2014) analyzed fatal crash involvement rates of drivers age 55 or older and licensing policies in 46 US states. A mandatory in-person license renewal policy, as well as a policy requiring drivers to pass a vision test when in-person renewal was not required, were both associated with an approximate 31% reduction in the fatal crash involvement rates of drivers age 85 or older. More frequent license renewal and mandatory reporting by health-care providers were not associated with statistically significant reductions in fatal crash involvement rates of older drivers. In addition, no policy examined had a significant impact on fatal crash involvement of drivers younger than 85 years, echoing the results of Grabowski et al. (2004).

Bell, Qiao, and Zarzaur (2015) conducted a cross-sectional study of older driver licensing policy to examine the impact of policy on fatal crash rates among adults age 65 or older in the US. The authors conducted a statistical analysis modeling motor vehicle fatality rates for the population over age 65 as a function of state transportation policies and demographic, health system, population health, and travel and climate characteristics. While lower fatality rates were significantly associated with higher average temperature, higher gas prices and a greater number of emergency medicine physicians to population size, no individual component (shortened renewal period, in-person renewal, or vision testing) of older driver licensing policy was significantly associated with lower fatal crash rates. In fact, the authors found that those states with age-based licensing laws were associated with higher motor vehicle fatality rates for the population of adults age 65 or older.

Several studies in Australia have also investigated the effectiveness of age-based licensing policies for reducing older driver crash rates and fatalities (Langford, Bohensky, Koppel, & Newstead, 2008; Langford, Fitzharris, Koppel, et al., 2004; Langford, Fitzharris, Newstead, & Koppel, 2004; Torpey, 1986). Collectively, these studies did not find any safety benefits of age-based licensing policies. For example, Langford, Fitzharris, Koppel, et al. (2004) examined whether different licensing policies were associated with different fatality rates in New South Wales, a state with mandatory age-based assessment, and Victoria, a state with no age-based testing requirements. The authors found no statistically significant difference in the overall fatality rates of drivers age 80 or older. In fact, when fatality rates were considered relative to the population of those age 80 or older, Victorian drivers had a lower overall fatality rate.

Researchers in Japan also explored the effects of age-based policies. A study by Ichikawa et al. (2015) examined the effectiveness of the mandated driving lesson for drivers age 70 or older described in the previous section. Trends in at-fault motor vehicle crash rate ratios for drivers age 65 or older were analyzed from 1986 to 2011. Results showed no downward trend in crash rate ratios of drivers age 70 or older relative to drivers age 65–69 following introduction of the mandated lesson.

Overall, results from countries throughout the world suggest that age-based licensing policies are ineffective in reducing crash risk and fatality rates of older drivers age 65–84 years. While there is evidence that policies can be effective for drivers age 85 or older, age-based licensing policies generally start approximately 10–15 years before an older adult reaches this age.

## Referrals

As discussed in Chapter 7, Physicians and Other Health Professionals, physicians or other health professionals, such as occupational and physical therapists, may report an older driver to a licensing authority if there is concern regarding the driving safety of the older adult. Chapter 9, Law Enforcement, discusses the role that law enforcement has in referring older drivers to the licensing authority if a driver appears to have functional declines that affect driving safety. The licensing authority can also act on unsolicited reports from family, friends, or other citizens regarding an older person's fitness to drive. The specific individuals allowed to refer an older adult to the licensing agency, as well as the process of reporting, vary by jurisdiction. Most states and provinces in the US and Canada accept the reports of medically at-risk drivers from family members of the older driver, and to a lesser extent friends and acquaintances of the older driver. Very few states or provinces accept anonymous reports. In addition, very few states provide absolute confidentiality for the person providing the report. While most states protect the identity of the referring individual to the fullest extent of the law, the majority of states and provinces allow the report to be used as evidence if necessary, and in many states, the referred driver can request a copy of the referral (AAAFTS, 2016).

In nearly half of the states in the US, standardized forms are available from respective State Departments of Motor Vehicles that members of the public can fill out to refer a potentially unsafe older driver to the licensing authority. Other states also accept letters (AAAFTS, 2016). Referrals for reexamination generally ask the person requesting reexamination for several details about the older driver, including the driver's full name, date of birth, address, driver license number, license plate number, and telephone number. A blank section is provided for the concerned person to explain why the request for an evaluation is being made, with most forms requesting as much detailed information as possible related to an incident or health condition about the driver that would indicate the inability to safely operate a vehicle. The person making the request is also required to provide full contact information as well as a signature certifying that the information provided is true (see, e.g., Michigan Department of State, 2014).

In addition to referrals from those mentioned above, automatic referrals are also generated based on the information collected in the licensing agency's database. For example, in Michigan, there are four reasons for which a driver may automatically be referred to the licensing agency for reexamination: involvement in a fatal crash; involvement in three or more negligent crashes within 24 months; accrual of 12 or more demerit points, which are points placed on a driver's license due to committing various traffic violations such as speeding or reckless driving, within 24 months; or a conviction for violating restrictions, terms, or conditions of the driver's license (State of Michigan, 2018).

The reexamination process varies by jurisdiction but most commonly has five steps (see, e.g., State of Michigan, 2018):

1. Referral to the licensing agency: The licensing agency is notified in writing of a driver who could pose a risk to himself or herself or the public.

2. Internal review of the referral to assess its validity: Licensing agency staff review the submitted information and determine if the referral appropriately justifies a reexamination of the driver. If the referral is deemed legitimate, the process continues. However, if there is no substantial evidence to move the reexamination forward, no further action is taken.
3. Driver scheduled for reexamination: A letter is mailed to the driver informing them of the reexamination. They are given a date, time, and place to appear for the reexamination.
4. Reexamination of the driver is conducted: All circumstances for the case are reviewed, including relevant medical documentation, driver history and crash records, and information received from the referral. Based on the jurisdiction's policies, a driver is liable to be subject to one or more of the following tests to maintain licensure: visual acuity, knowledge, cognitive assessments, and on-road driving evaluations. The licensing agency may also ask questions of the driver to gather more information about the nature of his or her specific situation.
5. Decision is made and licensing action is issued: Following the licensing agency's reexamination of the older driver, one of following several actions may occur.
   a. No action: The driver can continue driving with no additional intervention from the licensing agency.
   b. Medical probation: The driver maintains licensure but his or her medical condition is monitored by the licensing agency. The driver is required to authorize their physician to complete a medical evaluation form and submit it to the licensing agency on a prescribed basis.
   c. Limited-term license: The period of time between license expiration dates is shortened.
   d. Calendar reexamination: The driver must be reexamined regularly. This is usually the result of a progressive medical condition.
   e. Restriction: The driver remains licensed but is legally obligated to follow the restrictions placed on the license.
   f. Suspension: The license is placed on hold until a further action takes place, such as passing a vision test. The driver cannot legally drive during this time.
   g. Revocation: The license is terminated and the driver can no longer drive legally.

The length of a suspension or revocation is indefinite, but drivers who can provide evidence that they are fit to drive will be considered for licensure reinstatement. Following a reexamination, drivers have the right to a hearing and subsequent appeal if they disagree with the licensing decision.

Several states in the US have a Medical Advisory Board (MAB) that is responsible for reviewing cases of individuals referred to the licensing agency due to concerns over fitness to drive. For example, the MAB in Maryland is comprised of physicians with varied backgrounds who review cases of individuals with medical conditions that can impact safe driving. The MAB makes recommendations regarding the cases and advises the Maryland Motor Vehicle Administration on medical review processes but does not make the final decision on licensure (Soderstrom & Joyce, 2008).

## Screening and assessment

Similar to licensing policies, jurisdictions vary in the type of testing older adults must pass to maintain a driver's license, either upon a regularly scheduled renewal or if they have been referred to the licensing authority for reexamination. Tests of visual acuity, cognitive functioning, physical performance, knowledge, sign recognition, and driving competence have been implemented in various forms throughout the world. This section outlines the different methods of screening and assessment for older adults, as well as the threshold a driver must meet to maintain a license.

## *Vision screening and standards*

All US states and the District of Columbia, Canada, Australia, and countries in the EU require visual acuity testing for licensure (Carr, Schwartzberg, Manning, & Sempek, 2010; Owsley & McGwin, 2010). Drivers' visual acuity is assessed upon original licensure, and in many jurisdictions, upon license renewal. Throughout the US and Canada, visual acuity and visual field are commonly tested at the licensing agency; however, some jurisdictions allow the driver to submit a vision report from a vision specialist (AAAFTS, 2016). Visual acuity and visual field requirements vary but are usually 20/40 with both eyes for a nonrestricted license and a horizontal temporal field of at least 110 degrees from center, respectively (AAAFTS, 2016; Lococo et al., 2017). The use of corrective lenses is allowed and is then noted as a restriction on the license. Based on the outcome of the vision testing, there are several options: restrictions, such as daylight driving only, can be added to the license; the driver can be referred to a vision specialist such as a licensed optometrist or ophthalmologist for further testing; a temporary license may be issued for a period of 30 days to allow for further vision testing; an on-road driving assessment may be scheduled to determine if the driver can compensate for the visual deficit; or the license can be revoked.

## *Cognitive screening*

The likelihood of developing a form of cognitive impairment increases as one ages. As such, licensing agencies have an interest in monitoring older drivers for any cognitive decline that may pose a risk to safe driving. The following are two examples of cognitive screening tests that have been implemented to identify an older driver with a cognitive deficit that could affect driving. As previously mentioned, licensing policy in Japan requires older drivers to pass a cognitive screening test for dementia. This screening consists of the following: identifying the date, including year, month, day, day of the week, and time; a cued recall activity in which the older driver is asked to describe 16 objects they were shown; and drawing a clock. The total score on these activities places each older driver into one of three categories: cognitive function is not impaired, cognitive function is slightly impaired, or cognitive function is impaired (National Police Agency, 2018).

Maryland conducts a functional capacity test on drivers who have come to the attention of the MAB or the Division of Driver Wellness and Safety (Maryland Department of Transportation, 2018). Three of the five tests administered measure an aspect of cognitive functioning: the Motor Free Visual Perception Test, Trail Making B, and Cued Recall. Although licensing decisions are not based solely on their performance on these tests, poor results may trigger an on-road driving evaluation.

## Medical assessment by a physician or health professional

As discussed in Chapter 7, Physicians and Other Health Professionals, in some jurisdictions, medical assessments by a health professional are required as a condition of renewing a driver's license. For example, in Western Australia, drivers age 80 or older must have a *Medical Assessment Certificate: Senior driver's license renewal declaration* form filled out annually by a health professional who assesses their fitness to drive. The form allows the health professional to document the older driver's visual acuity, blood pressure, and any other medical conditions or clinical findings that may affect the ability for the older adult to operate a motor vehicle safely. There is also space to indicate that the older driver: meets the relevant medical criteria and is fit to drive; does not meet the relevant medical criteria and is not fit to drive; or is suitable to drive subject to certain conditions (Government of Western Australia Department of Transport, 2016). Several other jurisdictions around the world have standardized forms that must be filled out by a physician stating the older driver is medically fit to drive. The form must be returned to the licensing agency, which then reviews the form and makes a licensing decision based on the physician's assessment.

## On-road driving assessment

An on-road driving evaluation for older drivers has been used as an additional performance measure to assess fitness to drive. Jurisdictions vary on the rules regarding whether the driver can use his or her own vehicle for the test. In general, if the vehicle is in good condition and meets basic safety standards (e.g., the vehicle must be registered and insured, have no warning lights showing, no tire damage, and proper seat belts), it is allowed to be used for testing. A testing vehicle can sometimes be provided if the driver's own vehicle is not suitable. The route is generally predetermined by the licensing agency.

In many US states and other countries, a physician informs the licensing agency of this request based on medical concerns regarding fitness to drive. For example, in New Zealand, drivers age 75 or older must complete an on-road driving assessment if requested by their general practitioner (Keall & Woodbury, 2014). This assessment lasts approximately 20 minutes, during which the older drivers' ability to detect traffic hazards, control the vehicle, and follow the rules of the road are assessed.

In California, an on-road driving test is conducted if drivers did not meet the minimum vision requirements or if they were referred for reexamination due to a physical or medical condition. One purpose of this driving test is to ensure the driver can compensate for any physical condition that might affect driving ability, such as poor vision, loss of a limb, or early stage dementia (State of California Department of Motor Vehicles, 2018). While most jurisdictions have a set route that is used when performing on-road driving tests, the Department of Motor Vehicles in California allows the older driver the option to work with the examiner to create a predetermined driving test route. If the older driver passes using this route, the license will be restricted to driving in that area.

### Written tests

Another method of assessing a driver is through written tests regarding the older driver's knowledge of traffic laws, rules, and regulations specific to the jurisdiction in which the older driver resides. A traffic sign recognition test is often incorporated into the knowledge tests and assesses the driver's knowledge of regulatory, warning, and information signs that are commonly seen while driving. Issues with older adults' understanding and recognition of signs and other traffic control devices can be found in Chapter 13, Roadway Design and Infrastructure.

### Self-reporting of medical conditions

In some jurisdictions, older drivers are legally obligated to disclose to the licensing agency certain medical conditions that may affect driving, such as a diagnosis of dementia. There are certain medical conditions that affect licensure which are not limited to older adults; however, the prevalence of such conditions is much higher in older adults than the general population. Examples of these conditions include syncope, dementia, Parkinson's disease, and significant visual impairment, such as glaucoma, cataracts, or macular degeneration.

Dugan et al. (2013) reported that a lack of awareness of self-report requirements and poor compliance when the driver is aware, limits the impact of this policy. However, there are repercussions for noncompliance of these laws. Licensing agencies in Australia caution that drivers who do not report a condition likely to affect safe driving adversely may suffer long-term financial, insurance, and legal consequences (Austroads, 2017). For example, in Queensland, Australia, drivers are required to notify the licensing agency immediately if they are diagnosed with a condition that may affect driving. If it is discovered that a driver fails to report the condition, he or she may be fined A$6000 and have his or her license revoked (Queensland Government Department of Transport and Main Roads, 2013).

## Resources provided by licensing agencies

Some licensing agencies in the US have recognized the need to focus on the burgeoning older driver population and have created departments with a specialized interest in addressing issues related to older drivers. For example, in California, there is a Senior Driver Ombudsman Section of the Department of Motor Vehicles. This section represents the interests of public safety for all California residents with a special interest in addressing issues related to older drivers (State of California

Department of Motor Vehicles, 2017). The ombudsmen work to ensure older drivers are treated fairly and consistently with respect to laws and regulations. They are available to assist individuals and also participate in outreach seminars to a variety of audiences to promote driver safety in California, with an emphasis on older driver issues.

A recommendation resulting from the North American License Policies Workshop (Eby & Molnar, 2008) was that in addition to making decisions regarding licensure, licensing agencies should also provide older adults with information regarding their driving as well as planning for the transition to non-driving. Currently, many licensing agencies throughout the US and Australia provide resources for older drivers and their families to access from their websites (see, e.g., Pennsylvania Department of Transportation, 2018; VicRoads, 2018). Older drivers are provided with information, including rehabilitation facilities providing driver evaluation and training resources, driver refresher courses, safe driving tips, self-assessment tools to evaluate driving abilities, and alternative transportation services available in their area. Many of these resources are reviewed in Chapter 5, Older Adults, and Chapter 6, Family Members, Friends, and Other Informal Caregivers.

## Conclusions

Given the negative outcomes associated with driving cessation, including depression, social isolation, and other poor health outcomes (see, e.g., Edwards, Lunsman, Perkins, Rebok, & Roth, 2009; Fonda, Wallace, & Herzog, 2001; Marottoli et al., 2000; Ragland, Satariano, & MacLeod, 2005), it is important to try to balance public safety with the ability for an older adult to continue safely driving. While policies vary throughout the world, the literature is consistent regarding the limited effectiveness of age-based licensing policies, at least for those drivers under age 85. It is widely accepted among aging driver researchers that final decisions regarding licensure should be based on functional performance rather than age (Eby & Molnar, 2008). However, there is inconsistency between the current licensing policies and the research regarding the limited effectiveness of the policies in reducing crash rates and fatalities for older drivers.

Due to the increasing population of older drivers now and in the coming years, licensing policy will continue to be studied and critiqued. Based on the research to date, there are no license screening or assessments available that can accurately and effectively discriminate between safe and at-risk older drivers. Dobbs (2008) suggested that continuing to focus on older drivers in general rather than medically at-risk drivers will result in a costly, ineffective, and overburdened system. Limited resources and financial constraints relative to staffing and equipment in the licensing agency setting will not allow for more extensive testing to identify individuals who are unfit to drive (Soderstrom, 2008; Lococo et al., 2017), which further necessitates accurate and efficient methods of identifying at-risk older drivers.

For nearly 20 years, there has been international support for developing a more targeted approach to identifying older drivers that may pose a risk to themselves or other road users [Organization for Economic Cooperation Development (OECD), 2001]. Researchers across the world have highlighted the potential benefits of a multifaceted, integrated process for identifying and subsequently managing at-risk older drivers (see, e.g., Eby & Molnar, 2008; Fildes et al., 2008; Langford, Braitman, et al., 2008). Rather than relying solely on the licensing agency, the responsibility for identification of at-risk older drivers must be shared with physicians, other health professionals, law enforcement, and the community (Eby & Molnar, 2010; OECD, 2001). The development of valid, reliable, and easy to administer screening tools is critical to ensuring that only older drivers who pose a potential safety risk are referred to the licensing agency, or other organizations, for further assessment. Appropriate and accurate screening would obviate the presumed need for mandatory age-based assessment of all older drivers. Responsibility for assessing fitness to drive for those identified as at-risk should also be shared with a broad range of professionals trained in the area of older driver safety, such as Certified Driver Rehabilitation Specialists and Occupational Therapists. In-depth, individualized assessments for at-risk older drivers provides the basis for identifying reasons for functional deficits the older driver is experiencing, determining the extent to which these impairments affect safe driving, recommending licensing actions to the licensing agency, and identifying options for continued mobility (Eby & Molnar, 2008). Although final licensing decisions rest with the licensing agency, a more comprehensive approach to older driver screening and assessment will help to alleviate the burden placed on licensing agencies and help keep older adults safely mobile. Collaboration between researchers and practitioners to further refine licensing policy is necessary, as is continued research into developing valid and reliable tools to provide to individuals working within the broader system of older driver safety and mobility.

## References

AAA Foundation for Traffic Safety (AAAFTS). *Driver licensing policies and practices.* (2016). <http://lpp.seniordrivers.org/index.cfm?selection = licenserenewal1> Accessed April, 2018.

Austroads. (2017). *Assessing fitness to drive.* Report no. AP-G56-17. Sydney, NSW: Austroads Ltd.

Bell, T. M., Qiao, N., & Zarzaur, B. L. (2015). Mature driver laws and state predictors of motor vehicle crash fatality rates among the elderly: A cross-sectional ecological study. *Traffic Injury Prevention, 16*(7), 669–676.

Carr, D. B., Schwartzberg, J. G., Manning, L., & Sempek, J. (2010). *Physician's guide to assessing and counseling older drivers* (2nd ed.). Washington, DC: National Highway Traffic Safety Administration.

Davey, J. A. (2007). Older people and transport: Coping without a car. *Ageing and Society, 27*(1), 49–65.

Dobbs, B. M. (2008). Aging baby boomers—A blessing or challenge for driver licensing authorities. *Traffic Injury Prevention, 9*(4), 379–386.

Dugan, E., Barton, K. N., Coyle, C., & Lee, C. M. (2013). US policies to enhance older driver safety: A systematic review of the literature. *Journal of Aging & Social Policy, 25*(4), 335–352.

Eby, D. W., & Molnar, L. J. (2010). Driving fitness and cognitive impairment: Issues for physicians. *Journal of the American Medical Association, 303*(16), 1642–1643.

Eby, D. W., & Molnar, L. J. (2008). In D. W. Eby, & L. J. Molnar (Eds.), *Proceedings of the North American license policies workshop*. Washington, DC: AAA Foundation for Traffic Safety.

Edwards, J. D., Lunsman, M., Perkins, M., Rebok, G. W., & Roth, D. L. (2009). Driving cessation and health trajectories in older adults. *Journals of Gerontology Series A: Biomedical Sciences and Medical Sciences, 64*(12), 1290–1295.

Fildes, B. N., Charlton, J., Pronk, N., Langford, J., Oxley, J., & Koppel, S. (2008). An Australasian model license reassessment procedure for identifying potentially unsafe drivers. *Traffic Injury Prevention, 9*(4), 350–359.

Fonda, S. J., Wallace, R. B., & Herzog, A. R. (2001). Changes in driving patterns and worsening depressive symptoms among older adults. *The Journals of Gerontology Series B: Psychological Sciences and Social Sciences, 56*(6), S343–S351.

Government of Western Australia Department of Transport. *Medical assessment certificate: Senior driver's license renewal declaration.* (2016). <https://www.transport.wa.gov.au/mediaFiles/licensing/LBU_F_DL_M108A_MedicalSeniors.pdf> Accessed April, 2018.

Governors Highway Safety Association. *Mature drivers.* (2017). <https://www.ghsa.org/state-laws/issues/mature%20drivers> Accessed April, 2018.

Grabowski, D. C., Campbell, C. M., & Morrisey, M. A. (2004). Elderly licensure laws and motor vehicle fatalities. *Journal of the American Medical Association, 291*(23), 2840–2846.

Hakamies-Blomqvist, L. E., Johansson, K., & Lundberg, C. (1996). Medical screening of older drivers as a traffic safety measure—A comparative Finnish–Swedish evaluation study. *Journal of the American Geriatrics Society, 44*(6), 650–653.

Ichikawa, M., Nakahara, S., & Inada, H. (2015). Impact of mandating a driving lesson for older drivers at license renewal in Japan. *Accident Analysis & Prevention, 75*, 55–60.

Insurance Institute for Highway Safety (IIHS). *Older drivers.* (2018). <http://www.iihs.org/iihs/topics/laws/olderdrivers?topicName = older-drivers> Accessed April, 2018.

Keall, M. D., & Woodbury, E. (2014). An analysis of changes in mobility and safety of older drivers associated with a specific older driver on-road licensing test: A population study. *BMC Public Health, 14*, 165.

Kosuge, R., Okamura, K., Kihira, M., Nakano, Y., & Fujita, G. (2017). Predictors of driving outcomes including both crash involvement and driving cessation in a prospective study of Japanese older drivers. *Accident Analysis & Prevention, 106*, 131–140.

Langford, J., Bohensky, M., Koppel, S., & Newstead, S. (2008). Do older drivers pose a risk to other road users? *Traffic Injury Prevention, 9*(3), 181–189.

Langford, J., Braitman, K., Charlton, J., Eberhard, J., O'Neill, D., Staplin, L., & Stutts, J. (2008). TRB Workshop 2007: Licensing authorities' options for managing older driver safety—practical advice from the researchers. *Traffic Injury Prevention, 9*(4), 278–281.

Langford, J., Fitzharris, M., Koppel, S., & Newstead, S. (2004). Effectiveness of mandatory license testing for older drivers in reducing crash risk among urban older Australian drivers. *Traffic Injury Prevention, 5*(4), 326–335.

Langford, J., Fitzharris, M., Newstead, S., & Koppel, S. (2004). Some consequences of different older driver licensing procedures in Australia. *Accident Analysis & Prevention, 36*(6), 993–1001.

Lococo, K. H., Stutts, J., Sifrit, K. J., & Staplin, L. (2017). *Medical review practices for driver licensing, volume 3: Guidelines and processes in the United States.* Report no. DOT HS812 402. Washington, DC: National Highway Traffic Safety Administration.

Marottoli, R. A., de Leon, C. F. M., Glass, T. A., Williams, C. S., Cooney, L. M., Jr, & Berkman, L. F. (2000). Consequences of driving cessation: Decreased out-of-home activity levels. *The Journals of Gerontology Series B: Psychological Sciences and Social Sciences, 55*(6), S334–S340.

Maryland Department of Transportation. *What is a functional capacity test (FCT) Screening?* (2018). <http://www.mva.maryland.gov/safety/older/fct-screening.htm> Accessed April, 2018.

Michigan Department of State. *Request for driver evaluation.* (2014). <https://www.michigan.gov/documents/OC-88 16727_7.pdf> Accessed April, 2018.

Mitchell, C. G. B. (2008). The licensing of older drivers in Europe—A case study. *Traffic Injury Prevention, 9*(4), 360–366.

National Police Agency. *Cognitive impairment screening test for senior drivers.* (2018). <http://www.npa.go.jp/policies/application/license_renewal/ninti/index2.htm> Accessed April, 2018.

Organization for Economic Cooperation Development (OECD). (2001). *Aging and transport: Mobility needs and safety issues.* Paris, France: OECD.

Owsley, C., & McGwin, G., Jr. (2010). Vision and driving. *Vision Research, 50*(23), 2348–2361.

Pennsylvania Department of Transportation. *Driver resources.* (2018). <http://www.dmv.pa.gov/Information-Centers/Medical-Reporting/Pages/Driver-Resources.aspx> Accessed April, 2018.

Queensland Government Department of Transport and Main Roads. (2013). *Medical condition reporting: Jet's law.* Brisbane, QLD: Queensland Department of Transport and Main Roads.

Ragland, D. R., Satariano, W. A., & MacLeod, K. E. (2005). Driving cessation and increased depressive symptoms. *Journal of Gerontology: Medical Sciences, 60a*(3), 399–403.

Siren, A., & Haustein, S. (2015). Driving licences and medical screening in old age: Review of literature and European licensing policies. *Journal of Transport & Health, 2*(1), 68–78.

Siren, A., & Meng, A. (2012). Cognitive screening of older drivers does not produce safety benefits. *Accident Analysis & Prevention, 45*, 634–638.

Siren, A., Haustein, S., Meng, A., Bell, D., Pokriefke, E., Lang, B., ... Strnadova, Z. (2013). *Driver licensing regulation.* Report of the EU project CONSOL. <https://pdfs.semanticscholar.org/5cba/23811288f1c79d886373c6d6cd10d414c4f5.pdf> Accessed April, 2018.

Soderstrom, C. A. (2008). Applying research to licensing agency screening of seniors for fitness to drive. *Gerontology & Geriatrics Education, 29*(4), 310–325.

Soderstrom, C. A., & Joyce, J. J. (2008). Medical review of fitness to drive in older drivers: The Maryland experience. *Traffic Injury Prevention, 9*(4), 342–349.

State of California Department of Motor Vehicles. *DMV senior guide for safe driving.* (2017). <https://www.dmv.ca.gov/portal/wcm/connect/8a431ac8-535b-4783-b006-a6c6cf58ef18/dl625senior.pdf?MOD = AJPERES> Accessed April, 2018.

State of California Department of Motor Vehicles. *Driving tests*. (2018). <https://www.dmv.ca.gov/portal/dmv/?1dmy&urile = wcm:path:/dmv_content_en/dmv/about/senior/driverlicense/drivetest> Accessed April, 2018.

State of Michigan. *Driver assessment reexamination process*. (2018). <https://www.michigan.gov/sos/0,4670,7-127-1627_8665_9066-23775--,00.html> Accessed April, 2018.

Tefft, B. C. (2014). Driver license renewal policies and fatal crash involvement rates of older drivers, United States, 1986–2011. *Injury Epidemiology*, *1*(1), 25.

Torpey, S. (1986). *Licence re-testing of older drivers*. Melbourne, VIC: Road Traffic Authority.

VicRoads. *Older drivers*. (2018). <https://www.vicroads.vic.gov.au/safety-and-road-rules/driver-safety/older-drivers> Accessed April, 2018.

White, S., & O'Neill, D. (2000). Health and relicensing policies for older drivers in the European Union. *Gerontology*, *46*, 145–152.

# Law enforcement

# 9

*The best car safety device is a rear-view mirror with a cop in it.*

*Dudley Moore*

## Introduction

Law enforcement is an essential component of society. Law enforcement personnel are charged with protecting property and keeping the public safe. In the United States (US), there are several types of law enforcement agencies, including local, county, state/province, and national agencies. While the specific focus and job duties depend to a large extent on the type of agency, personnel from all types of agencies have frequent contact with the community members in that agency's jurisdiction.

Police officers interact with the public through crime reporting and investigation, welfare checks, disaster response, traffic crash response and investigation, and traffic enforcement. As the population continues to age globally, law enforcement contact with older adults will be more frequent. A study of more than 2300 older adults in one US city examined non-traffic-related contacts with law enforcement over an 11-year period. The study found that 29% of the older adults in this sample experienced a total of 1651 separate contacts with police (Lachs et al., 2004). Nearly three-fourths of these contacts were as a victim of an alleged crime. Police contact with older adults is much higher when traffic-related incidents are considered. Nationally representative data from the US Department of Justice (Eith & Durose, 2011) showed that among all contacts with the public in 2008, about 60% were traffic-related. Further, the number of traffic-related contacts among older adults increased by 33% from 2002 to 2008. In another study of 141 officers in San Francisco, California, 89% reported interacting with older adults on at least a monthly basis (Brown, Ahalt, Steinman, Kelly, & Williams, 2014). With such frequent contact with older adults during events that are critical enough to need law enforcement involvement, police officers are increasingly called on to assess the cognitive, perceptual, and psychomotor status of older adults and to make appropriate decisions regarding their driving safety. Are police ready to take on such a role?

**Perspectives and Strategies for Promoting Safe Transportation among Older Adults.**
**DOI: https://doi.org/10.1016/B978-0-12-812153-5.00009-1**

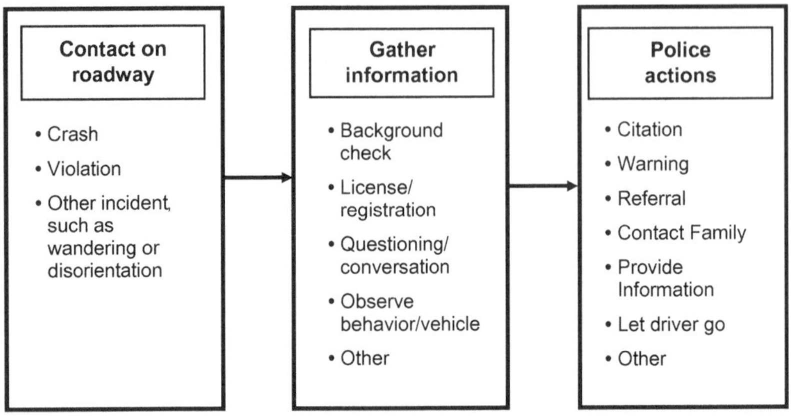


**Figure 9.1** The law enforcement/older driver traffic incident contact process.

## Law enforcement and older drivers

Traffic safety professionals have long recognized the importance of law enforcement in promoting safe transportation among older adults. In most jurisdictions around the globe, police play a vital role in helping to identify older adults who may be unsafe drivers. Fig. 9.1 shows schematically the process of law enforcement interaction with an older driver. The process starts with some incident on the roadway in which the older adult is a driver of a vehicle. Most commonly, these contacts are result from crashes or traffic law violations, but they can also result from something else, such as police observation of a driver who seems disoriented or lost. Once contact is made, police officers go through a process of information gathering and assessment. This information can come from an online check of records, such as with a law enforcement information network. Officers may also ask to see a driver license and/or other documents (e.g., registration) as well as interacting verbally with the older adults and observing their behavior and the condition of the vehicle. An officer then assesses the information and decides on a course of action. These actions can be one or more of the following: issuing a citation; giving a formal warning; referring the driver to the licensing authority or medical professionals; contacting caregivers, family, or friends; providing the driver with information or resources, such as a list of driver refresher courses; letting the driver go without documenting the contact; or some other action, such as arresting the driver or searching the vehicle (the last two being out the scope of this chapter).

## The importance of documenting traffic contacts

Several law enforcement authors (see, e.g., International Association of Chiefs of Police, 2004; McNeil & Ticer, 2005; National Sheriff's Association, 2003) have commented that it is common practice for law enforcement officers to release older drivers who have been stopped for minor offenses without issuing a citation or formal warning, when they might not have been so lenient for a younger driver. The reasoning was described by McNeil and Ticer (2005, p. 11): "These older drivers are released once the officer realizes that the driver is not a criminal or under the influence of drugs or alcohol. In addition, officers tend to be more lenient with older drivers because they remind them of their own parents or grandparents."

Data from the 2008 Police–Public Contact Survey, a nationally representative survey of people stopped by police, provided empirical support that older drivers are commonly allowed to leave a traffic contact without any enforcement action (Eith & Durose, 2011). Analysis of enforcement actions taken by police during traffic stops showed that drivers age 60 or older were allowed to proceed without any enforcement action 22.4% of the time, the highest percentage of any age group. This outcome happened in only 14.3% of traffic stops for drivers of other ages. Law enforcement and traffic safety organizations have argued that law enforcement personnel should treat older drivers in the same way that they treat drivers of other age groups (International Association of Directors of Law Enforcement Standards and Training (IADLEST), 2018; McNeil & Ticer, 2005; National Highway Traffic Safety Administration (NHTSA), 2013). Having their traffic stops documented is one of the best ways to identify an older driver who is beginning to have difficulty with driving safely. One role of law enforcement is to balance overall public safety with the needs of specific members of society, including older drivers (IADLEST, 2018). By establishing a history of traffic safety issues, authorities can be alerted to a potential problem driver and take remedial action, hopefully before the driver causes harm to him- or herself or others.

One particularly useful way to document a traffic contact is for law enforcement to refer older drivers who appear to have functional declines that may affect driving. This is especially important if the older driver has been in a crash that appears to be related to medical problems or poor functioning (International Association of Chiefs of Police, 2004). Law enforcement should be aware of the policies, procedures, and appropriate organizations in their jurisdictions for making these referrals. Referred drivers are usually assessed by a licensing agency and/or a medical professional (as discussed in Chapters 7 and 8) and either some licensing action is taken (revocation, suspension, periodic review, or restrictions) or the driver is cleared with full driving privileges maintained. Several studies have assessed the referral process in the US and Australia (e.g., Di Stefano, Cai, & Williams, 2012; Lococo, Decina, Branche, & Wagner, 2013; Meuser, Carr, & Ulfarsson, 2009; Muir et al., 2016; Soderstrom et al., 2009, 2010). Collectively, these studies found most police referrals of older drivers result from crashes; the most common declining ability among referred drivers was cognition, followed by movement abilities; very few referred older drivers retain full driving privileges after the assessment (4%–17% depending on the study); and another 10%–20% were allowed to drive with some restrictions. These results lead to two important conclusions: (1) many referred older drivers are likely not able to drive safely and are at higher risk of crash, highlighting the value of law enforcement use of the referral process and (2) not all referred drivers will lose full driving privileges.

## Education and training

It is generally agreed that law enforcement personnel could benefit from learning more about aging-related issues and older drivers. An analysis of a large police training academy's curriculum found that police recruits received no training specifically about helping older adults (Marion, 1998). The author concluded that recruits should be trained on how to deal with older adults, including aging demographic patterns, myths and facts about aging, and how to communicate with older adults. A recent study of 143 experienced police officers in a large US city assessed the self-reported aging-related health training received by officers (Brown et al., 2017). The study found that among these officers, 27% had received training on falls, 28% had been trained on aging-related health problems, 34% had been trained on dementia and perceptual problems, and 62% had received training on elder abuse. Another study of 126 officers in New Jersey investigated the types of aging-related training that officers received (Sever & Youdin, 2009). The study found that overall 88% of officers reported having received one or more types of aging-related training at some point in their career, with the following percentages reported by specific type of training: recruit (51.6%), in-service (45.2%), roll call (33.3%), specialized (18.3%), and field (8.7%). These results suggest that there is increasing recognition of the need for law enforcement personnel to receive training on the unique issues of our aging population, yet this training still may not be reaching a large percentage of law enforcement.

## Resources for helping law enforcement with older driver issues

Most of chapters in this book are relevant for educating law enforcement. Here, however, we review resources that have been specifically designed to educate, train, or otherwise help law enforcement with their interactions with older drivers. Most of these resources are intended to help law enforcement gather and assess information, but some are also designed to help officers decide on proper police actions and how to perform those actions better once a decision is made. NHTSA (2003) has compiled a list of older driver and law enforcement programs by state (https://one.nhtsa.gov/people/injury/olddrive/LawEnforcementOlderDriver03/index.htm), but this information has not been updated for many years.

### *Cues for law enforcement*

NHTSA was one of the first organizations to recognize the need among law enforcement for specific guidance on older drivers and published "Cues for Law Enforcement" (NHTSA, 1998). This document is now only available as a website: https://one.nhtsa.gov/people/injury/olddrive/cuesindex.html. This resource includes a brief background on older drivers, lists several barriers to safe mobility, and presents cues for detecting whether an older driver can safely operate a vehicle. According to the website, these cues were tested in the field by state police officers in a single county in Florida, but no further details of this effort are provided. The resource stresses the need for officers to both visually assess the driver and vehicle in combination with having a dialog with the driver. The cues presented in this resource are as follows:

- Does the driver know the current time of day, day of the week, month of the year, and year?
- Does the driver recall where he or she is coming from?
- Does the driver know his or her destination?
- Is the driver far from their residence?
- Does the driver have difficulty communicating, such as stumbling over words or rambling in short, unattached, meaningless sentences, or explanations of their driving ability?
- Is the driver's clothing disheveled, nonmatching, incomplete, or inappropriate for existing weather conditions?
- Does the driver exhibit poor personal hygiene?
- Does the driver launch into accusations of perceived victimization by criminals?
- Does the driver appear to be suffering from dementia such as Alzheimer's disease?
- Is the driver wearing an identification bracelet or necklace indicating dementia?
- Does the driver have large amounts of prescription medicines, prescribed by different doctors, visible in the motor vehicle?
- Does he or she have difficulty finding and removing driver's license, motor vehicle registration, insurance card from wallet/purse, or producing other requested documents?
- If the driver is out of the vehicle or exits the motor vehicle, does he or she take a long period of time to walk a short distance, stumble/fall, shake excessively, or lack coordination when accomplishing simple tasks?

The website also stresses that law enforcement can provide assistance to the older drivers through providing information about local agencies that can assist in driving assessment/rehabilitation, contacting and providing information to family members, recommending alternative sources of transportation, suggesting driving restrictions, and reminding drivers that they should assess their own ability to safely operate a motor vehicle.

## National Sheriffs' Association: older driver safety

The National Sheriffs Association (2003) published a six-page document to help educate law enforcement about aging drivers. This brief document provides discussions on aging drivers, facts about aging, crash statistics, law enforcement's role, the older driver's responsibilities, contact information for organizations on aging, driving, and law enforcement, and links to resources older driver issues.

## Turning the corner . . . and still driving: a review of law enforcement programs involving older driver safety

NHTSA and the National Sheriffs' Association developed a short guidebook to help law enforcement administrators develop local programs that train officers to address older driver issues more effectively (NHTSA, 2005). The guidebook provides background on the importance of driving and the lack of alternative transportation options for older adults, facts about the aging population, older driver crashes, and law enforcement's role in addressing older driver issues. The majority of the guidebook is devoted to reviewing several programs that have been implemented at Sheriffs' offices across the US and includes a succinct review of program features that can facilitate the success of a program. These features are involvement of partners and community, use of community liaisons, commitment from leadership, motivated employees, training staff, proactive organizations, inclusion of innovators, and adaptable organizations. The guidebook concludes with a listing of potential partners and resources about aging and driving.

## *International Association of Chiefs of Police (IACP, 2010) Alzheimer's initiative*

As part of larger initiative on law enforcement and Alzheimer's disease, the IACP developed the following webinars and roll-call videos related to older drivers (http://www.theiacp.org/Alzheimer-Training-Video):

- *Responding to Alzheimer's disease: The three stages of Alzheimer's disease.* This 9-minute webinar provides background information on Alzheimer's disease and its progression. It is presented by law enforcement personnel;
- *Responding to Alzheimer's disease: Situations in which law enforcement/first responders might encounter people with Alzheimer's disease.* This 25-minute video discusses several issues related to first responders and interacting with people who have Alzheimer's disease, presented by an experienced police officer;
- *Driver assessment (traffic stop): Learn to recognize signs of impaired driving due to Alzheimer's disease or dementia.* This 4.5-minute roll-call video presents a sample traffic stop with an older driver who has Alzheimer's disease and provides several suggestions on how to interact with the driver and take appropriate action;
- *Missing person (by car): Techniques for interviewing caregivers and search and rescue when someone with dementia goes missing by car.* Using a sample case of a missing driver with Alzheimer's disease, this 6-minute roll-call video provides facts about dementia and wandering, interacting with caregivers/family, and recommended law enforcement approaches to locating the lost driver.

## *Alzheimer's Association: Alzheimer's disease: guide for law enforcement*

This resource was developed as part of the Alzheimer's Association's (2006) Safe Return program under a grant from the U.S. Department of Justice. This five-page document briefly presents a background on Alzheimer's disease and wandering (including by car), the Safe Return program, types of incidents where law enforcement might encounter a person with Alzheimer's, and the tips for interacting with a person who is suspected of having Alzheimer's, including the following:

- Identify yourself as a law enforcement officer and explain why you've approached the person.
- Maintain good eye contact.

- Speak slowly in a nonthreatening, low-pitched voice.
- Loudness can convey anger; do not assume the person is hearing-impaired.
- Use short, simple words.
- Ask "yes" and "no" questions.
- Ask one question at a time, allowing plenty of time for response.
- If necessary, repeat your question using the exact wording as people with dementia may only grasp a part of the question at a time.
- Maintain a calm and quiet environment, devoid of chaos and excessive stimuli, by reducing radio volume, keeping squelch down, and avoiding use of sirens.
- Restraints should be used only as a last resort for the safety of the individual or others.
- Avoid correcting or "reality checks."

## NHTSA: educating law enforcement officers on older driver issues

Working with law enforcement, communication, and older driver experts, NHTSA (2013) updated and revised their *Older Driver Law Enforcement Instructor Training* program (IADLEST, 2018) so that law enforcement personnel could participate in an older driver training program in a self-paced, online environment. Although developed in 2013, the online training program was not available until 2017 (http://www.iadlest.org/Portals/0/Files/Documents/NHTSA/OlderDriver/player.html) and is hosted by the IADLEST, who provided the in-person training in the previous instructor-training program. The course has three modules. The first, "Reasons to Care," discusses aging demographics trends, older driver crash trends, the importance of driving to older adults and adverse consequences of driving cessation, and law enforcement's role in balancing public safety and quality of life for everyone. The second module, "Understanding and Interacting with Older Drivers," discusses common age-related perceptual, motor, and cognitive declines and their effects on driving abilities, and strategies for interacting with drivers who have functional declines. The third module, "Conducting Traffic Stops with Older Drivers," provides information on understanding the importance of stopping traffic violators, properly documenting traffic stops, identifying special needs/concerns related to older driver traffic stops, making appropriate referrals, and tips on communicating with older drivers. The interactive training program includes several videos, quizzes, and links to additional information to help improve understanding and allows the officer to earn a certificate of completion. Links to several resources are also included.

## Training, Research, and Education for Driving Safety (TREDS) law enforcement and older drivers training

The University of California, San Diego's Training, Research, and Education for Driving Safety (TREDS) program has developed several resources for training law enforcement on older driver issues (http://treds.ucsd.edu/law-enforcement). The hallmark of these resources is a 2-hour in-person course (titled Older Driver Safety: Law Enforcement's Role) that is certified in California to provide law enforcement with professional education credits. The course was developed based on focus groups with law enforcement and interviews with experts (Hill, Rybar, Stowe, & Jahns, 2016). According to the TREDS website, the course content includes demographics and safety risks with aging; medical conditions that can affect driving; older driver traffic stops: observations and communications; administration of TREDS-developed brief cognitive screen called the *Driver Orientation Screen for Cognitive Impairment* (DOSCI); use California-specific referral mechanisms; and resources for older drivers and families. There is also a 30-minute version of the course that just covers DOSCI and referral process. DOSCI is a nine-question screening tool designed to be used by law enforcement in the field to determine gross disorientation or cognitive impairment (Hill et al., 2016). The simple questions such as, "What state are we in now?" are each worth one point for a correct answer and scores are summed. Three summary score ranges are presented with recommended police actions for each range. TREDS also has developed several 9–30 minute videos related to law enforcement and older drivers with cognitive/medical impairment. These videos are available by request from TREDS.

TREDS personnel have published one article on an evaluation of their 2-hour training program and the use of DOSCI (Hill et al., 2016). The researchers conducted 103 training sessions with a total of 2018 officers who were required to attend the sessions over a 5-year period. Officers were asked to voluntarily complete two questionnaires—one before training ($n = 1905$) that asked about current behavior and confidence in managing older drivers, and one after the training ($n = 1985$) that asked about future intent and changes in confidence about dealing with older drivers. The study found that prior to training officers reported rarely referring older drivers to the licensing authority, whereas after the training officers reported that they intended to be more thorough when evaluating older drivers and were now more likely to refer older drivers to the proper authority. Officers also reported in the post questionnaire that they believed they were now more likely to be able to recognize medially impaired drivers. Finally, 90% of officers reported that they were likely or very likely to use the DOSCI tool. In a 2-year follow-up interview with 60 state troopers who had taken a training session, two-thirds reported carrying the DOSCI tool with them and 23% reported that they had used the DOSCI tool.

## Conclusions

Law enforcement plays a vital role in maintaining safe transportation for older adults. As a critical component of the justice system and as a first responder to many traffic-related incidents involving older drivers, law enforcement officers are especially positioned not only to be one of the first authorities to notice problem driving but also to be able to take positive steps in keeping the older driver and others on the roadways safe. We have argued that the best action to take with older drivers who are suspected of having declines that impact safe driving is to document the traffic stop so that evidence of potential driving–related problems is available early on (e.g., before a crash actually occurs). It is also recommended that law enforcement utilize the referral processes in their jurisdiction whenever they suspect that a driver is medically unsafe to drive. The processes, requirements, and necessary information for referrals will vary greatly by jurisdiction and the authority to which the person is being referred (licensing agency, medical board, etc.). Therefore, it is incumbent on each law enforcement agency to be aware of how referrals are made in their jurisdiction.

It is clear that law enforcement can benefit from training and education programs on older drivers issues and it is gratifying to see an increase in the number of resources and programs on these topics over the past 20 years. There is, however, a lack of formal evaluation of these resources and programs. Even though most of these resources were developed by experts in law enforcement, health, aging, and traffic safety, it is still important to assess the degree to which they change knowledge and, more importantly, the behaviors of law enforcement personnel. Ultimately, these evaluations should also attempt to assess the impact of these resources on older driver safety and mobility.

## References


Alzheimer's Association. (2006). *Alzheimer's disease: Guide for law enforcement.* Chicago, IL: Alzheimer's Association.

Brown, R. T., Ahalt, C., Rivera, J., Cenzer, I. S., Wilhelm, A., & Williams, B. A. (2017). Good cop, better cop: Evaluation of a geriatrics training program for police. *Journal of the American Geriatrics Society*, *65*(8), 1842–1847.

Brown, R. T., Ahalt, C., Steinman, M. A., Kelly, K., & Williams, B. A. (2014). Police on the front line of community geriatric healthcare: Challenges and opportunities. *Journal of the American Geriatrics Society*, *62*(11), 2191–2198.

Eith, C., & Durose, M. R. (2011). *Contacts between police and the public, 2008*. Report no. NCJ234599. Washington, DC: US Department of Justice, Bureau of Justice Statistics.

Hill, L. L., Rybar, J., Stowe, J., & Jahns, J. (2016). Development of a curriculum and roadside screening tool for law enforcement identification of medical impairment in aging drivers. *Injury Epidemiology*, *3*, 13.

International Association of Chiefs of Police. (2004). *Highway safety desk book*. Alexandria, VA: International Association of Chiefs of Police.

International Association of Chiefs of Police. (2010). *Alzheimer's initiatives training videos and webinars*. Alexandria, VA: International Association of Chiefs of Police. <http://www.theiacp.org/Alzheimer-Training-Video>. Accessed February, 2018.

International Association of Directors of Law Enforcement Standards and Training. *Older driver law enforcement instructor training*. (2018). <https://www.iadlest.org/training/older-driver-law-enforcement-training>. Accessed June, 2018.

Lachs, M., Bachman, R., Williams, C., Kossack, A., Bove, C., & O'Leary, J. (2004). Older adults as crime victims, perpetrators, witnesses, and complainants: A population-based study of police interactions. *Journal of Elder Abuse and Neglect*, *16*(4), 25–40.

Lococo, K. H., Decina, L. E., Branche, J., & Wagner, E. M. (2013). Medical review process and license disposition of drivers referred by law enforcement in Virginia. *Journal of Safety Research*, *45*, 47–53.

Marion, N. (1998). Police academy training: Are we teaching recruits what they need to know? *Policing: An International Journal of Police Strategies and Management*, *21*(1), 54–79.

McNeil, C., & Ticer, R. (2005). The older driver—Law enforcement challenges. *Experience, Fall*, 10–13.

Meuser, T. M., Carr, D. B., & Ulfarsson, G. F. (2009). Motor-vehicle crash history and licensing outcome for older drivers reported as medically impaired in Missouri. *Accident Analysis & Prevention*, *41*, 246–252.

Muir, C., Charlton, J. L., Odell, M., Keeffe, J., Wood, J., Bohensky, M., ... Rizzo, M. (2016). Medical review licensing outcome in drivers with visual field loss in Victoria, Australia. *Clinical and Experimental Ophthalmology*, *99*(5), 462–468.

National Highway Traffic Safety Administration. (2005). *Turning the corner...and still driving: A review of law enforcement programs involving older driver safety*. Report no. DOT HS 809 899. Washington, DC: US Department of Transportation.

National Highway Traffic Safety Administration. (2013). *Educating law enforcement officers on older driver issues*. Report no. DOT HS 811 684. Washington, DC: US Department of Transportation.

National Highway Traffic Safety Association. (1998). *Cues for law enforcement*. Report no. DOT HS 808 778. Washington, DC: US Department of Transportation. <https://one.nhtsa.gov/people/injury/olddrive/cuesindex.html>. Accessed February, 2018.

National Highway Traffic Safety Association. (2003). *A compendium of law enforcement older driver programs*. Washington, DC: US Department of Transportation. <https://one.nhtsa.gov/people/injury/olddrive/LawEnforcementOlderDriver03/index.htm>. Accessed February, 2018.

National Sheriffs Association (2003). *Older driver safety: NATI alerts*. Report number NATI-03-12. Alexandria, VA: National Sheriffs Association. <https://www.sheriffs.org/sites/default/files/uploads/TRIAD/Older%20Driver%20Safety.pdf>. Accessed February, 2018.

Sever, B., & Youdin, R. (2009). Police knowledge of older populations: The Impact of training, experience, and education. *Professional Issues in Criminal Justice: A Professional Journal*, *1*(2), 1–17.

Soderstrom, C. A., Scottino, M. A., Burch, C. A., Ho, S. M., Kerns, T. J., & Joyce, J. J. (2010). Pursuit of licensure by senior drivers referred by police to a state licensing agency's medical advisory board. *Annals of Advances in Automotive Medicine*, *54*, 351–358.

Soderstrom, C. A., Scottino, M. A., Joyce, J. J., Burch, C. A., Ho, S. M., & Kerns, T. J. (2009). Police referral of drivers to the Maryland motor vehicle administration's medical advisory board. *Annals of Advances in Automotive Medicine*, *53*, 105–116.

Di Stefano, M., Cai, S., & Williams, T. (2012). Characteristics of drivers referred by police to VicRoads: Evidence for indicators of declining driving competence. *Injury Prevention*, *18*(Suppl 1), A16.

# Transportation service providers

# 10

*On a bus, your eyes, ears, and pores are open absorbing in the variety, the wonder, and the magic of the city. It's a wonderful way to get to know the city.*

*George Takei*

## Introduction

As noted in earlier chapters, driving oneself is the preferred method of getting around in the community among people of all ages. However, when people are no longer able or choose not to drive, they need to find other options for maintaining their mobility. These other options for community mobility are varied, and the range of offerings is rapidly changing as noted in Chapter 3, Use of Non-driving Transportation Options. In addition, older adults living in rural or small communities face special challenges given the combination of a high proportion of older adults, lower population densities, greater distances between destinations, and often scarce resources (Bond, Brown, & Wood, 2017). Even when public transportation is available in communities, older adults may face barriers to using it. For example, Broome, Nalder, Worrall, and Boldy (2010) identified several challenges for older adults including unsuitable timetables and scheduling (e.g., infrequent buses or unsuitable times), inappropriate bus stop locations (too far from home, too far apart), difficulty with entry and exit, inappropriate routing (e.g., lack of direct routes), lack of connections, driver not friendly or helpful, lack of bus shelters, inconvenience, lack of prior knowledge, and lack of service.

Other challenges have been recognized with regard to use of alternative transportation services more generally (e.g., see Brown, Duncan, Horner, Bond, & Wood, 2018; Burkhardt, McGavock, Nelson, & Mitchell, 2002; Eby, Molnar, & Kartje, 2009; Eby, Molnar, Kostyniuk, Louis, & Zanier, 2011; Kerschner & Hardin, 2006). For example, Brown et al. (2018) identified four major barriers to older adults' use of alternative transportation services from a review of the literature: (1) the preference for automobile use resulting from a lifetime of such use, as well as the desire to maintain independence and negative perceptions of alternative options (e.g., Hess, 2012); (2) the unavailability or inaccessibility of alternative services due to total absence of service, distance of stops from home, location of routes, or hours of operation (e.g., Hess, 2012; Rosenbloom, 2009); (3) mobility impairments that restrict one's ability to carry out daily activities (e.g., Rosenberg, Bombadier, Hoffman, & Belza, 2011); and (4) cognitive impairments that might result in people

**Perspectives and Strategies for Promoting Safe Transportation among Older Adults.**
**DOI: https://doi.org/10.1016/B978-0-12-812153-5.00010-8**

getting lost or confused, or having difficulty coping with more general activities (e.g., Centers for Disease Control and Prevention, 2013).

Given these challenges, transportation service providers are faced with how best to meet the needs of older adults, which are often unique to this segment of the population, and at the same time, still maintain their own viability. This chapter begins by describing what is meant by age-friendly transportation services and how the focus has changed over time. We then discuss the importance of transportation coordination and mobility management in ensuring continued mobility for older adults, and at the same time, meeting the needs of service providers. Travel training is highlighted as an especially promising and growing strategy.

## Age-friendly services

Almost 20 years ago, Kerschner and Harris (2007) introduced the concept of the "five A's of senior friendly transportation," focused largely on the use of public transportation.

As defined by the authors, these include

- Availability: Transportation exists and is available when needed.
- Accessibility: Transportation can be reached and used (bus stairs can be negotiated, bus seats are high enough, bus stop is readable, and van comes to the door).
- Acceptability: Standards relate to conditions such as cleanliness (bus is not dirty), safety (bus stops are located in safe areas), and user-friendliness (transit operators are courteous and helpful).
- Affordability: Costs (fees) are affordable, comparable to or less than driving a car, and vouchers or coupons help defray out-of-pocket expenses.
- Adaptability: Transportation can be modified or adjusted to meet special needs (wheelchair can be accommodated, trip chaining is possible).

Broome, Worrall, McKenna, and Boldy (2010) further delineated the characteristics of age-friendly transportation services, identifying seven priorities for older adults in Australia. From highest to lowest, these priorities include having

- Accessible entry to all vehicles without steps.
- Lower bus floors closer to the curb with no obstructions in the entrance/exit.
- Friendly and helpful bus drivers with good communication skills who understand the varying needs of passengers, wait until passengers are seated before driving, and pull in close to curb.
- Buses that run frequently and are available in morning, evening, and weekends.
- Bus stop locations located close to homes and destinations with few hills along the route.
- Age appropriate pedestrian infrastructure; appropriate training and information on how to use buses.
- Bus routes and destinations matched to the needs and interests of older adults.

In addition, Broome, Worrall, Fleming, and Boldy (2011) noted the importance of travel information that can be easily found, understood, and used to plan trips on the bus.

In other work by Johnson, Shaw, Berding, Gather, and Rebstock (2017) that focused on the European Union, Norway, and Sweden, age-friendly transportation systems were characterized as being affordable, available, barrier-free, comfortable, comprehensible, efficient, friendly, reliable, safe, secure, and transparent. The authors reviewed the extent to which these 11 qualities were addressed throughout Europe and found that 3 in particular—safety, barrier freedom, and affordability—stood out in terms of getting the strongest support from national governments.

Recently, age-friendly transportation services have been conceptualized within the broader context of age-friendly communities (e.g., see Kihl, Brennan, Gabhalwala, List, & Mittal, 2005; Fitzgerald & Caro, 2014; Scharlach, Davitt, Lehning, Greenfield, & Graham, 2014; World Health Organization, 2007). Fitzgerald and Caro (2014) described age-friendly cities or communities as offering "... a supportive environment that enables residents to grow older actively within their families, neighborhoods, and civil society and offers extensive opportunities for their participation in the community" (p. 2). The concept of age-friendly cities grew out of the World Health Organization's active aging framework (World Health Organization, 2007). Current age-friendly initiatives generally follow guidelines established by WHO, as well as United States (US) organizations such as AARP (Livable Communities; Kihl et al., 2005). In fact, according to Jeste et al. (2016), there are currently 287 communities in 33 countries that are part of World Health Organization's network of age-friendly communities, and an additional 77 communities in the United States (US) belong to AARP's network. While varying definitions of age-friendly communities are used across initiatives, they noted that most are focused on improving aspects of the physical environment including the availability of affordable and reliable transportation; and the social environment (e.g., building respect for older adults, providing opportunities for them to participate in decision-making). Transportation-specific criteria for age-friendly communities included having a range of options for people to get around in the community that are available, affordable, and reliable; sufficient frequency of runs and travel stops; age-friendly vehicles; specialized services for older adults; priority seating and passenger courtesy; trained drivers; safety and comfort; driving conditions for and courtesy toward older drivers; parking; and variation in types of public transit and community transportation (e.g., see Shiau & Huang, 2014). More details on age-friendly communities can be found in Chapter 14, Age-Friendly Communities.

The issue of how transportation services can be made more age-friendly has received considerable attention (e.g., Bond et al., 2017; Broome, Worrall, Boldy, & Fleming, 2010; Broome et al., 2011; Broome, Worrall, Fleming, & Boldy, 2012; Burkhardt et al., 2002; Eby et al., 2009, 2011; Kerschner & Hardin, 2006). For example, Broome et al. (2010) examined whether age-friendly changes to bus services in Hervey Bay, Australia improved bus use, usability, and social activity outcomes for older adults. Pre and post surveys of riders in Hervey Bay and a comparison community indicated that there was minimal change in frequency of bus use, self-rated ease of use, and social activity participation in Hervey Bay, although the majority of respondents reported that the buses had improved. Respondents in the comparison community reported decreased ease of use, minimal change in frequency of use, and decreased participation in social activities over a 3-year period. The authors concluded that the improvements in Hervey Bay may have allowed older users to maintain their ease of use and social activity.

In a related study, Broome et al. (2012) examined the effects of replacing a fixed-route bus service in Hervey Bay with a flexible route bus service. The authors monitored ticket sales over a 9-month period and conducted before and after satisfaction surveys. They found that bus use by older adults approximately doubled over an 8-month period following introduction of the flexible service. In addition, overall satisfaction with the bus service increased significantly. Broome and his colleagues also explored older adults' needs and preferences relative to transportation information (Broome et al., 2011). Based on qualitative interviews with 40 adults age 60 or older, they found that older adults obtain transportation information from a variety of sources including printed materials, telephone, internet, bus drivers, word of mouth, and experience. They concluded that transportation providers should consider providing information in a variety of ways, through numerous locations, and at various levels of complexity.

One promising approach to ensuring age-friendly services in rural and small communities is through flexible transportation (or transport) services (FTS). FTS have been described as a range of formal or informal transportation networks that exist in rural areas to address mobility gaps faced by disadvantaged populations (Velaga, Nelson, Wright, & Farrington, 2012). According to Bond et al. (2017), FTS have been implemented to this end across North America, Australia, and Great Britain, although the specific services may vary (e.g., ride-sharing, paratransit, and volunteer driver programs). A key challenge associated with implementing FTS is that providers must take on most financial or operational requirements on their own, without direct guidance from funders or authorities (Mulley, Nelson, Teal, Wright, & Daniels, 2012).

Wood, Brown, Bond, and Suguri (2016) conducted a national survey of 40 service providers in rural and small communities to examine the type of services available to older adults in these communities and how they are organized and delivered. They concluded that agencies offer a diverse set of transportation services ranging from demand-responsive to fixed-route to highly specialized services; program managers consider partnerships with other organizations, informal marketing, and personalized interactions with older adults to be essential to their ability to provide services and meet older adult needs; and agencies have limited resources but managers think there is great potential to increase older adult ridership if they can expand their services and strengthen their marketing, education, and outreach efforts.

In follow-up work, Bond et al. (2017) explored the effectiveness of flexible services, partnerships, and individualized outreach to address the challenges faced by older adults in small and rural communities. They used responses from the national survey conducted by Wood et al. (2016) to identify seven case studies for their investigation, consisting of a total of 14 semi-structured telephone interviews with service providers (including traditional transit operators, public health agencies, and nonprofit organizations). They found that providers generally reported positive outcomes for each of the three approaches, although most relied on anecdotal evidence, suggesting a need for better evaluation data relative to whether the needs of older adults are being effectively met. According to the authors, their most important finding was the local context is important for types of services provided in these communities and their ultimate effectiveness.

Brown et al. (2018) also used the seven case studies discussed above to explore service provider perspectives on six promising services for improving older adults' use of alternative transportation services (volunteer driver programs, time banking programs, travel training, door-through-door services, service coordination, and mobility management). They found that many of the respondents were from small agencies that lacked the resources necessary to effectively meet their clients' needs; most respondents emphasized the importance of individualized, personal outreach to build trust among older adults; many reported unmet need for their services but actual information on ridership was limited; and the effectiveness of particular strategies in addressing barriers to use was highly dependent on funding constraints, reputation, and possibly unmet need. The authors highlighted the importance of ample funding, services that are well understood by the community, and knowledge of the ridership base and its travel demands, as well as the need for more formalized program evaluation.

## Transportation coordination and mobility management

As described by AARP (2012), "... coordination means that different organizations work together to provide transportation in the community, sharing their resources, which will provide more transportation options and improve mobility for those with specialized needs, such as older adults" (p. 2). The concept of coordination has evolved somewhat over time. For example, in 2004, the Federal Transit Administration's Coordinating Council on Access and Mobility (CCAM), charged with coordinating federal programs that fund transportation to improve community mobility options, focused primarily on the supply or provider side (Mattson, Miller, Goodwill, Sriraj, & Hough, 2017). To that end, the coordination of specialized transportation services was defined as a process by which different agencies could work with each other to achieve more cost-effective delivery of services, greater capacity to serve unmet needs, improved service quality, and improved rider accessibility and understanding of services (Federal Transit Administration, 2018a). In 2017, CCAM laid out its updated vision as enabling equal access to coordinated transportation for all Americans and improving the availability, accessibility, and efficiency of transportation, to be achieved through four goals: to improve access to the community through transportation, enhance the cost-effectiveness of coordinated transportation, strengthen interagency partnerships, and establish future models for coordinated transportation (Federal Transit Administration, 2017).

This newer vision for coordinated transportation, as noted by Mattson et al. (2017), "... has been expanded to one of mobility management that focuses on customers and meeting their needs, and using the assets of a number of organizations, rather than on the production of transportation services" (p. 78). More specifically according to the authors, the transportation coordination infrastructure built by CCAM and its partners is based on the establishment of coordinated transportation planning processes, mobility management coordination practices, one call/one click transportation management centers, and state leadership activities, including state and regional transportation coordination councils.

Mobility management has been described as a systems approach to managing transportation resources (Ellis, 2009) directed at identifying service needs and the transportation options to meet those needs; assessing community transportation resources and ability of individuals to use them; filling service gaps; and providing access to training on how to use local transportation (National Center for Mobility Management, 2018). The vision of mobility management as an expanded view of coordination is a central focus of United We Ride, the interagency initiative established by CCAM to improve the availability, quality, and efficiency of services for older adults, people with disabilities, and low-income individuals (Federal Transit Administration, 2018b). Mattson et al. (2017) noted that the role of policy coordination represents a key difference between previous coordination efforts and mobility management, with the latter focusing on helping communities develop coordination plans, programs, policies, and local partnerships.

Consistent with the expanded vision of coordination, The National Aging and Disability Transportation Center (NADTC) (2017) identified two levels of "person-centered" mobility management for older adults: the individual level which involves one-on-one group education and counseling about transportation options and alternatives to driving; and the systems level which is described as a service to facilitate coordination among transportation and human service providers and ensure the availability of a range of transportation options and modes to support older adult mobility needs in communities throughout the US. To that end, the Center suggested that mobility management can and should be applied to a broad range of transportation options, as well as to situations in which there are limited mobility options such as in rural areas, and some suburban and even small metropolitan areas.

Mobility management has enjoyed a longer history outside of the US—specifically in many countries in Europe (Majumdar, Sen, & Park, 2012). There and elsewhere, it has been known as transportation demand management, a set of strategies for achieving more efficient use of transportation resources (Litman, 2003). According to Litman (2003), mobility management offers significant opportunities for developing countries because of its low costs and multiple benefits, especially relative to continual public investments in road and parking facility expansion to accommodate increased travel by personal automobile. He notes, however, that the specific mobility management strategies employed will necessarily vary depending on the demographic, geographic, and political conditions in a community.

Resources for mobility management have been compiled by the National Center for Mobility Management (NCMM), an initiative of the United We Ride program (which is supported by the Federal Transit Administration and operated through a consortium consisting of the American Public Transportation Association, Community Transportation Association of America, and Easter Seals; National Center for Mobility Management, 2018). The purpose of NCMM is to support Federal Transit Administration grantees, mobility managers, and partners in the adoption of proven, sustainable, and replicable transportation coordination, mobility management, and one-call–one-click transportation information practices. To this end, the NCMM website includes a series of modules on the following topics: what mobility management is understanding the customer, identifying transportation services in one's community; transportation for people with disabilities, transportation for job seekers and people with limited income, transportation for medical purposes, transportation for older adults, transportation for military veterans, and creating new service options.

Increased funding in the US for mobility management was made available through passage of the Safe, Accountable, Flexible, Efficient Transportation Equity Act: A Legacy for Users (SAFETEA-LU) in 2005 which included it as an eligible activity under Federal Transit Administration's three specialized transportation programs (S.5310, Job Access and Reserve Commute Program, and New Freedom; Ellis, 2009). SAFETEA-LU ended in 2012 but was replaced by the Moving Ahead for Progress in the 21st Century (MAP-21), which used the same definition of mobility management and provided additional funding for the transportation of older adults and people with disabilities (Majumdar et al., 2012). Support for mobility management has continued under MAP-21's replacement, the Fixing America's Surface Transportation Act, signed into US law on December 4, 2015.

Of special note in mobility management is the one call/one click service component, identified as a strategy to help people learn about, and in some cases, access transportation services and programs, in a way that is tailored to their individual needs (Rodman, Berez, & Nelson, 2016). In a project funded by the National Cooperative Highway Research Program, the authors examined the state of the practice of connecting specialized transportation users and rides, on a statewide, regional, and community level basis. Their goal was to provide best practices that Departments of Transportation could use to improve services.

## Travel training

Fixed-route public transit services (i.e., buses, trains, and subways) represent one of the most affordable and commonly available non-driving transportation options, at least in urban and suburban communities. However, many older adults are unfamiliar with how to use public transportation and/or the benefits that it can bring (Babka, Cooper, & Ragland, 2009; Burkhardt et al., 2002; Ling & Murray, 2010; Tuokko, McGee, Stepaniuk, & Benner, 2007; Wolf-Branigin, Wolf-Branigin, Culver, & Welch, 2012). Travel training programs provide instruction on how to use transit services. Such travel instruction has been described as short-term, intensive, individualized instruction for older adults and individuals with disabilities to increase their mobility and travel on public transportation independently (e.g., Ride Connection, 2009). Travel training programs have the potential to help older adults who need non-driving options to get around in the community, thereby maintaining their mobility and quality of life (Burkhardt et al., 2002; Hardin, 2005).

The travel training got its start in the US in the 1970s, becoming more prevalent with the passage of the 1990 Americans with Disabilities Act (Lubin, Alexander, & Harvey, 2017) and the Individuals with Disabilities Education Act Amendments of 1997, the latter of which includes travel training under the definition of "special education" (Groce, 2013). More recently, a number of federal programs have facilitated the expansion of travel training through targeted support and funding. Travel training programs have also been developed outside of the US, in Canada, the United Kingdom, the Netherlands, and other countries (Beyerle & Dupree, 2016).

Travel training programs in the US have been examined extensively by Burkhardt et al. (2014a, 2014b). They noted that in its simplest form, travel training is provided by transit operators through instructional pamphlets or videos provided on a website. However, as noted by Burkhardt et al. (2014b), the most promising travel training programs are more involved and include one or more of the following types of training and instruction:

- *Transit travel orientation:* An instructor works briefly with older adults to introduce them to the bus or train routes they would like to learn about, and help them plan out routes to desired locations.
- *Group travel training:* A group of older adults, usually from an organization such as a senior center or senior residential facility, is brought together and given general instruction on how to use the transit system. This type of training often involves a group outing with the participants and the instructor going to an entertainment or shopping location to become more familiar with transit travel.
- *Travel ambassador training:* An older adult volunteer who is familiar with using the transit system accompanies an older adult to his or her destinations and provides instruction on using the transit system.
- *One-on-one training:* This is an intensive type of travel training that begins with a personalized assessment of an older adult's functional abilities and mobility needs, followed by instruction tailored to the individual. The instructor rides along with the older adult to his or her desired destination until the older adult is comfortable making these transit trips by himself or herself. There is regular follow-up with the older adult to make sure that mobility needs are being met and identify additional training needs.

Regardless of the type of travel training program, the instructional components typically include information on the following aspects of using public transportation: entering and exiting the transit facility, paying fares, using special passes, purchasing tickets, reading schedules, locating seating, planning trips, ensuring personal safety, and transferring from one bus to another. There is also training for older adults who rely on mobility devices to learn how to use lifts or other assistive devices when using transit facilities.

Travel training programs have been associated with benefits for older adults, caregivers, public transportation agencies, and the larger community (e.g.,

Burkhardt et al., 2014a, 2014b; Wolf-Branigin & Wolf-Branigin, 2010). As summarized by Burkhardt et al. (2014a), the benefits to trainees include

- Expansion of travel options.
- Increased ability to go to places that may have been difficult to go to without using transit.
- Less need for relying on friends or family for rides.
- Potential increase in quality of life as one ages, such as the ability to age in place in their own homes or to travel more spontaneously.
- Improved ability to stay connected with friends and family.
- Saving money that may otherwise be spent on more expensive travel options such as taxis or paratransit.

The benefits of travel training also extend to family members and friends who provide voluntary assistance to older adults. Results from a Michigan survey indicated that more than 90%of unpaid, informal caregivers for older adults provided some form of transportation assistance, with the most common being driving older adults to their destinations (Eby et al., 2011). Informal caregiving can adversely affect the health and employment of caregivers (e.g., National Alliance for Caregiving & AARP, 2015). Travel training has the potential to reduce the burden on caregivers by providing an opportunity for at least some of these trips to be made by fixed route, thereby freeing up their time for other activities, as well as saving resources that would otherwise be spent on older adult care.

Travel training programs benefit communities by contributing to their collective health (Burkhardt et al., 2014a). That is, communities in which older adults are not meeting their transportation needs are likely to experience increased health care costs and a general decrease in quality of life of their members. At least one study has shown that when people lose mobility they spend less money in their community due to a lack of access to goods and services (Kim & Richardson, 2006).

Many evaluations of travel training programs have relied on pre and post surveys to assess changes in perceptions, as well as intended and/or actual transit use (e.g., Lubin et al., 2017; Shaheen, Allen, & Liu, 2008). For example, Shaheen et al. (2008) evaluated the effectiveness of a travel training program in California that focused on building self-efficacy in using the bus (more generally seen as an individual's faith in his or her ability; Bandura & Ramachaudran, 1994) through in-class instruction and a bus tour of selected route lines. They found that after training, 85% of respondents reported that they planned to take public transit more frequently in the future; respondents' comfort levels with regard to taking buses to key destinations within the community increased, as did their confidence with regard to finding transit information; automobile use significantly decreased as the primary mode of transportation and public transit use increased significantly; and use of transit information resources increased significantly.

Lubin et al. (2017) used surveys to examine a group travel training program piloted with 173 older adults (age 75–84) in New Jersey that included both classroom instruction and a field trip. Respondents reported that they were highly satisfied with the program, and increases were found in respondent knowledge and skills, as well as interest in, willingness to use, and actual use of public transit after program completion. Respondents also reported increased confidence to travel independently and greater access to new opportunities and activities.

Although efforts to explicitly quantify the benefits of travel training have been more limited, an evaluation of a travel training program in Australia found significant benefit to cost ratios (Stevens, Battellino, & Pedler, 2013). The authors took into account social (reduced social isolation), economic (increased earnings or consumption), travel (fare savings to traveler and subsidy reductions to government), caregiver (increased leisure time and employment opportunities), and environmental benefits (reduced carbon emissions). The average benefit to cost ratio was 3.4–1, with the largest proportion of benefits associated with reduced social isolation for older adults.

Noting the lack of an integrative framework for evaluating travel training programs, Park, Welch, and Sriraj (2016) reported on the development of a framework that can be used in both design and evaluation of travel training. The framework takes into account three major dimensions: the production and delivery of travel training programs (e.g., types of training providers, skills of instructors, and training models and contents), outcomes (e.g., benefits to trainees, providers, and the larger community), and moderators and mediators influencing the relationship between travel training and its outcomes (e.g., infrastructure, trainee characteristics, involvement of and collaboration and partnerships among stakeholders). They also point out that the framework can serve as the basis for a model that includes resources, activities, outputs, and short-, mid-, and long-term outcomes of travel training programs. According to the authors, the framework and model can be used to achieve three key purposes of program evaluation: assessment of program merits and worth, needed improvements, and oversight and compliance.

Despite the potential benefits of travel training, including evidence of economic benefits to public transportation providers who engage in effective travel training programs (Wolf-Branigin et al., 2012), travel training is a relatively new and underused strategy in most areas of the US. There have been efforts, however, to produce resources for organizations interested in developing new programs or improving existing programs. One such effort is a US project, sponsored by the Transit Cooperative Research Program, that led to the development of a handbook for transit agencies and human services providers on how to create, implement, sustain, and evaluate a travel training program for older adults (Burkhardt et al., 2014a). The handbook also contains information on several model programs. The information for this handbook came from several in-depth case studies, a review of the literature, and expert knowledge. A companion document describes the research supporting the information discussed in the handbook (Burkhardt et al., 2014b).

## Conclusions

Older adults may face significant barriers in their use of transportation services, especially once they are no longer able or choose not to drive themselves. This is further complicated in rural and small communities where distances are greater and resources are often lacking. Transportation service providers also face challenges in ensuring that services to older adults are available, affordable, accessible, acceptable, and adaptable, while at the same time, allowing them to retain their viability. Considerable efforts have been expended to identify the components of age-friendly transportation services and develop strategies for implementing them in communities of all sizes. While there have been many promising efforts and programs (e.g., mobility management and travel training), continuing research is clearly needed to delineate how various strategies can best be tailored to the specific context of the community, and how program effectiveness can be more rigorously evaluated using objective behavioral data (e.g., ridership) in combination with survey data on rider perceptions, attitudes, and satisfaction. In addition, given the scarcity of resources in most communities, continuing efforts to identify innovative partnerships and collaborations across agencies and organizations are warranted.

## References

AARP. *Meeting older adults' mobility needs: Transportation planning and coordination in rural communities.* (2012). Available at: <https://www.aarp.org/content/dam/aarp/livable-communities/learn/transportation/meeting-older-adults-mobility-needs-transportation-planning-and-coordination-in-rural-communities-2012-aarp.pdf> Accessed June, 2018.

Babka, R., Cooper, J., & Ragland, D. (2009). Evaluation of urban travel training for older adults. *Transportation Research Record, 2110*, 149–154.

Bandura, A., & Ramachaudran, V. S. (1994). Self-efficacy. In V. S. Ramachaudran (Ed.), *Encyclopedia of human behavior* (4, pp. 71–81). New York, NY: Academic Press.

Beyerle, R., & Dupree, J. E. (2016). *Bridging the gap: Increasing transportation access through training and technology. Community wayfinding: Pathways to understanding* (pp. 195–211). Cham: Springer.

Bond, M., Brown, J. R., & Wood, J. (2017). Adapting to challenge: Examining older adult transportation in rural communities. *Case Studies on Transport Policy*, *5*(4), 707–715.

Broome, K., Nalder, E., Worrall, L., & Boldy, D. (2010). Age-friendly buses? A comparison of reported barriers and facilitators to bus use for younger and older adults. *Australasian Journal on Ageing*, *29*(1), 33–38.

Broome, K., Worrall, L., Boldy, D., & Fleming, J. (2010). Outcomes of age-friendly changes to bus systems: An Australian case study. In *Presented at the TRANSED 2010: 12th international conference on mobility and transport for elderly and disabled persons.* Hong Kong, China.

Broome, K., Worrall, L., Fleming, J., & Boldy, D. (2011). Characteristics of age-friendly bus information. *Journal of Public Transportation*, *14*(4), 43–61.

Broome, K., Worrall, L., Fleming, J., & Boldy, D. (2012). Evaluation of flexible route bus transport for older people. *Transport Policy*, *21*, 85–91.

Broome, K., Worrall, L., McKenna, K., & Boldy, D. (2010). Priorities for an age-friendly bus system. *Canadian Journal on Aging*, *29*(3), 435–444.

Brown, J. R., Duncan, M., Horner, M. W., Bond, M., & Wood, J. (2018). Provider perspectives on six strategies to overcome the barriers to older adult use of alternative transportation services: Evidence from seven communities. *Case Studies on Transport Policy*, *6* (2), 237–245.

Burkhardt, J. E., Bernstein, D. J., Kulbicki, K., Eby, D. W., Molnar, L. J., Nelson, C. A., & McLary, J. M. (2014a). *Travel training for older adults Part I: A handbook.* TCRP report 168. Washington, DC: Transit Cooperative Research Program.

Burkhardt, J.E., Bernstein, D. J., Kulbicki, K., Eby, D. W., Molnar, L. J., Nelson, C. A., & McLary, J. M. (2014b). *Travel training for older adults Part II: Research report and case studies.* TCRP report 168. Washington, DC: Transit Cooperative Research Program.

Burkhardt, J. E., McGavock, A. T., Nelson, C. A., & Mitchell, C. G. (2002). *TCRP report 82: Improving public transit options for older persons* (Vol. 1). Washington, DC: Transit Cooperative Research Program.

Centers for Disease Control and Prevention. (2013). *The state of aging and health in America 2013*. Atlanta, GA: Centers for Disease Control and Prevention.

Eby, D. W., Molnar, L. J., & Kartje, P. S. (2009). *Maintaining safe mobility in an aging society*. New York, NY: CRC Press.

Eby, D. W., Molnar, L. J., Kostyniuk, L. P., St. Louis, R. M., & Zanier, N. (2011). *Recommendations for meeting the needs of Michigan's aging population.* Report no. RC-1562. Lansing, MI: Michigan Department of Transportation.

Ellis, E. (2009). *Mobility management*. Washington, DC: AARP Public Policy Institute. Available at: http://assets.aarp.org/rgcenter/ppi/liv-com/roundtable_091013_mobility.pdf. Accessed June, 2018.

Federal Transit Administration. *Coordinating council on access and mobility: Industry update.* (2017). Available at: <https://nationalcenterformobilitymanagement.org/wp-content/uploads/2013/11/CCAM-Transit-Industry-Update-Session-Notes-1-25-17.pdf> Accessed June, 2018.

Federal Transit Administration. (2018a). *What is coordinated transportation?* Washington, DC: Federal Transit Administration, US Department of Transportation. Available at: <https://www.transit.dot.gov/what-coordinated-transportation> Accessed July, 2018.

Federal Transit Administration. (2018b). *United we ride brochure*. Washington, DC: Federal Transit Administration, US Department of Transportation. Available at: <https://www.transit.dot.gov/ccam/resources/united-we-ride-brochure> Accessed June, 2018.

Fitzgerald, K. G., & Caro, F. G. (2014). An overview of age-friendly cities and communities around the world. *Journal of Aging & Social Policy*, *26*(1-2), 1–18.

Groce, M. (2013). Travel training: A new idea or coming of age. In *Presented at 2013 association of travel instruction conference*. Chicago, IL.

Hardin, J. (2005). Helping seniors take the bus: Innovative transit travel training programs. *Community Transportation*, *23*(7), 33–35.

Hess, D. B. (2012). Walking to the bus: Perceived versus actual walking distance to bus stops for older adults. *Transportation*, *39*(2), 247–266.

Jeste, D. V., Blazer, D. G., Buckwalter, K. C., Cassidy, K. L. K., Fishman, L., Gwyther, L. P., ... Feather, J. (2016). Age-friendly communities initiative: Public health approach to promoting successful aging. *The American Journal of Geriatric Psychiatry, 24*(12), 1158–1170.

Johnson, R., Shaw, J., Berding, J., Gather, M., & Rebstock, M. (2017). European national government approaches to older people's transport system needs. *Transport Policy, 59*, 17–27.

Kerschner, H., & Hardin, J. (2006). *Transportation innovations for seniors: A synopsis of findings in rural America*. Pasadena, CA: Beverly Foundation and Community Transportation Association of America.

Kerschner, H., & Harris, J. (2007). Better options for older adults. *Public roads, 70*. FHWA-HRT-07-003. Washington, DC: Federal Highway Administration.

Kihl, M., Brennan, D., Gabhalwala, N., List, J., & Mittal, P. (2005). *Livable communities: An evaluation guide*. Washington, DC: AARP Public Policy Institute.

Kim, H., & Richardson, V. E. (2006). Driving cessation and consumption expenses in the later years. *Journal of Gerontology B: Social Sciences, 61*(6), S347–353.

Ling, D., & Murray, S. (2010). Sustaining independent mobility for elder people in an ageing population: managing the transition from car dependency to confident use of public transport. In *Paper presented at the 12th international conference on mobility and transport for elderly and disabled persons (TRANSED2010)*. Hong Kong, China.

Litman, T. (2003). *Mobility management*. Eschborn, Germany: GTZ Transport and Mobility Group.

Lubin, A., Alexander, K., & Harvey, E. (2017). Achieving mobility access for older adults through group travel instruction. *Transportation Research Record, 2650*, 18–24.

Majumdar, S. R., Sen, L., & Park, S. (2012). The feasibility of mobility management in the United States. *Public Works Management & Policy, 18*(3), 263–278.

Mattson, J., Miller, J., Goodwill, J., Sriraj, P. S., & Hough, J. (2017). Impacts of mobility management and human service transportation coordination efforts and end-user quality of life. *Journal of the Transportation Research Forum, 56*, 77–92.

Mulley, C., Nelson, J., Teal, R., Wright, S., & Daniels, R. (2012). Barriers to implementing flexible transport services: An international comparison of the experiences in Australia, Europe and USA. *Research in Transportation Business & Management, 3*, 3–11.

National Aging and Disability Transportation Center (NADTC). *NADTC webinar: Providing person-centered transportation information to older adults and people with disabilities*. (2017). Available at: <http://www.nadtc.org/wp-content/uploads/NADTC-Webinar-Transcript-Person-Centered-Transportation-Information-August-23-2017.pdf> Accessed July, 2018.

National Alliance for Caregiving & AARP. (2015). *Caregiving in the U.S.: A focused look at those caring for the 50+*. Bethesda, MD: National Alliance for Caregiving and AARP Public Policy Institute.

National Center for Mobility Management. *Promoting customer-centered mobility strategies*. (2018). Available at: https://nationalcenterformobilitymanagement.org/ Accessed July, 2018.

Park, C. H., Welch, E. W., & Sriraj, P. S. (2016). An integrative theory-driven framework for evaluating travel training programs. *Evaluation and Program Planning, 59*, 7–20.

Ride Connection, Inc. (2009). *A guide to travel training*. Portland, OR: Ride Connection Inc.

Rodman, W., Berez, D., & Nelson, S.M. (2016). *The national mobility management initiative: State dots connecting specialized transportation users and rides*. Report no. NCHRP 20-65 Task 60. Boston, MA: Nelson/Nygaard Consulting Associates.

Rosenberg, D. E., Bombadier, C. H., Hoffman, J. M., & Belza, B. (2011). Physical activity among persons aging with mobility disabilities: Shaping a research agenda. *Journal of Aging Research*, *2011*, 708510.

Rosenbloom, S. (2009). Meeting transportation needs in an aging-friendly community. *Generations*, *33*(2), 33–43.

Scharlach, A. E., Davitt, J. K., Lehning, A. J., Greenfield, E. A., & Graham, C. L. (2014). Does the village model help to foster age-friendly communities? *Journal of Aging & Social Policy*, *26*(1-2), 181–196.

Shaheen, S., Allen, D., & Liu, J. (2008). Public transit training: A mechanism to increase ridership among older adults. In *Presented at the Transportation Research Board 88th annual meeting*. Washington, DC.

Shiau, T. A., & Huang, W. K. (2014). User perspective of age-friendly transportation: A case study of Taipei City. *Transport Policy*, *36*, 184–191.

Stevens, N., Battellino, H., & Pedler, K. (2013). Evaluating travel training in Northern Sydney: Methodological and practical issues. In *Presented at the* 36th *Australasian Transport Research Forum (ATRF)*. Brisbane, Queensland, Australia.

Tuokko, H., McGee, P., Stepaniuk, J., & Benner, E. (2007). *The older and wiser rider: An examination of transportation for older drivers*. British Columbia, Canada: Capital Regional District Traffic Safety Commission and BC Transit.

Velaga, N., Nelson, J., Wright, S., & Farrington, J. (2012). The potential role of flexible transport services in enhancing rural public transport provision. *Journal of Public Transportation*, *15*(1), 111–131.

Wolf-Branigin, K., & Wolf-Branigin, M. (2010). A travel training cost benefit model for people with disabilities, public transportation agencies and communities. In *International conference on mobility and transport for elderly and disabled persons conference proceedings*.

Wolf-Branigin, K., Wolf-Branigin, M., Culver, J. D., & Welch, K. (January-February 2012). Can travel training services save public transportation agencies money? *TR News*, *278*, 36–38

Wood, J., Brown, J., Bond, M., & Suguri, V. (2016). Older adult transportation in rural communities: Results of an agency survey. *Journal of Public Transportation*, *19*(2), 154–167.

World Health Organization. (2007). Global age-friendly cities: A guide. Geneva, Switzerland: World Health Organization.

# Federal, state, and local governments

# 11

*The care of human life and happiness, and not their destruction, is the first and only object of good government.*

*Thomas Jefferson*

## Introduction

Federal, state, and local governments play a critical role in fostering opportunities for older adults to maintain their mobility and independence as drivers, and as users of other mobility options when they can no longer or choose not to drive. As discussed in Chapter 8, Licensing Agencies, licensing agencies generally fall under the scope of state government and work as part of a larger system in helping to ensure the safety of all road users while enabling older adults to maintain their mobility. Part of that larger system includes various programs and policies operating at both the federal and local level, in addition to a host of other programs and policies at the state level.

In older adulthood, access to transportation services becomes even more important with the possibility of driving cessation on the horizon. Efforts to promote mobility among older adults are wide ranging and encompass a great variety of initiatives such as reducing the costs of paratransit services, as well as integrating land-use and transportation planning to improve accessibility of the transportation system. The funds necessary to provide programs at the state and local level come from a variety of sources and often originate at the federal level. In the United States (US), transportation policies and programs cut across various governmental departments at the federal level, such as the Department of Health and Human Services, Administration on Aging, and Department of Transportation. Funding for transportation for older adults varies annually and is subject to budget cuts that may ultimately hinder the ability of older adults to maintain independence, primarily in low-resource settings such as sparsely populated rural areas.

Due to competing interests and scarce resources, fiscal constraints at the federal, state, and local levels may limit the funds available to provide transportation programs and services to the growing population of older adults. The increasing need to find solutions for enhancing the mobility of older adults has been acknowledged to varying degrees at all levels of government (see Johnson, Shaw, Berding, Gather, & Rebstock, 2017). However, current research regarding the utility of transportation systems in several countries throughout the world has led to the similar conclusion that these systems are failing to meet the mobility needs of older adults

**Perspectives and Strategies for Promoting Safe Transportation among Older Adults.**
**DOI: https://doi.org/10.1016/B978-0-12-812153-5.00011-X**

(Council of Canadian Academies, 2017; Holley-Moore & Creighton, 2015; Rosenbloom, 2009; Wong, Szeto, Yang, Li, & Wong, 2018).

This chapter discusses the role that federal, state, and local governments have in helping older adults maintain mobility throughout all stages of the driving continuum. The key challenges and opportunities for providing adequate mobility options are discussed, as well as promising initiatives that have been undertaken to ensure a transportation system that is robust enough to handle the changing needs of the population.

## Policy and planning

All levels of government have grappled with the transportation and mobility challenges associated with the aging of the population. The governments of many countries have developed long-term strategic plans to address the mobility needs of the growing older adult population. A primary goal is to reduce injuries and fatalities of road users, with special attention given to vulnerable populations such as older adults and those with mobility issues. Another goal is to improve the transportation system so that older adults have alternative ways to get to places they want or need to go when they can no longer or choose not to drive. High-level policy can take a system-wide approach to addressing the transportation issues of older adults and the population as a whole. A system-wide approach to solving transportation issues involves using an established set of principles to guide the implementation of various initiatives at all levels of government. An example of this is the Safe System approach, a policy framework that influences the development and implementation of traffic safety initiatives in which there is shared responsibility among everyone involved in the traffic safety system, from the engineers who design and construct the roadways to the users of the transport system (International Transport Forum (ITF), 2016). This approach has been adopted in several countries throughout the world and is discussed in detail later in this chapter.

Policy and planning at the local level is equally as important as the high-level policy described previously. State and local governments and the organizations that operate in partnership with these entities have insight into the specific needs of the community in which they serve and the unique challenges that must be overcome to provide safe and comprehensive opportunities for continued mobility for their community members. Examples of these policies include driver licensing regulations (see Chapter 8: Licensing Agencies), concession fares and priority seating on public transport (Wong et al., 2018), and building and upgrading sidewalks and walking paths (Satariano et al., 2012).

A comprehensive review of national-level transportation policy documents in the European Union, Norway, and Switzerland documented the extent to which the transport systems in 29 countries addressed the needs of older people (Johnson et al., 2017). The authors first identified 11 age-friendly qualities a transport system should have if it is to support older adults' mobility. These qualities were affordable, available, barrier-free (accessible), comfortable, comprehensible, efficient, friendly, reliable, safe, secure, and transparent (see Johnson et al., 2017 for definitions of each quality). Safety, accessibility, and affordability were the most frequently cited qualities addressed in policy documents to promote mobility of older adults across Europe, suggesting solutions that are more straightforward to promoting mobility such as guiderails, physical alterations of the transport space, and lowering the cost of transportation. In this respect, most policies are based on "tangible" qualities rather than "softer" social qualities. The authors argued that because older adults' mobility is largely influenced by subjective and contextual factors, the government should give more attention to interventions and policies that address other qualities that are deemed "softer" qualities, such as friendliness. The inclusion of such qualities in policymaking and the design of interventions could further efforts to promote mobility among the aging population.

Numerous jurisdictions throughout the world have established specialized work groups and formal committees to investigate the mobility needs of the aging population and provide recommendations for future transportation policy as it relates to older adults. The following examples of such groups and their policy recommendations are from Canada, Britain, and Australia. Each recognized the necessity of both short- and long-term planning, and the important role the government plays in providing a safe transportation system for all road users. The policy recommendations provided are extensive and demonstrate the tremendous variety of stakeholders involved in creating opportunities for the continued mobility of older adults.

The Conference Board of Canada (Munro, 2016) identified three core principles that should be acknowledged when developing transportation initiatives. The policies and strategies should (1) meet the transportation needs and preferences of older adults; (2) minimize risks associated with older adults' mobility, such as safety risks related to using other modes of transportation and escalating costs of alternative transport; and (3) respect the rights and dignity of older adults. Recommendations for enhancing mobility for older adults included the development of more accurate assessment standards for fitness to drive to assist health professionals in managing the driving safety of their patients; continued government funding for research into the effectiveness of transportation policies, procedures, and practices targeting older adults, such as age-based licensing; and transit agencies and the government should ensure proper dissemination of materials regarding the transportation services available in the community and how to use them.

An Older Drivers Task Force was established in Britain in 2014 with the aim of finding ways to help older drivers continue to drive safely for longer, acknowledging the fact that people are continuing to work until older ages, as well as increased life expectancy. The goal was to develop a National Older Drivers Strategy to "... improve the framework, advice, self-help and technology available to support the fast growing number of older drivers" (Older Drivers Task Force, 2016, p. 5). Policy recommendations provided in the strategy target different areas of the transportation system. Examples of recommendations included in the strategy were the age at which a driver must notify the licensing agency of a medical condition that may affect safe driving should be raised from 70 to 75; the United Kingdom should develop better guidelines for designing roads for older drivers; and vehicle manufactures should speed up the process of developing improved crash protection standards for older, more fragile people.

Similar to the Older Drivers Task Force in Britain, the Older Driver Safety Advisory Committee convened in 2011 to provide the government in Queensland, Australia with input to develop policies and initiatives to improve older driver safety outcomes. The committee reviewed key research on older driver issues, crash data, and policies directed at the older driver population. Based on this information, the committee provided policy recommendations for drivers age 75 and older. These recommendations included providing additional training to medical practitioners to support their ability to understand the impact of various eye conditions on driving, developing educational strategies to assist informal caregivers with discussions about driving safety, increasing the availability of alternative transportation options, and implementing guidelines on road design for older road users.

The Committee for the Conference on Transportation in an Aging Society (2005) outlined several recommendations to accomplish the goal of providing safe mobility to older adults. Chief among them was the necessity of leadership or decision-making in the political context, as this would enable a group to take ownership of the issue and advocate for changes to transportation policy. The need for leadership and commitment to advance the agenda for safe mobility among the aging population is echoed throughout transportation policy documents on a global scale (ITF, 2016; United Nations (UN) Secretary General's High-Level Advisory Group on Sustainable Transport, 2016) as well as locally (AARP, 2012). Leadership roles are often assumed by those holding governmental positions, such as federal congressional representatives, state governors, and local council people. In addition to leaders at all levels of government, researchers, lobbyists, nonprofit groups, and members of the public also play key roles in advocating for change to policy to support the mobility needs of older adults. Campaigns to change policy, transportation or otherwise, often begin as grassroots efforts by members of the public that are concerned about a similar issue. A study by Rosenbloom (2010) found that the current cohort of baby boomers are quite affected by their aging parents' decline in driving abilities and subsequent driving cessation, leaving this population concerned about how their parents will meet their mobility needs and also about the burden they will assume when their parents can no longer drive. Rosenbloom (2010) suggested that, due to the sheer magnitude of baby boomers in the US and the United Kingdom, this group could have a great impact on shaping future transportation policy by advocating for improvements to the transportation system.

Policy initiatives determine how resources are distributed among different levels of government. The allocation of funds affects several important areas of older adult mobility that are highlighted throughout this book. Policies and funds available impact decisions to build roadways that are engineered with older adults in mind, to design vehicles that are safer and easier to use, to develop new technologies to enhance older adult mobility, to create transportation alternatives, and to provide training and technical assistance for older adults and their caregivers

(Committee for the Conference on Transportation in an Aging Society, 2005). The following section provides a brief overview of funding for transportation services and programs for older adults.

## Funding

It is widely accepted that providing safe mobility for older people at some level is a vital function of the government (Committee for the Conference on Transportation in an Aging Society, 2005; Munro, 2016; Older Drivers Task Force, 2016; Spinney, Scott, & Newbold, 2009). In the United States, federal agencies administer programs that provide funds for a range of transportation services to both state and local organizations that, in turn, offer transportation services either directly or through private or public transportation providers (United States Government Accountability Office (US GAO), 2014). Currently, there are more than 80 federal programs in the United States that fund transportation services for the general public and for the transportation disadvantaged, such as older adults, people with disabilities, and those with lower income (Hemily, 2017; US GAO, 2012). In the United States, state transportation funds are provided in part by the federal government and health-care funds, under the umbrella of the Department of Health and Human Services, are often used to deliver transportation services and program to older adults for a variety of both medical and nonmedical reasons. For example, many organizations that provide paratransit services to older adults get a large portion of financial support from federal funding related to the Americans with Disabilities Act (Knodler et al., 2016).

State and local governments also provide funding for programs providing transportation for older adults, and these entities, along with public or private providers, administer services at the local level (Lynott, Fox-Grage, & Guzman, 2013; US GAO, 2014). Regional transit agencies, community-based organizations, health-care organizations, and private transit companies provide transportation options to older adults under varying circumstances. Programs can operate using a combination of resources from all levels of government, along with personal funds from the users of the programs and services (Knodler et al., 2016). Due to the variety of funding sources and sheer number of different organizations working to provide transportation options in any given area, there is a need for inter-organization coordination to ensure an effective and efficient system is in place. The benefits and challenges of inter-organization coordination will be discussed later in this chapter.

The distribution of funding at all levels of government, and the often complex nature of how the funds are allocated and used, emphasizes the importance of conducting research into the transportation needs of the older adult population at both a national level (e.g., exploring overall trends in driving patterns of older drivers in the US), as well as regional and local levels (e.g., ensuring older adults in a rural community have access to alternative transportation options). The following section describes the critical role of data and research for the appropriate allocation of resources.

## The role of data and research

Appropriate data collection and analysis enable agencies at all levels of government to prioritize actions that can have the greatest impact on improving the mobility needs of older adults. Research into the transportation needs of older adults provides the evidence for making policy recommendations, as well as decisions regarding the distribution of resources. In addition, research into the effectiveness of specific initiatives will allow for better policies and strategies to be designed (Munro, 2016). Indeed, the lack of data can be a barrier to adoption of effective transportation policy, as the evidence needed to inform and influence policymakers does not exist or is only anecdotal in nature.

Data are needed for a variety of reasons, including to ensure that available services are providing their intended effect of enhancing the mobility of older adults. A study by Bond, Brown, and Wood (2017) examined transportation agency strategies to serve older adults in rural and small communities better. Results showed that data regarding the characteristics of riders and trip purpose were not well tracked; therefore, it was difficult to assess whether current transportation options were sufficient in meeting the mobility needs of the population the organizations served. The overall goal of improving transportation for older adults is dependent upon more and better research about the transportation needs of community members, patterns of use of available transportation options, and effectiveness of policies and initiatives directed at older adults (Munro, 2016). In addition, research into identifying which transportation alternatives are preferred by older adults and most feasible to implement based on an area's demographics will aid policymakers in drafting laws and regulations that take into account the varying needs of older adults.

As previously stated, transportation programs and services obtain funding from a wide variety of sources within the federal, state, and local governments and other private entities. In the US, it is estimated that tens of thousands of government agencies, nonprofits, and private companies provide funding for transportation services (Rall & Myers, 2015). As such, there is no unifying database that identifies and tracks information about existing transportation programs that cater to the older adult population. Knowing this information could help to identify mobility needs within a community, understand how the various services within a community interact with one another, and determine how the availability of services impacts the mobility of older adults (Koffman, Weiner, Pfeiffer, & Chapman, 2010).

Koffman et al. (2010) stressed the importance of gathering better data about existing programs and presented three options for improved data gathering: (1) create a program to obtain consistent data from recipients of funding; (2) establish a basic set of required data items to be included in transportation inventories conducted for coordinated public transit–human services transportation plans; and (3) create a voluntary system of reporting under an initiative like the National Center on Senior Transportation. These data could then be used to inform decisions on resource allocation to ensure proper stewardship of limited funding as well as to provide information to policymakers about the transportation needs of older adults both within their jurisdiction and on a national level.

## Inter-organization coordination

This section expands upon the coordination of transportation services and policies related to mobility management discussed in Chapter 10, Transportation Service Providers. Organizations within federal, state, and local governments must work together to ensure mobility needs are met as well as reduce the risk of injuries and fatalities to older adults. In the United States, the need for inter-organization coordination to improve transportation services for disadvantaged populations, such as older adults and people with disabilities, was recognized as far back as the 1970s (see, e.g., US GAO, 1999, 2003). Coordination of transportation services "is a process in which two or more organizations interact to jointly accomplish their transportation objectives. When properly implemented, coordination can increase the efficiency of resource use, improve service delivery, and enhance customer knowledge of and access to transportation services" (Farber, Shinkle, Lynott, Fox-Grage, & Harrell, 2011, p. VIII). The need for inter-organization coordination continues today, as evidenced by *Beyond Traffic 2045*, a report about the future of the transportation system in the United States. This report highlighted a series of discussions with regional transportation stakeholders in 11 emerging megaregions, which are "... networks of urban clusters connected by economic and social relationships" (US DOT, 2017, p. 206). Stakeholders comprised citizens, elected officials, community leaders, city planners, business owners, and transportation industry leaders. A top issue discussed by stakeholders in nearly every megaregion was the importance of building collaborative relationships across boundaries to provide more efficient and effective service delivery (US DOT, 2017). Therefore, a policy recommendation provided within *Beyond Traffic 2045* is to strengthen the coordination of human service transportation services to meet the mobility needs of older adults and those with disabilities (US DOT, 2017).

Local transportation services are often delivered by many different organizations operating independently in the same community or region, resulting in a fragmented and duplicative transportation system that is difficult to navigate. For example, Knodler et al. (2016) highlighted the complexity of a mobility support system for older adults in Massachusetts and estimated that there are more than 570 different agencies and organizations to assist in providing information and mobility options to older adults operating in Massachusetts. In addition, a study in Michigan found that although there was an extensive transportation network for older adults (with every county in the state having some form of transportation service), gaps and barriers to services remained, largely due to lack of funding as well as lack of coordination among transportation providers (Eby, Molnar, Kostyniuk, St Louis, & Zanier, 2011). The large number, diversity, and dispersion of transportation programs can lead to underutilization of resources, overlap of services in one area and a shortage of services in another, inconsistent safety standards, and customer inconvenience (Rall & Myers, 2015).

Increased coordination is a goal of many state and federal policies and initiatives aimed at older adults and other transportation-disadvantaged populations (US GAO, 2014). To understand how policy supports local community coordination,

Schlossberg (2004) examined three jurisdictions with differing policy approaches toward coordinating transportation programs and services for transportation-disadvantaged populations. The three policy approaches included the following: (1) an incentive-based approach to coordination, in which the state government encourages and assists with coordination by providing grants and technical assistance to local and rural counties without imposing a statewide mandate; (2) a statewide mandate requiring all agencies receiving federal, state or local funds for transportation services to coordinate with other local agencies or organizations also providing transportation and receiving state funds; and (3) no policy or program facilitating local coordination of transportation services. Schlossberg (2004) concluded that the primary factors that facilitate successful coordination at the state government level were state programs that target coordination of transportation agencies and services and state financial support to fund the coordination process. He also highlighted the importance of having a full time, dedicated entity to work toward the goal of coordination of services.

A key strategy toward coordination has been the establishment of coordinating councils that operate at all levels of government and provide a forum for inter-organization collaboration. Coordinating councils are "... groups of diverse organizations that actively work together on an ongoing basis to better coordinate and provide transportation services to people who have mobility challenges" (Rall & Myers, 2015, p. 6). Examples of coordinating council members include representatives from state-level Departments of Transportation, Health and Human Services, Disabilities and Aging; state legislators; a representative from the Governor's Office; transit providers; nonprofit organizations; and individuals representing specific populations (such as older adults or those with disabilities). As of 2015, there were 20 states in the US with at least one active state-level coordinating council. A survey of stakeholders at state human service transportation agencies and within state coordinating councils determined the following factors to contribute to successful coordination: leadership of key decision makers, such as governors, managers, and staff who control agency funding; keeping members engaged and informed; and focusing on a small, attainable goal to create buy-in, which provides momentum for further collaboration (Rall & Myers, 2015).

Although inter-organization collaboration is necessary to achieve an effective and efficient transportation system that provides options for continued mobility of older adults, several barriers to collaboration and coordination of programs exist. These include lack of participation of important partner agencies, lack of funding to support council efforts, no mandate to coordinate fiscal resources, difficulty gaining buy-in from stakeholders, lack of understanding about the coordination process, and cultural differences in the language, motivations, and objectives of stakeholders from the transportation industry and those within human services (Rall & Myers, 2015). Lack of coordination is a significant obstacle to effectively meeting the mobility needs of people who need transportation services most (Hemily, 2017). As discussed in other chapters, rural areas present even greater challenges for meeting the mobility needs of the aging population. The great majority of older adults prefer to remain in their own homes as they age (Farber et al., 2011), and more than three quarters of older adults are aging in suburban or rural areas with few mobility options apart from a personal automobile (DeGood, 2011). Therefore, transportation services that allow older adults to remain in their own homes are a critical piece of extending the period of time an older adult can age in place while maintaining independence. Inter-organization coordination allows stakeholders to operate across their respective boundaries, which helps to ensure providers are working together to streamline programs and increase transportation options to older adults in the community.

Because the state government plays a pivotal role in implementing federally funded programs and delivering transportation services to older adults, Koffman, Raphael, and Weiner (2004) noted that promoting coordination of transportation services will likely require action at the state level with technical assistance from the federal government. In addition, similar to the findings by Schlossberg (2004), financial incentives provided to states from the federal government to increase coordination activities would help to overcome the barrier of lack of funding and to ensure coordination is a priority among state and local organizations.

## Promising initiatives

Numerous initiatives have been developed around the world to address the transportation and mobility needs of older adults. Initiatives range from local to global and therefore encompass a wide range of approaches to accommodate the varying needs of not only older adults but also the general public. For example, the UN is leading an effort on a global level to improve the safety of road users, as well as to allow people to access what they need for healthy and fulfilled lives. In 2015, the UN General Assembly adopted several goals and targets as part of the 2030 Agenda for Sustainable Development. One such target is to halve the number of deaths and injuries from traffic crashes throughout the world by 2020 (ITF, 2016). In addition, a target under the overarching goal of making cities and human settlements inclusive, safe, resilient, and sustainable is: “By 2030, provide access to safe, affordable, accessible and sustainable transport systems for all, improving road safety, notably by expanding public transport, with special attention to the needs of those in vulnerable situations, women, children, persons with disabilities and older persons” (United Nations (UN) Secretary General’s High-Level Advisory Group on Sustainable Transport, 2016, p. 12). Meeting this target will require government at all levels across the world to engage in policy discussions to develop strategies and action plans to improve access to and safety of transport systems for specific subpopulations.

A promising initiative to reducing injuries and fatalities of road users is the Safe System approach, which was pioneered in Sweden and the Netherlands in the 1980s and 1990s (ITF, 2016). The ITF (2016) describes a Safe System as “... the vision or aspiration that zero fatalities and serious injuries from road crashes are ultimately possible” (p. 30). This strategy represents a shift away from the traditional approach to road safety, which primarily emphasizes the responsibility of the road user, to a system that recognizes road safety as the outcome of the interaction between many different components that influence crash risk. The Safe System approach is a broader, systemic approach to addressing road safety issues and takes into account a variety of underlying factors that affect road safety, including the responsibility of governments to protect their citizens. The principles of the Safe System approach are (Welle et al., 2018)

1. No death or serious injury is acceptable: The mobility system should be safe and efficient for all road users.
2. Road safety is a shared responsibility: A safe transport system depends on shared responsibility between governments, the private sector, civil society, and road users. This includes those who design, build, manage, and use roads and vehicles as well as those who provide postcrash care.
3. Humans are fallible: Human error on the road is inevitable and can lead to crashes.
4. The human body is vulnerable in a crash: There are limits on the amount of force a human body can withstand in a crash before serious harm occurs.
5. It is a proactive approach to road safety: Rather than waiting for an event to occur and reacting, this approach creates layers of protection within the system to prevent injuries and fatalities resulting from crashes.

The Safe System approach to road safety can be used to develop action plans in the following areas: land-use planning; improved mobility options; enforcement, laws, and regulation; vehicle design and technology; street design and engineering; speed management; education and capacity building; and postcrash emergency response and care (Welle et al., 2018). The ITF recommends a Safe System to be designed to meet the needs of the growing population of older adults. Examples of ways to make traveling safer for older adults using the Safe System approach include limiting vehicle speed, reducing the width of pedestrian crossings and extending crossing time for older pedestrians, and to have safe, accessible and well-lit transit design (ITF, 2016). Using the Safe System policy framework, Langford and Oxley (2006) provided countermeasures aimed at preventing crashes and reducing the severity of crash outcomes for older drivers. The recommended countermeasures include improving the design of urban intersections, emphasizing crashworthiness in vehicle purchasing decisions, reducing speeds at intersections, and improving assessment procedures to identify at-risk older drivers.

The governments of several countries, states, and cities throughout the world have now adopted the Safe System approach and have called the policy framework various names, for example, Vision Zero, Towards Zero, and Road to Zero. The adoption of the Safe System approach has led to success in reducing injuries and fatalities in many countries throughout the world. Of 53 countries analyzed, those adopting the Safe System approach achieved both the lowest rate of traffic fatalities and the largest reductions in fatalities in over 20 years (Welle et al., 2018). Welle et al. (2018) estimated that nearly one million lives could be saved each year if all governments adopted this approach. *Sustainable & Safe: A Vision and Guidance for Zero Road Deaths* (Welle et al., 2018) provides guidance for policymakers on the application of the Safe System approach to road safety. The report can be used at several levels of government and applied in a variety of settings, including urban, rural, and intercity areas. Mirroring the chief recommendation provided by the Committee for the Conference for Transportation in an Aging Society, the ITF also believes strong and sustained leadership is vital to the success of a country shifting transportation and road safety policy to a Safe System. In addition, the World Health Organization (WHO) (2015) recommends that a lead agency be designated to develop a national road safety strategy and oversee its implementation to ensure the objectives are operationalized consistently throughout the country.

Other promising initiatives to keep older adults safely mobile are operating at state, regional, and local levels of government. Several states in the US have been recognized for their commitment to developing more unified and comprehensive approaches to promoting safe mobility of older adults, including California, Florida, Iowa, Maryland, New York, and Oregon (Stutts, 2005). In addition, the state of Michigan has developed a statewide strategy to promote safe mobility of older adults throughout all phases of the driving continuum. Researchers from the University of Michigan Transportation Research Institute (UMTRI) collaborated with the Michigan Department of Transportation and Michigan Department of State (MDOS), with input from over 20 partner organizations, to develop, implement, and evaluate a sustainable statewide safety education and intervention strategy with the following goals: help aging adults who are able to drive safely continue to do so; facilitate the transition from driving to non-driving for those who are unable or choose not to drive; and support the use of community mobility options for those who no longer drive. This strategy is titled *Safe Drivers Smart Options: Keys to Lifelong Mobility* (SDSO, Eby, Molnar, Kostyniuk, Zanier, & St Louis, 2016; State of Michigan, 2018). The strategy was based on the model shown in Fig. 11.1 that was developed by UMTRI. The primary method of delivery for the strategy is the SDSO website (www.michigan.gov/agingdriver), which houses resources and materials that support the primary goals of the strategy and are targeted toward aging drivers, caregivers, and professionals that work with older adults, such as physicians, other health-care workers, and law enforcement officers. The website also provides information on training, programs, and activities that are considered best practice for supporting aging drivers. SDSO is currently being implemented across Michigan and is managed by MDOS. The strategy has won several awards since its implementation, including the Public Affairs and Consumer Education Regional Award for Excellence in Government Partnership from the American Association of Motor Vehicle Administrators (State of Michigan, 2018).

The Community Transportation Pilot Grant Program in Ontario, Canada is an initiative that provides financial assistance to Ontario municipalities to partner with local community organizations to leverage and coordinate existing transportation services (Ontario Ministry of Transportation, 2018). The three goals of the program are to (1) improve mobility options for people who do not have access to transportation, including older adults and those with disabilities; (2) build capacity to better meet local transportation demand, primarily in areas where providing conventional or specialized transit service is challenging or not possible; and (3) create networks of coordinated community transportation services using existing services and pooling resources to provide more mobility options to a greater amount of people. As

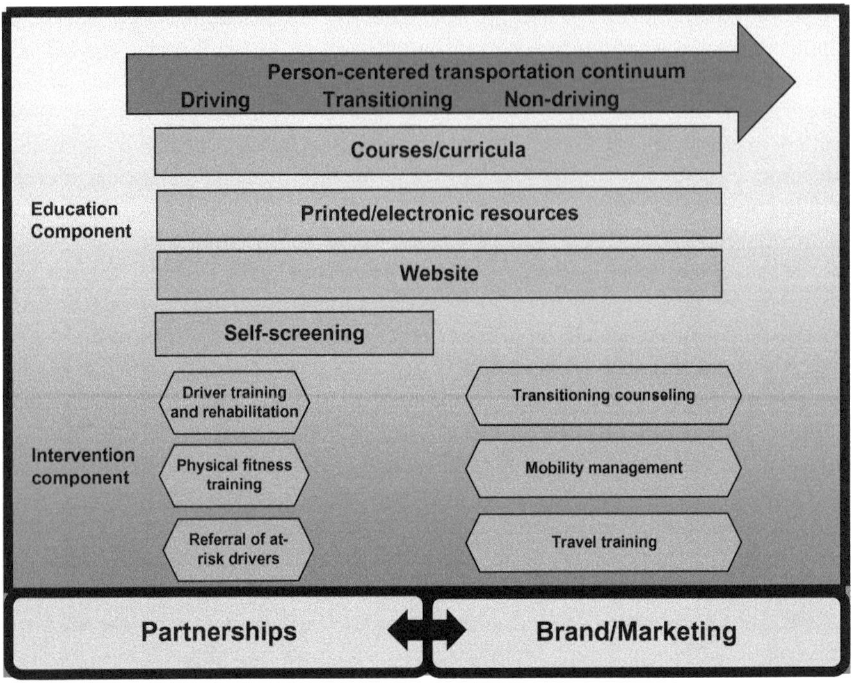


**Figure 11.1** A graphical depiction of the model that underlies the Michigan strategy to promote safe mobility for older adults called *Safe Drivers Smart Options: Keys to Lifelong Mobility*.

part of the initial 2-year pilot period from 2015 to 2017, 22 municipalities received, on average, approximately $88,000 (Canadian dollars) in grant funding of which the majority of funding was used to provide new transportation services where none had existed or enhanced existing services. The Ontario Ministry of Transportation (2018) conducted an evaluation of the program to assess the effectiveness of the community transportation service delivery model. Survey results showed that all pilot jurisdictions had a high or moderately high impact on improving community mobility, primarily by leveraging resources and partnerships to provide more transportation to community facilities, such as social and health services, older adults' community housing facilities, health-care clinics, and retail shopping centers. Throughout a 12-month period, 25,172 rides were provided to older adults. Overall, the pilot jurisdictions were able to customize transportation services effectively to meet the unique needs of their respective communities, strengthen community networks and improve administration of services through partnerships and coordination with other organizations, and increase transportation capacity and mobility options by sharing resources and assets with partner organizations (Ontario Ministry of Transportation, 2018). To help develop and sustain these efforts, pilot municipalities indicated they needed access to new or increased funding, sufficient time to pilot services and establish ridership, and more opportunity to build partnerships with private and nonprofit organizations.

A policy approach recommended in *Beyond Traffic 2045* (US DOT, 2017) is to promote integrated transportation and land-use planning as a method to preserve and create quality, affordable, and accessible transportation options for all members of the community. With input from nearly 1200 stakeholders, including community members and subject matter experts, the Atlanta Regional Commission (ARC) in the state of Georgia developed a regional strategic plan that recognizes the importance of combining land-use and transportation planning to support healthy aging, increase community mobility, and to allow older adults the opportunity to age in place (Atlanta Regional Commission Division of Aging and Health Resources, 2017). The ARC is the federally designated Metropolitan Planning Organization and intergovernmental coordination agency for the 10-county Atlanta region and also serves as the region's Area Agency on Aging (ARC, 2017). Given the breadth and scope of ARC, its unique position helps to focus on the region's leadership, attention, and resources on critical issues of common concern, with one major issue being the rapid growth of the aging population.

By 2030, one in five people in the Atlanta region will be over the age of 60 (Keyes, Rader, & Berger, 2011), and the desire to age in place is evidenced by a recent survey of older adults in the metro Atlanta region, which showed that 74% of older adults plan to stay in the region as they age (ARC, 2017). To prepare for this demographic shift while recognizing the desire for older adults to age in place, the ARC established the Lifelong Communities Initiative in 2007 (Lawler & Berger, 2009) and continues to uphold and implement its core principles current programs and policies to (1) promote housing and transportation options, (2) encourage healthy lifestyles, and (3) expand access to services (Keyes & Berger, 2013). The Lifelong Communities Initiative is an approach combining planning, community organizing, and policy reform at all levels of government to encourage the development of programs and infrastructure that allows people of all ages to remain in their homes and communities for as long as they desire (ARC, 2009; Keyes & Berger, 2013). A key element of Lifelong Communities is the development and promotion of alternative transportation options, as well as infrastructure that supports walkable communities for older adults and those with disabilities. ARC, which represents 78 local governments in the region, adopted the Lifelong Communities Initiative as regional policy, thereby committing to acknowledge and integrate the needs of older adults in every aspect of community and program planning as well as encouraging other local governments to do the same (Keyes & Berger, 2013).

## Conclusions

Addressing the challenges of developing and implementing transportation policy that supports the continued mobility of older adults throughout the driving continuum is a multifaceted issue that will only get more complex as the baby boomers age into older adulthood. All levels of government have acknowledged the growing demand for and importance of continued mobility and, to varying degrees, have made strides in planning and executing strategies to provide older adults with the opportunity for sustained mobility. The changing needs of the population are being addressed in international, national, state, and local policies. The primary policy operating in many jurisdictions throughout the world is the Safe System approach, which is "... at the center stage of road safety policy making at the global, regional, and national levels" (ITF, 2016, p. 18). To enable the implementation of this type of policy as well as others at local and regional levels, strong and consistent leadership is necessary.

Although increased access to public transportation options may be necessary to expand mobility options for older adults (Koffman et al., 2010), the issues that lend themselves to driving cessation, such decreased mobility or cognitive impairment, also affect one's ability to utilize public transportation. Policymakers and transportation leaders should consider this when planning for the future transportation system. It is also beneficial to include older adults as stakeholders in the planning process to gain perspective from current and future users of alternative transportation options.

Inter-organization coordination leads to better resource management strategies that not only improve the performance of various individual transportation services but also work to enhance overall mobility within a community (Burkhardt, Nelson, Murray, & Koffman, 2004). Therefore, continued governmental support and funding to facilitate inter-organization collaboration in planning and implementing mobility options for older adults at the state, regional, and local levels is critical. This includes collaboration within departments of state, regional, and local levels of government and with organizations in the private sector. Research into what makes inter-organization collaboration more or less successful in various community settings would also be beneficial to transportation leaders interested in developing partnerships to enhance mobility options.

Data and research will continue to play a dominant role in decision-making at all levels of government as they provide the necessary evidence to make informed policy decisions, to create new programs and services promoting older adult mobility, and to evaluate existing transportation policy and programs to ensure their stated objectives are being met. There are various mechanisms by which organizations receive funding from the government to implement transportation options to enhance the mobility of older adults. A greater emphasis on collecting data to understand the needs of a community, as well as information on how the programs are conducted and the financial resources are used to fund the program, would ensure scarce resources are allocated to areas in which the most impact can be made.

## References

AARP. (2012). *Meeting older adults' mobility needs: Transportation planning and coordination in rural communities*. Washington, DC: AARP.

Atlanta Regional Commission (ARC). (2009). *Lifelong communities: A regional guide to growth and longevity*. Atlanta, GA: Atlanta Regional Commission.

Atlanta Regional Commission (ARC). (2017). *The journey continues: Atlanta Regional Commission 2016 state of the region annual report*. Atlanta, GA: Atlanta Regional Commission.

Atlanta Regional Commission Division of Aging and Health Resources. (2017). *Live beyond expectations: Regional strategic plan.* Atlanta, GA: Atlanta Regional Commission.

Bond, M., Brown, J. R., & Wood, J. (2017). Adapting to challenge: Examining older adult transportation in rural communities. *Case Studies on Transport Policy*, *5*(4), 707–715.

Burkhardt, J. E., Nelson, C. A., Murray, G., & Koffman, D. (2004). *Toolkit for rural community coordinated transportation services.* TCRP report 101. Washington, DC: Transportation Research Board.

Committee for the Conference on Transportation in an Aging Society (2005). *Safe Mobility for Older Americans.* Conference Proceedings 2. Washington DC: Transportation Research Board.

Council of Canadian Academies. (2017). *Older Canadians on the move.* Ottawa, ON: The Expert Panel on the Transportation Needs of an Aging Population, Council of Canadian Academies.

DeGood, K. (2011). *Aging in place, stuck without options: Fixing the mobility crisis threatening the baby boom generation.* Washington, DC: Transportation for America.

Eby, D. W., Molnar, L. J., Kostyniuk, L. P., St Louis, R. M., & Zanier, N. (2011). *Recommendations for meeting the transportation needs of Michigan's aging population.* Lansing, MI: Michigan Department of Transportation.

Eby, D. W., Molnar, L. J., Kostyniuk, L. P., Zanier, N., & St Louis, R. M. (2016). *Safe Drivers Smart Options: Keys to Lifelong Mobility.* Report no. UMTRI-2016-18. Ann Arbor, MI: University of Michigan Transportation Research Institute.

Farber, N., Shinkle, D., Lynott, J., Fox-Grage, W., & Harrell, R. (2011). *Aging in place: A state survey of livability policies and practices.* Washington, DC: National Conference of State Legislators and AARP Public Policy Institute.

Hemily, B. (2017). *Reference manual for planning and design of a Travel Management Coordination Center (TMCC).* FTA report no. 0117. Washington, DC: Federal Transit Administration.

Holley-Moore, G., & Creighton, H. (2015). *The future of transport in an ageing society.* London, England: Age UK.

International Transport Forum (ITF). (2016). *Zero road deaths and serious injuries: Leading a paradigm shift to a Safe System.* Paris: Organisation for Economic Co-operation and Development Publishing.

Johnson, R., Shaw, J., Berding, J., Gather, M., & Rebstock, M. (2017). European national government approaches to older people's transport system needs. *Transport Policy*, *59*, 17–27.

Keyes, L., & Berger, C. (2013). *Atlanta Regional Commission's Lifelong Communities Initiative: Creating Communities for All Ages and Abilities.* Atlanta, GA: The Atlanta Regional Commission.

Keyes, L., & Berger, C. (2011). Creating communities: Atlanta's lifelong community initiative. *Physical & Occupational Therapy in Geriatrics*, *29*(1), 59–74.

Knodler Jr, M. A., Collura, J., Rothenberg, H. A., Tupper, S., Peabody, D., Riessman, R., & Kennedy, J. R. (2016). *Coping with the aging driving population.* Report no. SPRII.06.23. Boston, MA: Massachusetts Department of Transportation.

Koffman, D., Raphael, D., & Weiner, R. (2004). *The impact of federal programs on transportation for older adults.* Report no. 2004-17. Washington, DC: AARP Public Policy Institute.

Koffman, D., Weiner, R., Pfeiffer, A., & Chapman, S. (2010). *Funding the public transportation needs of an aging population.* San Francisco, CA: Nelson/Nygaard Consulting Associates.

Langford, J., & Oxley, J. (2006). Using the Safe System approach to keep older drivers safely mobile. *IATSS Research*, *30*(2), 97–109.

Lawler, K., & Berger, C. (2009). Creating lifelong communities: One region's response to the opportunity of longevity. *Public Policy and Aging Report*, *19*(1), 9–14.

Lynott, J., Fox-Grage, W., & Guzman, S. (2013). *Weaving it together: A tapestry of transportation funding for older adults*. Washington, DC: AARP Public Policy Institute.

Munro, D. (2016). *Managing mobility. Transportation in an aging society*. Ottawa, ON: The Conference Board of Canada.

Older Drivers Task Force. (2016). *Support safe driving into old age: A national older driver strategy*. Brussels, Belgium: Ageas.

Ontario Ministry of Transportation. (2018). *Community transportation pilot grant program: Survey and final reporting evaluation*. Ontario, Canada: Ministry of Transportation.

Rall, J., & Myers, A. (2015). *State human service transportation coordinating councils: An overview and state profiles, 2014 update*. Denver, CO and Washington, DC: National Conference of State Legislatures.

Rosenbloom, S. (2009). Meeting transportation needs in an aging-friendly community. *Generations*, *33*(2), 33–43.

Rosenbloom, S. (2010). How adult children in the UK and the US view the driving cessation of their parents: Is a policy window opening? *Journal of Transport Geography*, *18*(5), 634–641.

Satariano, W. A., Guralnik, J. M., Jackson, R. J., Marottoli, R. A., Phelan, E. A., & Prohaska, T. R. (2012). Mobility and aging: New directions for public health action. *American Journal of Public Health*, *102*(8), 1508–1515.

Schlossberg, M. (2004). Coordination as a strategy for serving the transportation disadvantaged: A comparative framework of local and state roles. *Public Works Management & Policy*, *9*(2), 132–144.

Spinney, J. E., Scott, D. M., & Newbold, K. B. (2009). Transport mobility benefits and quality of life: A time-use perspective of elderly Canadians. *Transport Policy*, *16*(1), 1–11.

State of Michigan. *Safe drivers smart options: Keys to lifelong mobility*. (2018). <https://www.michigan.gov/agingdriver> Accessed June, 2018.

Stutts, J. C. (2005). *Improving the safety of older road users: A synthesis of highway practice*. NCHRP synthesis 348. Washington, DC: Transportation Research Board.

United Nations (UN) Secretary General's High-Level Advisory Group on Sustainable Transport. (2016). *Mobilizing sustainable transport for development: Analysis and policy recommendations from the United Nations Secretary General's High-Level Advisory Group on Sustainable Transport*. New York, NY: United Nations.

United States Department of Transportation (US DOT). (2017). *Beyond traffic 2045*. Washington, DC: United States Department of Transportation.

United States Government Accountability Office (US GAO). (1999). *Transportation coordination: Benefits and barriers exist, and planning efforts progress slowly*. Report no. GAO/RCED-00-1. Washington, DC: United States General Accounting Office.

United States Government Accountability Office (US GAO). (2003). *Transportation disadvantaged populations: Many federal programs fund transportation services, but obstacles to coordination persist*. Report no. GAO/RCED-03-698T. Washington, DC: United States General Accounting Office.

United States Government Accountability Office (US GAO). (2012). *Transportation disadvantaged populations: Federal coordination efforts could be further strengthened*. Report no. GAO-12-647. Washington, DC: United States General Accounting Office.

United States Government Accountability Office (US GAO). (2014). *Transportation for older adults: Measuring results could help determine if coordination efforts improve mobility.* No. GAO-15-158. Washington, DC: United States General Accounting Office.

Welle, B., Sharpin, A. B., Adriazola, C., Bhatt, A., Alveano, S., Obelheiro, M., . . . Bose, D. (2018). *Sustainable & safe: A vision and guidance for zero road deaths.* Washington, DC: World Resources Institute and World Bank.

Wong, R. C. P., Szeto, W. Y., Yang, L., Li, Y. C., & Wong, S. C. (2018). Public transport policy measures for improving elderly mobility. *Transport Policy, 63*, 73–79.

World Health Organization (WHO). (2015). *Global status report on road safety 2015.* Geneva, Switzerland: World Health Organization.

# Part III

# Strategies

# In-vehicle and self-driving technologies

12

*Everything in life is somewhere else, and you get there in a car.*

*E. B. White*

## Introduction

Nearly a decade ago, Eby, Molnar, and Kartje (2009) predicted that the automobile industry would "... respond to the coming wave of aging baby boomers by designing vehicles that take into account the functional declines with aging." (pg 107). Indeed, the industry has responded to the aging of society, and this response has largely been in the form of new in-vehicle technologies that can make driving safer and more comfortable for older drivers. In the past few years, numerous organizations have published lists of in-vehicle technologies and features that they recommend for older drivers, including AAA (2015), AAA Foundation for Traffic Safety (AAAFTS) (Eby et al., 2015, 2016), AARP (2018), Carfax (Keegan, 2016), Cars.com (Burklow, 2016), Consumer Reports (Stockburger, 2018), Edmunds (Newcomb, 2015), The Hartford (2012), and US News and World Report (Trop & Threewitt, 2018). For example, based on the opinions of seven experts, The Hartford (2012) developed the following set of 10 recommended technologies for older drivers: smart headlights, emergency response, reverse monitoring, blind spot warning, lane departure warning, vehicle stability control, assistive parking, voice-activated controls, crash mitigation, and drowsy driver alerts. While this list and many of the other lists are based on expert opinion, formal research on older drivers' attitudes toward, use of, preferences for, and benefits of in-vehicle technologies has been increasing.

Perhaps one of the most important transportation advances in the past decade has been the development of self-driving vehicle technologies (also called autonomous vehicles). The potential of self-driving vehicles as a means for reducing traffic crashes and maintaining mobility among older adults is mentioned regularly in the media. In an article in the *New York Times*, Chris Urmson, now the former Director of Self-Driving Cars at Google, cited older drivers and blind people as the groups who would receive the greatest benefits from autonomous vehicles (Kessler, 2015). Several other media stories have cited the particular benefits of autonomous vehicles for the older adult demographic (see, e.g., Antoville, 2014; Berk, 2014; McLaughlin, 2014; O'Connor, 2013). Indeed, having access to a vehicle that can take passengers anywhere they want to go, at any time, and under any conditions

**Perspectives and Strategies for Promoting Safe Transportation among Older Adults.**
**DOI: https://doi.org/10.1016/B978-0-12-812153-5.00012-1**

would have profound impacts on societal transportation. Yet, it is important to keep in mind that fully automated vehicles do not yet exist and there will be significant hurdles to overcome to achieve truly driverless vehicles for older adults [National Highway Traffic Safety Administration (NHTSA), 2012].

In this chapter, we review the research on several in-vehicle technologies in relation to older drivers. We present the summary of technologies in two broad categories: technologies for crash avoidance and other driver assistance technologies. Where possible, this section will address older drivers' use of and opinions about the technologies, as well as research on the technologies' impact on behaviors or traffic safety. This section of the chapter draws heavily from previous reviews we have conducted (Eby & Molnar, 2014; Eby et al., 2009, 2015, 2016). The chapter also reviews the latest research and issues on developing self-driving vehicles and older adults. Finally, the chapter addresses the issue of educating older adults on using and understanding automotive technologies.

## In-vehicle technologies for crash avoidance

Several in-vehicle technologies are designed specifically to help driver avoid crashes. These systems use a suite of sensors and intelligent programming to detect driving situations where a crash is probable and then perform some action or set of actions that can range from providing a warning to the driver to taking over partial control of the vehicle such as slowing the car down to prevent a collision. Here, we review five technologies: lane departure warning/mitigation systems, curve speed warning systems, forward collision warning systems, blind spot warning systems, and cross-traffic alert systems.

### *Lane departure warning/mitigation*

Maintaining proper position in a travel lane is a fundamental aspect of safe driving. Technologies have been developed that can use sensors to determine a vehicle's position in a lane and provide warnings to the driver if he or she starts to drift over a lane line without using a signal, called lane departure warning systems (LeBlanc et al., 2006). In some versions of this technology, these systems may also actively help steer the vehicle back into the center of the lane, called lane departure mitigation systems. Recent work suggests that these systems are not commonly found in older drivers' vehicles. Two studies of a large cohort of older drivers in five United States (US) locations have found through self-report and visual inspection of vehicles that only about 6% of older drivers have a lane departure warning system, but those that have them use them nearly all of the time (Eby et al., 2018; Zanier et al., 2018).

While no research has yet to study the safety benefits of these systems specifically for older drivers, studies that have included drivers of all ages estimate that use of these systems by all drivers could reduce lane departure crashes with serious injuries by up to 30% and fatal crashes of this type by up to 20% (Blower, 2014; Jermakian, 2011; Kusano & Gabler, 2014; Kusano, Gorman, Sherony, & Gabler, 2014). One would expect that these benefits would be even greater for older drivers. Naturalistic studies with drivers of all ages, including those aged 60–70 years, using vehicles equipped with lane departure warning systems in real-world driving have also shown safety benefits. Collectively these studies report that, as compared to not using the system, lane positioning was better when dialing a mobile phone and in non-distracted driving situations, drivers used turn signals more often, there were fewer unintentional lane marker crossings, and drivers thought the system was useful (Blaschke, Breyer, Färber, Freyer, & Limbacher, 2009; LeBlanc et al., 2006).

Older drivers opinions about lane departure warning systems have been assessed through focus groups and questionnaires conducted in a number of countries (see, e.g., Braitman, McCartt, Zuby, & Singer, 2010; Eby et al., 2018; Eichelberger & McCartt, 2014a; Gish, Vrkljan, Grenier, & Van Miltenburg, 2017; Regan, Mitsopoulos, Haworth, & Young, 2002; Strand, Nilsson, Karlsson, & Nilsson, 2011). These studies find that older drivers use the system frequently, like them overall, and report that lane departure warning systems make them a safer driver; are useful when driving; increase their use of turn signals; reduce driving stress; sometimes give false alarms; and do not work in all driving situations, such as bad weather. Many older drivers report that they would want a lane departure system on their next vehicle.

Based on these results, lane departure warning/mitigation systems could improve driving safety for older adults, particularly among older drivers on drowsiness-inducing medications or who are easily fatigued. More research on these systems that include older drivers using these systems in real-world conditions over a long period of time is needed in order to more firmly establish the safety benefits for older drivers. Further, as stated by Eby et al. (2015), "... for these systems to be accepted by older adults they will need to be operationally robust (i.e., work under most driving conditions), the number of false alarms will need to be small, and drivers should be able to selectively use the system under the conditions that they choose, allowing them to turn off the system in bad weather or on roads that have poor lane markings" (pg 30).

## Curve speed warning

Curve speed warning systems combine global positioning system (GPS)–based vehicle location information with speed data to determine if a driver is approaching a curve at an unsafe speed and, if so, presents a warning to the driver to slow down. Only, a few studies have assessed older drivers' use of or thoughts about curve speed warning systems (LeBlanc et al., 2006; McElheny, Blanco, & Hankey, 2006; Sayer et al., 2010). These studies include drivers age 60 and older who drove vehicles equipped with a curve speed warning system on either a test track or in normal, everyday driving for up to 3 weeks. Results showed that when compared to not using the system, there were mixed results about the effect on driving speeds on curves, with two studies showing no effect and one study showing reduced speeds when the warnings were activated. Older drivers reported liking the system and wanting a curve speed warning system in a future vehicle. There is very little evidence of the value of these systems for older drivers.

## *Forward collision warning/mitigation*

Forward collision warnings systems use a number of sensors to determine the location of objects in front of a vehicle and how quickly the vehicle is approaching those objects. When the system determines that the vehicle has a high probability of crashing into a forward object, it will provide a warning for the driver to brake or make an evasive maneuver and, in some systems, actually apply the brakes without input from the driver (mitigation). Thus, these systems are designed to prevent imminent crashes directly. Studies in the US have estimated that the forward collision systems could prevent as many as 20% of crashes and reduce injuries and fatalities by a significant amount if they were installed in all vehicles (Blower, 2014; Jermakian, 2011; Kusano & Gabler, 2014). Unfortunately, available data show that forward collision warning/mitigation systems are only in about 5%–7% of older driver vehicles in a large US cohort study (Eby et al., 2018; Zanier et al., 2018).

Older driver's behaviors when using a forward collision system have been studied in driving simulators using scenarios in which hard braking is necessary (such as a pedestrian stepping in the vehicle's path) and in naturalistic driving studies in real-world traffic in several countries (Adell, Vàrhelyi, & Fontana, 2011; Cotté, Meyer, & Coughlin, 2001; Dingus et al., 1997; Ervin et al., 2005; Kramer, Cassavaugh, Horrey, & Mayhugh, 2007; LeBlanc, Bao, Sayer, & Bogard, 2013; Lester et al., 2015; Maltz & Shinar, 2004; Sayer et al., 2010; Wilschut, Kroon, de Goede, Cremers, & Hoedemaeker, 2014). The general positive findings from these studies are older drivers maintain longer headway in all driving but will follow more closely when using a forward collision system; older drivers have significantly slower response times to system warnings as compared to drivers of younger ages; forward collision systems reduce the likelihood of a crash in a simulator; older drivers were better able to detect pedestrians and other obstacles in the roadway; and the systems improve safety in the real world and did not increase distraction. These studies also show that when using the systems, there were more hard braking events at traffic signals, more lane line crossings, older drivers wanted warnings earlier than younger drivers, and forward collision systems sometimes gave false warnings, but older drivers were more tolerant of the events and were more favorable to the systems than younger drivers.

The opinions and perceptions of older drivers regarding forward collision warning/mitigation systems have been investigated in a number of focus group and questionnaire studies of drivers who have experience using these systems (Braitman et al., 2010; Cicchino & McCartt, 2015; Eby et al., 2018; Eichelberger & McCartt, 2014a, 2014b; Gish et al., 2017; Strand et al., 2011). The studies differed in the ages defining the older drivers, and many of the studies also include younger drivers in reporting results. The following conclusions can be gleaned from these studies: a large majority of older drivers always or often use the system when driving (these system usually default to on when the vehicle is started); nearly all older drivers report that the system makes them a safer driver; about one-half think the system always worked properly (but some also believed that they got false alarms); and older drivers reported that the forward collision systems made them more aware of the distances that they follow behind vehicles, and some reported that they increased their following distances when using the system, perhaps to decrease the likelihood that they would receive a warning.

The research evidence is strong that these systems provide a significant safety benefit for older drivers. Further, older drivers report liking these systems, feel safer when using the system, and that the systems have prevented crashes. As with other technologies, future development should attempt to reduce the number of false alarms.

## Blind spot warning

Studies show that older drivers check blind spots around their vehicles much less frequently (about one-half as often) than younger drivers before changing lanes or merging (Lavallière, Laurendeau, Simoneau, & Teasdale, 2011; Lavallière, Reimer, et al., 2011). Blind spot warning systems are designed to help drivers know when a vehicle or other object is in location that may be difficult for a driver to see. These systems usually display a warning light near, or in, the side view mirrors when objects are detected. According to Jermakian (2011), blind spot warning systems could prevent up to 20,000 injuries and 400 deaths each year in the US. Recent work, however, has shown that blind spot warning systems were included in only about 10% of vehicles in a cohort of 2990 older drivers (age 65–79) across five US locations (Eby et al., 2018; Zanier et al., 2018).

As with other in-vehicle technologies, behaviors associated with blind spot warning systems have been investigated with older drivers in simulators, on test tracks, and in naturalistic driving (Guo, Wotring, & Antin, 2010; Kessler et al., 2012; Kiefer & Hankey, 2008; Sayer et al., 2010). These studies show that use of these systems among older drivers increased the frequency of mirror checking prior to lane changes, increased situational awareness of traffic in adjacent lanes, and decreased the use of signals. This latter finding may indicate that older drivers tended to over-rely on the warning during lanes changes and possibly believe that using signals was not important. This unintended negative consequence, however, has been shown to be alleviated when blind spot warning systems are paired with lane departure warnings systems (Sayer et al., 2010).

Older drivers' opinions of blind spot warning systems have been assessed in studies in the US and Europe through interviews with vehicle owners who have this system in their car (Braitman et al., 2010; Cicchino & McCartt, 2015; Eby et al., 2018; Strand et al., 2011; Trübswetter & Bengler, 2013). These studies tend to find mixed results with some older drivers reporting that they ignore the warning while others believe that it is helpful, some reporting that the warning signal is distracting while others do not, and some reporting that the systems are reliable while other older drivers have reported that the systems do not work well in inclement weather conditions. On the other hand, older drivers report that these systems make them a safer, less-stressed driver, and several older drivers have reported that the system had helped them avoid a collision during a lane change.

Given that the blind spot warning systems address a known and significant functional decline associated with aging—turning the neck and/or torso to check blind spots—these systems are recommended for older drivers. There is clear evidence that these systems can prevent crashes and they can help older drivers be more aware of surrounding traffic. Educational or technological solutions should be utilized to counteract the possibility of less frequent signal use, such as combining these systems with lane departure warning systems.

### *Cross-traffic alert*

Backing out of a parking space can be difficult for older drivers, particularly those who have difficulty turning their heads or torsos to see out the back of the vehicle. Cross-traffic alert systems detect traffic and other objects, such as bicyclists and pedestrians, that are approaching the vehicle from the side and give warnings to the driver or may also automatically apply the brakes (Seto et al., 2012). Eby et al. (2018) found that these systems were reported to be in about 6% of primary vehicles being driven by older adults.

The one study that has addressed older driver behaviors associated with the use of cross-traffic alert systems in actual traffic systems found that significantly more drivers stopped appropriately when cross-traffic was present and found a small decrease in stress levels as compared to not using the system (Reimer, Mehler, & Coughlin, 2010). Some recent US studies have assessed opinions about cross-traffic alert systems through questionnaires with older drivers who owned vehicles equipped with these systems (Cicchino & McCartt, 2015; Eby et al., 2018). These studies reported that cross-traffic alert systems are used frequently, are easy to learn, help drivers see traffic from behind, help to avoid crashes, are useful for backing up, and do produce some false alarms.

There is too little information addressing older drivers' use and perceptions of cross-traffic alerts, but the available information suggests that these systems might be very useful for older drivers. Future systems should address the high false alarm rates and these systems should be tested with older drivers using the systems in normal driving.

## Other driver assistance technologies

There are a number of other technologies that are designed to assist drivers with the driving task or make driving easier. Many of these technologies can also help to prevent crashes. Here, we review what is known about older driver use and thoughts about the following systems: rearview camera/rear parking sensor, semiautonomous parking assist, navigation assistance, adaptive cruise control, automatic crash notification, adaptive headlights, voice-activated controls, and drowsiness/fatigue monitoring.

## *Rearview camera/rear parking sensor systems*

NHTSA (Austin, 2008) estimates that about 300 fatalities and 18,000 injuries are caused each year by drivers backing up. Rearview camera/rear parking sensor systems utilize small cameras and proximity sensors placed at the rear of the vehicle and display this information to the driver using a video screen and/or alerts (usually auditory or visual). Citing the safety benefits of rearview camera/rear parking sensor systems, Canada and US have both passed laws that require new vehicles (model year 2016 for Canada, and May, 2018 for the US) to be equipped with these camera systems (Wikipedia, 2018). Indeed, rearview camera systems were one of the most common in-vehicle technologies found in older drivers' vehicles, with both self-report and visual inspection finding these systems in about 40% of vehicles (Eby et al., 2018; Zanier et al., 2018).

The backing-up behaviors and use of these systems have been addressed in a number of studies. Laboratory/controlled setting studies report the following: drivers rarely look at the video display and often hit objects placed behind the car when backing up unless the system has proximity sensors that alert the drivers to obstacles; there was no difference in backing speed or acceleration; and parking ability was improved as determined by a number of measures (Hurwitz et al., 2010; Llaneras, Neurauter, & Green, 2011; Mazzae, Barickman, Baldwin, & Ranney, 2008; McLaughlin, Hankey, Green, & Kiefer, 2003).

The thoughts and perceptions of older drivers who have these systems in their vehicles have been investigated in several US studies (AAAFTS, 2008; Cicchino, Eichelberger, & McCartt, 2015; Eby et al., 2018; Hurwitz et al., 2010; McLaughlin et al., 2003; Mazzae et al., 2008; Mueller, Sangrar, & Vrkljan, in press). Collectively, these studies find that rearview camera/rear parking sensor systems are used frequently and rarely turned off, are easy to learn, are rated as having high usability, are perceived as helpful for avoiding crashes, relieve stress for many older drivers, are helpful for backing into parking space and in parallel parking, produce little distraction, and are generally highly regarded.

Rearview camera/rear parking sensor systems are clearly useful for older adults and are helpful in overcoming the difficulties with parking and backing up reported by older drivers. It is important, however, that the systems include more than just a video camera display, which tends not to be used by older drivers. Combining such a display with other information, such as obstacle alerts, greatly improves the value of these systems for older drivers.

## *Semiautonomous parking assist*

Like many people, older drivers have difficulty parallel parking, find it to be particularly stressful, and will try to avoid this type of parking (see, e.g., Baldock, Mathias, McLean, & Berndt, 2006; Douissembekov, Gabaude, Rogé, Navarro, & Michael, 2014). Semiautonomous parking assist systems are designed to make parallel parking easier by having the vehicle control the steering while the driver controls the brake and throttle. These systems are rarely found in older drivers vehicles. Two studies on the same large cohort of older drivers found prevalence rates of 1% (self-report; Eby et al., 2018) and 2% (visual inspection; Zanier et al., 2018). Only a handful of studies have investigated older drivers' use and perceptions of these systems (Eby et al., 2018; Kawabata et al., 2008; Reimer et al., 2010; Tachibana, 2011; Totzke, Jessberger, Mühlbacher, & Krüger, 2011; Totzke, Müehlbacher, & Krüger, 2010). Using testing in real-world driving and interviews with older drivers who have these systems, the studies conclude that the systems are not used very often; they can reduce stress and mental workload when parallel parking; and parking behavior is improved both with and without using the system.

Despite the fact that very few older drivers have these systems in their vehicles, the research supports a conclusion that these systems are useful for older drivers, at least among those who want to parallel-park their vehicle. Those older drivers who have used these systems report generally positive outcomes.

## Navigation assistance

Older drivers, particularly those who have some level of cognitive decline, occasionally get lost or have difficulties with wayfinding (Bryden, Charlton, Oxley, & Lowndes, 2013; Cushman, Stein, & Duffy, 2008; Eby, Silverstein, Molnar, LeBlanc, & Adler, 2012; Hunt, Brown, & Gilman, 2010; Uc, Rizzo, Anderson, Shi, & Dawson, 2004). Navigation assistance systems are designed to use GPS data along with road map information (and in some systems real-time traffic information), to determine the best route to a destination and then provide navigation instructions (usually both visually and verbally) to the driver as he or she drives (Kostyniuk, Streff, & Eby, 1997). Navigation assistance systems have been widely available in new vehicles for more than a decade and are commonly found in vehicles driven by older adults (Eby et al., 2018; Zanier et al., 2018).

Navigation assistance systems' use and perceptions among older drives have been evaluated in the real driving conditions in many studies (Dingus et al., 1997; Eby & Kostyniuk, 1998,1999; Kostyniuk, Eby, Christoff, & Hopp, 1997; Oxley, Barham, & Ayala, 1995) as well as in focus group/interview studies (Chan & Rose, 2002; Eby et al., 2018; Emmerson, Guo, Blythe, Namdeo, & Edwards, 2013; Kessler et al., 2012; Stinchcombe et al., 2017; Vrkljan & Polgar, 2007; Willstrand et al., 2015). These studies tend to find that these systems are used frequently by older drivers; older divers tend to figure out how to use them on their own, through dealer instructions, or from family/friends and take longer to learn as compared to younger drivers; older driver are more likely to travel to places which are unfamiliar when using the systems; older driver report more positive feelings, such as confidence, when using the systems; older drivers tended to use the systems in collaboration with a passenger, usually a spouse; older drivers express some concerns about distraction, and some have concerns about getting lost if the system stopped working.

Navigation assistance systems have been shown to provide clear benefits for older drivers, particularly in helping them be more comfortable driving in unfamiliar areas. Interfaces for these systems are fairly easy to use and learn, and many older drivers are currently using these systems. Future research should begin to understand how these systems might be used as an intervention for drivers who have become lost, as is common in drivers with declining cognitive ability (e.g., Yi, Lee, Parsons, & Falkmer, 2014).

## Adaptive cruise control

Unlike conventional cruise control, adaptive cruise control systems will automatically maintain a set headway from the vehicle in front by operating the brake and throttle without input from the driver (Fancher et al., 1998). In many systems, the driver can select the headway for which they are most comfortable, and the system will maintain that headway in traffic. These systems are not forward collision mitigation systems, so the driver has to maintain his or her attention on developing traffic situations and be ready to apply the brake if a vehicle stops suddenly. Adaptive cruise control was found in 5%–6% of vehicles being driven by a large cohort of older drivers in the US (Eby et al., 2018; Zanier et al., 2018).

Much of the behavioral research on adaptive cruise control has utilized driving simulators and samples that include older drivers but not separate analyses of these drivers (de Winter, Happee, Martens, & Stanton, 2014; Hoedemaeker & Brookhuis, 1998; Piccinini, Rodrigues, Leitão, & Simões, 2014, 2015; Rajaonah, Anceaux, & Vienne, 2006; Stanton & Young, 2005; Xiong, Boyle, Moeckli, Dow, & Brown, 2012). In these studies, conducted in both the US and Europe, comparisons are made between driving with and without a simulated adaptive cruise control system. Collectively, these studies report that while use of these systems reduces stress and workload, they also decrease drivers' awareness of what is going on around them, including the changing traffic patterns; drivers travel at faster speeds; and people do not understand the systems' limitations and were more likely to collide with simulated vehicles suddenly stopping. On-road, naturalistic driving studies using vehicles equipped with either adaptive cruise control systems alone or combined with a forward collision mitigation systems report that these systems are safe and positively received, particularly for the two systems combined (Ervin et al., 2005; Fancher et al., 1998; Kessler et al., 2012; Rakha, Hankey, Patterson, & van Aerde, 2001).

Subjective data from older drivers who have used adaptive cruise control or have this type of system installed in his or her own vehicle are generally positive (AAAFTS, 2008; Cicchino & McCartt, 2015; Eby et al., 2018; Eichelberger & McCartt, 2014a, 2014b; Kamalanathsharma, Rakha, & Zohdy, 2015; Motamedi & Wang, 2017; Strand et al., 2011). These studies report that adaptive cruise control systems are used frequently (about half of the time) and most often on freeways; older drivers tend to use the longest headway setting; are perceived to make drivering safer; do not induce drivers to spend less time looking away from the roadway; and are considered easy to use. Further, as many as 40% of older drivers do not understand that the system alone will not prevent a collision with a stopped vehicle.

The research shows that older drivers like and use adaptive cruise control systems and that these systems can make driving comfortable and enjoyable. The research also shows that older drivers (and others) do not generally understand that adaptive cruise control systems will not stop the vehicle in emergency situations. As such, these systems are recommended for older drivers as long as these systems come with an effective training/educational program or the system is paired with a forward collision mitigation system that will stop the vehicle automatically in emergency situations.

## Advanced automatic crash notification

Some researchers have discussed the golden hour for motor vehicle occupants that are injured in a crash (see, e.g., Martinez, Toh, Cano, Calafate, & Manzoni, 2010), that is, the time it takes from the crash occurring to injured people receiving care at the hospital. After the first hour, the chances of survival decrease. Martinez et al. (2010) argue that it takes about 5 minutes on average for first responders to be notified of the crash and 15 minutes to extricate injured occupants. Advanced automotive crash notification systems use cellular technology that, within seconds, automatically notify emergency personnel that a crash has occurred, and the advanced systems can also send data about the crash severity and type, which can help emergency personnel send the correct equipment for extricating vehicle occupants and save valuable time. The following reductions in fatalities for fully implemented advanced crash notification system have been estimated for several countries/jurisdictions: 9%–15% for Korea (Jeong, Oh, & Lee, 2014), 2%–6% for the US (Clark & Cushing, 2002; Lee, Wu, Kang, & Craig, 2017), 4%–8% for Finland (Sihvola, Luoma, Schirokof, Salo, & Karkola, 2009), and 2%–4% for South Australia (Ponte, Ryan, & Anderson, 2016). No studies have estimated the potential benefits directly for older adults, but given the increased frailty and fragility in older adulthood, it is reasonable to assume that the fatality reductions might be greater for older adults. These systems, however, are not commonly found in vehicles driven by older adults. In one study of older drivers, crash notification systems were reported to be in only 10% of vehicles being driving by older adults (Eby et al., 2018). Automatic crash notification is recommended for older drivers, particularly for those who live in rural areas or other locations where first responders may not be close by.

## Adaptive headlights

Adaptive headlight systems are a class of technologies designed to help drivers see better at night. Included in this class are systems that direct the headlights toward turns and curves, systems that automatically dim high-beam light for oncoming traffic, and systems that control the shape of the headlight beams to improve visibility and reduce glare (Band & Perel, 2007). A number of studies have estimated that adaptive headlight systems could reduce nighttime crashes by 2%–5% (Jermakian, 2011; Mehler, Reimer, Lavallière, Dobres, & Coughlin, 2014; Sullivan & Flannagan, 2007). Given the known difficulties that many older drivers report about driving at nighttime, there is a surprising lack of information on how these systems are used by older drivers. One study that utilized a small sample of drivers, one-half of whom were older adults, assessed pedestrian detection and perceptions while using an adaptive headlight system in real traffic at night (Sivak, Flannagan, Traube, Aoki, & Sayer, 1994). The study found a 14% improvement in detection ability, and drivers were generally indifferent about the system. More recent studies have assessed the use and opinions of adaptive headlight systems from older drivers using questionnaires (Braitman et al., 2010; Eby et al., 2018). These studies report that a large majority of older drivers think these systems make them safer; allow them to more easily see lane lines, pedestrians, overhead signs, the roadway on hills, and in general at night; most older drivers preferred the system over standard headlights; small percentage thought the system helped them better negotiate curves; and some older drivers reported that when using the system, they were more likely to drive at night and they drove faster.

Adaptive headlight systems are tentatively recommended for older drivers, but more research is needed on the behaviors associated with the use of these systems among older drivers. One particular question of interest is whether or not these systems allow older drivers to be more comfortable and capable of driving at night as compared to the use of traditional headlight.

## Voice-activated controls

Controlling technology through spoken commands has become more commonplace since the release of *Siri* on Apple's iPhones in 2011 and the Amazon Echo that includes *Alexa* in 2014. Voice-activated control systems are similar technologies that have been developed to enhance the interface between the driver and various vehicle technologies, such as selecting destinations for the navigation assistance system or adjusting the radio. Voice control systems are designed to make interfaces easier and safer than manual controls. About 19% of the older drivers in one study reported to have a voice control system in their vehicle (Eby et al., 2018). Research among young and middle-age drivers comparing voice and manual controls in simulators report that voice controls reduce cognitive distraction, but distraction is still much higher than driving without manipulating anything, and reaction times were slower using voice controls (He et al., 2014; Itoh, Miki, Yoshitsugu, Kubo, & Mashimo, 2004; Jenness, Lattanzio, O'Toole, Taylor, & Pax, 2002; Lee, Caven, Haake, & Brown, 2001; Maciej & Vollrath, 2009; Strayer et al., 2013).

Little research in use and opinions of voice control system among older drivers has been conducted, but the study of Eby et al. (2018) found that voice control systems are used infrequently, with 39% of older drivers who have these systems reporting that they never use them and 37% did not believe that voice controls made them a safer driver. On-road studies, some of which have included older drivers (Chiang, Brooks, & Weir, 2005; Mehler, Reimer, Lavallière, et al., 2014; Mehler, Reimer, Dobres, et al., 2014; Neurauter, Hankey, Schalk, & Wallace, 2012; Perez, Viita, Hankey, Voran-Nowak, & Tengler, 2011; Ranney, Mazzae, Baldwin, & Salaani, 2007; Reimer et al., 2013; Schreiner, Blanco, & Hankey, 2004; Strayer et al., 2013; Strayer, Turrill, Coleman, Ortiz, & Cooper, 2014), report that voice controls can produce high levels of cognitive distraction; voice controls are safer and faster to use than manual controls in many situations; and these systems are liked by drivers. Thus, voice control systems appear to be easier and safer than manual controls, but they still produce significant cognitive distraction when they are being used.

Vehicles will continue to include greater and more complex technologies and developing safer and easier ways to interface with these technologies will be critical. Voice-activated controls are found to be safer and easier than manual controls, and for this reason, these systems are recommended for older drivers. These systems continue to be developed, and they are becoming more able to respond appropriately to intuitive and natural speech. Developers of future systems should include older adults when testing the systems.

## *Drowsiness/fatigue warnings*

As compared to other age groups, older drivers are rarely involved in crashes related to being drowsy, and few report falling asleep while driving (McGwin & Brown, 1999; Stutts, Martell, & Staplin, 2009; Wheaton, Chapman, Presley-Cantrell, Croft, & Roehler, 2013). A myriad of approaches are being developed to detect and warn drivers that they are getting too drowsy to safely drive (see Balkin, Horrey, Graeber, Czeisler, & Dinges, 2011, for a brief review). Research shows that these systems are generally good at detecting when a driver is drowsy but not good at detecting the level of drowsiness, which is important to know in order to present warnings that are relevant to a driver who is about to fall asleep (Balkin et al., 2011; Horberry, Hartley, Kruger, & Mabbott, 2001; Williamson & Chamberlain, 2005). These systems continue to be developed.

Fatigue warning systems, on the other hand, are currently available in motor vehicles. These systems analyze driving behaviors, such as lane keeping, speed variance, and driving time, and, when certain thresholds are reached, will warn the driver that he or she may be getting fatigued. A recent study of nearly 3000 older drivers in the US found that fatigue/drowsy warning systems were reported to be present in only about 1% of vehicle driven by older drivers, but 70% of those drivers who had them thought the system made them a safer driver (Eby et al., 2018). Other questionnaire and focus group research that included older drivers in their samples have found that many drivers have received fatigue warnings and report that a large majority of these warnings were false alarms, some are confused by the warnings, more than half ignore the warnings, and small percentage report that the warnings induced them to pay closer attention to their driving (Eichelberger & McCartt, 2014b; Strand et al., 2011).

There is little evidence that these systems afford any safety or convenience benefits for older adults and are therefore not recommended in their current state of development. However, a system that could reliably determine when an older driver is too drowsy or fatigued to drive safely would likely provide great benefits for older adults, especially those on medications.

# Self-driving technologies

One of the most intriguing and potentially useful developments in vehicle technology in the past several decades is the self-driving vehicle, also called the autonomous vehicle. Large amounts of research funding from government and industry are being devoted to developing this technology, and the field is advancing quickly. As discussed previously, many professionals believe that self-driving vehicles will help to solve many of society's problems, including promoting safe mobility for older adults. Indeed, once a so-called fully automated vehicle is developed—that is, one that can take a person anywhere they want go, at any time, in any weather—many of the issues about older adult mobility will be alleviated. Vehicles with full automation, however, are not yet available.

## *Levels of automation*

We have already discussed some in-vehicle systems that take over partial control of driving, such as forward collision mitigation systems. NHTSA 2018 and the Society of Automotive Engineers International (SAE) (2016) define vehicle automation as having the following six levels:

- *Level 0 (no automation):* The driver controls all vehicle functions.
- *Level 1 (driver assistance):* The driver controls all vehicle functions but is given some assistance from an in-vehicle technology. The vehicle can control only one vehicle function, such as steering or braking, but not both.
- *Level 2 (partial automation):* The driver still needs to be engaged in the driving task at all times, but the vehicle can control more than one function of the vehicle under certain circumstances.
- *Level 3 (conditional automation):* The vehicle can perform all driving functions under certain circumstances, but the driver needs to be able to quickly take back control of the vehicle when circumstances change. There are vehicles on the road today with this level of automation, such as the Tesla's equipped with the Autopilot technology.
- *Level 4 (high automation):* The vehicle can perform all driving functions under certain circumstances and there is no need for the driver to monitor the anything under these circumstances.
- *Level 5 (full automation):* The vehicle is self-driving in all circumstances. There is no need for a driver and all occupants in the vehicle are passengers.

In vehicles with automation levels of 1–3, there is a need for the driver to still be engaged in what is happening around the vehicle and what the vehicle is

**Figure 12.1** Level 4 automated vehicle being tested at the University of Michigan. Photography by David W. Eby.

currently doing so that he or she can effectively and safely take back control of the vehicle when necessary. In level 4 automation, the need for driver input would be dependent upon the specific circumstances under which this level of automation operates. For example, the University of Michigan is pilot testing level 4 automated vehicles to shuttle students on specific route during good weather. These vehicles do not need driver input on these specific routes. Fig. 12.1 shows one of these vehicles. With level 5 automation, society will begin to see some of the many safety, mobility, and environmental benefits of self-driving vehicles. It will, however, likely take several decades for these higher levels of automation to significantly penetrate the vehicle fleet (see, e.g., Bansal & Kockelman, 2017).

## Older driver opinions of self-driving vehicles

As the development of self-driving technologies has continued, there has been a lot of interest in what people think about these technologies. Many surveys have been conducted worldwide on a variety of topics related to self-driving vehicles (see Kyriakidis, Happee, & de Winter, 2015, for a review). Here, we review recent studies that have either included a large proportion of older adults in their sample or have presented results for older drivers separately.

Schoetttle and Sivak (2015) surveyed opinions of 505 drivers using an online survey tool. About 27% of the respondents were of age 60 or older. The study found that when asked about their preferred level of automation among three levels of automation (roughly corresponding to level 0, levels 2/3, and level 5), about 50% of older drivers choose no automation, 39% chose partial, and 11% choose full automation. The study also reported that 77% of older drivers reported that they were moderately or very concerned about riding in fully automated vehicles, and there was less concern for partially automated vehicles (54% were moderately or very concerned). Nearly all older drivers wanted automated vehicles to have controls that they could take over to control the vehicle if they so desired.

A study of 2954 drivers in the US (52% were age 55 or older) that investigated preferences toward automated vehicles found somewhat different results (Abraham et al., 2016). Respondents were asked about the maximum level of automation that they were comfortable with. Among drivers age 65–74, 4% were reported "no automation," 12% reported "only in emergency," 56% only to "help driver," 14% reported "partial automation," and 14% reported "full autonomy." Results were similar for respondents age 75 or older.

A study in the United Kingdom of 1000 drivers (age range 18–85) explored opinions of autonomous vehicles using an online survey (Hulse, Xie, & Galea, 2018). The study reported that attitudes toward automated vehicles were generally positive but less positive with increasing age, and about one-quarter of respondents reported that they needed to learn more about the safety aspects of automated vehicles.

Finally, a study in Germany (Hartwich, Beggiato, & Krems, 2018) utilized a driving simulator to investigate comfort, enjoyment, and acceptance for a younger (25–35 years) and older group (65–85 years) of drivers. The study utilized two "driving styles" for the automated vehicle: familiar (speed profiles were within the boundaries for a specific participant based on his or her manual driving patterns in the simulator) and unfamiliar (a style that was outside the speed profile bounds from manual driving). After driving/riding in the simulator under these various conditions, respondents completed a series of questionnaires. The study found that as compared to manual driving, full automation increased driving comfort for both age groups and decreased younger driver enjoyment, and younger drivers were more likely to prefer their familiar driving style while older drivers preferred the unfamiliar style.

## *Transfer of control studies*

In all levels of automation other than full automation, the driver will need to drive the vehicle at least under some circumstances. This switch between the automated control of the vehicle to the driver being in control, called transfer or takeover of control, is starting to be investigated using older drivers (Clark & Feng, 2017; Köber, Gold, Lechner, & Bengler, 2016; Miller et al., 2016; Molnar et al., 2017). These studies have used driving simulators that are programmed to travel urban roadway and occasionally encounter situations that the automation cannot handle, such as construction, poor lane markings, or malfunctioning traffic control. At these times, the vehicle alerts the driver that they need to take over the operation of the vehicle. In some studies, participants are given secondary tasks to engage in while the vehicle is self-driving, and in other studies, participants are free to do whatever they choose. All of these studies compared older drivers with at least one other driver age group. These studies found when given no specific task to engage in while in automated driving, both young and older drivers will choose to engage in a non-driving task; older drivers benefited more than younger drivers from having a longer takeover interval before the vehicle relinquished control; many older drivers missed takeover situations; older drivers were more likely not to reengage automation after a transfer event; in one study, older drivers reacted just as fast as the younger drivers to the transfer alert, but they had more hard braking events when assuming control; in another study, older and middle-age drivers were significantly slower than young drivers in reacting to the transfer alert; both younger and older drivers reacted faster and more appropriately to transfer alerts as they became more familiar with the transfer situations; and older drivers found the transfer of control to be more challenging.

## Training and education

It has long been known that older drivers have greater difficulty learning how to use advanced in-vehicle technologies and that they also lack a complete understanding of the operation and limitations of these systems (AAAFTS, 2008; Caird, 2004; Dickie & Boyle, 2009; Kostyniuk et al., 1997; McDonald et al., 2016; Piccinini et al., 2015; Shaw, Polgar, Vrkljan, & Jacobson, 2010). For example, a nationwide study of drivers of all ages reported that only 17% and 38% of drivers correctly understood adaptive cruise control systems and forward collision warning systems, respectively (McDonald et al., 2016).

The question of how older drivers learn to use technologies has been investigated in several questionnaire-based studies of older adults who have advanced technologies in their vehicles (AAAFTS, 2008; Braitman et al., 2010; Eby et al., 2018; Eichelberger & McCartt, 2014a). These studies find a wide range of ways in which older drivers learn about technologies. Eichelberger and McCartt (2014a) reported that for owners of vehicles with adaptive cruise control (about a third of whom were older drivers), 75% used the owner's manual, 60% learned through the dealer, 56% figured it out themselves, 16% used the Internet, 11% learned from a family/friend, and 9% consulted digital media. Cicchino and McCartt (2015) reported that users of several crash avoidance systems (about one-third older drivers) found similar results, with 77% using the owner's manual, 54% figuring it out themselves, and 30% learning from the dealer. Abraham et al. (2016) found that drivers (over one-half of which were age 55 or older) reported learning to use in-vehicle technologies by using the owner's manual (63%), on their own (59%), or through the dealer (24%). Work by the AAAFTS (2008) found that the top three ways older adults learned to use several in-vehicle technologies were through the owner's manual, the dealer, and by trial or error on the roadway. A recent study of nearly 3000 older drivers (Eby et al., 2018) found similar results across a range of technologies (see Fig. 12.2). As shown in this figure, a large majority of older drivers report that they learn the systems on their own, except for voice controls. The second most commonly reported method across the technologies was the owner's manual, followed by the dealer. Interestingly, less than 1% of older drivers reported using the Internet to learn how to use systems, about 11% reported never learning how to use systems, and nearly one-half of older drivers never learned to use semiautonomous parking assist systems.

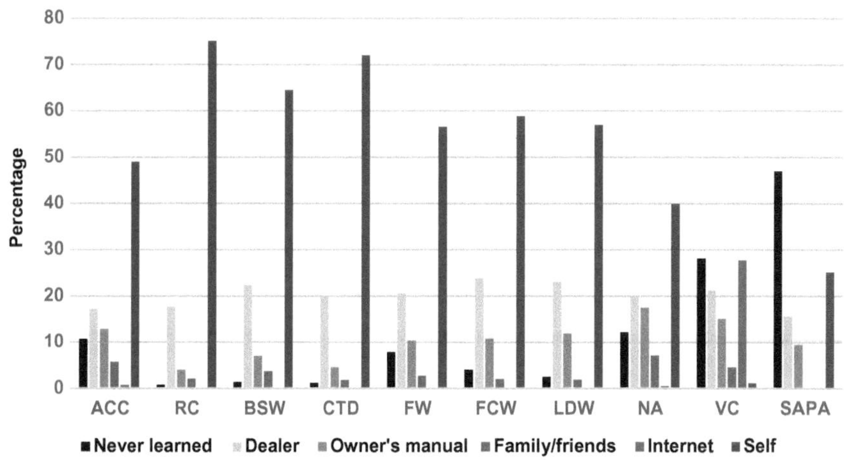


**Figure 12.2** Ways in which older drivers learn to use in-vehicle technologies. *ACC*, Adaptive cruise control; *RC*, Rearview camera/rear parking sensor; *BSW*, Blind spot warning; *CTD*, Cross-traffic detection; *FW*, Fatigue warning; *FCW*, Forward collision warning; *LDW*, Lane departure warning; *NA*, Navigation assistance; *VC*, Voice controls; and *SAPA*, Semiautonomous parking assist.
From Eby, D. W., Molnar, L. J., Zakrajsek, J., Ryan, L., Zanier, N., St. Louis, R. M., . . . on behalf of the LongROAD Research Team. (2018). Prevalence, attitudes, and knowledge of in-vehicle technologies and vehicle adaptations among older drivers. *Accident Analysis & Prevention*, *113*, 54–62.

Collectively, these results show that society needs to improve how we teach people, and especially older drivers, about new in-vehicle technologies (Coughlin, 2009; Eby & Molnar, 2014; Reimer, 2014). A lack of understand can decrease the safety and convenience benefits of these technologies. It is not surprising that so many older adults resort to learning technologies on their own given the known issues with owner's manuals (long and difficult to understand) and dealers (often not enough time or knowledge to fully train drivers when they first purchase the vehicle). Websites have recently been developed that are intended to help teach people about in-vehicle technologies, such as *My Car Does What?* (National Safety Council, 2018). Use of the Internet affords many advantages, including an easy and relatively inexpensive way to widely distribute information and the ability to personalize the information for the person using the website. Unfortunately, at least for the current generation of older drivers, very few currently use the Internet for this purpose.

# Conclusions

The development of vehicle technologies to improve safety, comfort, and convenience over the past decade has begun to be responsive to the needs and capabilities of older drivers. There are still, unfortunately, significant gaps in understanding how older drivers use and adapt their driving to vehicle technologies. In the future, researchers should endeavor to include an older driver age group in their studies and analyze data so that the findings can be interpreted for these older drivers. Further, as we have discussed elsewhere (Eby et al., 2015), it is important to define the older driver age group using ages that are in-line with the aging and transportation literature that categorize an older driver as starting at age 65 or 70. It is also time to start considering how the oldest-old (drivers age 80 and older) use and think about in-vehicle technologies, as this is one of the fastest growing segments of many countries (National Institute of Aging, 2011).

There is also a lack of information about the long-term use of technologies under real-world driving conditions. Many technologies are projected to improve safety, yet there are limited studies addressing the safety of in-vehicle technologies utilizing objective measures of safety in real-world driving conditions (Mehler, Reimer, Dobres, et al., 2014). The actual benefits of technologies may not match the projected benefits because in actual driving people may not use the technologies as they were intended or they may change their driving behaviors in unexpected ways in response to the technologies. Thus, several traffic safety researchers have noted that more information is needed about how in-vehicle technologies are used in naturalistic driving (see, e.g., Kostyniuk et al., 1997; Mehler, Reimer, Dobres, et al., 2014; Paris et al., 2014).

The expectations for self-driving vehicles to solve the issues of older adult mobility continue to be high. Questionnaire data suggest that older drivers in many countries have mixed feelings about self-driving vehicles, and these feelings are moderated by their trust and acceptance of the technologies as well as their experiences. Older drivers are more reluctant than drivers of other ages to be willing to relinquish all vehicle control to technology. On the other hand, older drivers seem to recognize, perhaps more than drivers of other ages, the potential value of fully automated vehicles. Until the time of fully automated vehicles, however, more research is needed on understanding the issues of transfer of control and how to execute this process in a way that is safe and non-stressful for older drivers.

Many technologies employ novel concepts, and most have limits to their operation. It is clear from the research that society is doing a poor job of educating the public about not only future technologies but also technologies that are currently in vehicles. Far too many older drivers report not ever learning to use technologies or learning through trial and error. This leads to two conclusions. First, new approaches should be developed not only to help older drivers learn about technologies but also to motivate them to seek out this instruction. Second, effort should be made to improve the interfaces and operation of technologies so that their use is more intuitive (see, e.g., Baerentsen, 2000; Hurtienne & Blessing, 2007). Intuitive interfaces utilize what a person already knows so that the operation of the technology seems obvious and requires little to no education.

# References


AAA. (2015). *Smart features for older drivers*. Heathrow, FL: AAA.

AAAFTS. (2008). *Use of advanced in-vehicle technology by younger and older early adopters*. Washington, DC: AAA Foundation for Traffic Safety.

AARP. (2018). *Top technologies for mature drivers*. Washington, DC: AARP. <https://www.aarp.org/auto/driver-safety/top-auto-tech/> Accessed February, 2018.

Abraham, H., Lee, C., Brady, S., Fitzgerald, C., Mehler, B., Reimer, B., & Coughlin, J. F. (2016). *Autonomous vehicles, trust, and driving alternatives: A survey of consumer preferences*. White paper 2016-6. Cambridge MA: MIT AgeLab.

Adell, E., Vàrhelyi, A., & Fontana, M. D. (2011). The effects of a driver assistance system for safe speed and safe distance—A real-life field study. *Transportation Research Part C, 19*, 145–155.

Antoville, A. (2014). Self-driving cares: A solution for aging drivers. *Compassionate Aging*. http://www.compassionateaging.org/self-driving-cars-a-solution-for-aging-drivers/. Accessed February, 2018.

Austin, R. (2008). *Fatalities and injuries in motor vehicle backing crashes: Report to Congress*. Report no. DOT HS 811 144. Washington, DC: NHTSA.

Baerentsen, K. B. (2000). Intuitive use interfaces. *Scandinavian Journal of Information Systems, 12*, 29–60.

Baldock, M. R. J., Mathias, J. L., McLean, A. J., & Berndt, A. (2006). Self-regulation of driving and its relationship to driving ability among older adults. *Accident Analysis & Prevention, 38*, 1038–1045.

Balkin, T. J., Horrey, W. J., Graeber, R. C., Czeisler, C. A., & Dinges, D. F. (2011). The challenges and opportunities of technological approaches to fatigue management. *Accident Analysis & Prevention, 43*, 565–572.

Band, D., & Perel, M. (2007). Senior mobility series: Article 8 new vehicle technologies may help older drivers. *Public Roads, 71*, 1–14.

Bansal, P., & Kockelman, K. M. (2017). Forecasting Americans' long-term adoption of connected and autonomous vehicle technologies. *Transportation Research Part A, 95*, 49–63.

Berk, B. (2014, April). Self-driving cars could keep seniors in the driver's seat. *The dallas morning news*. ⟨http://www.dallasnews.com/opinion/latestcolumns/20140415 self driving-cars-could-keep-seniors-in-the-drivers-seat.ece⟩ Accessed February, 2018.

Blaschke, C., Breyer, F., Färber., Freyer, J., & Limbacher, R. (2009). Driver distraction based lane-keeping assistance. *Transportation Research Part F, 12*, 288–299.

Blower, D. (2014). *Assessment of the effectiveness of advanced collision avoidance technologies*. Report no. UMTRI-2014-3. Ann Arbor, MI: University of Michigan Transportation Research Institute.

Braitman, K. A., McCartt, A. T., Zuby, D. S., & Singer, J. (2010). Volvo and Infiniti drivers' experience with select crash avoidance technologies. *Traffic Injury Prevention, 11*, 270–278.

Bryden, K. J., Charlton, J. L., Oxley, J. A., & Lowndes, G. J. (2013). Self-reported wayfinding ability of older adults. *Accident Analysis & Prevention, 59*, 277–282.

Burklow, J. (2016). *10 Helpful safety features for mature drivers*. Chicago, IL: Cars.com. https://www.cars.com/articles/10-helpful-safety-features-for-mature-drivers-1420684729725/. Accessed February, 2018.

Caird, J. K. (2004). *In-vehicle intelligent transportation systems: Safety and mobility of older drivers. Transportation in an aging society: A decade of experience*. Washington, DC: Transportation Research Board.

Chan, M., & Rose, G. (2002). *Navigation and travel behaviour: Findings from focus group results*. Report no. ITS-WP-01-18. Sydney, NSW: Institute of Transport and Logistics Studies, Faculty of Economics and Business.

Chiang, D. P., Brooks, A. M., & Weir, D. H. (2005). *Comparison of visual-manual and voice interaction with contemporary navigation system HMIs*. Report no. 2005-01-0433. Warrendale, PA: SAE International.

Cicchino, J. B., Eichelberger, A. H., & McCartt, A. T. (2015). Buick Lucerne drivers' experiences with rear parking sensors. *Traffic Injury Prevention*, *16*, 196–201.

Cicchino, J. B., & McCartt, A. T. (2015). Experiences of model year 2011 Dodge and Jeep owners with collision avoidance and related technologies. *Traffic Injury Prevention*, *16* (3), 298–303.

Clark, D. E., & Cushing, B. M. (2002). Predicted effect of automatic crash notification on traffic mortality. *Accident Analysis & Prevention*, *34*, 507–513.

Clark, H., & Feng, J. (2017). Age differences in the takeover of vehicle control and engagement in non-driving-related activities in simulated driving with conditional automation. *Accident Analysis & Prevention*, *106*, 468–479.

Cotté, N., Meyer, J., & Coughlin, J. F. (2001). *Older and younger drivers' reliance on collision warning systems. Proceedings of the Human Factors and Ergonomics Society 45th annual meeting*. Santa Monica, CA: Human Factors and Ergonomics Society.

Coughlin, J. F. (2009). Longevity, lifestyle, and anticipating the new demands of aging on the transportation system. *Public Works Management & Policy*, *13*, 301–311.

Cushman, L. A., Stein, K., & Duffy, C. J. (2008). Detecting navigational deficits in cognitive aging and Alzheimer disease using virtual reality. *Neurology*, *71*, 888–895.

Dickie, D. A., & Boyle, L. N. (2009). Drivers' understanding of adaptive cruise control limitations. *Proceedings of the Human Factors and Ergonomics Society annual meeting*, *53*, 1806–1810.

Dingus, T., Hulse, M. C., Mollnehauer, M. A., Fleischman, R. N., McGehee, D. V., & Manakkal, N. (1997). Effects of age, system experience, and navigation technique on driving with an advanced traveler information system. *Human Factors*, *39*, 177–179.

Douissembekov, E., Gabaude, C., Rogé, J., Navarro, J., & Michael, G. A. (2014). Parking and manoeuvring among older drivers: A survey investigating special needs and difficulties. *Transportation Research Part F: Traffic Psychology and Behaviour*, *26*, 238–245.

Eby, D. W., & Kostyniuk, L. P. (1998). Maintaining older driver mobility and well-being with traveler information systems. *Transportation Quarterly*, *52*, 45–53.

Eby, D. W., & Kostyniuk, L. P. (1999). An on-the-road comparison of in-vehicle navigation assistance systems. *Human Factors*, *41*, 295–311.

Eby, D. W., & Molnar, L. J. (2014). Has the time come for an older driver vehicle? *Journal of Ergonomics.*, *S3*, 002.

Eby, D. W., Molnar, L. J., & Kartje, P. S. (2009). *Maintaining safe mobility in an aging society*. New York, NY: CRC Press.

Eby, D. W., Molnar, L. J., Zakrajsek, J., Ryan, L., Zanier, N., St. Louis, R. M., … on behalf of the LongROAD Research Team. (2018). Prevalence, attitudes, and knowledge of in-vehicle technologies and vehicle adaptations among older drivers. *Accident Analysis & Prevention*, *113*, 54–62.

Eby, D. W., Molnar, L. J., Zhang, L., St. Louis, R. M., Zanier, N., & Kostyniuk, L. P. (2015). *Keeping older adults driving safely: A research synthesis of advanced in-vehicle technologies*. Washington, DC: AAA Foundation for Traffic Safety.

Eby, D. W., Molnar, L. J., Zhang, L., St. Louis, R. M., Zanier, N., ... Stanciu, S. (2016). Use, perceptions, and benefits of automotive technologies among aging drivers. *Injury Epidemiology*, *3*(28), 1–20.

Eby, D. W., Silverstein, N. M., Molnar, L. J., LeBlanc, D., & Adler, G. (2012). Driving behaviors in early stage dementia: A study using in-vehicle technology. *Accident Analysis & Prevention*, *49*, 324–331.

Eichelberger, A. H., & McCartt, A. T. (2014a). ). Toyota drivers' experiences with dynamic radar, cruise control, the pre-collision system, and lane-keeping assist. Arlington, VA: Insurance Institute for Highway Safety.

Eichelberger, A. H., & McCartt, A. T. (2014b). Volvo drivers' experiences with advanced crash avoidance and related technologies. *Traffic Injury Prevention*, *15*(2), 187–195.

Emmerson, C., Guo, W., Blythe, P., Namdeo, A., & Edwards, S. (2013). Fork in the road: In-vehicle navigation systems and older drivers. *Transportation Research Part F*, *21*, 173–180.

Ervin, R. D., Sayer, J., LeBlanc, D., Bogard, S., Mefford, M., Hagan, M., ... Winkler, C. (2005). *Automotive collision avoidance system field operational test report: Methodology and results*. Report no. DOT HS 809 900. Washington, DC: US Department of Transportation.

Fancher, P., Ervin, R., Sayer, J., Hagan, M., Bogard, S., Bareket, Z., ... Haugen, J. (1998). *Intelligent cruise control field operational test (final report)*. Report no. UMTRI-98-17. Ann Arbor, MI: University of Michigan Transportation Research Institute.

Gish, J., Vrkljan, B., Grenier, A., & Van Miltenburg, B. (2017). Driving with advanced vehicle technology: A qualitative investigation of older drivers' perceptions and motivations for use. *Accident Analysis & Prevention*, *106*, 498–504.

Guo, F., Wotring, B. M., & Antin, J. F. (2010). *Evaluation of lane change collision avoidance systems using the national advanced driving simulator*. Report no. DOT HS 811 332. Washington, DC: National Highway Traffic Safety Administration.

Hartwich, F., Beggiato, M., & Krems, J. F. (2018). Driving comfort, enjoyment, and acceptance of automated driving—Effects of drivers' age and driving style familiarity. *Ergonomics*, *61*(8), 1017–1032.

He, J., Chaparro, A., Nguyen, B., Burge, R. J., Chandall, J., Chaparro, B., & Cao, S. (2014). Texting while driving: Is speech-based text entry less risky than handheld text entry? *Accident Analysis & Prevention*, *72*, 287–295.

Hoedemaeker, M., & Brookhuis, K. A. (1998). Behavioural adaptation to driving with an adaptive cruise control (ACC). *Transportation Research Part F*, *1*, 95–106.

Horberry, T., Hartley, L., Kruger, G. P., & Mabbott, N. (2001). *Fatigue detection technologies for drivers: A review of existing operator-centered systems. Proceedings people in control: An international conference on human interfaces in control rooms, cockpits, and command centers*. Washington, DC: IEEE.

Hulse, L. M., Xie, H., & Galea, E. R. (2018). Perceptions of autonomous vehicles: Relationships with road users, risk, gender and age. *Safety Science*, *102*, 1–13.

Hunt, L. A., Brown, A. E., & Gilman, I. P. (2010). Drivers with dementia and outcomes of becoming lost while driving. *American Journal of Occupational Therapy*, *64*, 225–232.

Hurtienne, J., & Blessing, L. (2007). *Design for intuitive use—Testing image schema theory for user interface design. Proceedings of the international conference on engineering design*. Paris France: ICED.

Hurwitz, D. S., Pradhan, A., Fischer, D. L., Knodler, M. A., Muttart, J. W., Menon, R., & Meissner, U. (2010). Backing collisions: A study of drivers' eye and backing behaviour using combined rear-view camera and sensor systems. *Injury Prevention*, *16*, 79–84.

Itoh, K., Miki, Y., Yoshitsugu, N., Kubo, N., & Mashimo, S. (2004). *Evaluation of a voice-activated system using a driving simulator*. Report no. 2004-01-0232. Warrendale, PA: SAE International.

Jenness, J. W., Lattanzio, R. J., O'Toole, M., Taylor, N., & Pax, C. (2002). Effects of manual versus voice-activated dialing during simulated driving. *Perceptual and Motor Skills*, *94*, 363–379.

Jeong, E., Oh, C., & Lee, J. (2014). Evaluation of safety benefits of automatic crash information notification systems on freeways. *International Journal of Automotive Technology*, *15*, 495–503.

Jermakian, J. S. (2011). Crash avoidance potential of four vehicle technologies. *Accident Analysis & Prevention*, *43*, 732–740.

Kamalanathsharma, R. K., Rakha, H. A., & Zohdy, I. H. (2015). Survey of in-vehicle technology use: Results and findings. *International Journal of Transportation Science and Technology*, *4*(2), 135–150.

Kawabata, Y., Endo, T., Makno, Y., Satonaka, H., Tanaka, Y., & Katoh, M. (2008). *Improvement of reverse parking assist with automatic steering. Proceedings of the 15th World Congress on intelligent transport systems and ITS America annual meeting 2008*. Washington, DC: ITS America.

Keegan, M. (2016). 10 Must-have technologies for senior drivers. ⟨https://www.carfax.com/blog/10-technologies-for-senior-drivers⟩ Accessed February, 2018.

Kessler, A. M. (2015, January, 14). In Detroit, Google makes a case for driverless cars. *The New York Times*. ⟨http://www.nytimes.com/2015/01/15/business/in-detroit-google-makes-a-case-for-driverless-cars.html?_r = 0⟩ Accessed February, 2018.

Kessler, C., Etemad, A., Alessendretti, G., Heinig, K., Selpi., Brouwer, R., ... Benmimoun, M. (2012). *European large-scale field operational tests on in-vehicle systems: Deliverable D11.3*. Aachen, Germany: euroFOT Consortium.

Kiefer, R. J., & Hankey, J. M. (2008). Lane change behavior with a side blind zone alert. *Accident Analysis & Prevention*, *40*, 683–690.

Köber, M., Gold, C., Lechner, D., & Bengler, K. (2016). The influence of age on the take-over of vehicle control in highly automated driving. *Transportation Research Part F*, *39*, 19–32.

Kostyniuk, L. P., Eby, D. W., Christoff, C., & Hopp, M. L. (1997). *An evaluation of driver response to the TetraStar navigation assistance system by age and sex*. Report no. UMTRI-97-33. Ann Arbor, MI: University of Michigan Transportation Research Institute.

Kostyniuk, L. P., Streff, F. M., & Eby, D. W. (1997). *The older driver and navigation assistance technologies*. Report no. UMTRI-97-47. Ann Arbor, MI: University of Michigan Transportation Research Institute.

Kramer, A. F., Cassavaugh, N., Horrey, W. J., & Mayhugh, J. L. (2007). Influence of age and proximity warning devices on collision avoidance in simulated driving. *Human Factors*, *49*, 935–949.

Kusano, K., & Gabler, H. C. (2014). Comprehensive target populations for current active safety systems using national crash databases. *Traffic Injury Prevention*, *15*, 753–761.

Kusano, K., Gorman, T. I., Sherony, R., & Gabler, H. C. (2014). Potential occupant injury reduction in the U.S. vehicle fleet for lane departure warning-equipped vehicles in single-vehicle crashes. *Traffic Injury Prevention*, *15*, S157–S164.

Kyriakidis, M., Happee, R., & de Winter, J. C. F. (2015). Public opinion on automated driving: Results of an international questionnaire among 5000 respondents. *Transportation Research Part F, 32*, 127–140.

Lavallière, M., Laurendeau, D., Simoneau, M., & Teasdale, N. (2011). Changing lanes in a simulator: Effects of aging on the control of the vehicle and visual inspection of mirrors and blind spot. *Traffic Injury Prevention, 12*(2), 191–200.

Lavallière, M., Reimer, B., Mehler, B., D'Ambrosio, L., Wang, Y., Teasdale, N., & Coughlin, J. F. (2011). *The effect of age and gender on visual search during lane changing. Proceedings driving assessment 2011: 6th international driving symposium on human factors in driver assessment, training, and vehicle design*. Ames, IA: University of Iowa.

LeBlanc, D., Sayer, J., Winkler, C., Ervin, R., Bogard, S., Devonshire, J., ... Gordon, T. (2006). *Road departure crash warning system field operational test: Methodology and results*. Report no. UMTRI-2006-9-1. Ann Arbor, MI: University of Michigan Transportation Research Institute.

LeBlanc, D. J., Bao, S., Sayer, J. R., & Bogard, S. (2013). Longitudinal driving behavior with integrated crash-warning system. *Transportation Research Record: Journal of the Transportation Research Board, 2365*, 17–21.

Lee, E., Wu, J., Kang, T., & Craig, M. (2017). Estimate of mortality reduction with implementation of advanced automatic collision notification. *Traffic Injury Prevention, 18* (suppl s1), S24–S30.

Lee, J. D., Caven, B., Haake, S., & Brown, T. L. (2001). Speech-based interaction with in-vehicle computer: The effect of speech-based E-mail on drivers' attention to the roadway. *Human Factors: The Journal of the Human Factors and Ergonomics Society, 43* (4), 631–640.

Lester, B. D., Sager, L. N., Dawson, J., Hacker, S. D., Aksan, N., Rizzo, M., & Kitazaki, S. (2015). Pilot results on forward collision warning system effectiveness in older drivers. In: *Proceedings of the international driving symposium on human factors, driving assessment, training, and vehicle design* (pp. 345–351).

Llaneras, R. E., Neurauter, M. L., & Green, C. A. (2011). *Factors moderating the effectiveness of rear vision systems: What performance-shaping factors contribute to drivers' detection and response to unexpected in-path obstacles when backing?* Report no. 2011-01-0549. SAE Technical Papers.

Maciej, J., & Vollrath, M. (2009). Comparison of manual vs. speech-based interaction with in-vehicle information systems. *Accident Analysis & Prevention, 41*, 924–930.

Maltz, M., & Shinar, D. (2004). Imperfect in-vehicle collision avoidance warning systems can aid drivers. *Human Factors, 46*(2), 357–366.

Martinez, F. J., Toh, C.-K., Cano, J.-C., Calafate, C. T., & Manzoni, P. (2010). Emergency services in future intelligent transportation systems based on vehicular communication networks. *IEEE Intelligent Transportation Systems Magazine, Summer*, 6–20.

Mazzae, E. N., Barickman, F., Baldwin, G. H., & Ranney, T. (2008). *On-road study of drivers' use of rearview video systems (ORSDURVS)*. Report no. DOT HS 811 024. Washington, DC: National Highway Traffic Safety Administration.

McDonald, A. B., McGehee, D. V., Chrysler, S. T., Askelson, N. M., Angell, L. S., & Seppelt, B. D. (2016). National survey identifying gaps in consumer knowledge of advanced vehicle safety systems. *Transportation Research Record, 2559*, 1–6.

McElheny, M., Blanco, M., & Hankey, J. M. (2006). On-road evaluation of an in-vehicle curve warning device. *Proceedings of the Human Factors and Ergonomics Society 50th annual meeting, 50*, 2414–2418).

McGwin, G., & Brown, D. B. (1999). Characteristics of traffic crashes among young, middle-aged, an older drivers. *Accident Analysis & Prevention*, *31*, 181–198.

McLaughlin, D. (2014, July, 16). 17 Ways driverless cars could change America. *The federalist*. ⟨http://thefederalist.com/2014/07/16/17-ways-driverless-cars-could-change-america/⟩ Accessed February, 2018.

McLaughlin, S. B., Hankey, J. M., Green, C. A., & Kiefer, R. J. (2003). *Driver performance evaluation of two rear parking aids. Proceedings of the 18th international technical conference on the enhanced safety of vehicles*. Washington, DC: National Highway Traffic Safety Administration.

Mehler, B., Reimer, B., Dobres, J., McAnulty, H., Mehler, A., Munger, D., & Coughlin, J. F. (2014). *Further evaluation of the effects of a production level "voice-command" interface on driver behavior: Replication and a consideration of the significance of training method*. MIT AgeLab technical report no. 2014-2. Cambridge, MA: Massachusetts Institute of Technology.

Mehler, B., Reimer, B., Lavallière, M., Dobres, J., & Coughlin, J. F. (2014). *Evaluating technologies relevant to the enhancement of driver safety*. Washington, DC: AAA Foundation for Traffic Safety.

Miller, D., Johns, M., Ive, P., Gowda, N., Sirkin, D., Sibi, S., ... Ju, W. (2016). *Exploring transitional automation with new and older drivers*. Report no. 2016-01-1442. Warrendale, PA: SAE International.

Molnar, L. J., Pradhan, A. K., Eby, D. W., Ryan, L. H., St. Louis, R. M., ... Zhang, L. (2017). *Age-related differences in driver behavior associated with automated vehicles and the transfer of control between automated and manual control: A simulator evaluation*. Report no. UMTRI-2017-04. Ann Arbor, MI: University of Michigan Transportation Research Institute.

Motamedi, A., & Wang, J.-H. (2017). Older adult drivers' challenges and in-vehicle technology acceptance. *International Journal for Traffic and Transport Engineering*, *7*(4), 498–515.

Mueller, A. S., Sangrar, R., & Vrkljan, B. (in press). Rearview camera system use among older drivers: A naturalistic observation study. *Transportation Research Part F: Traffic Psychology and Behaviour*. https://doi.org/10.1016/j.trf.2017.06.014.

National Highway Traffic Safety Administration (NHTSA). (2012). *Preliminary statement of policy concerning automated vehicles*. Washington, DC: NHTSA.

National Highway Traffic Safety Administration (NHTSA). (2018). *The road to full automation*. Washington, DC: NHTSA. https://www.nhtsa.gov/technology-innovation/automated-vehicles-safety. Accessed March, 2018.

National Institute of Aging. (2011). Global health and aging. *NIA publication no. 11-7737*. Washington, DC: National Institute of Aging, National Institute of Health.

National Safety Council (2018). *My car does what: Know more. Drive safer*. Itasca, IL: National Safety Council. ⟨https://mycardoeswhat.org/⟩ Accessed March, 2018.

Neurauter, M. L., Hankey, J. M., Schalk, T. B., & Wallace, G. (2012). Outbound texting: Comparison of speech-based approach and handheld touch-screen equivalent. *Transportation Research Record*, *2321*, 23–30.

Newcomb, D. *Car technology that helps older drivers*. (2015). ⟨https://www.edmunds.com/car-technology/car-technology-that-helps-older-drivers.html⟩ Accessed February, 2018.

O'Connor, A. (2013). *Would a driverless car be right for you?* AARP. ⟨http://www.aarp.org/home-family/getting-around/info-03-2013/driverless-cars-are-we-close.html⟩ Accessed February, 2018.

Oxley, P. R., Barham, P. A., & Ayala, B. E. (1995). *The use of route guidance systems by elderly drivers. Proceedings of the 1994 World Congress on applications of transport telemetrics and intelligent vehicle-highway systems*. Boston, MA: Artech House.

Paris, J. C., Bellet, T., Cour, M., Marin-Lamellet, C., Deleurence, P., Moreau, F., ... Claverie, B. (2014). *Driving assistances for senior drivers: A human centered design approach*. Paper no. 18291. Transport Research Arena 2014.

Perez, M. A., Viita, D., Hankey, J. M., Voran-Nowak, S., & Tengler, S. C. (2011). *Voice- and visual-manual-control navigation system evaluation based on user performance in destination entry and navigation tasks. TRB 90th annual meeting compendium of papers DVD*. Washington, DC: Transportation Research Board.

Piccinini, G. F. B., Rodrigues, C. M., Leitão, M., & Simões, A. (2014). Driver's behavioral adaptation to adaptive cruise control (ACC): The case of speed and time headway. *Journal of Safety Research, 49*, 77–84.

Piccinini, G. F. B., Rodrigues, C. M., Leitão, M., & Simões, A. (2015). Reaction to a critical situation during driving with adaptive cruise control for users and non-users of the system. *Safety Science, 72*, 116–126.

Ponte, G., Ryan, G. A., & Anderson, R. W. G. (2016). An estimate of the effectiveness of an in-vehicle collision notification system in reducing road crash fatalities in South Australia. *Traffic Injury Prevention, 17*(3), 258–263.

Rajaonah, B., Anceaux, F., & Vienne, F. (2006). Trust and the use of adaptive cruise control: A study of a cut-in situation. *Cognition, Technology, and Work, 8*, 146–155.

Rakha, H., Hankey, J., Patterson, A., & van Aerde, M. (2001). Field evaluation of safety impacts of adaptive cruise control. *ITS Journal, 6*(3), 225–259.

Ranney, T. A., Mazzae, E. N., Baldwin, G. H. S., & Salaani, M. K. (2007). *Characteristics of voice-based interfaces for in-vehicle systems and their effects on driving performance*. Report DOT HS 810 867. Washington, DC: National Highway Traffic Safety Administration.

Regan, M. A., Mitsopoulos, E., Haworth, N. & Young, C. (2002). *Acceptability of in-vehicle intelligent transport systems to Victorian car drivers*. Report no. 02/02. Melbourne, VIC, Australia: Monash University Accident Research Centre.

Reimer, B. (2014). Driver assistance systems and the transition to automated vehicles: A path to increase older adult safety and mobility? *Public Policy and Aging Report, 24*, 27–31.

Reimer, B., Mehler, B., & Coughlin, J. F. (2010). *An evaluation of driver reactions to new vehicle parking assist technologies developed to reduce driver stress*. Cambridge, MA: New England University Transportation Center, Massachusetts Institute of Technology.

Reimer, B., Mehler, B., McAnulty, H., Munger, D., Mehler, A., Perez, E. A. G., ... Coughlin, J. F. (2013). *A preliminary assessment of perceived and objectively scaled workload of a voice-based driver interface. Proceedings of the seventh international driving symposium on human factors in driver assessment, training, and vehicle design*. Ames, IA: University of Iowa.

Sayer, J. R., Buonarosa, M. J., Bao, S., Bogard, S. E., LeBlanc, D. J., Blankespoor, A. D., ... Winkler, C. B. (2010). *Integrated vehicle-based safety systems light-vehicle field operational test methodology and results report*. Report no. UMTRI-2010-30. Ann Arbor, MI: University of Michigan Transportation Research Institute.

Schoetttle, B., & Sivak, M. (2015). *Motorists' preferences for different levels of vehicle automation*. Report no. UMTRI-2015-22. Ann Arbor, MI: University of Michigan Transportation Research Institute.

Schreiner, C., Blanco, M., & Hankey, J. M. (2004). *Investigation of driving behavior changes associated with manual and voice-activated phone-dialing in a real-world environment. Proceedings 14th annual meeting and exposition ITS America*. Washington, DC: ITS America.

Seto, Y., Sugano, T., Gokan, T., Sakui, H., Akatsu, Y., & Kobayashi, M. (2012). *Development of a backup collision intervention system. Proceedings of the 19th intelligent transport systems World Congress*. Washington, DC: ITS America.

Shaw, L., Polgar, J. M., Vrkljan, B., & Jacobson, J. (2010). Seniors' perceptions of vehicle safety risks and needs. *The American Journal of Occupational Therapy*, *64*(2), 215–224.

Sihvola, N., Luoma, J., Schirokof, A., Salo, J., & Karkola, K. (2009). In-depth evaluation of the effects of an automatic emergency call system on road fatalities. *European Transport Research Review*, *1*(3), 99–105.

Sivak, M., Flannagan, M. J., Traube, E. C., Aoki, M., & Sayer, J. R. (1994). *Evaluation of an active headlight system*. Report no. UMTRI-94-17. Ann Arbor, MI: University of Michigan Transportation Research Institute.

Society of Automotive Engineers International (SAE). (2016). *Taxonomy and definitions for terms related to driving automation systems for on-road motor vehicles*. Report no. 2016-09-30. Warrendale, PA: SAE.

Stanton, N. A., & Young, M. S. (2005). Driver behavior with adaptive cruise control. *Ergonomics*, *10*, 1294–1313.

Stinchcombe, A., Gagnon, S., Kateb, M., Curtis, M., Porter, M. M., Polgar, J., & Bédard, M. (2017). Letting in-vehicle navigation lead the way: Older drivers' perceptions of and ability to follow a GPS navigation system. *Accident Analysis & Prevention*, *106*, 515–520.

Stockburger, J. *Top 25 new cars for senior drivers*. (2018). ⟨https://www.consumerreports.org/elderly-driving/top-25-new-cars-for-senior-drivers/⟩ Accessed February, 2018.

Strand, N., Nilsson, J., Karlsson, I. C. M., & Nilsson, L. (2011). *Interaction with and use of driver assistance systems: A study of end-user experiences. Proceedings of the 18th ITS World Congress*. Washington, DC: ITS America.

Strayer, D. L., Cooper, J. M., Turrill, J., Coleman, J., Mederios-Ward, N., & Biondi, F. (2013). *Measuring cognitive distraction in the automobile*. Washington, DC: AAA Foundation for Traffic Safety.

Strayer, D. L., Turrill, J., Coleman, J. R., Ortiz, E. V., & Cooper, J. M. (2014). *Measuring cognitive distraction in the automobile II: Assessing in-vehicle voice-based interactive technologies*. Washington, DC: AAA Foundation for Traffic Safety.

Stutts, J., Martell, C., & Staplin, L. (2009). *Identifying behaviors and situations with increased crash risk for older drivers*. Report no. DOT HS 811 093. Washington, DC: National Highway Traffic safety Administration.

Sullivan, J. M., & Flannagan, M. J. (2007). Determining the potential safety benefits of improved lighting in three pedestrian crash scenarios. *Accident Analysis & Prevention*, *39*, 638–647.

Tachibana, H. (2011). *The development of a parking support system considering driving characteristics. Proceedings of the SAE 2011 World Congress and exhibition*. Warrendale, PA: SAE International.

The Hartford. (2012). *Top technologies for mature drivers: Expert ranking*. Hartford, CT: The Hartford Financial Services Group, Inc. http://www.thehartford.com/mature-market-excellence/vehicle-technology. Accessed February, 2018.

Totzke, I., Jessberger, S., Mühlbacher., & Krüger, H.-P. (2011). Semi-autonomous advanced parking assistants: Do they really have to be learned if steering is automated? *IET Intelligent Transport Systems*, *5*(2), 141–147.

Totzke, I., Müehlbacher., & Krüger, H.-P. (2010). *Semi-autonomous advanced parking assist: A source of drivers' distraction? Human factors: A system view of human, technology and organization: Annual conference of the Europe chapter of the Human Factors and Ergonomics Society*. Santa Monica, CA: Human Factors and Ergonomics Society.

Trop, J. & Threewitt, C. *9 Best new cars for older drivers*. (2018). ⟨https://cars.usnews.com/cars-trucks/best-cars-for-older-drivers⟩ Accessed February, 2018.

Trübswetter, N., & Bengler, K. (2013). *Why should I use ADAS? Advanced driver assistance systems and the elderly: Knowledge, experience, and usage barriers. Proceedings of the seventh international driving symposium on human factors in driver assessment, training, and vehicle design*. Ames, IA: University of Iowa.

Uc, E. Y., Rizzo, M., Anderson, S. W., Shi, Q., & Dawson, J. D. (2004). Driver route-following and safety errors in early Alzheimer disease. *Neurology*, *63*, 832–837.

Vrkljan, B. H., & Polgar, J. M. (2007). Driving, navigation, and vehicular technology: Experiences of older drivers and their co-pilots. *Traffic Injury Prevention*, *8*, 403–410.

Wheaton, A. G., Chapman, D. P., Presley-Cantrell, L. R., Croft, J. B., & Roehler, D. R. (2013). Drowsy driving—19 states and the District of Columbia. *Morbidity and Mortality Weekly Report*, *61*(51–52), 1033–1037.

Wikipedia. *Backup cameras*. (2018). ⟨https://en.wikipedia.org/wiki/Backup_camera⟩ Accessed February, 2018.

Williamson, A., & Chamberlain, T. (2005). *Review of On-Road Driver Fatigue Monitoring Devices*. Kensington, New South Wales: NSW Injury Risk Management Research Centre, University of New South Wales.

Willstrand, T. D., Bellet, T., Broberg, T., Stave, C., Paris, J.-C., Peters, B., & Marin-Lamellet, C. (2015). What ADAS are the most promising for our future older drivers? Evidences reported from France and Sweden. *Proceedings of the 3rd international symposium on future active safety technology towards zero traffic accidents*, 523–530).

Wilschut, E. S., Kroon, L., de Goede, M., Cremers, A., & Hoedemaeker, M. (2014). The older adult road user: Recommendations for driver assistance. In *Proceedings of the international interdisciplinary conference on ageing and safe mobility*. ⟨https://repository.tudelft.nl/view/tno/uuid:3137581b-a0d7-467f-a900-8ad6ab522df6/⟩ Accessed March, 2018.

de Winter, J. C. F., Happee, R., Martens, M. H., & Stanton, N. A. (2014). Effects of adaptive cruise control and highly automated driving on workload and situation awareness: A review of the empirical evidence. *Transportation Research Part F: Traffic Psychology and Behaviour*, *27*, 196–217.

Xiong, H., Boyle, L. N., Moeckli, J., Dow, B. R., & Brown, T. L. (2012). Use patterns among early adopters of adaptive cruise control. *Human Factors: The Journal of the Human Factors and Ergonomics Society*, *54*, 722–733.

Yi, J., Lee, H. C.-Y., Parsons, R., & Falkmer, T. (2014). The effects of the global positioning system on the driving performance of people with mild Alzheimer's disease. *Gerontology*, *61*, 79–88.

Zanier, N., Molnar, L. J., Eby, D. W., Zakrajsek, J., Ryan, L., St. Louis, R. M., … the LongROAD Research Team. (2018). *Observed maintenance, damage, technologies, and adaptations among vehicles of older drivers: A LongROAD study. Research brief*. Washington, DC: AAA Foundation for Traffic Safety.

# Roadway design and infrastructure

# 13

*Life is a journey that must be traveled no matter how bad the roads and accommodations.*

*Oliver Goldsmith*

## Introduction

Constructed roadways and other infrastructure to support transportation have been around since ancient times. Constructed roads can be traced as far back in history as 4000 BC to stone-paved roads in Iraq and timber-paved roads in England (Lay & Benson, 2016). Indeed, ancient civilizations are often judged by the extensiveness and quality of their transportation systems. Several ancient civilizations were considered exceptional road builders, and the names of some of these roads are still familiar today, including the Romans and the Apian Way, the Persians and the Royal Road, China and the Great Silk Road, and the Incan Andes Roads (Lay & Benson, 2016). Modern road building began in France and Britain in the late 1700s and appeared in the United States (US) in the early 1800s (Lay & Benson, 2016). Starting in the mid-1900s, many developed countries passed legislation to develop and manage national roadway systems, such as the *National Roads Act 1974* in Australia (Australasian Legal Information Institute, 2018), the *Highway Act 1959* in the United Kingdom (UK) (National Archives, 2018), and the *Federal Aid Highway Act of 1956*, which started development of the Interstate Highway System in the US (Wikipedia, 2018).

While this legislation provided funding and administrative support for updating and developing new roadways, these roadways were designed for the drivers of the mid-20th century and not for the aging populations that many countries are experiencing today. There is convincing worldwide evidence that older drivers have difficulties with some roadway features, particularly complex intersections (see, e.g., Cicchino & McCartt, 2015; Clarke, Ward, Bartle, & Truman, 2010; Fildes, Lee, Kenny, & Foddy, 1994; Lombardi, Horrey, & Courtney, 2017; Preusser, Williams, Ferguson, Ulmer, & Weinstein, 1998; Rakotonirainy, Steinhardt, Delhomme, Darvell, & Schramm, 2012; Staplin, Lococo, McKnight, McKnight, & Odenheimer, 1998). For example, a nationwide study in the US examined a census of fatal two-vehicle crashes between 2011 and 2014 for age-related differences (Lombardi et al., 2017). The researchers analyzed more than 48,000 drivers involved in fatal intersection crashes and calculated crash involvement ratios by age group. The study found that drivers age 70–74 were about 20% more likely

**Perspectives and Strategies for Promoting Safe Transportation among Older Adults.**
**DOI: https://doi.org/10.1016/B978-0-12-812153-5.00013-3**

than drivers age 20–24 to be in fatal intersection crashes. The study also found that the fatal intersection crashes of older drivers were more likely to be on rural roadways, have a fewer number of lanes, more likely to have traffic controls present, be on lower speed roadways, be at fault, and occur during the daytime in good weather. Researchers in Queensland, Australia, analyzed 191,709 crashes and compared crash characteristics between middle-age drivers (age 40–59) and older drivers (age 60 + ) and found that older drivers were significantly more likely to be involved in both conventional and circular intersection crashes (Rakotonirainy et al., 2012). Similar results have been found for the UK (Clarke et al., 2010).

Survey and focus group results in several countries have indicated that older drivers report that they have some difficulties with roadway design features, including making left turns at unprotected intersections, locating and reading signage and pavement markings, and knowing the proper lane to be in for left turns and roundabouts (Benekohal, Resende, Shim, Michaels, & Weeks, 1992; Dissanayake & Perera, 2011; Fildes et al., 1994; Insurance Institute for Highway Safety, 2013; Kwigizile et al., 2017; Musselwhite & Haddad, 2010). For example, a survey of 284 older drivers in Kansas, US, found that nearly one-half of respondents reported that making unprotected left turns was challenging as compared to only 1% reporting that left turns with a green arrow was challenging (Dissanayake & Perera, 2011). A qualitative study of 29 older drivers in the UK explored problematic driving issues (Musselwhite & Haddad, 2010). The study found that older drivers reported the following issues with roadway design features: road signs, event signs, and work-zone signs were considered distracting; road signs were often inappropriately placed, requiring the older drivers to read the sign while doing other tasks such as turning; and road sign language was confusing and lacked continuity. A workshop of older and former drivers in Canberra, Australia, found that there were a number of roadway features that were a problem for older drivers, including inadequate roads signs, lettering too small on signs and roadway markings, difficult to understand signs, and inadequate roadway lighting, particularly for seeing pedestrians (Fildes et al., 1994).

The fact that roadways were not designed to accommodate the declining abilities of older drivers has long been recognized (see, e.g., Transportation Research Board, 1988). Several jurisdictions have proposed that improved roadway designs could enhance older driver safety. In the US, the Federal Highway Administration (FHWA) has sponsored a number of efforts to develop research-based guidelines and recommendations to help engineers design and improve roadways to accommodate older drivers and aging pedestrians (Brewer, Murillo, & Pate, 2014; Harkey et al., 2001; Staplin, Lococo, & Byington, 1998; Staplin, Lococo, Byington, & Harkey, 2001). The RAC Foundation in the UK published a report of recommendations for improving the safe mobility of older drivers (Box, Gandolfi, & Mitchell, 2010). Among many recommendations, the report advocated strongly for improving roadway design elements to match the capabilities of older road users better. The jurisdictions of Australasia (Australia, New Zealand, and neighboring islands) have implemented a "safe system" approach (Organisation for Economic Co-operation and Development, 2008) to reduce roadway injuries and fatalities (Oxley, Langford,

& Charlton, 2010). An important component of this approach is to optimize the safety of roadways, as described by the Commonwealth of Australia (2017):

> *A Safe System ensures that the forces in collisions do not exceed the limits of human tolerance. Speeds must be managed so that humans are not exposed to impact forces beyond their physical tolerance. System designers and operators need to take into account the limits of the human body in designing and maintaining roads, vehicles and speeds. (n.p.)*

Oxley et al. (2010) have argued that the safe system approach in Australia is particularly pertinent for improving older drivers safety and that improvements to infrastructure and road design that better match the characteristics of older drivers will need to be based on the following: designs should reflect the capabilities of older drivers; design improvements should be made to environments that have been shown to be difficult for older drivers, such as intersections; and efforts should be made to facilitate the accessibility and availability of non-driving community mobility options.

This chapter reviews research and practice in roadway design infrastructure in relation to older drivers. Covered here are traffic control devices, intersections, work zones, and crashes that are caused by a driver travelling the wrong way on a roadway, a type of crash in which older drivers are overrepresented.

## Traffic control devices

According to the FHWA (2009), traffic control devices have several purposes: to promote safety and efficiency by guiding travel of all road users; to inform all road users of regulations; to provide warnings for needed road user behaviors to minimize the occurrences of crashes; and to provide tourist-oriented information and services. FHWA further states that for a traffic control device to be effective, it should meet the following five criteria for all road users, including older adults:

- Fulfill a need;
- Command attention;
- Convey a clear, simple meaning;
- Command respect from road users; and
- Give adequate time for proper response.

The history of traffic control devices in the US dates back to the early 1900s when motor vehicles were just starting to become more common. This fascinating history is well documented by Professor H. Gene Hawkins, Jr. of Texas A&M University on his website *Manual on Uniform Traffic Control Devices (MUTCD) History* (Hawkins, 2016), the FHWA (2017a), and McShane (1999). Given that signs, pavement markings, and signals are commonplace on today's roadways, it is hard to imagine that, prior to the early 1900s, roadways did not have traffic control devices. Early on, those who could afford automobiles often discovered that they had difficulty navigating to locations because they did not have information on how to get to other towns and locales. In various cities, automobile clubs were formed (as early as 1899) with a primary purpose of placing and maintaining directional signing on roadways for motorists. As the density of motor vehicles on roadways increased, particularly in cities such as Detroit, Los Angeles, New York, Chicago, and Cleveland, and traffic crashes became more common, officials in these cities began to develop and install their own set of traffic control devices. According to FHWA (2017a), between 1911 and 1920, the first centerline was painted on a street, the first stop-sign was installed, and the first three-color traffic light was used in Detroit; the first electric traffic light was installed in Cleveland; and the first official state route signs were installed in Wisconsin. With so many organizations and jurisdictions developing their own versions of traffic control devices, drivers from one area did not necessarily understand traffic control devices in another area. On some roadways, an auto club may have used one set of traffic control devices while another club used a different set. It became clear that standardization was needed. In the 1920s and 1930s, state transportation officials started to meet and develop requirements for traffic control devices that would be used across the country, resulting in the publication of the *Manual on Uniform Traffic Control Devices [MUTCD]* (American Association of State Highway Officials, 1935). This manual has been continuously updated as practices have changed, and the most recent version is the 2009 edition, with corrections of errors in 2012. One of the most significant recent factors influencing changes to the MUTCD is the aging of the population (Brewer et al., 2014; Harkey et al., 2001; Staplin et al., 1998, 2001).

## Signs

Roadway signs play a critical role in letting road users know about upcoming behaviors, providing warnings about safety-critical areas, and notifying users about laws and regulations. As with other forms of communication, for signs to be effective, they must be noticed by the road user (conspicuity), they must be easy to read and/or deciphered (legibility), and they must be properly understood (comprehension; Dewar & Olson, 2007). Problems with any of these components of communication can reduce the effectiveness of the sign.

Sign conspicuity is affected by the sign's location, size, color/brightness, and other objects nearby (clutter). Studies in Canada and Australia have investigated the effects of clutter on sign conspicuity among older adults (Edqvist & Johnston, 2008; Ho, Scialfa, Caird, & Graw, 2001; McPhee, Scialfa, Dennis, Ho, & Caird, 2004). These studies reported that all drivers had a more difficult time noticing signs with increasing visual clutter, but this effect was greater for older drivers, particularly when the driver was engaged in other tasks such as talking with a passenger. A study of older drivers with and without early-stage Alzheimer's disease investigated how well drivers noticed signs during actual driving (Uc, Rizzo, Anderson, Shi, & Dawson, 2005). Participants drove a set course and verbally identified roadway signs and landmarks. The researchers found that drivers with early Alzheimer's identified significantly fewer signs, including signs defined as being highly salient to the driving task such as speed limit signs.

Traffic signs use shape, color, size, lettering, and symbols to convey meaning. In the US (FHWA, 2009), there are 13 allowable colors for signs, each with a different general meaning (e.g., red means stop or prohibition; green indicates movements permitted or direction guidance; and blue indicates road user services guidance, tourist information, and evacuation routes). In the US, there are also nine sign shapes that have different uses and convey different meanings (see Table 13.1). Although there is some consistency in meaning/use of colors and shapes across the globe, it is not universal, and studies have found that international travelers often have difficulty understanding traffic signs in foreign countries (see, e.g., Al-Madani & Al-Janahi, 2002; Choocharukul & Sriroongvikrai, 2017; Shinar, Dewar, Summala, & Zakowska, 2003).

Comprehension of traffic signs may be lower among older drivers (Ben-Bassat & Shinar, 2015; Dewar, Kline, & Swanson, 1994; Shinar et al., 2003). In a large study of traffic sign symbol recognition, Shinar et al. (2003) assessed accuracy among five groups of people in four countries: novice drivers, tourists, older drivers (age 65 or older), problem drivers with traffic repeat violations, and students. In three of the four countries, older drivers had the lowest overall percentage of perfectly identifying traffic sign symbols (in the fourth country all groups were about the same). Further, in all countries, the older driver group had among the highest percentage of reporting the opposite meaning of traffic sign symbols. A study in Israel investigated traffic sign comprehension as a function of age and of whether the signs were in a roadway context or with a white background (Ben-Bassat & Shinar, 2015). These authors reported

**Table 13.1** Shapes of traffic signs in the US and their use/meaning (FHWA, 2009)

| Sign shape | Use/Meaning | Sign shape | Use/Meaning |
|---|---|---|---|
|  | Stop |  | Grade crossing |
| 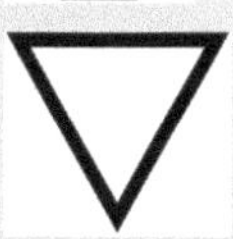 | Yield |  | Warning |
|  | Grade crossing advance warning |  | Regulatory, guide, or warning |
| 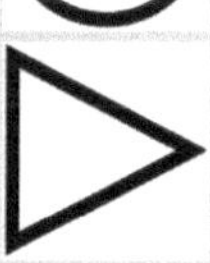 | No passing | 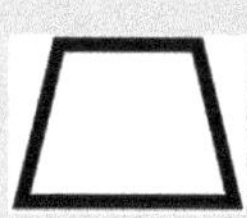 | Recreational, cultural interest area, national forest route |
| 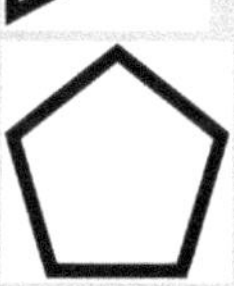 | School advance warning | | |

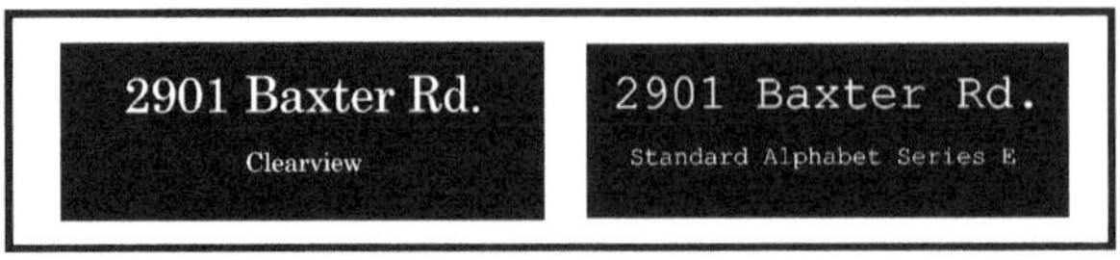


**Figure 13.1** Comparison of two font types used in US roadway signs.

that accuracy of comprehension did not vary by the context for the signs, but correct responses were higher for younger drivers (82%) than for older drivers (76%). The study also found that older drivers took nearly twice as long to respond to the signs as compared to younger drivers. A study in five Middle Eastern countries, however, reported that traffic sign comprehension increased with age, even when driving experience was taken into account (Al-Madani & Al-Janahi, 2002). However, the oldest age group in this study was age 45 and older and the study did not report the age range of respondents, so these results may not be applicable to drivers age 65 and older (an age group that makes up a small proportion of the populations of these countries).

As discussed in Chapter 1, The Challenges, older drivers tend to have greater difficulty seeing at night, so it is not surprising that many studies have shown that older drivers have more difficulty reading highway signs (legibility) at night as compared to younger drivers (see, e.g., Chrysler, Danielson, & Kirby, 1996; Evans & Ginsburg, 1985; Schieber & Kline, 1994; Sivak, Olson, & Pastalan, 1981). For example, in a field study in the US, researchers found that the legibility distances for older drivers were 65% of the distances for younger drivers for the same signs (Chrysler et al., 1996). Other studies have investigated the effects of traffic sign legibility as a function of text size, contrast, and font type among older drivers (see, e.g., Dobres, Chrysler, Wolfe, Chahine, & Reimer, 2017; Garvey, Klena, Eie, Meeker, & Pietrucha, 2016; Holick, Chrysler, Park, & Carlson, 2006; Ohyama & Sagawa, 2016; Schnell, Yekhshatyan, & Daiker, 2009). Collectively, these studies reported that older drivers had better sign legibility with increasing text size; legibility was best with positive contrast (light letters on a darker background); and a font type known as Clearview provided better visibility than the font known as Standard Alphabet Series E used in many jurisdictions in the US (see Fig. 13.1), at least when used with positive contrast.

Organizations in several countries have examined the research on aging drivers, age-related functional declines, and traffic control devices and have developed recommendations for best practice (Box et al., 2010; Brewer & Bedsole, 2015; FHWA, 2003a; Fildes, Oxley, Corben, & Langford, 2004; Rigdon, Atkinson, Bosack, O'Donnell, & Lambert, 2014). Table 13.2 shows a sampling of these recommendations along with the aging-driver issue addressed by each recommendation.

## *Pavement markings*

According to the MUTCD (FHWA, 2009), pavement markings are designed to provide guidance, warnings, regulations, or other information to the road users and may work in conjunction with traffic signs and signals or may be used alone. The

**Table 13.2** Recommendations for traffic control devices to accommodate older drivers

| Recommendation | Aging-driver issue |
|---|---|
| **Signs** | |
| At intersections with poor sight distance and/ or visibility, use advance warning signs | Declines in visual abilities and slower decision times |
| At intersections with multiple lanes and high traffic, use overhead placement of lane-use signs | Declines in attentional and visual abilities |
| For intersections, use multiple advance warning signs for merges, exit, and entry ramps | Declines in attentional and visual abilities |
| Use Clearview fonts on guide and street signs | Declines in visual abilities |
| Use combination lane-use/destination overhead guide signs at intersections with complex design | Declines in processing speed and wayfinding abilities |
| Use retroreflective sheeting backgrounds on guide and warning signs | Declines in visual abilities, particularly contrast sensitivity and difficulties seeing at night |
| At intersections with medians or offset turn lanes, large signs should be used (see FHWA, 2003a for sizes) | Declines in visual and cognitive abilities |
| Use NO TURN ON RED signs where intersection geometry might result in unexpected conflicts | Declines in ability to turn head |
| Use redundant street sign names for major intersections | Decreased reaction time and slowed information processing |
| Use mixed case lettering for signs | Declines in visual abilities |
| **Pavement markings** | |
| Use route markings on appropriate travel lanes at major freeway junctions | Decreased reaction time and slowed information processing |
| Use highly reflective materials for pavements markings | Declines in visual abilities |
| When a lane becomes a mandatory turn/exit lane on a freeway, a dotted lane line should be used in addition to advanced warning signs | Declines in visual abilities, particularly peripheral vision |
| Use black contrast markings when pavement color is light to increase visibility | Declines in visual abilities, particularly contrast sensitivity |
| Use curve warning markings to supplement curve warning signs | Declines in visual abilities, particularly peripheral vision |
| **Signals** | |
| Use backplates on traffic signals with retroreflective borders to reduce red-light-running crashes for all drivers | Declines in visual and attentional abilities |
| Use protected-only left-turn signals for all left turning movements, whenever appropriate | Declines in visual perception, speed of processing, and reaction time |

MUTCD also points out that the main limitation of pavement markings is that they have limited visibility under certain roadway conditions such as at night or in the presence of snow or debris. Visibility can also be reduced as the pavement marking materials degrade with time and high levels of traffic.

As with signs, every aspect of pavement markings from the color to the width and pattern has specific meanings. For example, in many jurisdictions, different colors are used in pavement marking for different purposes. In the US, five colors are used (FHWA, 2009): white (the separation of traffic moving in the same direction and the edge of the roadway), yellow (separation of traffic moving in opposite directions and the separation of two-way turn lanes), red (truck escape ramps or one-way roadways lanes that should not be entered from the direction of the pavement marking), blue (handicap parking), and purple (to indicate toll plaza lanes for vehicles with electronic toll collection accounts). Black can also be used but only for increasing the contrast of other pavement markings on roadways that are light. Nighttime visibility of pavement markings can be enhanced through the use of retroreflective materials (e.g., Carlson, Miles, Pratt, & Pike, 2005) and is required in the US unless the area is adequately lit at nighttime (FHWA, 2009).

Much of the research on pavement markings and older drivers has focused on visibility, and study results show that older drivers have more difficulty seeing pavement markings at night and in bad weather than younger drivers. (e.g., Benekohal et al., 1992; Berces & Robertson, 2012; Diamandouros & Gatscha, 2016; Graham, Harrold, & King, 1996; Horberry, Anderson, & Regan, 2006; Molino, Opiela, Andersen, & Moyer, 2003; Schnell, Aktan, & Lee, 2003; Zwahlen & Schnell, 1999). For example, a field study conducted on an abandoned runway examined pavement marking detection distances at nighttime between younger and older drivers with various retroreflective materials (Zwahlen & Schnell, 1999). The study found that detection distances were about 30%–39% longer (i.e., better visibility) for the younger drivers across the various type of retroreflectivity and high/low beam conditions. A similar study in New Zealand that compared nonreflective and retroreflective pavement markings found that older drivers had about a 23% worse visibility score than younger drivers (Dravitzki, Wilkie, & Lester, 2006).

As with signs, a number of publications have provided recommendations and/or best practices regarding pavement markings to help older drivers (Box et al., 2010; Brewer & Bedsole, 2015; FHWA, 2003a; Fildes et al., 2004; Rigdon et al., 2014). Table 13.2 shows a sampling of these recommendations along with the aging-driver issue addressed by each recommendation.

## Signals

Traffic signals are designed to inform and guide road users. Signals are unique, however, in that they are usually lighted and dynamic. According to the FHWA (2009), traffic signals include displays for controlling intersection traffic, pedestrian displays, beacons that flash, signals for controlling lane direction, and so on

(Brewer et al., 2014). Traffic signals have a number of advantages over other traffic control devices, including (FHWA, 2009):

- Providing for the orderly movement of traffic,
- Increasing the capacity of an intersection to handle traffic,
- Reducing the frequency and severity of certain types of crashes,
- Coordinating the near continuous movement of traffic at a defined speed along a given route, and
- Interrupting heavy traffic at intervals to permit other traffic a right-of-way.

As discussed in the *Handbook for Designing Roadways for the Aging Population* (Brewer et al., 2014), there is little research on traffic signals and aging drivers. After review of research on visual declines with age, these authors concluded, "... evidence suggests ... that aging individuals have reduced levels of sensitivity to intensity and contrast, but not to color" (p. 174). Thus, aging drivers should have little difficulty perceiving traffic signal colors but are likely to have more difficulty simply seeing illuminated signals, as compared to younger drivers. The handbook reviews extensive research on traffic signal intensity and size and provides recommendations, and the interested reader is referred to the handbook for more details.

Protected left turns (or right turns in countries like Australia and Japan where driving is done on the opposite side of the road compared to the US) utilize a colored arrow signal (usually green) to indicate whether or not a driver may turn with the right-of-way. This type of signal eliminates the need for the driver to make judgments about traffic gaps before proceeding into a turn. Permissive left turns, on the other hand, are usually red lights or flashing red lights and allow the driver to make a turn when the traffic is clear. As discussed in Chapter 1, The Challenges, yielding the right-of-way is the most common error leading to older driver crashes (e.g., Mayhew, Simpson, & Ferguson, 2006; Thompson, Baldock, Mathias, & Wundersitz, 2013). There is some evidence that older drivers have a less accurate understanding of these types of signals than other drivers do (Brehmer, Kacir, Noyce, & Manser, 2003). A computer-based survey of 2465 drivers (7% age 65 or older) in eight US cities addressed the understanding of protected/permissive left-turn signals. Drivers were presented color photographs of intersections and given a description of the scenario such as "if you wanted to turn left and you see the traffic signals shown, you would...." and the respondent could answer "stop," "yield and wait for the gap," "stop then wait for the gap," or "stop." While high percentages of drivers of all ages responded correctly to the protected left-turn signal scenarios, drivers age 65 and older had a lower percentage of correct responses (82.5%) compared to drivers age 22–44 (88.6%). Results were much worse for permissive left-turn signals (a variety of signal types). In these scenarios, older drivers were only correct in 51.4% of judgments as compared to drivers age 22–44 (57.5%).

Several publications provide recommendations and/or best practices regarding signals to help older drivers (Box et al., 2010; Brewer & Bedsole, 2015; FHWA, 2003a; Fildes et al., 2004; Rigdon et al., 2014). Table 13.2 shows a few example recommendations along with the aging-driver issue addressed by each recommendation. For a full list, the reader is referred to these documents.

## Intersections

It is well established that intersections pose greater challenges for older drivers than for younger drivers and that the result is higher crash rates at these roadway elements (see, e.g., Cicchino & McCartt, 2015; Mayhew et al., 2006; Rakotonirainy et al., 2012; Thompson et al., 2013). Studies that have examined older driver behaviors at intersections either using video cameras or an on-board observer (e.g., Porter & Whitton, 2002; Staplin, Gish, Decina, Lococo, & McKnight, 1998) have reported the following problem behaviors for older drivers: not completely stopping at a stop sign, improper turn path, improper signaling, failing to yield, improper approaches to intersections, failing to clear the intersection, and leaving on turn signal after the turn. Studies that have analyzed driver errors in intersection crashes have found that these same errors are also commonly found as contributors to older drivers crashes (Braitman, Kirley, Ferguson, & Chaudhary, 2007; Cicchino & McCartt, 2015; Koppel, Bohensky, Langford, & Taranto, 2011; Kwigizile et al., 2017; Mayhew et al., 2006; Oxley, Fildes, Corben, & Langford, 2006; Rakotonirainy et al., 2012; Thompson et al., 2013). For example, a study of crashes in Australia and New Zealand found the following 10 contributing factors and their proportions in older-driver intersection crashes: inappropriate gap selection (76%), high task complexity and the presence of other road users (50%), high approach speeds of conflicting traffic (40%), high traffic volumes (40%), limit or restricted sight distance (34%), inadequate intersection definition (8%), red-light running/inappropriate response to signals (8%), inappropriate pavement markings (8%), poor channelization (6%), and road width restrictions (6%).

Given the known challenges that older drivers face when maneuvering through intersections, recommendations for improving roadways for older drivers in many countries have a large focus on intersection design changes (Box et al., 2010; Brewer & Bedsole, 2015; Brewer et al., 2014; FHWA, 2003a; Fildes et al., 2004; Rigdon et al., 2014). As an example, the US-based *Desk Reference: Handbook for Designing Roadways for the Aging Population* (Brewer & Bedsole, 2015) provides 31 pages of intersection-based recommendations (more than 42% of the total pages in the desk reference).

Work at the University of Florida has begun to examine the effects of some of the guidelines proposed by the FHWA (Brewer et al., 2014; Harkey et al., 2001) to improve intersections for older drivers. One of the studies used a driving simulator with younger (age 25–45) and older (age 65–85) drivers (Shechtman et al., 2007). Participants drove the simulator through turns at four pairs of intersections. In each pair, one intersection was "improved" by implementing four of the Harkey et al.'s (2001) recommendations (extended receiving lane, right-turn channelization and an acceleration, left-turn offset, and separate lane signals with a protected left-turn phase), while the other intersection was the same basic design without the improvements. The researchers measured both driving errors and vehicle kinematics and both measures were analyzed to assess driving performance. At specific intersection pairs, participants were asked to perform the same maneuver (left or right turn).

The study found that there were fewer driving errors and greater lateral control (better vehicle handling) for most of the improved intersections, with no age differences. The authors concluded that the improved intersections benefitted both younger and older drivers.

This same research team also investigated improved versus non-improved intersections between younger and older drivers using an instrumented vehicle being driven through actual intersections (Classen et al., 2007). The study used five pairs of intersections with the improved intersections including the four design changes previously discussed along with a non-skewed angle intersection (changing a skewed intersection to make the roads intersect at 90 degrees). Vehicle kinematic and driving error data were collected with respect to vehicle positioning, lane maintenance, speed, yielding, signaling, visual scanning, adjustment to stimuli/traffic control devices, and gap acceptance. The kinematic data generally showed better vehicle handling and confidence, with older drivers showing a greater positive effect. Fewer driving errors were found for the improved intersections, again with older drivers showing a greater benefit. As with the simulator study, the authors concluded that for intersection design recommendations addressed in the study, both older and younger drivers benefitted, providing support for policy to implement these changes whenever feasible. Table 13.3 provides a sample of other recommendations and/or best practices regarding older drivers and intersection design changes (Box et al., 2010; Brewer & Bedsole, 2015; Brewer et al., 2014; FHWA, 2003a; Fildes et al., 2004; Rigdon et al., 2014).

**Table 13.3** Recommendations for intersection design changes to accommodate older drivers

| **Recommendation** | **Aging-driver issue** |
|---|---|
| Use right-angle intersections whenever feasible | Reduction in neck flexibility and decreased cognitive processing speed and reaction time |
| Use raised channelization for left and right turns when possible | Declines in visual abilities, particularly acuity and contrast sensitivity |
| Ensure adequate sight distance at intersections | Declines in visual abilities |
| Use offset left-turn lanes (or right-turn lanes in countries like Australia and Japan) whenever possible | Declines in visual abilities, particularly motion and depth perception |
| If possible at intersections where roadways intersect at 90 degrees, a corner curb radius of 25–30 ft should be used | Declines in psychomotor functioning |
| Use reduced left-turn conflict designs for intersections (i.e., designs in which left turns at intersections are reduced or eliminated. See Brewer et al., 2014, p. 218, for example) | Declines in visual and cognitive abilities |

## Roundabouts

Roundabouts are designed to make traffic flow at an intersection more efficient and to reduce the frequency and severity of crashes, particularly injury crashes. Roundabouts appeared first in Europe and are now becoming commonplace in many countries, including the US (Rodegerdts et al., 2007). One reason for the implementation of roundabouts is that they may reduce or eliminate some of the difficulties that older drivers have with negotiating intersections, such as making turns across traffic and understanding traffic control devices. Indeed, research confirms that roundabouts improve safety across the globe for all ages, including older drivers (Brilon, 2016; Elvik, 2003; Rodegerdts et al., 2007). For example, in a meta-analysis of 28 studies outside of the US where signalized intersections were replaced by roundabouts, Elvik (2003) concluded that roundabouts were associated with a 30%–50% reduction in injury crashes and a 50%–70% reduction in fatal crashes across all ages.

With such clear safety benefits, one would think that older drivers would value roundabouts, but this does not seem to be the case. Studies have found that older drivers reported feeling less safe in roundabouts than signalized intersections (Tollazzi, Renčelj, Rodešek, & Zalar, 2010); older drivers had a more negative general perception of roundabouts (Retting, Luttrell, & Russell, 2002; Retting, Mandavilli, Russel, & McCartt, 2006; Retting, McCartt, & Kyrychenko, 2007; Savolainen, Kawa, & Gates, 2012); older drivers considered roundabouts difficult to negotiate and were often confused about the rules governing these intersections (Hanscom, 2010; Lord, van Schalkwyk, Chrysler, & Staplin, 2007; McKnight, Khattak, & Bishu, 2008); older drivers reported moderate levels of nervousness when negotiating roundabouts (Parker, McDonald, Rabbitt, & Sutcliffe, 2000); older drivers made more errors negotiating roundabouts as compared to traffic-light controlled intersections (Broberg & Willstrand, 2014); and older drivers often took alternate routes in order to avoid roundabouts (Hu, McCartt, Jermakian, & Mandavilli, 2014). Undoubtedly, some of these negative outcomes arise from a lack of familiarity with roundabouts and will improve as drivers gain more experience. One study, however, has shown that older drivers' confusion with roundabouts can persist at least up to a year after construction (Hu et al., 2014).

How can we improve older drivers' experiences negotiating roundabouts? One approach is to couple the introduction of new roundabouts with educational and outreach efforts (Hawley, Smith, & Goodwin, in press; Pochowski & Myers, 2010; Veneziano & Ewan, 2015). A wide range of materials and methods have been used in the educational programs, and evaluations have shown that drivers report they are useful. However, none have been evaluated to determine if they improve opinions about or behaviors while negotiating roundabouts. Further research in this area is needed.

A second approach is to improve the design and traffic control information of roundabouts to better accommodate older drivers. In the US, the *Handbook for Designing Roadways for the Aging Population* (Brewer et al., 2014) suggests the following to improve older drivers' use and experiences of roundabouts, some of which are shown being implemented in Fig. 13.2:

- Where possible, roundabouts should be limited to one-lane entrances and exits and one lane of circulating traffic.
- To control for wrong-way movements, calm traffic, and provide a pedestrian refuge, raised splitter islands should be used instead of pavement markings to delineate the channelization.
- The sides and tops of curbs on the splitter islands and the central island should be treated with retroreflective markings and be maintained at a minimum luminance contrast.
- Advanced roundabout warning signs should be used on all approaches to the roundabout.
- A roundabout directional arrow sign should be used to direct traffic in the proper direction (counter-clockwise in the US) around the central island. This sign display should be placed on the central island in direct view of a driver's entry point.
- A roundabout circulation plaque should be placed immediately below a yield sign on both sides of the road at each entrance to the roundabout.

A laboratory study of 31 older drivers examined perceived safety, comfort, and confidence with regard to several roundabout design countermeasures (Lord et al., 2007). Participants viewed video presentations of a vehicle negotiating roundabouts, with the design alternatives edited into the video. Two countermeasures were investigated for each of the following five design elements: advanced warning signs, roundabout lane control signs, directional (one-way) signs, yield treatments, and

**Figure 13.2** A US roundabout showing several recommended best practices for older drivers including one-lane entrance and exit, raised splitter islands, a directional arrow sign in the central island, and a street sign name with an arrow pointing to the exit leg.
Source: Photography by Gregory Kostyniuk.

exit treatments. Participants viewed a series of pair comparisons—first the intersection without the enhancement (base condition) and then the same intersection with one of the countermeasures—and provided ratings of the perceived change between the two intersections in the pair on a seven-point scale with the midpoint indicating "no change." The study found that the countermeasures were more positively judged than the base condition for the advanced warning signs, roundabout control, and directional control signs. For the yield and exit sign treatment countermeasures, only one of the two countermeasures was more positively judged as compared to the base condition. These countermeasures were text under the yield sign that stated "TO THE TRAFFIC IN CIRCLE" and a street sign name with an arrow pointing to the exit leg. The authors concluded that design elements that improve path guidance in roundabouts have the potential to improve the safety, comfort, and confidence of older drivers negotiating these types of intersections. Further research is also needed in this area.

## Work/construction zones

Although work zones are not necessarily intersections, they do represent temporary roadway locations where conflicts can occur and lead to crashes. According to the FHWA (2017b), in 2015, there were 96,626 crashes in work zones in the US, and in 26,127 of these crashes, someone was injured or killed. Some older drivers report having problems driving in work zones. For example, a survey of older drivers (age 50–97) in the US found that about one-fifth reported having problems negotiating work zones, and about 30% indicated that work zones needed to be better lit at night (Knoblauch, Nitzburg, & Seifert, 1997).

Behavioral data also point to the problems that older drivers have with work zones. A study using a driving simulator compared the behaviors of middle-age drivers (age 35–50) and older drivers (age 65–80) while driving through work zones that varied in terms of the types of barriers, warnings, and configurations (Reyes & Khan, 2008). The study found that as compared to middle-age drivers, older drivers, approached and entered work zones more slowly, had greater variability in speed negotiating the work zone and drove more than 12 in closer to the barriers. Studies analyzing crash data also suggest that older drivers are overrepresented in work zone crashes, particularly in fatal crashes (Akepati & Dissanayake, 2011; Harb, Radwan, Yan, Pande, & Abdel-Aty, 2008, Li & Bai, 2008). For example, Li and Bai (2008) analyzed at-fault driver data from fatal and injury work zone crashes between 1992 and 2004 in Kansas and found that drivers age 65 and older were involved in 18% of fatal and 8% of injury work zone crashes. Drivers age 55–64 were involved in only 4% of fatal and 7% of injury crashes. A study in Florida analyzed work zone crash data for the years 2002–04 (Harb et al., 2008). Using multiple regression modeling, these researchers calculated relative crash involvement ratios and found that older drivers had among the highest ratios of crash involvement for work zone crashes involving both one and two vehicles. Further investigation into at-fault two-vehicle crashes showed that older drivers who were female had the second highest crash involvement ratios second only to young male drivers.

Jurisdictions have long recognized that work zones present difficulties and cause stress for not only older drivers but also drivers of all ages and have developed countermeasures to address these issues (Brewer et al., 2014; FHWA, 2003b; Fildes et al., 2004). One approach is to provide better education to drivers. For example, the FHWA (2003b) has produced a two-page document that presents the following best practices for drivers in work zones:

- Stay alert and minimize distractions,
- Keep headlights on,
- Pay attention to the road,
- Merge into the proper lane,
- Do not tailgate,
- Obey the posted speed limit,
- Change lanes safely,
- Follow instructions from flaggers,
- Expect the unexpected, and
- Be patient.

This document also presents and describes the meaning of the most common signs used in work zones. The other approach is to provide recommendations on how to establish and maintain a safer work zone that takes into account the declining abilities of older drivers. Extensive recommendations from both Australia and the US have been published (Brewer et al., 2014; Fildes et al., 2004).

## Wrong-way driver crashes

Crashes in which a driver has entered a roadway and driven in the opposite direction than is allowed (wrong-way driver crashes) are a relatively uncommon crash-type but are more likely to result in greater injury severity than other crashes (Baratian-Ghorghi, Zhou, & Shaw, 2014; Das, Avelar, Dixon, & Sun, 2018). Several recent studies have examined the characteristics of wrong-way driver crashes and have found that they are more common at night, involve an impaired driver, occur on non-freeway roads, more likely among male drivers, and occur on weekends (see Baratian-Ghorghi et al., 2014 for a summary of this work). Research has also found that wrong-way driver crashes often involve older drivers. Some of these results are summarized as follows:

- An analysis of wrong-way driver crashes on Interstate roadways in Alabama between 2009 and 2013 found that drivers age 65 and older were involved in 26% of these crashes, the highest of any age group (Pour-Rouholamin, Zhou, Zhang, & Turochy, 2016).
- A study in France examined wrong-way driver crashes on divided roads between 2008 and 2012 and found that older drivers were about 16 times more likely to be involved in these crashes than drivers under age 25 (Kemel, 2015).

- The results of an analysis of wrong-way driver crash characteristics in Japan found that in wrong-way crashes caused by a wrong entry onto the roads, 61% were with a driver age 60 or older, and in wrong-way crashes caused by confusion with an ordinary road, 86% involved an older driver (Xing, 2014).
- Florida wrong-way driver crash data between 2003 and 2010 were analyzed by whether they occurred on arterials or freeways and driver characteristics (Ponnaluri, 2018). The study found that for arterial roadways, drivers age 61–80 years were about 1.3 times more likely and drivers age 81 or older were 1.9 times more likely to be in wrong-way driver crashes as compared to drivers age 20 or younger. On freeways, however, drivers age 61–80 years were nearly three times as likely and drivers age 81 or older were 11 times more likely to be involved in wrong-way driver crashes.
- A study of wrong-way driver crashes in Illinois on divided highways analyzed wrong-way driver crashes on freeways from 2009 to 2013 and found that older drivers accounted for nearly 27% of these crashes and were more than 6 times more likely to be involved in these crashes as compared to drivers age 25 or younger (Zhang, Pour-Rouholamin, & Zhou, 2017).

Preventing wrong-way driver crashes is of great interest to many jurisdictions. Because of the high involvement of impaired drivers and drivers with age-related declines in ability, educational and training interventions are not likely to be that useful. Instead, jurisdictions have implemented roadway design- and infrastructure-based countermeasures (see, e.g., Cooner, Cothron, & Ranft, 2004; Das et al., 2018; Moler, 2002; Pour-Rouholamin, Zhou, Shaw, & Tobias, 2014, 2015; Zhou & Pour-Rouholamin, 2014). The following presents some of these ideas, noting that these are not specific to older drivers:

- Use WRONG WAY arrows,
- Use red raised pavement markers,
- Use solid stop lines,
- Make warning signs and pavement markers bigger and more retroreflective,
- Ensure signs and markings are not worn or faded,
- Entrance/Exit ramp separation,
- Use GPS navigation to alert drivers to wrong-way movements,
- Use radio-based alerts for wrong-way drivers,
- Use flashing message signs triggered by a wrong-way vehicle, and
- Provide consistent messages and alerts that are intuitive to the driver.

# Conclusions

This chapter has briefly reviewed information about maintaining older driver safety and well-being from the perspective of roadway design and infrastructure. The roadway environment comprises one-third of the well-known Haddon Matrix (Haddon, 1980) and, in conjunction with driver-based and vehicle-based countermeasures, plays a critical role in the safe transportation of older drivers. This chapter has presented several recommended roadway treatments for making roadways easier and safer for older drivers to negotiate, yet these represent only a small fraction of the full set of recommendations. Two excellent resources are recommended for the reader interested in more detail—one from the US (Brewer et al., 2014) and one from Australia (Fildes et al., 2004).

It should be noted that roadway design changes are expensive and often require significant time to implement. It is our hope that as roadways need replacement or upgrading, jurisdictions will begin to consider roadway treatments shown to improve safety for older drivers. Such improvements will benefit not only older drivers but also road users of all ages. It is also important for jurisdictions to engage in education and outreach with older drivers to ensure not only that new roadway design features are understood by older drivers but that the safety and convenience benefits are also communicated.

## References

Akepati, S. R., & Dissanayake, S. (2011). *Characteristics of the [sic] work zones crashes. T & DI Congress 2011 proceedings* (pp. 1286–1295)). Reston, VA: American Society of Civil Engineers.

Al-Madani, H., & Al-Janahi, A.-R. (2002). Assessment of drivers' comprehension of traffic signs based on their traffic, personal and social characteristics. *Transportation Research Part F*, *5*, 63–76.

American Association of State Highway Officials. (1935). *Manual on uniform traffic control devices for streets and highways.* Washington, DC: American Association of State Highway Officials.

Australasian Legal Information Institute. (2018). *National Roads Act 1974.* Sydney, NSW, Australia: AustLII. http://www8.austlii.edu.au/cgi-bin/viewdb/au/legis/cth/num_act/nra1974151/. Accessed March, 2018.

Baratian-Ghorghi, F., Zhou, H., & Shaw, J. S. (2014). Overview of wrong-way driver fatal crashes in the United States. *ITE Journal*, *84*(8), 41–47.

Ben-Bassat, T., & Shinar, D. (2015). The effect of context and drivers' age on highway traffic sign comprehension. *Transportation Research Part F*, *33*, 117–127.

Benekohal, R. F., Resende, P., Shim, E., Michaels, R. M., & Weeks, B. (1992). *Highway operations problems of elderly drivers in Illinois.* Report no. FHWA-IL-92-023. Springfield, IL: Federal Highway Administration.

Berces, A., & Robertson, S. (2012). Keeping people safer through better visibility: Advances in retroreflectivity for road signage, pavement markings and vehicle visibility delivering safer roads. In *Proceedings of the Australasian road safety research, policing, and education conference* 2012. Wellington, New Zealand.

Box, E., Gandolfi, J., & Mitchell, K. (2010). *Maintaining safe mobility for the ageing population: The role of the private car.* London, Great Britain. Royal Automobile Club Foundation for Motoring Limited.

Braitman, K. A., Kirley, B. B., Ferguson, S., & Chaudhary, N. K. (2007). Factors leading to older drivers' intersection crashes. *Traffic Injury Prevention*, *8*, 267–274.

Brehmer, C. L., Kacir, K. C., Noyce, D. A., & Manser, M. P. (2003). *Evaluation of traffic signal displays for protected/permissive left-turn control.* NCHRP report no. 493. Washington, DC: Transportation Research Board.

Brewer, M. & Bedsole, L. (2015). *Desk reference to the handbook for designing roadways for the aging population.* Report no. FHWA-SA-15-088. Washington, DC: US Department of Transportation.

Brewer, M., Murillo, D., & Pate, A. (2014). *Handbook for designing roadways for the aging population.* Report no. FHWA-SA-14-015. Washington, DC: US Department of Transportation.

Brilon, W. (2016). Safety of roundabouts: International overview. In *TRB 95th annual meeting compendium of papers*. Paper no. 16-0648. Washington, DC: The National Academies of Sciences.

Broberg, T., & Willstrand, T. D. (2014). Safe mobility for elderly drivers—Considerations based on expert and self-assessment. *Accident Analysis & Prevention*, *66*, 104–113.

Carlson, P. J., Miles, J. D., Pratt, M. P., & Pike, A. M. (2005). *Evaluation of wet-weather pavement markings: First year report*. Report no. FHWA/TX-06/0-5008-1. Austin, TX: Texas Department of Transportation.

Choocharukul, K., & Sriroongvikrai, K. (2017). Road safety awareness and comprehension of road signs for international tourist's perspectives: A case study in Thailand. *Transportation Research Procedia*, *25*, 4518–4528.

Chrysler, S. T., Danielson, S. M., & Kirby, V. M. (1996). *Age differences in visual abilities in nighttime driving field conditions. Proceedings of the human factors and ergonomics society 40th annual meeting* (pp. 923–927)). Santa Monica, CA: Human Factors and Ergonomics Society.

Cicchino, J. B., & McCartt, A. T. (2015). Critical older driver errors in a national sample of serious U.S. crashes. *Accident Analysis & Prevention*, *80*, 211–219.

Clarke, D. D., Ward, P., Bartle, C., & Truman, W. (2010). Older drivers' road traffic crashes in the UK. *Accident Analysis & Prevention*, *42*, 1018–1024.

Classen, S., Schechtman, O., Stephens, B., David, E., Justiss, M., Bendix, R., ... Mann, W. (2007). The impact of roadway intersection design on driving performance of young and senior adults. *Traffic Injury Prevention*, *8*(1), 69–77.

Commonwealth of Australia. *The safe system approach*. (2017). ⟨http://roadsafety.gov.au/nrss/safe-system.aspx⟩ Accessed 3/12/2018. Accessed March, 2018.

Cooner, S. A., Cothron, A. S., & Ranft, S. E. (2004). *Countermeasures for wrong-way movement of freeways: Overview of project activities and findings*. Report no. FHWA/TX-04/4128-1. Austin, TX: Texas Department of Transportation.

Das, S., Avelar, R., Dixon, K., & Sun, Z. (2018). Investigation on the wrong way driving crash patterns using multiple correspondence analysis. *Accident Analysis & Prevention*, *111*, 43–55.

Dewar, R., & Olson, P. (2007). Traffic control devices. In R. Dewar, & P. Olson (Eds.), *Human factors in traffic safety*. Tucson, AZ: Lawyers and Judges Publishing Company.

Dewar, R. E., Kline, D. W., & Swanson, H. A. (1994). Age differences in comprehension of traffic sign symbols. *Transportation Research Record*, *1456*, 1–10.

Diamandouros, K., & Gatscha, M. (2016). Rainvision: The impact of road markings on driver behavior—Wet night visibility. *Transportation Research Procedia*, *14*, 4344–4353.

Dissanayake, S., & Perera, L. (2011). A survey based stud of factors related to older driver highway safety. *Journal of Transportation Safety & Security*, *3*(2), 77–94.

Dobres, J., Chrysler, S. T., Wolfe, B., Chahine, N., & Reimer, B. (2017). Empirical assessment of the legibility of the highway gothic and Clearview signage fonts. *Transportation Research Record*, *2624*, 1–8.

Dravitzki, V. K., Wilkie, S. M., & Lester, T. J. (2006). *The safety benefits of brighter road-markings*. Land transport New Zealand research report 310. Wellington, New Zealand: Land Transport New Zealand.

Edqvist, J., & Johnston, I. (2008). Visual clutter in road environments—What it does and what to do about it. *Proceedings 2008 Australasian road safety research, policing and education conference*, 733–738).

Elvik, R. (2003). Effects of road safety of converting intersections to roundabouts: Review of evidence from non-US studies. *Transportation Research Record*, *1847*, 1–10.

Evans, D. W., & Ginsburg, A. P. (1985). Contrast sensitivity predicts age-related differences in highway-sign discriminability. *Human Factors, 27*(6), 637–642.
Federal Highway Administration (FHWA). (2003a). *A pocket guide to improve traffic control and mobility for our older population*. Report no. FHWA-OP-03-098. Washington, DC: US Department of Transportation.
Federal Highway Administration (FHWA). (2003b). *Work zone safety for drivers*. Report no FHWA-SA-03-012. Washington, DC: US Department of Transportation.
Federal Highway Administration (FHWA). (2009). *Manual on uniform traffic control devices for streets and highways (2009 ed.)*. Washington, DC: US Department of Transportation.
Federal Highway Administration (FHWA). (2017a). *The evolution of MUTCD*. Washington, DC: US Department of Transportation. https://mutcd.fhwa.dot.gov/kno-history.htm. Accessed 3/13/2018. Accessed March, 2018.
Federal Highway Administration (FHWA). (2017b). *Facts and statistics—Work zone safety*. Washington, DC: Federal Highway Administration. https://ops.fhwa.dot.gov/wz/resources/facts_stats/safety.htm. Accessed March, 2018.
Fildes, B. N., Lee, S. J., Kenny, D., & Foddy, W. (1994). *Survey of older road users: Behavioural & travel issues*. Report no. 57. Clayton, VIC: Monash University Accident Research Centre.
Fildes, B. N., Oxley, J., Corben, B., & Langford, J. (2004). *Road environment and design for older drivers: Stage II. Volume 1—Overview. Volume 2—Handbook of suggestions for road design changes*. Report no. AP-R261/04. Sydney, Australia: Austroads.
Garvey, P. M., Klena, M. J., Eie, W.-Y., Meeker, D. T., & Pietrucha, M. T. (2016). Legibility of the Clearview typeface and FHWA Standard Alphabets on negative- and positive-contrast signs. *Transportation Research Record, 2555*, 28–37.
Graham, J. R., Harrold, J. K., & King, L. E. (1996). Pavement marking retroreflectivity requirements for older drivers. *Transportation Research Record, 1529*, 65–70.
Haddon, W., Jr. (1980). Advances in the epidemiology of injuries as a basis for public policy. *Public Health Report, 95*, 411–421.
Hanscom, F. R. (2010). Drivers' understanding of innovative roundabout traffic control devices. *ITE Journal, 80*(7), 40–44.
Harb, R., Radwan, E., Yan, X., Pande, A., & Abdel-Aty, M. (2008). *Journal of Transportation Engineering, 134*, 5.
Harkey, D., Staplin, L., Lococo, K., Srinivasan, R., Baek, J., Paul, M., . . . Tantillo, M. (2001). *Highway design handbook for older drivers and pedestrians*. Report no. FHWA-RD-01-103. Washington, DC: US Department of Transportation.
Hawkins, H. G., Jr. (2016). *MUTCD history*. College Station, TX: Texas A&M University. https://ceprofs.civil.tamu.edu/ghawkins/MUTCD-History.htm. Accessed March, 2018.
Hawley, C. A., Smith, R., & Goodwin, L. (in press). Road safety education of older drivers: Evaluation of a classroom-based training initiative. *Transportation Research Part F* https://doi.org/10.1016/j.trf.2017.11.009.
Ho, G., Scialfa, C. T., Caird, J. K., & Graw, T. (2001). Visual search for traffic signs: The effects of clutter, luminance, and aging. *Human Factors, 43*(2), 194–207.
Holick, A. J., Chrysler, S. T., Park, E. S., & Carlson, P. J. (2006). *Evaluation of the Clearview font for negative contrast traffic signs*. Report no. FHWA/TX-06/0-4984-1. Austin, TX: Texas Department of Transportation.
Horberry, T., Anderson, J., & Regan, M. A. (2006). The possible safety benefits of enhanced road markings: A driving simulator evaluation. *Transportation Research Part F, 9*, 77–87.
Hu, W., McCartt, A. T., Jermakian, J. S., & Mandavilli, S. (2014). Public opinion, traffic performance, the environment, and safety after construction of double-lane roundabouts. *Transportation Research Record, 2402*, 47–55.

Insurance Institute for Highway Safety. (2013). Two-lane roundabouts bring benefits but also some confusion. *Status Report, 48*(2).

Kemel, E. (2015). Wrong-way driving crashes on French divided roads. *Accident Analysis & Prevention, 75*, 69–76.

Knoblauch, R., Nitzburg, M., & Seifert, R. (1997). *An investigation of older driver freeway needs and capabilities*. Report no. FHWA-RD-95-194. Washington, DC: Federal Highway Administration.

Koppel, S., Bohensky, M., Langford, J., & Taranto, D. (2011). Older drivers, crashes and injuries. *Traffic Injury Prevention, 12*, 459–467.

Kwigizile, V., Oh, J-S., Van Houten, R., Kwayu, K., Lyimo, S., Bagdade, J., & McArthur, A. (2017). *Association of Michigan's older adult crashes with roadway features*. Report no. SPR-1653. Lansing, MI: Michigan Department of Transportation.

Lay, M. G., & Benson, F. J. (2016). *Roads and highways*. Encyclopedia Britannica Inc. https://www.britannica.com/technology/road. Accessed March, 2018.

Li, Y., & Bai, Y. (2008). *Fatal and injury crash characteristics in highway work zones. Transportation Research Board annual meeting CD-ROM*. Washington, DC: The National Academies.

Lombardi, D. A., Horrey, W. J., & Courtney, T. K. (2017). Age-related differences in fatal intersection crashes in the United States. *Accident Analysis & Prevention, 99*, 20–29.

Lord, D., van Schalkwyk, I., Chrysler, S., & Staplin, L. (2007). A strategy to reduce older driver injuries at intersections using more accommodating roundabout design practices. *Accident Analysis & Prevention, 39*, 427–432.

Mayhew, D. R., Simpson, H. M., & Ferguson, S. A. (2006). Collisions involving senior drivers: High-risk conditions and locations. *Traffic Injury Prevention, 7*, 117–124.

McKnight, G. A., Khattak, A. J., & Bishu, R. (2008). Driver characteristics associated with knowledge of correct roundabout negotiation. *Transportation Research Record, 2078*, 96–99.

McPhee, L. C., Scialfa, C. T., Dennis, W. M., Ho, G., & Caird, J. K. (2004). Age differences in visual search for traffic signs during a simulated conversation. *Human Factors, 46*(4), 674–685.

McShane, C. (1999). The origins and globalization of traffic control devices. *Journal of Urban History, 25*(3), 379–404.

Moler, S. (2002). Stop. You're going the wrong way!. *Public Roads, 66*(2), 1–9.

Molino, J. A., Opiela, K. S., Andersen, C. K., & Moyer, M. J. (2003). Relative luminance of retroreflective raised pavement markers and pavement marking stripes on simulated rural two-lane roads. *Transportation Research Record, 1844*, 45–51.

Musselwhite, C. B. A., & Haddad, H. (2010). Exploring older drivers' perceptions of driving. *European Journal of Ageing, 7*, 181–188.

National Archives. (2018). *Highways Act 1959*. Surry, UK: National Archives. https://www.legislation.gov.uk/ukpga/Eliz2/7-8/25/enacted. Accessed March, 2018.

Ohyama, J., & Sagawa, K. (2016). The effects of letter design features and aging on legibility. *Perception, 45*(6), 642–656.

Organisation for Economic Co-operation and Development. (2008). *Towards zero: Ambitious road safety targets and the safe system approach*. Paris, France: OECD.

Oxley, J., Fildes, B., Corben, B., & Langford, J. (2006). Intersection design for older drivers. *Transportation Research Part F, 9*, 335–346.

Oxley, J., Langford, J., & Charlton, J. (2010). The safe mobility of older drivers: A challenge for urban road designers. *Journal of Transport Geography, 18*, 642–648.

Parker, D., McDonald, L., Rabbitt, P., & Sutcliffe, P. (2000). Elderly drivers and their accidents: The Aging Driver Questionnaire. *Accident Analysis & Prevention, 32*, 751–759.

Pochowski, A., & Myers, E. J. (2010). Review of state roundabout programs. *Transportation Research Record*, *2182*, 121–128.

Ponnaluri, R. V. (2018). Modeling wrong-way crashes and fatalities on arterials and freeways. *IATSS Research*, *42*(1), 8–17.

Porter, M. M., & Whitton, M. J. (2002). Assessment of driving with global positioning system and video technology in young, middle-aged, and older drivers. *Journal of Gerontology*, *57A*, M578–M582.

Pour-Rouholamin, M., Zhou, H., Shaw, J., & Tobias, P. (2014). Overview of safety countermeasures for wrong-way driving crashes. *ITE Journal*, *84*(12), 31–38.

Pour-Rouholamin, M., Zhou, H., Shaw, J., & Tobias, P. (2015). Current practices of safety countermeasures for wrong-way driving crashes. In *Transportation Research Board 94th annual meeting compendium of papers*. Paper no. 15-3648. Washington, DC: The National Academies of Sciences.

Pour-Rouholamin, M., Zhou, H., Zhang, B., & Turochy, R. E. (2016). Comprehensive analysis of wrong-way driving crashes on Alabama interstates. *Transportation Research Record*, *2610*, 50–58.

Preusser, D. F., Williams, A. F., Ferguson, S. A., Ulmer, R. G., & Weinstein, H. B. (1998). Fatal crash risk for older drivers at intersections. *Accident Analysis & Prevention*, *30*, 151–159.

Rakotonirainy, A., Steinhardt, D., Delhomme, P., Darvell, M., & Schramm, A. (2012). Older drivers' crashes in Queensland, Australia. *Accident Analysis & Prevention*, *48*, 423–429.

Retting, R. A., Luttrell, G., & Russell, E. (2002). Public opinion and traffic flow impacts of newly installed modern roundabouts in the United States. *ITE Journal*, *72*(9), 30–37.

Retting, R. A., Mandavilli, S., Russel, E. R., & McCartt, A. T. (2006). Roundabouts, traffic flow, and public opinion—Evidence from the U.S. *Traffic Engineering and Control*, *47* (7), 268–272.

Retting, R. A., McCartt, A. T., & Kyrychenko, S. Y. (2007). Long-term trends in public opinion following construction of roundabouts. *Transportation Research Record*, *2019*, 219–224.

Reyes, M.L. & Khan, S.A. (2008). *Examining driver behavior in response to work zone interventions: A driving simulator study*. Final report SWZDI 2008-01. Ames, IA: Iowa State University.

Rigdon, H., Atkinson, J., Bosack, J., O'Donnell, C., & Lambert, J. (2014). *North American conference on elderly mobility—Noteworthy practices guide*. Report no. FHWA-SA-14-095. Washington, DC: Federal Highway Administration.

Rodegerdts, L., Blogg, M., Wemple, E., Myers, E., Kyte, M., Dixon, M., ... & Carter, D. (2007). *Roundabouts in the United States*. NCHRP report 572. Washington, DC: The National Academies of Sciences.

Savolainen, P. T., Kawa, J. M., & Gates, T. J. (2012). Examining statewide public perceptions of roundabouts through a web-based survey. *Transportation Research Record*, *2312*, 25–33.

Schieber, F., & Kline, D. W. (1994). *Age differences in the legibility of symbol highway signs as a function of Luminance and glare level: A preliminary report. Proceedings of the human factors and ergonomics society 38th annual meeting* (pp. 133–136)). Santa Monica, CA: Human Factors and Ergonomics Society.

Schnell, T., Aktan, F., & Lee, Y.-C. (2003). Nighttime visibility and retroreflectance of pavement markings in dry, wet, and rainy conditions. *Transportation Research Record*, *1824*, 144–155.

Schnell, T., Yekhshatyan, L., & Daiker, R. (2009). Effect of luminance and text size on information acquisition time from traffic signs. *Transportation Research Record*, *2122*, 52–62.

Shechtman, O., Classen, S., Stephens, B., Bendixen, R., Belchior, P., Sandhu, M., ... Mann, W. (2007). The impact of intersection design on simulated driving performance of young and senior adults. *Traffic Injury Prevention*, *8*, 78–86.

Shinar, D., Dewar, R. E., Summala, H., & Zakowska, L. (2003). Traffic sign symbol comprehension: A cross-cultural study. *Ergonomics*, *46*, 1549–1565.

Sivak, M., Olson, P. L., & Pastalan, L. A. (1981). Effect of driver's age on nighttime legibility of highway signs. *Human Factors*, *23*(1), 59–64.

Staplin, L., Gish, K. W., Decina, L. E., Lococo, K. H., & McKnight, A. S. (1998). *Intersection negotiation problems of older drivers: Volume I. Final technical report.* Report no. DOT HS 808 850. Washington, DC: US Department of Transportation.

Staplin, L., Lococo, K., & Byington, S. (1998). *Older driver highway design handbook.* Report no. FHWA-RD-97-135. Washington, DC: US Department of Transportation.

Staplin, L., Lococo, K., Byington, S., & Harkey, D. (2001). *Guidelines and recommendation to accommodate older drivers and pedestrians.* Report no. FHWA-RD-01-051. Washington, DC: US Department of Transportation.

Staplin, L., Lococo, K. H., McKnight, A. J., McKnight, A. S., & Odenheimer, G. L. (1998). *Intersection negotiation problems of older drivers, Volume II: Background synthesis on age and intersection driving difficulties.* Report no. DOT HS 808 850. Washington, DC: US Department of Transportation.

Thompson, J. P., Baldock, M. R. J., Mathias, J. L., & Wundersitz, L. N. (2013). An examination of the environmental, driver and vehicle factors associated with the serious and fatal crashes of older rural drivers. *Accident Analysis & Prevention*, *50*, 768–775.

Tollazzi, T., Renčelj, M., Rodešek, V., & Zalar, B. (2010). Traffic safety of older drivers in various types of road intersections. *Promet—Traffic & Transportation*, *22*(3), 193–201.

Transportation Research Board. (1988). *Special report 218: Transportation in an aging society: Improving mobility and safety for older persons* (Vol. 1). Washington, DC: The National Research Council.

Uc, E. Y., Rizzo, M., Anderson, S. W., Shi, Q., & Dawson, J. D. (2005). Driver landmark and traffic sign identification in early Alzheimer's disease. *Journal of Neurology, Neurosurgery, and Psychiatry*, *76*, 764–768.

Veneziano, D. & Ewan, L. (2015). *Approaches to roundabout education and outreach.* In *Paper presented at the 94th annual meeting of the Transportation Research Board.* Washington, DC.

Wikipedia. *The interstate highway system.* (2018). ⟨https://en.wikipedia.org/wiki/Interstate_Highway_System⟩. Accessed 03/09/2018. Accessed March, 2018.

Xing, J. (2014). Characteristics of wrong-way driving on motorways in Japan. *IET Intelligent Transport Systems*, *9*(1), 3.

Zhang, B., Pour-Rouholamin, M., & Zhou, H. (2017). Investigation of confounding factors contributing to wrong-way driving crashes on partially and uncontrolled-access divided highways. In *Transportation Research Board 96th annual meeting compendium of papers.* Paper no. 17-05146. Washington, DC: The National Academies of Sciences.

Zhou, H., & Pour-Rouholamin, M. (2014). *Guidelines for reducing wrong-way crashes on freeways.* Report no. FHWA-ICT-010. Springfield, IL: Illinois Department of Transportation.

Zwahlen, H. T., & Schnell, T. (1999). Visibility of road marking as a function of age, retroreflectivity under low-beam and high-beam illumination at night. *Transportation Research Record*, *1692*, 152–162.

# Age-friendly communities

# 14

*A community is the mental and spiritual condition of knowing that the place is shared, and that the people who share the place define and limit the possibilities of each other's lives. It is the knowledge that people have of each other, their concern for each other, their trust in each other, the freedom with which they come and go among themselves.*

*Wendell Berry*

## Introduction

According to a survey of adults age 65 or older in the United States (US), 87% reported a preference to remain in their home and community as they age (Harrell, Lynott, Guzman, & Lampkin, 2014). This finding highlights the increased importance of the surrounding environment on the health and well-being of aging adults. Due to aging of the population coupled with the rise in urbanization, the World Health Organization (WHO) (2007) has spearheaded a movement over the past two decades to encourage cities and communities worldwide to acknowledge the influx of aging adults and design communities that allow this population to actively age in place. An age-friendly community is defined by WHO (2015) as "... an inclusive and accessible community environment that optimizes opportunities for health, participation, and security for all people, in order that quality of life and dignity are ensured as people age" (p. 3). An age-friendly community employs policies, services, settings, and structures to support and enable people to age in place while staying connected to their community (WHO, 2007). As introduced in Chapter 10, Transportation Service Providers, but explored more fully in this chapter, transportation is a critical component of an age-friendly city and is identified as one of eight key domains of health and well-being in a community setting (WHO, 2007, 2015). The ability to remain mobile is an essential element that allows older adults to stay engaged and contribute to the community, maintain their independence, and avoid the mental health impacts of social isolation.

Efforts to make cities and communities more age friendly have gained significant momentum in recent years. Although an age-friendly community is intended to account for all community members, emphasis is placed on the needs of older adults and those with disabilities. Older adults, in particular, require supportive and enabling living environments to compensate for declines in physical abilities as well as social changes associated with aging (WHO, 2007). One advantage of

**Perspectives and Strategies for Promoting Safe Transportation among Older Adults.**
**DOI: https://doi.org/10.1016/B978-0-12-812153-5.00014-5**

designing a community focused on the needs of older adults is that design improvements are not exclusive to older adults but can be beneficial for the community as a whole.

This chapter provides a brief history of the concept of age-friendly communities and cities, provides examples of how cities are implementing age-friendly transportation elements into their urban planning and infrastructure, the importance of evaluating the efforts and outcomes of communities that have taken active steps in designing and incorporating age-friendly components into the built environment, and the impact that technology will have on transportation in an age-friendly community.

## Background of age-friendly communities

As mentioned in Chapter 10, Transportation Service Providers, the concept of an age-friendly community is based on WHO's policy framework for active aging, in which active aging is defined as "... the process of optimizing opportunities for health, participation, and security in order to enhance quality of life as people age" (WHO, 2002, p. 12). This framework lists six influences on active aging including economic, social, behavioral, and personal determinants, as well as health and social services, and the physical environment. Using this framework as a guide, WHO launched an international project in 2006 to understand age-friendly features of cities and the advantages and barriers experienced by older adults living in urbanized settings. This effort included focus groups with older adults, caregivers, and service providers in 33 cities across the world. The result of this project was the *Global Age-friendly Cities Guide* (WHO, 2007) which operationalized the active aging policy framework by providing age-friendly checklists and concrete examples of how a city can adapt to meet the needs of older adults (Warth, 2016). Transportation was identified as a key factor influencing active aging and was a theme that was interwoven with many other topics of focus group discussion due to its importance in connecting older adults with their community. One of the eight checklists provided by WHO focuses exclusively on age-friendly transportation and provides examples of how to enable a community to ensure continued mobility for older adults. Age-friendly transportation features of a community span the transportation continuum to ensure that older adults can continue to drive as long as they can safely do so and also have access to alternative transportation options when they can no longer or choose not to drive. Specific examples include the following: public transportation is affordable, reliable, and frequent; ensure all areas of the city are well-serviced with adequate, well-connected transport routes within the city and between neighboring cities; provide and promote driver refresher courses; ensure priority parking spaces are provided close to buildings and transport stops; ensure roads are well-maintained, wide, and well-lit; and provide information to older adults about the range of alternative transportation options available in the community (WHO, 2007).

In 2010, WHO established the Global Network for Age-Friendly Cities and Communities to connect local governments using WHO's approach to age-friendly cities (Warth, 2016). This network provides a platform for the exchange of experiences and for mutual learning and support between cities and communities committed to implementing age-friendly features to create a physical and social environment that encourages active aging. According to the most recent membership numbers from WHO (2018a), the Global Network includes 600 cities and communities in 38 countries covering over 190 million people throughout the world.

In addition to the efforts of WHO, numerous other frameworks and guides for creating age-friendly communities have been developed throughout the past two decades (see, e.g., Australian Local Government Association, 2006; City of Edmonton, 2017; Kihl, Brennan, List, Gabhawala, & Mittal, 2005; Menec, Means, Keating, Parkhurst, & Eales, 2011; National Association of Area Agencies on Aging, 2007; New Zealand Ministry of Social Development, 2007; Pollack, 1999; WHO, 2007). For example, in 2012 in the US, AARP launched the Network of Age-Friendly States and Communities, an affiliate of WHO's Global Network for Age-Friendly Cities and Communities, which "... encourages states, cities, towns and counties to prepare for the rapid aging of the US population by paying increased attention to the environmental, economic and social factors that influence the health and well-being of older adults" (AARP, 2018, para. 2). AARP provides a tool kit to members of the network which contains examples for developing action plans that are unique to the needs of each community, offers guidance for developing a framework linking back to the action plan, and explains the evaluation phases each member community must conduct to monitor and assess their progress. More generally, guides such as those offered by AARP and others are intended to assist community leaders, planners, and policymakers in incorporating age-friendly features into their community to minimize barriers to older adult mobility. There is agreement within all frameworks and guides that transportation plays a critical role in creating an age-friendly community in which older adults are able to maintain their independence for as long as possible (Steels, 2015).

## Planning for an age-friendly community

The development of an age-friendly community comprises four stages: planning, implementation, continual improvement, and evaluation (Jeste et al., 2016). This section discusses the planning process and the necessary involvement of a variety of stakeholders to achieve a feasible action plan. Given the current and anticipated increase in the proportion of older adults in the population, policymakers and city planners are encouraged to reflect on key issues facing an aging community and plan for an environment that is inclusive of the needs of older adults.

Numerous states, cities, and communities throughout the world have devised strategic plans that focus on creating age-friendly communities (see, e.g., Brimbank City Council, 2017; City of Auburn Hills, 2015; Queensland Government, 2016).

A critical component to the planning process is the involvement of older adults within the community (Buffel, Phillipson, & Scharf, 2012; Steels, 2015; WHO, 2002). Including older adults as full partners in the planning process ensures that the plan and subsequent age-friendly programs and adaptations reflect the real concerns and issues of the community members most likely to be affected by the proposed action plan. Input to guide the planning of age-friendly city features has been gathered from older adults in a variety of ways including focus groups; online, telephone, and paper-and-pencil surveys; and community forums in which older adults are encouraged to express their opinions regarding the facilitators and barriers to aging in their community and their ideas for solutions for making their community more age-friendly.

An example of including older adults in the planning process comes from the state of Queensland in Australia. The Queensland Government (2016) elicited feedback from over 9000 community members through an online community survey, a "senior summit", the Queensland Seniors Facebook page, meetings and forums with stakeholders, and other engagement activities. As a result, issues regarding transportation (defined as the ability to get "out and about") were identified as the main barriers that could prevent older adults from "being more involved and participating more actively in life" (Queensland Government, 2016, p. 5). Suggestions for how to address this concern were also provided by community members and included the following: provide more subsidies to reduce transport costs, increase community transportation options, improve accessibility of public transportation for those with mobility issues, and improve parking options (Queensland Government, 2016). Based on the feedback and suggested improvements, the action plan specified 11 action items to implement to meet the goal of allowing older adults to remain mobile using a range of affordable, user-friendly transportation services. Examples of planned actions included cutting the cost of public transportation fees, improving access to passenger transportation infrastructure and services, and testing a new flexible demand responsive public transportation service tailored to better meet community needs (Queensland Government, 2016).

Leadership and collaboration are vital to the successful development of an age-friendly community. In addition to involvement from older adults, it is important to bring together a wide range of stakeholders to work together to optimize age-friendly strategies that can be implemented throughout the community, such as housing, transportation, and outdoor spaces (Steels, 2015). Local government is uniquely positioned to support age-friendly communities by promoting awareness of the concept of age-friendly communities; coordinating decision making within their local community; and developing and implementing community design plans, strategies and policies that support age-friendly communities (Australian Local Government Association, 2006; National Association of Area Agencies on Aging, 2007). Officials from the federal and state levels of government, business representatives, nonprofit organizations, advocacy groups, and service providers who work with older adults also have important roles in planning.

Participation of other groups with relevant expertise is also desirable (National Association for Area Agencies on Aging, 2007). For example, urban design and the built environment play an integral role in allowing older adults to age in place and maintain their mobility and independence. Therefore, it would be beneficial to include a city planner who understands the importance of land-use patterns and the built environment in terms of accessibility and mobility. Older adults are particularly vulnerable to features and conditions in the environment in which they live (Clarke & Nieuwenhuijsen, 2009). For example, mobility limitations can create unique challenges for older adults when crossing a busy intersection, navigating cracked sidewalks, or entering a building that can only be accessed via steps (Menec et al., 2011). Creating age-friendly infrastructure to address these issues is fundamental to meeting the mobility needs of older adults. This requires an integrated approach to the planning and design of road networks, safe intersection crossings, level pavements, and the location of amenities and services (Holley-Moore & Creighton, 2015). The ultimate goal is to devise a leadership team in which stakeholders can work together with a shared vision to exchange knowledge and combine resources to achieve the outcome of creating a more age-friendly environment.

A baseline assessment of existing community services must be conducted to better understand the areas to target for age-friendly improvements. A comprehensive inventory of current initiatives allows a community to leverage existing resources and build upon existing efforts. An assessment can be done through consultation with the stakeholder group as well as involving community members as in the example from Queensland. A program created specifically to elicit feedback from community-dwelling older adults is called the AdvantAge Initiative. The AdvantAge Initiative uses a survey, which can be customized to suit the needs of the local community, to assess the perceptions and experiences of community members to identify barriers to aging in place and develop a plan for age-friendly adaptations to the physical and social environment [Center for Home Care Policy and Research (CHCPR), 2018]. The survey findings assist stakeholders in identifying community assets and opportunities for action, and in developing responses to identified issues of aging in the community. Approximately 50 communities across the US have used this service (CHCPR, 2018).

Age-friendly action plans like those referenced in the beginning of this section generally follow a standard format in which information regarding community input is shared, key priority areas are identified (typically within the eight domains for age-friendly communities established by WHO (2007) which are civic participation and employment, communication and information, community support and health services, housing, respect and inclusion, social participation, outdoor spaces, and buildings, and transportation), and action items are presented. Communities are encouraged to create timelines, identify those responsible for executing the specific action item, develop a monitoring plan, and state indicators of progress. This leads to the final key component in the planning process, which is establishing outcome measures and developing evaluation methods to ensure the action items stated in the plan are having their intended purpose of achieving the goals of an age-friendly community. The importance of conducting a proper evaluation of age-friendly community initiatives is discussed later in this chapter.

## Innovative strategies and programs

To achieve a community that is conducive to the continued health and well-being of aging adults, several adaptations to the social and physical environment of cities, towns, and neighborhoods have been proposed. Recent years have seen a proliferation of initiatives in cities and communities aimed at enhancing the ability of older adults to age in place. Current age-friendly initiatives generally follow guidelines established by WHO or AARP. The following paragraphs describe age-friendly transportation adaptations that have been implemented in cities and communities throughout the world to address common issues that aging adults encounter when utilizing the transportation system as a driver, pedestrian, or passenger on public transportation.

Several studies in various countries have shown that older adults are not able to walk fast enough to safely cross the street in the allotted pedestrian crossing time, which requires a pedestrian to walk at approximately 1.22 m/s (Asher, Aresu, Falaschetti, & Mindell, 2012; Duim, Lebrão, & Antunes, 2017; Hoxie & Rubenstein, 1994; Romero-Ortuno, Cogan, Cunningham, & Kenny, 2010; Webb, Bell, Lacey, & Abell, 2017). The inability to safely traverse the roadway in a specified amount of time can lead to limited independence and reduced opportunities for physical activity and social interaction. Therefore, authors recommended increasing the length of time an individual is given to cross the street to accommodate for the needs of older adults and people with disabilities.

While the latest edition of Manual on Uniform Traffic Control Devices (discussed more fully in Chapter 13, Roadway Design and Infrastructure) in the US specifies a walking speed of 1.07 m/s for designating the clearance time for pedestrians at traffic signals [US Department of Transportation (US DOT), 2009], recommendations from a study by Fitzpatrick, Turner, and Brewer (2007) suggested a walking speed of 0.90 m/s to accommodate older adults. Increasing the length of time an individual has to cross the street may seem like a simple and effective design change to increase safety and accessibility for older adults; however, doing so leads to concern about creating inefficiency in traffic flow and unnecessary delays at crosswalks, primarily if there is low probability of slower-walking pedestrians accessing the crosswalk (Godavarthy & Russell, 2016).

An innovative, age-friendly design approach to providing a safer environment for older adults to cross the street, while being mindful of disrupting traffic flow, has been implemented throughout the last several years in Singapore (Land Transport Authority, 2018). Green Man Plus is a program that allows older adults and people with disabilities more time to cross the street when they activate the Green Man Plus function at the crosswalk. Older adults and people with disabilities are provided with concession cards that they can tap on the reader mounted above the standard push button on the traffic light pole. Once the card reader verifies that the card is valid, the system will extend the length of time in which the individual has to cross the street. This typically ranges from 3 to 13 extra seconds to cross, depending on the size of the street. On average, most of the selected pedestrian crossings provide the pedestrian with 6 extra seconds to safety cross the street (Land Transport Authority, 2018). This type of on-demand approach to lengthening the crossing time for specific segments of the population allows traffic to operate at its normal pace and is only altered when a qualified individual activates the system. The Land Transport Authority continues to implement this system at crosswalks throughout Singapore and aims to have at least 1000 installed by the end of 2018 (Ministerial Committee on Ageing, 2016).

In 2015, AARP recognized the age-friendly transportation practices of the city of Edmonton in Alberta, Canada, a member of WHO's Global Network for Age-Friendly Cities and Communities (AARP, 2015). Edmonton has been providing age-friendly transportation programs to older adults since the mid-1990s, and the city has now implemented a set of interlinked programs to provide an age-friendly transportation environment to meet the mobility needs of the aging population now and into the future. The programs address the mobility needs of aging adults as they are considering or have already transitioned to alternative forms of transportation. Public transportation options that suit the preferences and needs of older adults will become increasingly important in the coming years as the proportion of non-driving older adults continues to grow. The city of Edmonton has acknowledged the important role that public transportation can have in the lives of older adults and actively works to educate the aging population about the transportation resources available in the community and how to use public transportation to meet their mobility needs. The educational programs are free to the public and include individual and group training, primarily for older adults and those with mobility issues, on accessing the public transportation system; workshops that provide information about older driver issues, transit options, and planning for driving retirement; and "Seniors' Transportation Information Hubs," located in activity centers, housing complexes, shopping malls, and other areas, which provide informational materials about the transit system and available services (AARP, 2015).

In addition to increases in mobility limitations, as the population continues to age, there is likely to be more people with cognitive impairment accessing the public transportation system when they can no longer safely drive. Using public transportation presents additional challenges for older adults experiencing cognitive decline as they may have difficultly remembering routes, handling fares, and interacting with other passengers (Holley-Moore & Creighton, 2015). Several researchers have highlighted the critical role transit operators have in ensuring the age-friendliness of public transportation (Broome, Worrall, McKenna, & Boldy, 2010; Shiau & Huang, 2014; WHO, 2007). As such, every transit operator in Edmonton has been trained to respond to user mobility issues and the unique needs of older adult customers, including those with balance, speech, visual, hearing, or cognitive difficulties. The Edmonton Transit Service has several tools available for customers with mobility or cognitive limitations (City of Edmonton, 2018):

- The Bus Hailer Kit is for transit passengers with visual or cognitive limitations. A plastic sleeve displays three route numbers on each side which tells the driver which route number the passenger needs. This helps those with cognitive limitations remember their route

numbers. For visually impaired passengers, each numerical card has the Braille equivalent of that number in the corner.
- Customer Communication Cards are designed for passengers who have difficulty verbalizing their transit trip needs due to cognitive or physical limitations. These cards allow passengers to discreetly request a stop announcement or inform the driver of physical or cognitive limitations.
- Mobility Cards allow passengers with physical limitations to request the ramp or kneeling feature as the driver pulls up to the bus stop. A Mobility Card is a small, reflective, dual colored card with a "K" on one side that is orange, and an "R" on the other side that is green. As the bus pulls up to the stop, showing the orange "K" side of the card alerts the driver that the passenger is requesting to have the bus lowered (kneel the bus), and showing the green "R" side lets the driver know that the passenger is requesting the ramp to be lowered.

These examples provide only a small glimpse into the myriad age-friendly designs and programs that have been implemented around the world. For more examples, visit WHO's Global Database of Age-friendly Practices (WHO, 2018b). In order to know if the age-friendly elements of a community are having their intended effect of providing a space that encourages and supports active aging, an evaluation must be conducted. The following section describes this process.

## Evaluating age-friendly communities

A key task in monitoring and determining the success of age-friendly policies, programs, and services is conducting an evaluation. As stated earlier, communities throughout the world have implemented age-friendly initiatives in all eight WHO domains; however, there is little research regarding the impact of age-friendly initiatives on the community. While there are numerous documents that provide substantial detail about the different types of age-friendly initiatives implemented in various communities, findings from a review by Steels (2015) and others (Beard & Petitot, 2010; Orpana, Chawla, Gallagher, & Escaravage, 2016; Smith, Lehning, & Dunkle, 2013) found that there was a lack of documentation on the effectiveness of specific approaches to creating a more age-friendly environment as well as the specific evaluation of age-friendly policies and interventions. To ensure that resources for age-friendly initiatives are put to best use, it is crucial that the policies and interventions that are adopted are subject to rigorous evaluation (Beard & Petitot, 2010).

As age-friendly initiatives have become more abundant in recent years, more emphasis is now being placed on evaluating the effectiveness and outcomes of age-friendly strategies to determine the extent to which age-friendly adaptations have had an impact on community-dwelling older adults (Buckner et al., 2017; Orpana, et al., 2016; Public Health Agency of Canada (PHAC), 2015; Ruza, Kim, Leung, Kam, & Ng, 2014; Smith et al., 2013; WHO, 2015). Evaluating the age-friendliness of a community is a complex task and one that is highly context-specific as each community has a unique set of needs, circumstances, and implemented programs. To provide guidance in assessing and monitoring progress of age-friendly initiatives, several frameworks and guides have been published (Kihl et al., 2005; Neal & Wernher, 2014; PHAC, 2015). A requirement for participation in WHO's Global Network for Age-friendly Cities and Communities and AARP's Network of Age-Friendly States and Communities is that the community formally commit to a process of continual improvement and evaluation (Neal & Wernher, 2014). This involves a 5-year program cycle in which members submit mandatory evaluation reports that summarize activities, program refinements, and amendments to the action plan.

One criticism of community evaluations is that inputs and outputs of age-friendly initiatives are successfully enumerated, but measurement of short-, medium-, and long-term outcomes is lacking. For example, a community may acknowledge that older adults who no longer drive have limited access to shopping and decide to add a bus stop (output) at the local grocery store. Further evaluation should then be conducted to examine whether the addition of the bus stop resulted in increased perceived access to goods and services and reduced social isolation (short-term outcomes) for older adults, and ultimately if this change had an impact on the physical and mental well-being of older adults in the community (long-term outcome).

According to Plouffe and Kalache (2011), development and use of outcome indicators to track changes and effects in communities engaged in age-friendly initiatives will be vital to demonstrate the effectiveness of initiatives as policy interventions to promote active aging. An indicator is defined as a specific, observable, and measurable characteristic or change that represents progress toward a goal (PHAC, 2015). More recently there has been a push by researchers to develop such indicators to evaluate age-friendly initiatives. Many evaluation approaches and resulting indicators are structured around the eight WHO domains but are often adapted (Handler, 2014; Ruza et al., 2014). For example, Orpana et al. (2016) developed a list of 39 indicators across the eight WHO domains and an additional four indicators related to long-term health and social outcomes. Based on these results, a guide was developed to share the indicators and propose approaches to measuring the indicators (PHAC, 2015).

Regardless of the specific set of tools a community uses to conduct an evaluation of its age-friendly initiatives, results of the evaluation can identify successes and areas for improvement or adjustment as well as provide overall direction for the initiative. Proper evaluation also enables a community to demonstrate the impact of its age-friendly initiatives on the health and well-being of its residents and provide information to stakeholders to aid in the process of further developing an age-friendly community.

## Smart cities and the role of technology

The concept of a "smart city" has experienced rapid growth in the past few years as an increasing number of cities have begun to integrate technology and data into city operations. Federal initiatives, such as the US DOT's *Smart City Challenge* (US DOT, 2017) and National Science Foundation's (NSF) (2017) *Smart and Connected Communities Program* have spurred research into the innovative use of data, applications, and technology to ultimately improve the quality of life of residents in these communities. NSF defines a smart and connected community as one that "... synergistically integrates intelligent technologies with the natural and built environments, including infrastructure, to improve the social, economic, and environmental well-being of those who live, work, or travel within it" (NSF, 2017, p. 2). With a focus on improving the quality of life of all citizens in the community, a smart and connected community pairs well with the concept of an age-friendly community.

Increasingly, cities throughout the world are committing to leveraging technology and data to increase the efficiency and accessibility of the transportation system (US DOT, 2017). Initiatives are wide ranging and include projects such as connected vehicle testing environments to enhance safety and mobility throughout the transportation system, as well as projects to design and build digital applications to allow residents to more easily access the transportation system (see, e.g., City of Columbus, 2018). Smart city initiatives are important for people of all ages; however, older adults in particular could benefit from the resulting technologies and services provided.

Researchers at the Center for Assistive Technology and Environmental Access have teamed with the Center for Geographic Information Systems at the Georgia Institute of Technology to develop a software application to make urban areas more accessible for older adults (Becker, 2017). Recognizing the importance of the built environment on older adult mobility, the application, known as ALIGN (Application for Locational Intelligence and Geospatial Navigation), provides users with environmental information on over 50 accessibility factors that could impact one's ability to navigate a route. Such factors include uphill climbs, unshaded sidewalks, traffic signals, and curb cuts. Real-time data about traffic and weather conditions, as well as crowd-sourced information on actual route conditions, are also incorporated into the application (Becker, 2017). The aim is to reduce barriers to mobility by allowing users to select a route based on their abilities and personal preferences. Within an age-friendly community framework, this type of technology could be greatly beneficial to older adults as the information provided would allow an increased likelihood of community engagement, access to goods and services, and decreased social isolation.

The use of smartphones and applications has risen dramatically over the last decade. Results from a survey of over 3000 older adults in the US showed that 42% of adults age 65 or older reported owning a smartphone, an increase from 18% in 2003. In addition, 67% of older adults reported using the Internet (Anderson & Perrin, 2017). Technologies such as ALIGN have the potential to have a positive impact on the ability of older adults to age in place in their communities; however, older adults must have access to devices that support the technology as well as knowledge of how to use the technology. Although the rise in ownership and use of smartphones and the Internet is encouraging, older adults remain a disparate and heterogeneous group with regard to their use of digital technology use because their past employment, motivation, and existing knowledge varies (Lee & Coughlin, 2015). Furthermore, advanced age (80 + years), lower household income, and lower education levels are negatively associated with adoption of these technologies (Anderson & Perrin, 2017). Increasing the technological abilities of those with access to smartphones will enable more access to and widespread use of smart city resources and technologies. Finally, to ensure that technology is suitable and usable for older adults, it recommended that older adults be involved in all stages of designing technology that is geared toward the aging population (Rogers & Fisk, 2010).

There is also potential for communities to harness technological advances to aid in the research and planning process of age-friendly initiatives. New technologies can assist in the development phase, for example, by providing data on objective measures of mobility through use of individual global positioning system (GPS) monitors installed in the older adult's vehicle (Li et al., 2017) or attached to the older adult (Yen et al., 2015). Information gathered from GPS monitors do not rely on individual recall, allow assessment of individual trips into the community, and can provide information on specific location and speed of movement. Collectively, these data could inform the development of age-friendly community initiatives that address potential barriers to mobility.

## Conclusions

This chapter provided an overview of age-friendly communities and how transportation and mobility issues factor heavily into this concept. Population aging and increased urbanization have prompted federal, state, and local governments to evaluate the built environment and plan for a future in which older adults are able to maintain their independence, stay socially and civically engaged, and contribute to their community. Age-friendly initiatives will benefit from continued research into the factors that facilitate or hinder older adult mobility throughout the driving continuum. Although making cities more age-friendly is beneficial for residents of all ages, creating an age-friendly space is just one of a number of competing societal and governmental concerns. Consistent government leadership and support is necessary to enable longer term planning and implementation of age-friendly community initiatives. In addition, engagement with a broad group of stakeholders, including older adults, is necessary so that the age-friendly agenda can be integrated into different sectors of the government and community.

The concept of smart and connected communities is continuing to evolve and gain momentum in cities throughout the world. Smart cities initiatives place transportation as one of the major components of smart- and connected-related policies and operations, and this will continue into the future as transportation cuts across several domains of health, well-being, and overall community liveability. Emerging mobile technologies and tools are also likely to create new paradigms of smart connectivity in the decades to come. Continuing to develop technologies that enhance the quality of life of older adults, as well as leveraging data to generate age-friendly solutions to reduce barriers and increase mobility, will have a positive impact on the ability for aging adults to continue to play an active role in the communities in which they live.

## References

AARP. (2015). *Age-friendly: Inspiring communities report*. Washington, DC: AARP.
AARP. *AARP network of age-friendly states and communities*. (2018). ⟨https://www.aarp.org/livable-communities/network-age-friendly-communities/⟩ Accessed July, 2018.
Anderson, M., & Perrin, A. (2017). *Tech adoption climbs among older adults*. Washington, DC: Pew Research Center.
Asher, L., Aresu, M., Falaschetti, E., & Mindell, J. (2012). Most older pedestrians are unable to cross the road in time: A cross-sectional study. *Age and Ageing*, *41*(5), 690–694.
Australian Local Government Association. (2006). *Age-friendly built environments: Opportunities for local governments*. Deakin, ACT: Australian Local Government Association.
Beard, J. R., & Petitot, C. (2010). Ageing and urbanization: Can cities be designed to foster active ageing? *Public Health Reviews*, *32*(2), 427.
Becker, T. J. *Smart cities. Georgia tech research horizons, issue 1*. (2017). ⟨http://www.rh.gatech.edu/features/smart-cities⟩ Accessed July, 2018.
Brimbank City Council. (2017). *Brimbank age friendly city plan 2018–2022*. Sunshine, VIC: Brimbank City Council.
Broome, K., Worrall, L., McKenna, K., & Boldy, D. (2010). Priorities for an age-friendly bus system. *Canadian Journal on Aging/La Revue Canadienne du Vieillissement*, *29*(3), 435–444.
Buckner, S., Pope, D., Mattocks, C., Lafortune, L., Dherani, M., & Bruce, N. (2017). Developing age-friendly cities: An evidence-based evaluation tool. *Journal of Population Ageing*, 1–21.
Buffel, T., Phillipson, C., & Scharf, T. (2012). Ageing in urban environments: Developing 'age-friendly' cities. *Critical Social Policy*, *32*(4), 597–617.
Center for Home Care Policy and Research (CHCPR). *What is the AdvantAge initiative?* (2018). ⟨https://apps.vnsny.org/advantage/advantage.html⟩ Accessed July, 2018.
City of Auburn Hills. (2015). *City of auburn hills age-friendly 2015 action plan*. Auburn Hills, MI: City of Auburn Hills—Senior Services Department.
City of Columbus. (2018). *Project management plan for the Smart Columbus Demonstration Program*. Washington, DC: US Department of Transportation.
City of Edmonton. (2017). *Age-friendly Edmonton: Access design guide*. Edmonton, AB: Age-Friendly Edmonton.
City of Edmonton. *Customer mobility travel tools*. (2018). ⟨https://www.edmonton.ca/ets/customer-mobility-travel-tools.aspx⟩ Accessed July, 2018.
Clarke, P., & Nieuwenhuijsen, E. R. (2009). Environments for healthy ageing: A critical review. *Maturitas*, *64*(1), 14–19.
Duim, E., Lebrão, M. L., & Antunes, J. L. F. (2017). Walking speed of older people and pedestrian crossing time. *Journal of Transport & Health*, *5*, 70–76.
Fitzpatrick, K., Turner, S., & Brewer, M. A. (2007). Improving pedestrian safety at unsignalized intersections. *Institute of Transportation Engineers. ITE Journal*, *77*(5), 34–41.

Godavarthy, R. P., & Russell, E. R. (2016). Study of pedestrian hybrid beacon's effectiveness for motorists at midblock pedestrian crossings. *Journal of Traffic and Transportation Engineering (English Edition)*, *3*(6), 531–539.

Handler, S. (2014). *A research & evaluation framework for age-friendly cities*. Manchester, England: UK Urban Ageing Consortium.

Harrell, R., Lynott, J., Guzman, S., & Lampkin, C. (2014). *What is livable? Community preferences of older adults*. Washington, DC: AARP Public Policy Institute.

Holley-Moore, G., & Creighton, H. (2015). *The future of transport in an ageing society*. London, England: Age UK & ILC-UK.

Hoxie, R. E., & Rubenstein, L. Z. (1994). Are older pedestrians allowed enough time to cross intersections safely? *Journal of the American Geriatrics Society*, *42*(3), 241–244.

Jeste, D. V., Blazer, D. G., II, Buckwalter, K. C., Cassidy, K. L. K., Fishman, L., Gwyther, L. P., . . . Feather, J. (2016). Age-friendly communities initiative: Public health approach to promoting successful aging. *The American Journal of Geriatric Psychiatry*, *24*(12), 1158–1170.

Kihl, M., Brennan, D., List, J., Gabhawala, N., & Mittal, P. (2005). *Livable communities: An evaluation guide*. Washington, DC: AARP Public Policy Institute.

Land Transport Authority. *Green man +*. (2018). ⟨https://www.onemotoring.com.sg/content/onemotoring/en/on_the_roads/traffic_management/green_man_plus.html⟩ Accessed July, 2018.

Lee, C., & Coughlin, J. F. (2015). PERSPECTIVE: Older adults' adoption of technology: An integrated approach to identifying determinants and barriers. *Journal of Product Innovation Management*, *32*(5), 747–759.

Li, G., Eby, D. W., Santos, R., Mielenz, T. J., Molnar, L. J., Strogatz, D., . . . for the Long ROAD Research Team. (2017). Longitudinal Research on Aging Drivers (LongROAD): Study design and methods. *Injury Epidemiology*, *4*, 22.

Menec, V. H., Means, R., Keating, N., Parkhurst, G., & Eales, J. (2011). Conceptualizing age-friendly communities. *Canadian Journal on Aging/La Revue Canadienne du Vieillissement*, *30*(3), 479–493.

Ministerial Committee on Ageing. (2016). *I feel young in my Singapore! Action plan for successful ageing*. Singapore: Ministry of Health.

National Association of Area Agencies on Aging. (2007). *A blueprint for action: Developing a livable community for all ages*. Washington, DC: National Association of Area Agencies on Aging.

National Science Foundation (NSF). *Smart and connected communities program solicitation*. (2017). ⟨https://www.nsf.gov/pubs/2018/nsf18520/nsf18520.pdf⟩ Accessed July, 2018.

Neal, M. B., & Wernher, I. (2014). *Evaluating your age-friendly community program: A step-by-step guide*. Washington, DC: AARP.

New Zealand Ministry of Social Development. (2007). *Positive ageing indicators 2007*. Wellington, NZ: Ministry of Social Development.

Orpana, H., Chawla, M., Gallagher, E., & Escaravage, E. (2016). Developing indicators for evaluation of age-friendly communities in Canada: Process and results. *Health Promotion and Chronic Disease Prevention in Canada: Research, Policy and Practice*, *36*(10), 214.

Plouffe, L. A., & Kalache, A. (2011). Making communities age friendly: State and municipal initiatives in Canada and other countries. *Gaceta Sanitaria*, *25*, 131–137.

Pollack, P. B. (1999). *Liveable communities: An evaluation guide*. Washington, DC: AARP Public Policy Institute.

Public Health Agency of Canada (PHAC). (2015). *Age-friendly communities evaluation guide: Using indicators to measure progress*. Ottawa, ON: Public Health Agency of Canada.

Queensland Government. (2016). *Queensland: An age friendly community—Action plan.* Brisbane, QLD: Queensland Government.
Rogers, W. A., & Fisk, A. D. (2010). Toward a psychological science of advanced technology design for older adults. *Journals of Gerontology Series B: Psychological Sciences and Social Sciences*, *65*(6), 645–653.
Romero-Ortuno, R., Cogan, L., Cunningham, C. U., & Kenny, R. A. (2010). Do older pedestrians have enough time to cross roads in Dublin? A critique of the Traffic Management Guidelines based on clinical research findings. *Age and Ageing*, *39*(1), 80–86.
Ruza, J., Kim, J. I., Leung, I., Kam, C., & Ng, S. Y. M. (2014). Sustainable, age-friendly cities: An evaluation framework and case study application on Palo Alto, California. *Sustainable Cities and Society*, *14*, 390–396.
Shiau, T. A., & Huang, W. K. (2014). User perspective of age-friendly transportation: A case study of Taipei City. *Transport Policy*, *36*, 184–191.
Smith, R. J., Lehning, A. J., & Dunkle, R. E. (2013). Conceptualizing age-friendly community characteristics in a sample of urban elders: An exploratory factor analysis. *Journal of Gerontological Social Work*, *56*(2), 90–111.
Steels, S. (2015). Key characteristics of age-friendly cities and communities: A review. *Cities*, *47*, 45–52.
US Department of Transportation (US DOT). (2009). *Manual on uniform traffic control devices; for streets and highways*. Washington, DC: US Department of Transportation, Federal Highway Administration.
US Department of Transportation (US DOT). (2017). *Smart city challenge: Lessons for building cities of the future*. Washington, DC: US Department of Transportation.
Warth, L. (2016). The WHO global network of age-friendly cities and communities: Origins, developments and challenges. In T. Moulaert, & S. Garon (Eds.), *Age-friendly cities and communities in international comparison* (pp. 37–46). Switzerland: Springer International Publishing.
Webb, E. A., Bell, S., Lacey, R. E., & Abell, J. G. (2017). Crossing the road in time: Inequalities in older people's walking speeds. *Journal of Transport & Health*, *5*, 77–83.
World Health Organization (WHO). (2002). *Active ageing: A policy framework*. Geneva, Switzerland: World Health Organization.
World Health Organization (WHO). (2007). Global age-friendly cities: A guide. Geneva, Switzerland: World Health Organization.
World Health Organization (WHO). (2015). Measuring the age-friendliness of cities: A guide to using core indicators. Geneva, Switzerland: World Health Organization.
World Health Organization (WHO). *About the global network for age-friendly cities and communities*. (2018a). ⟨https://extranet.who.int/agefriendlyworld/who-network/⟩ Accessed July, 2018.
World Health Organization (WHO). *Global database for age-friendly practices*. (2018b). ⟨https://extranet.who.int/agefriendlyworld/afp/⟩ Accessed July, 2018.
Yen, I. H., Leung, C. W., Lan, M., Sarrafzadeh, M., Kayekjian, K. C., & Duru, O. K. (2015). A pilot study using global positioning systems (GPS) devices and surveys to ascertain older adults' travel patterns. *Journal of Applied Gerontology*, *34*(3), NP190–NP201.

# Part IV

# Where Do We Go From Here?

# Where do we go from here?

# 15

*The institutions that represent the core of our society—the design of our cities, the transportation system, the work force, our education, retirement, tax policies—are not designed to support a barrel. They were designed to support a pyramid.*

*Jack Rowe*

## An aging global society

The demographic statistics, population pyramids, and gerontological modeling document the aging of the world's population. These stark data, however, do not capture the experience of living in a society that has forever been transformed. All of us are a part of the new aging world. A recent film entitled *Coming of Age in an Aging America* asks the question: "What will it mean for us all to grow up, live and age in a society where a third of the population is over age 65?" (Herbes-Sommers, 2017). This engaging and optimistic film presents a clear description of the issues facing an aging America, issues that are also applicable to countries around the globe. But the film does not stop there; it also presents insights into how society might "reconfigure" its thinking and actions related to society's core institutions to better serve all age groups. A key theme of the film is that the solutions to the issues of an aging society are interwoven into the very fabric of society itself and not focused solely on older adults. As stated in *Coming of Age in an Aging America* by James Jackson, Daniel Katz Distinguished University Professor of Psychology at the University of Michigan: "The aging society is not just about older people. In fact, it is about all people." Our intent throughout this book has been to apply this same sentiment to the issues surrounding safe transportation for older adults.

## Revisiting a framework for promoting and understanding older adult safe transportation

In Chapter 4, A Framework for Promoting Older Adult Safe Transportation, we introduced a framework for promoting safe transportation among older adults (see Fig. 4.1). This framework depicts the many stakeholders, including older adults themselves, that impact safe transportation before, during, and after the transition to non-driving community mobility. Influencing the actions and abilities of these stakeholders are three overarching factors that impact society: communities, technology, and

**Perspectives and Strategies for Promoting Safe Transportation among Older Adults.**
**DOI: https://doi.org/10.1016/B978-0-12-812153-5.00015-7**

roadways. These factors were discussed in detail in Chapter 11, Federal, state, and local government, Chapter 12, In-vehicle and self-driving technologies, Chapter 13, Roadway design and infrastructure. A key component of the model is the connection of stakeholders with not only older adults but with each other. For example, informal caregivers (family and friends of older adults) often seek the advice of other stakeholder groups regarding transportation issues. Indeed, a statewide survey in Michigan (Eby, Molnar, Kostyniuk, St. Louis, & Zanier, 2017) found that high proportions of informal caregivers who provided transportation assistance to older adults seek information from health-care professionals (54.5%), other family/friends (38.5%), senior centers (30.8%), and government agencies (23.9%). Likewise, as discussed in Chapter 8, Licensing agencies are bound by the laws enacted by governments; most often receive referrals from health professionals and law enforcement; frequently require a medical assessment as a component of the process for determining fitness to drive; and in many cases will refer older adults who are having driving difficulties to transportation service providers. Similar connections exist for each of the stakeholder groups. Missing from the framework are the researchers, practitioners, educators, and thought leaders who develop new knowledge, programs, and ideas that help to solve the problems of safe transportation in an aging society and communicate this information to the stakeholders who need it. As such, these professions are interwoven into all aspects of the framework.

## Themes

While each chapter provides detailed information on specific topics, several themes that cut across chapters are evident. One is that today's challenges with safe transportation for older adults have their roots in history. Not only have concerns about aging drivers been expressed for more than 80 years (DeSilva, 1938, 1939; DeSilva & Forbes, 1937; Forbes, 1938), societal systems that evolved over the past several decades, such as the development of suburban areas where many parents first choose to raise families and now want to remain as they age into older adulthood, have contributed to many of the transportation challenges that society faces today. It is important to keep in mind that the actions taken by society today will also contribute, both positively and negatively, to the transportation issues of the future.

Another theme is that the personal automobile will continue to be a crucial component of personal mobility, at least for the next several decades and likely longer. Older adults will continue to want to drive themselves, and when they cannot drive, they will prefer to travel as a passenger in a personal vehicle to meet their transportation needs. Transportation systems change slowly, in part because changes are expensive and in part because of the disruptions that changes will inevitably cause. A related theme is that current nondriving options for transportation are inadequate and underfunded, as discussed in Chapter 3, Use of nondriving transportation options, and Chapter 10, Transportation service providers. If society had community mobility options that were available, accessible, acceptable, affordable, and adaptable for large segments of the older adult population, then many of the challenges discussed in this book would be resolved. More funding, however, will not be enough. There are systemic issues, such as the lack of age-friendliness design in many communities, that will need to be addressed to realize a future transportation system that works well for all users.

Many stakeholders are looking to the introduction of automated vehicles as a solution to many of the challenges of aging and safe transportation. As this technology continues to evolve, there is a fundamental need to empirically demonstrate its value for older adults, who currently have little trust in it. As higher levels of vehicle automation are achieved, particularly fully automated vehicles, there will still be a need to address the challenges of using this technology for helping older adults stay mobile and independent, including the following issues that older adults or people with disabilities will face: difficulty entering and exiting the vehicle, particularly when mobility devices are being used; difficulty moving from home to the vehicle and the vehicle to a destination, particularly when the person has significant functional decline; comfort and safety of the vehicle seating; handling of emergency situations; and communication between the vehicle and occupant, particularly when the older adult has cognitive or auditory declines.

The transportation systems that now exist will need even greater investment in the future to simply maintain the present systems. Global warming, population expansion, and the development of megaregions (discussed in Chapter 1: The Challenges) will put greater stress on current systems. Worn signage, faded pavement markings, and deteriorating roadways will reduce safely for all road users and can inhibit the development of innovative countermeasures to improve safety. For example, some of the new in-vehicle, advanced technologies discussed in Chapter 12, In-vehicle and self-driving technologies, rely on being able to accurately sense lane markings and signage. The effectiveness of these systems is greatly reduced when vehicles are traveling on poorly maintained roadways.

Education and training are mentioned in nearly every chapter, highlighting the importance of these activities for the safe transportation of older adults. Education and training materials related to aging and driving are available for all of the stakeholder groups included in the framework, yet there is a need to keep this information current. New research findings are published each year and new programs across the globe continue to be developed and implemented. Processing and synthesizing this large volume of new information can be daunting. As such, there can be several benefits associated with efforts to consolidate information through a process of scrutinizing new research and evaluating programs to determine their value and generalizability, organizing this information into a meaningful framework, and then providing access to the information to appropriate stakeholders. Several examples of such an approach are the *Clearinghouse for Older Road User Safety* website mentioned in Chapter 6, Family members, friends, and other informal caregivers (Roadway Safety Foundation, 2018); *Safe Drivers Smart Options: Keys to Lifelong Mobility* (Eby, Molnar, Kostyniuk, Zanier, & St Louis, 2016; State of Michigan, 2018) discussed in Chapter 11, Federal, state, and local government; and AARP's *Promising Approaches for Promoting Lifelong Community Mobility* (Molnar, Eby, St. Louis, & Neumeyer, 2007).

One of the most persistent challenges in the area of older drivers is determining how to objectively assess a person's ability to drive safely and identify the point at which driving privileges should be revoked. As discussed in Chapter 7, Physicians and other health professionals, and Chapter 8, Licensing agencies, several attempts have been made to develop a battery of tests that can be used to identify those who should stop driving without also falsely identifying a large proportion of drivers as unsafe when they are actually safe. The quest for this elusive set of objective tests continues. Even in the absence of this battery, the screening and assessment process could benefit from greater standardization.

Communities are composed of families and friends who are now and will continue to be intimately involved in the safe transportation of older adults. Whether we call this informal caregiving or simply being part of a family or group of friends, these people are indispensable to the older adult as discussed in Chapter 5, Older adults. There is a great need to develop a better understanding of informal caregiving related to transportation to develop better ways to support families and friends in both providing this care and in reducing the adverse economic and health impacts that the provision of care can produce.

As discussed in Chapter 11, Federal, state, and local government, and Chapter 14, Age-friendly communities, strong and consistent leadership was identified as a necessary factor in building effective coalitions of stakeholders and successful coordinations among organizations. From the process of planning for an aging society to implementing policy that enables older adults to maintain mobility, leadership of key decision makers is vital to advancing the agenda for safe transportation among older adults. Leadership, particularly local government, can also play an important role in safe transportation by leading the organizing and vetting of resources that are relevant to the potentially unique needs of local stakeholders.

Finally, a greater emphasis needs to be placed on planning for future mobility as discussed in Chapters 5, Older adults, and Chapter 14, Age-friendly communities. It is often said that people should plan for secure future mobility in the same way that they plan for a secure financial future in older adulthood. This is, perhaps, the wrong approach. A 2017 survey of Americans found that 39% reported having no retirement savings and another 18% had less than $1000 saved for retirement (GoBankRates, 2017). Other studies show that older adults simply do not want to even contemplate giving up driving (e.g., Kostyniuk & Shope, 2003). Therefore, an important first step will be to develop strategies focused on reducing the resistance to thinking about future mobility so that planning can start to take place.

## Research needs

It is an axiom among researchers that all research reports should end with a statement about further research needs. Notwithstanding the job-security underlying such statements, there is, in fact, always a need to better understand our world. Much of this book focused on reviewing and synthesizing research findings on a number of topics related to aging and safe transportation and, therefore, most chapters also identified areas in which further research and program development are needed. In recent years, several transportation-related groups and organizations from Europe, North America, Australia, and elsewhere have developed lists of research needs and activities (Classen, Eby, Molnar, Dobbs, & Winter, 2011; Dickerson et al., 2007; Dickerson, Molnar, Bédard, Eby, Berg-Weger, et al., 2017; Dickerson, Molnar, Bédard, Eby, Classen, et al., 2017; Mjelde et al., 2017; National Highway Traffic Safety Administration, 2010, 2014; National Institute on Aging, 2018; Older Driver Safety Advisory Committee, 2012; Road Safety Foundation, 2016; TRIP, 2018). Collectively, the research needs can be categorized into seven areas: improving vehicles, improving roadways, improving screening and assessment, improving stakeholder knowledge, improving policy, improving transportation options, and improving collaborations. Here, we summarize recommended research, new programs, and actions identified by these groups. Readers interested in the complete lists should consult the cited documents.

## Improve vehicles

- Continue the development of advanced vehicle technologies that can help overcome common functional declines associated with aging.
- Develop a better understanding of how transportation technologies are used by older drivers, what changes in behavior occur with continued use, and what safety benefits can be achieved in real-world use of these technologies.
- Determine which technologies are valued by older drivers and which are not.
- Develop more effective ways to educate older drivers on the use and benefits of transportation technology.
- Determine the safety and comfort-related benefits of various vehicle modifications and communicate this information to stakeholders.
- Gain a better understanding of the unique issues for older adults' use of automated and connected vehicles and develop strategies to maximize benefits and safety among older users.

## Improve roadways

- Implement older driver–based guidelines when building or replacing roadway segments.
- Maintain and/or replace worn or old signage, pavements markings, and signals.
- Evaluate new roadway design features with older drivers to determine if they provide the expected benefits.

## Improve screening and assessment

- Develop and validate driver screening tools and protocols that can be implemented in real-world settings.
- Standardize and validate fitness-to-drive evaluations among health professionals.
- Determine appropriate and feasible guidelines for reassessment intervals for drivers with progressive diseases such as Alzheimer's disease.
- Better identify perceptual, cognitive, and psychomotor factors that increase the risk of older driver crashes.
- Establish the effectiveness of Medical Advisory Boards in helping to determine fitness-to-drive.

## Improve the process of transiting to non-driving

- Gain a better understanding of the consequences of stopping driving.
- Determine the effects of all factors that impact the decision to reduce and ultimately cease driving and use this information to facilitate the transitioning process.
- Evaluate the safety effects (and other effects) of older driver self-regulation.

## Improve policy

- Continue to evaluate the effects of age-based licensing and renewal requirements.
- Evaluate the effects of medical professional reporting policies and modify these policies based on empirical information.
- Determine the effects of driver referral processes, including public safety and quality-of-life for older drivers.
- Develop and evaluate policies that encourage the appropriate reporting of potentially at-risk older drivers.
- Encourage empirically based older driver policies.

## Improve non-driving mobility

- Determine the factors that influence the market for alternative transportation services.
- Better understand the characteristics that make transportation options more appealing, easier to use, and safer for older adults.
- Develop and evaluate community models that incorporate a continuum of senior friendly transportation services.
- Develop, integrate, and better advertise travel training programs for older adults that help them learn about and be more comfortable using transportation options.
- Develop and understand how older adults use and can benefit from ridehailing and ride-sharing transportation options.
- Develop better strategies to use existing and future transportation options to benefit older adults.
- Expand the evaluation of aging friendly, community-based models to assess outcomes related to healthy aging.
- Ensure that public transit vehicles and facilities are assessable and accommodating to older adults.
- Better understand issues associated with rural transportation options and older adults and develop innovative solutions that address these issues.
- Develop more effective strategies and countermeasures to improve the safety of older pedestrians and bicyclists.

## Improve collaborations

- Develop strategies to build coalitions that include representation from a wide range of stakeholders to enhance safe transportation among older adults.
- Address the system-wide (e.g., funding) and psychological (e.g., lack of familiarity with other fields) barriers that hinder effective coalition building.

- Promote jurisdiction-wide stakeholder inclusions when developing strategies, policies, and practices for promoting safe transportation among older adults.
- An often overlooked stakeholder—the older adults themselves—should be represented when developing strategies, policies, and practices.
- Encourage jurisdictions to establish stakeholder partnerships in order to develop jurisdiction-wide strategies to promote safe transportation for older society members.

# Final words

Dr. Cynthia J. Brown of the University of Alabama at Birmingham Division of Gerontology stated in reference to work published in the Journal of the American Medical Association (Brown & Flood, 2013), "Mobility is one of the cornerstones of healthy aging" (University of Alabama at Birmingham, 2013, np). Although Dr. Brown was referring specifically to walking mobility, this statement applies equally to community transportation. Being able to get around in one's community, regardless of the mode of travel, enables people to satisfy important needs and to live the lives that they choose. Unfortunately, aging impacts one's community mobility, particularly if an older adult is dependent on being able to drive. As licensing agencies frequently remind us—driving is a privilege and not a right. Several transportation and aging experts have commented that transportation represents a basic need for people and is necessary for independence, autonomy, and quality of life (Dickerson et al., 2007). When driving is no longer safe, the need for transportation still remains. Empowering transportation solutions for older adults will be essential for healthy aging. As society continues to age, the transportation issues presented in this book will continue to be relevant topics of research, policy, intervention, and discussion.

As we hope this book illustrates, transportation and mobility are interwoven into the very fabric of society, and at multiple levels. These levels are made up of older adults themselves who need to get around in the community to stay independent yet connected, as well as the various individuals and groups who have a stake in their continued mobility and well-being including family members, friends, and other informal caregivers; physicians and other health providers; licensing agencies; law enforcement; and transportation service providers. It is clear that the challenges and the solutions to maintaining safe mobility for aging adults, whether through driving or other options, affect and are affected by all of the stakeholder groups we have identified and discussed. Just as we as researchers can benefit from an interdisciplinary perspective, we as a society need to include all of the various groups who have a stake in the safe mobility of older adults as we work to understand the issues and put in place effective strategies. It is our hope that the framework presented in this book for thinking about and addressing the issue of safe mobility will be useful to researchers, practitioners, and policy makers as they grapple with the challenges of an aging society and work to ensure the safety and welfare of older adults.

# References


Brown, C. J., & Flood, K. L. (2013). Mobility limitation in the older patient: A clinical review. *Journal of the American Medical Association, 310*(11), 1168–1177.

Classen, S., Eby, D. W., Molnar, L. J., Dobbs, B., & Winter, S. (2011). Transportation and aging: Evaluating stakeholders' perspective on advancing safe mobility. *South African Journal of Occupational Therapy, 41*(3), 18–24.

DeSilva, H. R. (1938). Age and highway accidents. *The Scientific Monthly, 47*(6), 536–545.

DeSilva, H. R. (1939). Normal versus accident drivers. *The Journal of Psychology, 7*, 337–342.

DeSilva, H. R., & Forbes T. W. (1937). *Testing results*. Project no. 6S46-18S59. Boston, MA: Harvard Traffic Bureau and W. P. A. of Massachusetts.

Dickerson, A. E., Molnar, L. J., Bédard, M., Eby, D. W., Berg-Weger, M., Choi, M., ... Silverstein, N. M. (2017). Transportation and aging: An updated research agenda for advancing safe mobility among older adults transitioning from driving to non-driving. *The Gerontologist*. Available from https://doi.org/10.1093/geront/gnx120.

Dickerson, A. E., Molnar, L. J., Bédard, M., Eby, D. W., Classen, S., & Polgar, J. M. (2017). Transportation and aging: An updated research agenda for advancing safe mobility. *Journal of Applied Gerontology*. Available from https://doi.org/10.1177/0733464817739154.

Dickerson, A. E., Molnar, L. J., Eby, D. W., Adler, G., Bédard, M., Berg-Weger, M., ... Trujillo, L. (2007). Transportation and aging: A research agenda for advancing safe mobility. *The Gerontologist, 47*, 578–590.

Eby, D. W., Molnar, L. J., Kostyniuk, L. P., St. Louis, R. M., & Zanier, N. (2017). Characteristics of informal caregivers who provide transportation assistance to older adults. *PLoS ONE, 12*(9), e0184085.

Eby, D. W., Molnar, L. J., Kostyniuk, L. P., Zanier, N., & St Louis, R. M. (2016). *Safe drivers smart options: Keys to lifelong mobility*. Report no. UMTRI-2016-18. Ann Arbor, MI: University of Michigan Transportation Research Institute.

Forbes, T. W. (1938). Age performance relationships among accident-repeater automobile drivers. *Journal of Consulting Psychology, 2*(5), 143–148.

GoBankingRates (2017). *More than half of Americans have less than $1,000 in savings in 2017*. ⟨https://www.gobankingrates.com/saving-money/savings-advice/half-americans-less-savings-2017/⟩ Accessed July, 2018.

Herbes-Sommers, C. (2017). *Coming of age in an aging America (video)*. Cambridge, MA: Vital Pictures, Inc. http://www.theagingamericaproject.com/. Accessed July, 2018.

Kostyniuk, L. P., & Shope, J. T. (2003). Driving alternatives: Older drivers in Michigan. *Journal of Safety Research, 34*(4), 404–417.

Mjelde, J. W., Dudensing, R., Brooks, J., Battista, G., Carrillo, M., Counsil, B., ... Ullerich, S. (2017). *Economics of transportation research needs for rural elderly and transportation disadvantaged populations*. Report no. TTI-2017-1. College Station, TX: Texas A&M Transportation Institute.

Molnar, L. J., Eby, D. W., St. Louis, R. M., & Neumeyer, A. L. (2007). *Promising approaches for promoting lifelong community mobility*. Washington, DC: AARP.

National Highway Traffic Safety Administration. (2010). *Older driver program: Five-year strategic plan, 2012–2017*. Report no. DOT HS 811 432. Washington, DC: US Department of Transportation.

National Highway Traffic Safety Administration. (2014). *Uniform guidelines for state highway safety programs: Older driver safety*. Report no. DOT HS 812 007D. Washington, DC: US Department of Transportation.

National Institute on Aging. (2018). *Research goal B: Continue to develop and disseminate information about interventions to reduce disease and disability and improve the health and quality of life of older adults*. Washington, DC: National Institute on Aging. https://www.nia.nih.gov/about/living-long-well-21st-century-strategic-directions-research-aging/research-goal-b-continue. Accessed July, 2018.

Older Driver Safety Advisory Committee. (2012). *Results of consultation: Improving the safety of older drivers*. Brisbane, QLD, Australia: The State of Queensland Government.

Road Safety Foundation. (2016). *Supporting safe driving into old age: A national older driver strategy*. Hampshire, United Kingdom: Road Safety Foundation.

Roadway Safety Foundation. (2018). *Clearinghouse for Older Road User Safety (ChORUS)*. Washington, DC: Roadway Safety Foundation. https://www.roadsafeseniors.org/. Accessed July, 2018.

State of Michigan. *Safe drivers smart options: Keys to lifelong mobility*. (2018). ⟨https://www.michigan.gov/agingdriver⟩ Accessed July, 2018.

TRIP. (2018). *Preserving the mobility and safety of older Americans*. Washington, DC: TRIP.

University of Alabama at Birmingham. (2013, September, 17). Mobility is key to healthy aging. *ScienceDaily*. https://www.sciencedaily.com/releases/2013/09/130917161634.htm. Accessed July, 2018.

# Index

*Note*: Page numbers followed by "*f*" and "*t*" refer to figures and tables, respectively.

Kolibri 360 GmbH
Ferdinand-Jühlke-Straße 7
99095 Erfurt, Deutschland
produktsicherheit@kolibri360.de